A·N·N·U·A·L E·D·I·T·I·O·N·S

Production and Operations Management

Second Edition

01/02

D0082420

EDITOR

P. K. Shukla
Chapman University

Dr. P. K. Shukla is associate professor of management at Chapman University. He received his bachelor's degree from California State University, Long Beach, his master's degree from the University of Southern California, and his doctorate from the University of California at Los Angeles. He is certified in Production and Inventory Management by APICS—The Educational Society for Resource Management. His research and consulting interests include operational and strategic planning. Dr. Shukla resides in Villa Park, California, with his wife and children.

McGraw-Hill/Dushkin
530 Old Whitfield Street, Guilford, Connecticut 06437

Visit us on the Internet
http://www.dushkin.com

Credits

1. Performance Improvement and Electronic Commerce
Unit photo—Courtesy of Tom Way/IBM Microelectronics.

2. Quality
Unit photo—Courtesy of TRW, Inc.

3. Human Resources Management for Productivity
Unit photo—© 2001 by PhotoDisc, Inc.

4. Forecasting and Product Design
Unit photo—© 2001 by PhotoDisc, Inc.

5. Capacity, Location, Logistics, and Layout Planning
Unit photo—© 2001 by PhotoDisc, Inc.

6. Inventory and Supply Chain Management
Unit photo—Courtesy of TRW, Inc.

7. Emerging Trends in Production and Operations Management
Unit photo—Courtesy of Digital Stock.

Copyright

Cataloging in Publication Data
Main entry under title: Annual Editions: Production and Operations Management. 2001/2002.
     1. Operations research. 2. Production scheduling. 3. Management science. I. Shukla, P. K., *comp.*
II. Title: Production and operations management.
ISBN 0–07–243288–8   658′.4034   ISSN 1525–3627

Second Edition

Cover image © 2001 by PhotoDisc, Inc.

Printed in the United States of America   1234567890BAHBAH54321   Printed on Recycled Paper

To the Reader

In publishing ANNUAL EDITIONS we recognize the enormous role played by the magazines, newspapers, and journals of the public press in providing current, first-rate educational information in a broad spectrum of interest areas. Many of these articles are appropriate for students, researchers, and professionals seeking accurate, current material to help bridge the gap between principles and theories and the real world. These articles, however, become more useful for study when those of lasting value are carefully collected, organized, indexed, and reproduced in a low-cost format, which provides easy and permanent access when the material is needed. That is the role played by ANNUAL EDITIONS.

Organizations today are faced with challenges to improve performance and to increase customer service. Firms must provide greater quality and faster delivery than ever before and simultaneously reduce costs. Important decisions are required in forecasting demand accurately, human resources management, capacity, location, logistics, and layout planning. Supply chain management has emerged as a major area of importance for all firms. The Internet has provided new challenges and opportunities for electronic commerce; both business-to-consumer and business-to-business sales opportunities have been created. These challenges are dealt with by the utilization of operations and production management concepts.

The field of production management has its roots in scientific management principles from the early 1900s that were developed when the United States economy was primarily manufacturing-based. As the economy shifted to more service-based and information-based sectors, the focus shifted away from production management to operations management within service organizations. As we see greater globalization, firms must now ensure that they are world class to remain competitive. With the dynamic environment in the field, managers need to keep up with these new developments. This second edition of *Annual Editions: Production and Operations Management* is designed to provide students and managers with a concise review of recent developments in theory and company illustrations of practice.

This publication contains a number of features designed to be useful for managers and students interested in production and operations management. These features include a *topic guide* for locating articles on a specific subject and a *table of contents* with abstracts that summarize each article, highlighting key ideas in bold italics. Also, there are selected *World Wide Web sites* that can be used to further explore the topics. These sites are cross-referenced by number to the topic guide.

Annual Editions: Production and Operations Management 01/02 is organized into seven units, each dealing with specific interrelated topics in production and operations management. The units cover performance improvement and electronic commerce; quality; human resources management for productivity; forecasting and product design; decisions on capacity, location, logistics, and layout planning; inventory and supply chain management; and emerging trends in operations and production management. These seven units cover the major decision areas and considerations faced by managers in the field. The units are interrelated and cumulatively provide the reader with concepts of management within both manufacturing and service environments. Each unit begins with an overview that provides the necessary background information and basic core concepts. These unit overviews allow the reader to place the selections in the context of the book. Important topics are emphasized, and key points to consider address major themes.

This is the second edition of *Annual Editions: Production and Operations Management* and it is designed to provide the reader with the most complete and current selection of readings available on the subject. We would like to know what you think. Please take a few minutes to complete and return the postage-paid *article rating form* at the back of the volume. Any book can be improved, and we need your help to improve *Annual Editions: Production and Operations Management*.

P. K. Shukla

P. K. Shukla
Editor

Contents

To the Reader iv
Topic Guide 2
● Selected World Wide Web Sites 4

Overview 6

1. **An Empirical Assessment of the Production/Operations Manager's Job,** Brian D'Netto, Amrik S. Sohal, and John Trevillyan, *Production and Inventory Management Journal,* First Quarter, 1998.   8
Findings from a survey of production/operations managers indicate that the modern production manager is vastly different from the traditional profile. *The nature of the job has changed from a department-centered approach to cross-functional linkages* with marketing, engineering, human resources, finance, and accounting.

2. **Reengineer or Perish,** G. Berton Latamore, *APICS—The Performance Advantage,* January 1999.   13
Michael Hammer, the originator of both reengineering and process-centering, is interviewed in this article. He comments on how *reengineering the supply chain* is the *key to manufacturing success* in the new millennium.

3. **Hurry Up and Wait,** Kelly Barron, *Forbes,* October 16, 2000.   17
Time is a scarce resource for customers and frustration occurs when customers are forced to wait in lines. Firms *need to value customer time* and use concepts like queuing theory to reduce waiting time.

4. **Do You Have What It Takes To Be Lean?** William Feld, *APICS—The Performance Advantage,* May 2000.   22
Most firms have had difficulty in achieving successful lean manufacturing. Benchmarks, primary elements, principles, and a road map for successful *lean manufacturing implementation are presented. Performance measurement* is viewed as vital for successful implementation.

5. **Rally of the Dolls: It Worked for Toyota. Can It Work for Toys?** Alex Taylor III, *Fortune,* January 11, 1999.   26
Alexander Doll Company has turned around its operations and finances from bankruptcy to profitability, and it has improved its operations processes by utilizing the same *lean production system concepts* used by *Toyota Motor Corporation.*

6. **Using ERP Data to Get [Close] to Customers,** G. Berton Latamore, *APICS—The Performance Advantage,* September 2000.   28
Enterprise Resource Planning (ERP) systems provide valuable data to shop-floor personnel. Firms using ERP data are improving response to order changes, customer needs, and market conditions.

UNIT 1

Performance Improvement and Electronic Commerce

Six articles in this section examine some of the elements in improving the process of business operations: reengineering the supply chain, benchmarking, job design, and the management of services.

The concepts in bold italics are developed in the article. For further expansion please refer to the Topic Guide and the Index.

UNIT 2

Quality

Seven selections consider job design, tracking quality, effective service strategies, and improving the various job processes.

Overview — 32

7. **Fool Proof Service: Poka-Yoke,** Richard B. Chase and Douglas M. Stewart, *USC Business*, Spring 1994. — 34
This article reviews the Japanese concept of *quality management* called "poka-yoke." In essence, it builds a step into a process that must be completed before the next stage can be performed. In other words, it ensures that each phase of an operation is done correctly.

8. **A Conversation With Joseph Juran,** Thomas A. Stewart, *Fortune*, January 11, 1999. — 37
Joseph Juran, a pioneer in quality control, presents his views on *why quality matters,* why quality takes so long, the cost of quality, control versus creativity, and perfection.

9. **One More Time: Eight Things You Should Remember About Quality,** John P. Mello Jr., *Harvard Management Update*, May 1998. — 39
John Mello identifies eight suggestions for *gaining organizational commitment to quality* by involvement of customers, top management, and workers. Examples of several firms provide support to the view that more than just quality standards are needed.

10. **ISO 9000 Myth and Reality: A Reasonable Approach to ISO 9000,** Frank C. Barnes, *SAM Advanced Management Journal*, Spring 1998. — 42
Frank Barnes presents a background on *ISO 9000 quality system standards,* discusses benefits and costs, and makes recommendations based upon data collected on actual savings to firms of different sizes.

11. **2-D or Not 2-D?** Srikumar S. Rao, *Forbes*, November 15, 1999. — 49
Bar codes, introduced over 20 years ago, have been improved to "2-D" bar codes. The *enhanced bar codes* allow for more *data capacity,* reduce paperwork with inventories, and reduce costs.

12. **Jac Nasser's Biggest Test,** Alex Taylor III, *Fortune*, September 18, 2000. — 51
Ford CEO Jac Nasser faced a crisis in 2000 with *Ford Explorer SUV tire failures* and rollovers. Unlike other CEOs faced with litigation and congressional hearings, Nasser chose to speak openly about the crisis.

13. **Cause of Tire Failures Still a Matter of Dispute,** Terril Yue Jones, *Los Angeles Times*, October 22, 2000. — 55
Ford and Bridgestone/Firestone disputed *the cause of tire failures* in 1999 and 2000. Explanations for the tire cracks ranged from manufacturing flaws and poor design to improper tire inflation and maintenance.

The concepts in bold italics are developed in the article. For further expansion please refer to the Topic Guide and the Index.

Overview   60

14. **How Will Kawai's Hand-Built Grand Play Against Steinway?** Sonni Efron, *Los Angeles Times*, November 3, 2000.   62
Kawai Musical Instrument Manufacturing Company has mass-produced affordable family pianos for 72 years. Kawai plans to introduce a limited number of high quality hand-built pianos to compete against Steinway.

15. **Less Stress, More Productivity,** Phillip M. Perry, *Area Development*, May 1999.   64
Employee stress affects productivity in addition to employee job satisfaction. Suggestions are presented to reduce stress and to increase productivity.

16. **How Great Machines Are Born,** Stuart F. Brown, *Fortune*, March 1, 1999.   66
Friendly machines, based upon human factors and ergonomics, have been developed for use in the home and in industry. The designs are efficient and often safer, and users say the machines are a joy to use.

17. **Characteristics of the Manufacturing Environment That Influence Team Success,** Mark Pagell and Jeffrey A. LePine, *Production and Inventory Management Journal*, Third Quarter, 1999.   71
Work performed through teams is common in many firms. In this article, Mark Pagell and Jeffrey LePine analyze characteristics of *the manufacturing environment* that influence team success. They examine three categories: operational system, informal communication, and new or unusual problems.

18. **The Legal Limitations to Self-Directed Work Teams in Production Planning and Control,** Steven E. Abraham and Michael S. Spencer, *Production and Inventory Management Journal*, First Quarter, 1998.   76
The use of employee-driven problem-solving teams, or quality circles, is a central component of Just-In-Time (JIT) and total quality management (TQM). The authors identify the *legal limitations to self-directed work teams* with a review of case law.

Overview   82

19. **Managing the New Product Development Process: Strategic Imperatives,** Melissa A. Schilling and Charles W. L. Hill, *Academy of Management Executive*, August 1998.   84
For many industries, *new product development* is now the single *most important factor* driving success or failure. The authors present models of the new product development (NPD) process and recommend strategic imperatives to reduce delays and failures.

20. **BMW Drives New Web Strategy,** Dan Carmel, *EC World*, October 2000.   98
Dan Carmel reports on how BMW lets customers "build" their own cars online, thereby gathering *marketing research on customer preferences.* This data is then linked to production for better model designs and communications to customers.

UNIT 3

Human Resources Management for Productivity

Five articles in this section discuss the various challenges faced by human resources when targeting productivity. Some of the topics considered are: job design, product design, self-directed work teams, and ergonomic machines.

UNIT 4

Forecasting and Product Design

Six articles in this section assess the importance of new product development, the impact of effective management on the project, the role of forecasting, and the need for improving the necessary processes.

The concepts in bold italics are developed in the article. For further expansion please refer to the Topic Guide and the Index.

21. Bringing Discipline to Project Management, Jeffrey **100**
Elton and Justin Roe, *Harvard Business Review,*
March/April 1998.
Project delays and excessive costs can be reduced or eliminated
through ***proper project management*** as well as by managers'
taking a comprehensive view of managing problems, according to
Eliyahu Goldratt, who has outlined his new theories in the book,
Critical Chain.

22. New Era About to Dawn for International Space **105**
Station, Peter Pae, *Los Angeles Times,* October 29,
2000.
The ***International Space Station*** is a multination $25 billion
project. Peter Pae reports that cost estimates have far exceeded
original figures. Some critics propose that the project should be
shut down.

23. Seven Keys to Better Forecasting, Mark A. Moon, **108**
John T. Mentzer, Carlo D. Smith, and Michael S. Garver,
Business Horizons, September/October 1998.
Sales forecasting is important for company success, especially fi-
nancial health. The authors review seven key focus points that will
help any company to ***improve its forecasting performance.***

24. Vitamin Efficiency, Amy Doan, *Forbes,* November 1, **117**
1999.
Longs Drug Stores slashed its inventory without running short by
using a ***demand forecasting system.*** The system provided
up-to-the-day sales predictions that cut inventory and lowered replenishment costs, according to Amy Doan.

UNIT 5

Capacity, Location, Logistics, and Layout Planning

Five selections in this section
discuss the importance of
creating the proper atmosphere
for a productive company.

Overview **120**

25. Not All Projections Bad for Overgrown Theater **122**
Chains, Claudia Eller and James Bates, *Los Angeles
Times,* September 8, 2000.
The authors report that movie theatre chains increased the number
of screens rapidly from 1980 to 1999, but ticket sales did not
keep pace with the increase in ***capacity.*** Many chains filed Chapter 11 bankruptcy petitions in 2000.

26. State Declares First Stage 3 Power Alert, Nancy **124**
Rivera Brooks and Nancy Vogel, *Los Angeles Times,* December
8, 2000.
California faces a crisis with ***high energy demand and limited electricity capacity.*** The authors report that the state declared its first Stage 3 power alert in December 2000, when the
state dipped into its last 1.5 percent of reserves.

The concepts in bold italics are developed in the article. For further expansion please refer to the Topic Guide and the Index.

27. Changes in Performance Measures on the Factory Floor, Robert F. Marsh and Jack R. Meredith, *Production and Inventory Management Journal*, First Quarter, 1998.
Robert Marsh and Jack Meredith review cellular manufacturing, where some production is moved from a job shop to a line process design. With a **move to cells,** managers can change performance measures on the factory floor, leading to **lower costs and shorter lead times.**

128

28. Using Queueing Network Models to Set Lot-Sizing Policies for Printed Circuit Board Assembly Operations, Maged M. Dessouky, *Production and Inventory Management Journal*, Third Quarter, 1998.
To implement Just-In-Time (JIT) manufacturing, **small lot sizes** often need to be run. Queueing network models can be used to set lot-sizing policies, as illustrated in this article about a printed circuit board assembly operation.

134

29. A New Route for Boeing's Latest Model, Peter Pae, *Los Angeles Times*, November 19, 2000.
Boeing Corporation is manufacturing its 717 jet on a **moving assembly line,** hoping to improve the plane's prospects by speeding production and cutting costs. Peter Pae explains that with the old, nonmoving, assembly line, mechanics wasted a lot of time looking for tools and parts.

140

Overview

142

30. Introducing JIT Manufacturing: It's Easier Than You Think, Luciana Beard and Stephen A. Butler, *Business Horizons*, September/October 2000.
Some firms have assumed that **JIT** (Just-In-Time) would be too difficult to implement and abandoned its consideration. Luciana Beard and Stephen Butler claim that the benefits of JIT warrant its consideration, and they offer examples to show that introducing JIT is easier than some managers think.

144

31. Tailored Just-In-Time and MRP Systems in Carpet Manufacturing, Z. Kevin Weng, *Production and Inventory Management Journal*, First Quarter, 1998.
This article shows how **JIT** can be **applied to low-tech industries** and how it can be used alongside a traditional material-requirements planning system.

148

32. The Critical Importance of Master Production Scheduling, Steve Wilson and Chuck Davenport, *APICS—The Performance Advantage*, October 1998.
For proper supply chain management, **master production scheduling (MPS) is one of the most critical points.** The evolution of master planning, inputs, and the potential for problems without proper MPS are identified.

153

UNIT 6

Inventory and Supply Chain Management

Six articles in this section consider the importance of proper and effective inventory control, the value of Just-In-Time manufacturing, and the general need for a well-designed supply chain system.

The concepts in bold italics are developed in the article. For further expansion please refer to the Topic Guide and the Index.

ix

33. The Manager's Guide to Supply Chain Management, 157
F. Ian Stuart and David M. McCutcheon, *Business Horizons,* March/April 2000.
Supply chain management has been growing in importance to manufacturing firms. The authors identify objectives, supply cost reduction advantages, relationship choices, and supporting practices. They also present a contingency model for **supply chain decisions.**

34. Squeezing the Most Out of Supply Chains, 167
Michael S. McGarr, *EC World,* December 2000.
Supply chain management can benefit from the use of software tools that identify best practices for firms, a supply chain partner-strategic certification process, and steps for managing **supply chain partnerships.**

35. Saturn's Supply-Chain Innovation: High Value in After-Sales Service, Morris A. Cohen, Carl Cull, Hau L. Lee, and Don Willen, *Sloan Management Review,* Summer 2000. 172
A case study is presented on innovations in Saturn Corporation's after-sales service business. Results indicate that Saturn's innovations have resulted in efficient **supply chain management,** satisfied customers, and brand loyalty.

36. From Supply Chain to Value Net, David Bovel and Joseph Martha, *Journal of Business Strategy,* July/August 2000. 180
Supply chain management should lead to strategic advantages, but too many firms have utilized a traditional approach that misses opportunities, according to the authors. A **value net** is proposed to create value for all participants.

Overview 184

37. Electronics Manufacturing: A Well-Integrated IT Approach, Bruce Reinhart, *APICS—The Performance Advantage,* October 1998. 186
For proper supply chain planning, an effective and efficient use of **information technology** (IT) is required. Bruce Reinhart examines the IT requirements to support customer requirements and company concerns for cost savings.

38. Are You Ready for the E-Supply Chain? Jim Turcotte, Bob Silveri, and Tom Jobson, *APICS—The Performance Advantage,* August 1998. 189
The authors examine how the growth of the Internet will affect the managing of supply chains. **Information technology terms and concepts** are reviewed along with recommendations for **e-supply chain success.**

UNIT 7

Emerging Trends in Production and Operations Management

Six articles in this section look at some of the challenges facing an effective production management system.

The concepts in bold italics are developed in the article. For further expansion please refer to the Topic Guide and the Index.

39. The Global Six, *Business Week,* January 25, 1999.   **193**
This article reviews the mergers that are taking place in the ***automobile manufacturing*** industry and predicts that the "Global Six" will remain: General Motors, Ford Motor, DaimlerChrysler, Volkswagen, Toyota Motor, and Honda Motor.

40. Thinking Machines, Otis Port, *Business Week,* August   **197**
7, 2000.
Computer hardware and software have increased in capabilities with artificial intelligence, neural networks, and robotics. This special report presents examples of ***"smart manufacturing"*** to show how thinking machines are affecting factories.

41. One Giant Leap for Machinekind? Usha Lee McFarling,   **202**
Los Angeles Times, August 31, 2000.
Computer scientists have created ***self-evolving and self-generating robotic machines*** that will greatly alter manufacturing. Usha McFarling reports that these robotic creatures are powered by motors and are controlled by a neural network on a microchip.

**42. Environmental Management: New Challenges for   205
Production and Inventory Managers,** R. Anthony Inman, *Production and Inventory Management Journal,* Third Quarter, 1999.
According to the author, increased interest in ***environmental preservation*** has presented new challenges for production and inventory managers. Environmental programs will have an impact on their decisions on production planning and control, inventory control, and distribution.

Index   **209**
Test Your Knowledge Form   **212**
Article Rating Form   **213**

The concepts in bold italics are developed in the article. For further expansion please refer to the Topic Guide and the Index.

Topic Guide

This topic guide suggests how the selections in this book relate to the subjects covered in your course.

The Web icon (●) under the topic articles easily identifies the relevant Web sites, which are numbered and annotated on the next two pages. By linking the articles and the Web sites by topic, this ANNUAL EDITIONS reader becomes a powerful learning and research tool.

TOPIC AREA	TREATED IN	TOPIC AREA	TREATED IN
Decisions: Capacity, Location, Logistics, Layout	3. Hurry Up and Wait 25. Not All Projections Bad for Overgrown Theatre Chains 26. State Declares First Stage 3 Power Alert 27. Changes in Performance Measures on the Factory Floor 28. Using Queueing Network Models to Set Lot-Sizing Policies 29. New Route for Boeing's Latest Model ● **4, 6, 7, 10, 20, 28, 29, 30**		20. BMW Drives New Web Strategy 34. Squeezing the Most out of Supply Chains 37. Electronic Manufacturing 38. Are You Ready for the E-Supply Chain? 40. Thinking Machines 41. One Giant Leap for Machinekind? ● **3, 33, 34, 35, 36, 37**
Forecasting	23. Seven Keys to Better Forecasting 24. Vitamin Efficiency 26. State Declares First Stage 3 Power Alert 39. Global Six ● **7, 8, 9, 25, 26, 27**	**Job Design**	1. Empirical Assessment of the Production/Operations Manager's Job 5. Rally of the Dolls 7. Fool Proof Service 8. Conversation With Joseph Juran 9. One More Time 14. How Will Kawai's Hand-Built Grand Play Against Steinway? 15. Less Stress, More Productivity 16. How Great Machines Are Born 17. Characteristics of the Manufacturing Environment 18. Legal Limitations to Self-Directed Work Teams 40. Thinking Machines 41. One Giant Leap for Machinekind? ● **1, 2, 3, 6, 7, 10, 12, 13, 14, 22, 23, 24**
Global Issues	1. Empirical Assessment of the Production/Operations Manager's Job 8. Conversation With Joseph Juran 10. ISO 9000 Myth and Reality 12. Jac Nasser's Biggest Test 13. Cause of Tire Failures Still a Matter of Dispute 14. How Will Kawai's Hand-Built Grand Play Against Steinway? 20. BMW Drives New Web Strategy 22. New Era About to Dawn for International Space Station 39. Global Six ● **17, 35, 36, 37**		
		Managing Services	3. Hurry Up and Wait 7. Fool Proof Service 15. Less Stress, More Productivity 24. Vitamin Efficiency 25. Not All Projections Bad for Overgrown Theatre Chains ● **30**
Information Technology and Electronic Commerce	2. Reengineer or Perish 6. Using ERP Data to Get [Close] to Customers 11. 2-D or Not 2-D? 16. How Great Machines Are Born	**Process Improvement**	1. Empirical Assessment of the Production/Operations Manager's Job 2. Reengineer or Perish 3. Hurry Up and Wait

TOPIC AREA	TREATED IN	TOPIC AREA	TREATED IN
	4. Do You Have What It Takes to Be Lean?	**Quality**	7. Fool Proof Service
	5. Rally of the Dolls		8. Conversation With Joseph Juran
	7. Fool Proof Service		9. One More Time
	8. Conversation With Joseph Juran		10. ISO 9000 Myth and Reality
	9. One More Time		11. 2-D or Not 2-D?
	11. 2-D or Not 2-D?		12. Jac Nasser's Biggest Test
	18. Legal Limitations to Self-Directed Work Teams		13. Cause of Tire Failures Still a Matter of Dispute
	19. Managing the New Product Development Process		14. How Will Kawai's Hand-Built Grand Play Against Steinway?
	29. New Route for Boeing's Latest Model		19. Managing the New Product Development Process
	35. Saturn's Supply-Chain Innovation		● *1, 2, 3, 6, 10, 12, 13, 15, 16, 17, 18, 19, 24*
	● *1, 2, 6, 7, 11, 20, 22, 23, 24, 30*		
Product Design	3. Hurry Up and Wait	**Supply Chain Management/ Inventory, Master Production Scheduling (MPS), Materials Research Planning (MRP)**	2. Reengineer or Perish
	13. Cause of Tire Failures Still a Matter of Dispute		28. Using Queuing Network Models to Set Lot-Sizing Policies
	14. How Will Kawai's Hand-Built Grand Play Against Steinway?		30. Introducing JIT Manufacturing
	16. How Great Machines Are Born		31. Tailored Just-In-Time and MRP Systems in Carpet Manufacturing
	19. Managing the New Product Development Process		32. Critical Importance of Master Production Scheduling
	20. BMW Drives New Web Strategy		33. Manager's Guide to Supply Chain Management
	39. Global Six		34. Squeezing the Most out of Supply Chains
	42. Environmental Management		35. Saturn's Supply-Chain Innovation
	● *1, 2, 3, 10, 18, 19, 25, 26, 27*		36. From Supply Chain to Value Net
Project Management	17. Characteristics of the Manufacturing Environment		37. Electronics Manufacturing
	19. Managing the New Product Development Process		38. Are You Ready for the E-Supply Chain?
	21. Bringing Discipline to Project Management		● *4, 6, 7, 9, 10, 11, 13, 14, 19, 21, 22, 28, 29, 30, 31, 32, 33*
	22. New Era About to Dawn for International Space Station		
	29. New Route for Boeing's Latest Model		
	● *1, 2, 3, 4, 6, 7, 26*		

DUSHKIN ONLINE

AE: Production and Operations Management

The following World Wide Web sites have been carefully researched and selected to support the articles found in this reader. The sites are cross-referenced by number and the Web icon (◉) in the topic guide. In addition, it is possible to link directly to these Web sites through our DUSHKIN ONLINE support site at *http://www.dushkin.com/online/*.

The following sites were available at the time of publication. Visit our Web site—we update DUSHKIN ONLINE regularly to reflect any changes.

General Sources

1. American National Standards Institute (ANSI)
http://web.ansi.org/default.htm
ANSI Online is designed to provide convenient access to timely information on the ANSI Federation and the latest national and international standards-related activities.

2. APICS Online
http://www.apics.org
APICS is the Educational Society for Resource Management. The *Performance Advantage* magazine is located here as well as a link to certification testing information.

3. Data Interchange Standards Association (DISA)
http://www.disa.org
DISA is a not-for-profit organization that supports the development of EDI standards in electronic commerce.

4. Introduction to Operations Management
http://members.tripod.co.uk/tomi/whatis.html
Here is an excellent starting place for understanding the basics of operations management. This TOMI site uses interesting examples on the Web to illustrate its points.

5. Operations Management Center (OMC)
http://www.mhhe.com/pom
OMC is a supersite developed by McGraw-Hill/Irwin that contains a number of resources. Available are links to OM resource sites by topic; full text of OM articles from *Business Week*; a number of links to OM publications, organizations, and news feeds; and virtual tours of OM companies. The site also allows for interactive feedback that effectively works to improve content and coverage.

Performance Improvement and Electronic Commerce

6. Agile Manufacturing Project at MIT
http://web.mit.edu/ctpid/www/agile/atlanta.html
This interesting paper describes the research plan, methods, and early progress of two coordinated Agile Pathfinders focused on the aircraft and automobile industry respectively. The paper's working hypothesis is that a network of companies can improve its performance if participants take proactive steps during early product design.

7. American Productivity and Quality Center (APQC)
http://www.apqc.org
APQC is a nonprofit education and research organization. Its Web site shows how benchmarking and best practices can help an organization improve its processes and performance.

8. Business Forecasting
http://forecasting.cwru.edu
Use this page to access the thinking of business researchers who, using statistics, economics, psychology, and related disciplines, attempt to predict the future.

9. Demystifying Supply Chain Management
http://www.manufacturing.net/magazine/logistic/archives/1998/scmr/myst.htm
Peter J. Metz shows that SCM is, in fact, a logical development of lasting value, and not just a buzzword.

10. Design for Competitive Advantage TOC
http://dfca.larc.nasa.gov/dfc/toc.html
The table of contents of Ed Dean's book *Design for Competitive Advantage* leads to chapters on technologies of business, quality, cost, and others.

11. Galaxy: Manufacturing and Processing
http://galaxy.einet.net/GJ/mnfg.html
Billed as "the professional's guide to a world of information," Galaxy is a rich source of links to engineering and technology (cryogenics, quality control and more).

12. Kaizen
http://akao.larc.nasa.gov/dfc/kai.html
This selection explains *kaizen* and its relationship to Total Quality Control.

13. Voice of the Shuttle: Postindustrial Business Theory Page
http://vos.ucsb.edu/shuttle/commerce.html
Subjects covered at this Web page include the team concept, the quality movement, outsourcing, diversity management, restructuring, reengineering, downsizing, knowledge work, knowledge management, and learning organizations.

14. WARIA, the Workflow and Reengineering International Association
http://www.waria.com
This nonprofit organization tries to make sense of what is happening at the intersection of business process reengineering, workflow, and electronic commerce.

Quality

15. American Society for Quality (ASQ)
http://www.asq.org
Subtitled "Your Quality Resource," ASQ covers the field. The site includes a glossary, quality-related sites, and a quality forum, as well as standards and certification.

16. Concept Corner
http://members.tripod.co.uk/tomi/concepts.html
Concept Corner provides an introduction to Internet sites that help explain concepts, tools, and techniques that may be applied within the subject of operations management.

17. International Organization for Standardization (ISO)
http://www.iso.ch/welcome.html
Through ISO's home page find out everything you need to know about ISO, ISO 9000, and ISO 14000.

18. John Grout's Poka-Yoke Page
http://www.campbell.berry.edu/faculty/jgrout/pokayoke.shtml
Find out about mistake-proofing, zero defect quality (ZDQ), and fail-safing here. Choose from 20 selections, including Poka-Yoke Resources, Bad Designs, and Quality Links.

19. Plan-Do-Check-Act
http://www.inform.umd.edu/CampusInfor/Departments/ cqi/Outlook/Tech/pdca.html
This article offers a clear explanation of PDCA as well as an example of how to put this concept of Continuous Quality Improvement (CQI) to work.

Human Resources Management for Productivity

20. Ergonomics, HCI, and Human Factors: Working Environments
http://www.workspace-resources.com/work00.htm
Workspace Resources offers information about the societal changes that have been made in the commercial office.

21. Just-in-Time Manufacturing
http://dali.ece.curtin.edu.au/~clive/public_html/jit/jit.htm
Curtin University of Technology offers this introduction to the basic concepts of a JIT manufacturing system.

22. Quality Circles
http://www.nw.com.au/~jingde/homepa6.htm
This interesting Web page from Australia is all about the behavioral science technique called quality circles.

23. SDWT: Self-Directed Work Teams
http://users.ids.net/~brim/sdwtt.html
This very complete site links to discussions of the what and why of SDWT, skills and steps needed for success, examples of teams, work teams in public, and related resources.

24. TQM: Total Quality Management Diagnostics
http://www.skyenet.net/~leg/tqm.htm
Offered at this Web site is a simplified TQM diagnostic model.

Forecasting and Product Design

25. New Product Development: Practice and Research
http://www.eas.asu.edu/~kdooley/nsfnpd/practices.html
These are the results of a research project that surveyed over 40 New Product Development programs. From this page link to a description of the theory behind this work.

26. Project Management Institute (PMI)
http://www.pmi.org
PMI aims to build professionalism into project management and this Web site is part of that endeavor. Download *A Guide to the Project Management Body of Knowledge* here. The site also contains links to other organizations.

27. STORES June 1998: Editor's Choice
http://www.stores.org/eng/archives/jun98edch.html
This article on sales forecasting, "Retailers, Suppliers Push Joint Sales Forecasting" by Ginger Koloszyyc, introduces the concept of information sharing known as collaborative planning, forecasting, and replenishing (CPFR).

Capacity, Location, Logistics, and Layout Planning

28. Manufacturers Information Net
http://mfginfo.com/newhome2.htm
A complete source of information for industry and services related to manufacturing is provided at the site.

29. Warwick Business School—Focus on Research
http://users.wbs.ac.uk/om/research/

Visit this page for some downloadable research papers. Topics on operations strategy, capacity management, supply chain management, service quality and design, and performance measurement are covered.

30. TWIGG's Operations Management Index (TOMI)
http://members.tripod.co.uk/tomi/index.html
This Index is an entry point to operations management resources on the Web, providing information on topics like purchasing, product development, and quality.

Inventory and SupplyChain Management

31. System 21 Manufacturing
http://jbaworld.com/solutions/infosheets/masterprodsched.htm
This description of System 21 manufacturing is an example of using the computer in a manufacturing environment.

32. MAGI: Master Production Scheduling
http://www.magimfg.com/Master_Production_Scheduler.htm
MAGI, the Manufacturing Action Group Inc., opens windows and shows you the screens it uses in setting up this Web program of master production scheduling.

33. Informs: Institute for Operations Research and the Management Sciences
http://www.informs.org
From the home page of Informs you can link to research on operations research and management science (OR/MS) and also explore articles that have appeared in the press.

Emerging Trends in Production and Operations Management

34. Centre for Intelligent Machines
http://www.cim.mcgill.ca/index_nf.html
CIM's mission is to excel in the field of intelligent machines, stressing basic research, technology development, and education. Domains such as robotics, automation, artificial intelligence, and computer vision systems are explored.

35. International Center for Research on the Management of Technology (ICRMOT)
http://web.mit.edu/icrmot/www/
ICRMOT will demonstrate its scope at this site. Specific research themes include managing complex global projects, capturing the value of technological innovation, and creating and delivering technology-based services.

36. Information Technology Association of America
http://www.itaa.org
An interesting article available at this Web site is one about global information technology spending. The ITAA provides information about the IT industry and links to other sites.

37. KPMG United States
http://www.us.kpmg.com/cm/article-archives/actual-articles/ global.html
KPMG, knowledge management experts, offers this article, "Tips for Improving Global Supply Chains," at their United States Web site.

We highly recommend that you review our Web site for expanded information and our other product lines. We are continually updating and adding links to our Web site in order to offer you the most usable and useful information that will support and expand the value of your Annual Editions. You can reach us at:
http://www.dushkin. com/annualeditions/.

Unit Selections

1. **An Empirical Assessment of the Production/Operations Manager's Job,** Brian D'Netto, Amrik S. Sohal, and John Trevillyan
2. **Reengineer or Perish,** G. Berton Latamore
3. **Hurry Up and Wait,** Kelly Barron
4. **Do You Have What It Takes to Be Lean?** William Feld
5. **Rally of the Dolls: It Worked for Toyota. Can It Work for Toys?** Alex Taylor III
6. **Using ERP Data to Get [Close] to Customers,** G. Berton Latamore

Key Points to Consider

❖ What forces within the United States and globally have pressured firms to seek performance improvement?

❖ What are the similarities and differences in the performance improvement approaches presented in this unit?

❖ What are the opportunities and challenges to firms from electronic commerce?

 **Links**   **www.dushkin.com/online/**

6. **Agile Manufacturing Project at MIT**
   http://web.mit.edu/ctpid/www/agile/atlanta.html

7. **American Productivity and Quality Center (APQC)**
   http://www.apqc.org

8. **Business Forecasting**
   http://forecasting.cwru.edu

9. **Demystifying Supply Chain Management**
   http://www.manufacturing.net/magazine/logistic/archives/1998/scmr/myst.htm

10. **Design for Competitive Advantage TOC**
    http://dfca.larc.nasa.gov/dfc/toc.html

11. **Galaxy: Manufacturing and Processing**
    http://galaxy.einet.net/GJ/mnfg.html

12. **Kaizen**
    http://akao.larc.nasa.gov/dfc/kai.html

13. **Voice of the Shuttle: Postindustrial Business Theory Page**
    http://vos.ucsb.edu/shuttle/commerce.html

14. **WARIA, the Workflow and Reengineering International Association**
    http://www.waria.com

These sites are annotated on pages 4 and 5.

Given the increased challenges facing managers and firms today, a greater emphasis is placed upon production and operations management. Organizations today are faced with the need to improve performance and to increase customer service. Firms must provide greater quality, faster delivery, and simultaneously reduce costs. Firms recognize that they can not ensure their survival by maintaining the status quo. Performance improvement is necessary and the operations area of a firm plays a vital role in securing this improvement. The Internet has emerged as a great opportunity and a challenge for firms. Electronic commerce incorporates business-to-consumer and business-to-business sales. This unit examines the job of a production/operations manager, reviews approaches for performance improvement, developments in electronic commerce, and presents case illustrations from firms.

The job of a production/operations manager is of great importance today. In the first article of unit 1, Brian D'Netto et al. provide an empirical assessment of the activities of a production/ operations manager. The article contrasts the reality of the job in practice with the traditional profile of a production manager.

Various approaches have been proposed over the last two decades to increase performance improvement. This unit presents articles that review approaches such as reengineering, the use of queueing theory to reduce customer waiting time, and lean manufacturing. These newer approaches focus upon critical examination of existing processes, comparison of a firm's performance to that of leading firms, and a focus upon continuous improvement. The newer approaches toward performance improvement recognize that slow, gradual change will not meet the demands of a competitive marketplace. Major changes are often necessary in firms and these changes need to be implemented quickly and carefully. The articles in this unit emphasize how the operations and production area of a firm is central to attempts at change. Although these newer approaches involve commitments of time, effort, and capital, the long-term gains can be substantial.

G. Berton Latamore's article examines the use of information technology and enterprise resource planning (ERP) software to get more data to shop floor personnel. The article by Alex Taylor presents illustrations of firms that have succeeded at or that are in the process of improving performance. The approaches developed for performance improvement should be equally adaptable to service firms as they are to manufacturing firms.

AN EMPIRICAL ASSESSMENT OF THE PRODUCTION/OPERATIONS MANAGER'S JOB

BRIAN D'NETTO, PHD
AMRIK S. SOHAL, PHD
Department of Management, Monash University, Victoria 3145, Australia

JOHN TREVILLYAN
Monash Mt. Eliza Business School, Monash University, Victoria 3145, Australia

Past assessments of the production manager's job have been very unfavorable. Two earlier studies of the British manufacturing industry have found that the malaise of the manufacturing industry was undoubtedly due, in part, to a marked lack of well-qualified and ambitious people in production management [3, 6]. These studies also indicated that when compared to other managers in the organization, production/operations managers see their job as less glamorous, with less pleasant working conditions, poor career prospects and low pay. In a study on Australian manufacturing managers, Sohal and Marriott [8] had indicated that manufacturing managers are ill-prepared for managing the major changes taking place in technology and work practices. These authors argue that some explanation for poor performance lies in the human resource development function of manufacturing organizations.

Studies on the changing nature of the production manager's job have indicated that the modern production manager is a vastly different individual from the traditional profile of a production manager, i.e., the old-fashioned autocrat that worked himself up from the shop floor [6]. Today, a production manager must have technical knowledge relevant to his/her industry, highly developed interpersonal skills, knowledge of advanced manufacturing technology, knowledge of other functional areas within the organization and an ability to accept and guide change. Gone are the days when the production manager could concern himself/herself only with getting the product out. He/she now needs to produce continually changing products on time, more cheaply and with increasingly better quality. The continuous improvement of the manufacturing operation is an essential part of any production manager's responsibilities.

The nature of the production manager's job has changed from a traditional department-centered approach to cross-functional linkages with marketing, engineering, human resources, finance and accounting. Cross-functional linkages represent the latest challenge in current market needs; the need for more new products faster, with fewer modifications and a shorter product life cycle [1]. Production managers must have expertise in the use of new technologies and philosophies such as programmable automation (PA), Just-in-Time (JIT), computer-integrated manufacturing (CIM), statistical process control (SPC), and total quality management (TQM). Entry-level jobs in manufacturing management are being replaced by jobs in the areas of quality planning and control and purchasing management. In view of the dynamic nature of the environment, an individual must be ready to change jobs and even functional areas several times in a career lifetime. With the increase in cross-functional integration, production managers need to constantly update their knowledge and skills base, particularly along the chain of product development through product distribution [4]. Manufacturing professionals must relate not only to people in other functional areas, but also to other organizations including vendors, customers, government institutions and regulatory bodies. Thus, the ability to communicate effectively, motivate other people, manage projects and work on multidisciplinary teams are essential attributes for effective performance [2, 7].

While several authors have documented changes in the production function, there has been very little empirical research to assess the current job of the production manager. In the present study, we sought to make an empirical assessment of the job of the production/operations manager. Specifically, the study focused on the educational qualifications, career progression, job content, and reward perceptions of production/operations managers in Australia.

CHARACTERISTICS OF THE SAMPLE

The total sample in this study consisted of 600 large, medium and small organizations in Australia. A modified version of the questionnaire used in a previous study [6] was mailed to the production/operations managers in the organizations included in the sample. From the 600 mailed, 254 completed and useable questionnaires were received, yielding an overall response rate of 42.3%. Pertinent facts included: 68.1% of the respondents represented manufacturing organizations, while 31.9% represented non-manufacturing; 25 different industries were included in the sample; and 64.6% of the companies were Australian owned. As to size, 30.3% of the organizations had under 100 employees, 40.9% had between 101 and 400 employees, while 28.8% employed over 400 people. These findings indicate that small, medium and large organizations were included in the survey.

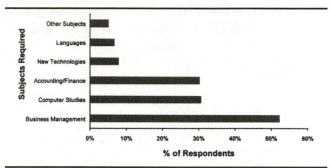

FIGURE 1: Subjects required for present job but not studied earlier

ASSESSMENT OF EDUCATIONAL QUALIFICATIONS AND CAREER STRUCTURES

The findings of the study indicated that Australian production/operations managers are well-qualified, with 78.8% of them having completed a diploma or higher degree. Given that over one-half of the respondents began their careers when they were younger than 19 years old, it appears that a large proportion of the respondents subsequently completed their tertiary education on a part-time basis. Over the past decade, both employees and organizations in Australia have realized the value and importance of higher education. Several companies have provided "study time allowances" and have also agreed to pay for the education of their employees. This could explain the high level of qualifications that production/operations managers possess.

Respondents were asked to identify subjects they felt were required for their present job, but were not studied earlier. The most important subjects identified were business management, computer studies and accounting/finance (see Figure 1). In fact, additional training in business management was also identified as the most important area for future career success.

With respect to career structures, early career mobility appears to be very high, with respondents having worked in several other functions before entering the production/operations function. However, once respondents joined the production/operations management function, they tended to remain in the same functional area; 76.3% of the respondents had been working in production/operations management for over ten years. This considerably long tenure in the same function, together with high levels of job satisfaction, indicates that production/operations managers in Australia do not find the job distasteful

TABLE 1: Control of Different Functions

Control of Functions	% of Respondents		
	Total	Partial	None
Direct Production/ Operations	67.8	25.2	7.0
Quality	48.1	47.2	4.7
Planning	44.5	52.4	3.1
Maintenance	40.6	41.3	18.1
Work Study	36.6	49.6	13.8
Costing (routine)	32.3	52.7	15.0
Purchasing and Supply	26.0	59.0	15.0
Personnel/HRM	24.8	64.9	10.3
Costing (new product/services)	24.0	61.8	14.2
Systems Design (product/information)	19.7	64.9	15.4
Development of New Product Services	16.1	69.7	14.2

as indicated in the earlier British studies. These findings are strengthened by the fact that 45.8% of the respondents entered the production function when they were quite young (less than 25 years old).

ASSESSMENT OF THE JOB CONTENT

An examination of the job content indicated that 67.8% of the respondents had total control of production/operations (see Table 1). However, less than one-half of the sample indicated that they had total control over quality, planning and maintenance.

The most important areas in which respondents believed their control should be increased were planning, systems design, human resources management (HRM) and quality (see Table 2).

Satisfaction with their relationship with other functions and with their jobs was expressed by 70% of the respondents. The greatest job satisfaction was derived from the key tasks of improving productivity, solving managerial problems, opportunities for personal initiative and opportunities for innovation (see Figure 2).

The current organizational restructuring and downsizing has increased the span of control, with 75.2% of the respondents supervising ten or more employees. Besides, with the increasing focus on the bottom line, the most important areas in which managers were responsible for making improvements were cost reduction, productivity and organization

of work and people. Nearly three-fourths of the respondents had defined targets for improvements and specific programs aimed at achieving these targets. However, only 45.7% of the respondents had staff allocated exclusively to the improvement program, while 92.9% of the respondents indicated that their department had its own budget.

ASSESSMENT OF SALARY LEVELS AND SATISFACTION WITH REWARDS

Annual salaries of the respondents varied considerably, from below $60,00 per annum to over $150,000 per annum. However, an interesting finding is that only 9% of the respondents had annual salaries of below $60,000. The results indicate that production/operations managers receive relatively high salaries, with 61.5% of the respondents earning over $90,000 per annum.

Respondents were asked to rate their level of satisfaction with 12 different rewards for their job, compared to the rewards for managers in other functions in the organization (see Table 3).

It is interesting to note that respondents had very positive perceptions of the rewards for their job. In fact, compensation (salary) for the job was perceived as being better than in other functional areas. Intrinsic rewards such as work variety, work importance, authority, control and autonomy appear to be very high. According to Herzberg [5], while extrinsic rewards such as compensation remove dissatis-

TABLE 2: Functions Requiring Change of Control

Change of Control Required	% of Respondents	
	Increased	No Change
Planning	53.2	46.8
Systems Design (product/information)	42.5	57.5
Personnel/HRM	41.3	58.7
Quality	40.2	59.8
Development of New Product Services	37.8	62.2
Direct Production/Operations	33.1	66.9
Costing (new product/services)	29.9	70.1
Work Study	29.2	70.8
Purchasing and Supply	28.0	72.0
Maintenance	24.8	75.2
Costing (routine)	22.4	77.6

faction, intrinsic rewards which flow from the work itself motivate individuals. Given that compensation is good, and intrinsic rewards are high, it is possible that production/operations managers are highly motivated. The results indicated that rewards that need some improvement are benefits, work load, feedback and advancement opportunities. While perceived inequities of benefits with other functions need to be investigated further, problems with the other three rewards could be due to the increasing pressure placed on the production/operations function during streamlining operations in which most Australian organizations are currently engaged. With the pressure to be more competitive, work load has increased. Lack of time can result in performance appraisals and feedback being largely ignored. Flatter organizational structures reduce advancement opportunities, especially if the incumbent does not possess adequate managerial skills and cannot move out of the production/operations management function.

AREAS FOR IMPROVEMENT

There were several areas identified by respondents which require improvement. First, only 4.3% of the respondents were female. It is sad to note that in spite of equal employment opportunity and affirmative action legislation, women have not been able to make inroads into this traditionally male-dominated profession. Second, while 78.8% of the respondents were well-qualified, nearly one-half of the sample were not members of any profes-

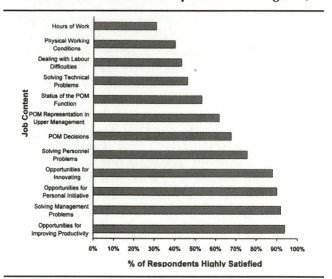

FIGURE 2: Level of job satisfaction

TABLE 3: Perceptions of Rewards (Percentages)

Rewards	Below Average	Average	Above Average
Compensation	17.7	32.7	49.6
Benefits	36.7	41.7	21.6
Social Interaction	18.9	24.4	56.7
Job Security	21.2	22.8	56.0
Status/Recognition	20.5	23.2	56.3
Work Variety	15.0	10.6	74.4
Work Importance	7.5	12.2	80.3
Work Load	33.9	20.5	45.6
Autonomy	7.5	12.2	80.3
Advancement Opportunities	25.5	31.1	43.4
Feedback	30.8	31.5	37.7
Working Conditions	19.7	31.5	48.8

sional institution. Professional institutions play a significant role in providing current information and discussing recent changes in the field. This low rate of membership could be an indication of the failure of production/operations managers to keep up with current trends in the field. This could be due to paucity of time, as respondents indicated that their work load was too high. Failure to keep abreast of current changes could explain why respondents indicated that solving technical problems was one of the areas which yielded the lowest job satisfaction. Third, while tertiary education appears to have provided technical skills, there is clearly a need for more skills in business management, computers, finance and accounting. Flatter organizational structures and increasing spans of control have made it necessary for managers to possess these skills. Over one-half of the respondents indicated that they required additional business management skills for their current and future jobs. The lack of management skills that production/operations managers possess could be the reason dealing with labor is one of the areas which yields the lowest job satisfaction. Besides, 18.9% of the managers indicated that they required foreign language skills. This could be a result of the high proportion of work force diversity in Australia. Fourth, while nearly three-fourths of the respondents had targets and programs for improvements, less than 50% had staff allocated exclusively to the improvement program. Improvement programs will not be successful unless adequate time and resources are devoted to them. In addition, managers indicated that they require control over planning, systems design, human resource management and quality in order to enhance their performance. Fifth, nearly one-third of the organizations did not have any written production/operations management policy. Over one-half of the respondents believed that the board of directors did not have knowledge of the production/operations management function. Without adequate knowledge at the board level, it is possible that important decisions affecting manufacturing strategy and policy will be made incorrectly.

CONCLUSION

The findings of this study indicate that there have been significant positive changes to both the individual and the job in the production/operations management function in Australia. The most important finding is that, overall, production/operations managers are well-qualified, have positive perceptions of their jobs and are generally satisfied with the rewards. Also, perceived intrinsic rewards from the job appear to be high. The job of the production manager in the future is likely to be very exciting. The rapid increase of technology, and the advent of the knowledge worker, is likely to require highly qualified individuals with outstanding managerial skills to effectively manage the production function. The importance of the production management function in organizations is likely to increase, and outstanding production managers will be required to create and maintain a sustainable competitive advantage.

REFERENCES

1. Bandyopadhyay, J. K. "Redesigning the POM Major to Prepare Manufacturing Managers of the 1990s." *Production and Inventory Management Journal* 35, no. 1 (1994): 16–30.

2. Calvacca, L. "Managing Change: What Production Executives Need to Know." *Folio: The Magazine for Magazine Management* 23, no. 19 (1995): 200–201.

3. Gill, R. W. T., and K. G. Lockyer. "The Career Development of the Production Manager in British Industry." London: *British Institute of Management*, 1978.

4. Gordon, J., and J. Wiseman. "Thriving on Competition." *Business Quarterly* (Spring 1995): 79–84.

5. Herzberg, F. *Motivation to Work*. New York: John Wiley, 1959.

6. Oakland, J. S., and A. Sohal. "The Education, Training, and Career of Production Managers in British Industry." *International Journal of Operations and Production Management* 9, no. 8 (1989): 63–90.

7. Rao, A. R. "Manufacturing Professionals of the 1990s: How Should They Be Prepared." *Report of the APICS Academic/Practitioner Liaison Committee*, 1989.

8. Sohal, A. S., and F. Marriott. "Manufacturing Management in Australia: The Human Resource Management Implications." *International Journal of Manpower* 14, no. 9 (1993): 41–55.

About the Authors—

BRIAN D'NETTO, PhD, is a lecturer in human resource management at Monash University. Prior to joining the university, he completed his PhD in human resource management at the State University of New York at Buffalo. He has worked in the field of human resource management in industry for seven years. Dr. D'Netto's current research interests include recruitment and selection, training and development, compensation and managing work-force diversity.

AMRIK S. SOHAL, PhD, leads the operations management group in the Department of Management at Monash University, where he is professor and Director of the Quality Management Research Unit. Dr. Sohal's previous academic appointments were with the Graduate School of Management at the University of Melbourne (Australia) and with the University of Bradford (UK). His current interests are in manufacturing/operations strategy, quality management, Just-in-Time systems and technology management. He has received research grants from the state and commonwealth governments and the Australian Research Council.

JOHN TREVILLYAN is the director of the Workplace Management Centre, Monash Mt. Eliza Business School. Mr. Trevillyan has directed programs in Australia, Papua New Guinea, Fiji, Indonesia and New Zealand for various groups and companies. He has also undertaken a number of consultancies for organizations in the areas of organizational culture, performance management, best practice management techniques and was a board member of a metropolitan public hospital. Mr. Tevillyan's areas of research include learning technologies, performance management and operations management.

Reengineer or Perish

By G. Berton Latamore

Emerging factors, such as shorter product cycles and the rise of the super customer, put increasing pressure on companies to reengineer business practices, says management guru Dr. Michael Hammer. Those companies experiencing success have reengineered the supply chain to speed cycle times, cut costs, improve asset use, and add more value to the customer.

THE IDEAS OF DR. MICHAEL HAMMER, one of the world's foremost business thinkers and the originator of both reengineering and process-centering, have transformed the modern business world. In 1992, *Business Week* named him one of the four preeminent management thinkers of the 1990s, and in 1996 *Time* magazine named him to its first list of America's 25 most influential individuals.

A former professor of computer science at the Massachusetts Institute of Technology, Hammer is the founder and director of several high-tech companies. He serves as an advisor to leaders of the world's most progressive companies and his public seminars are attended by thousands of people annually. He is the author of *Reengineering the Corporation: A Manifesto for Business Revolution* (with James Champy) (HarperBusiness, 1993); *The Reengineering Revolution: A Handbook* (HarperBusiness, 1995); and *Beyond Reengineering: How the Process-Centered Organization is Changing Our Work and Our Lives* (HarperBusiness, 1996).

In this exclusive interview with *APICS—The Performance Advantage,* Hammer discusses how reengineering the supply chain is the key to manufacturing success in the new millennium.

APICS—The Performance Advantage: **When you wrote** *Reengineering the Corporation,* **the U.S. economy was in recession. The first chapter focuses on why U.S. businesses were failing. Today, despite the economic problems of much of the rest of the world, the U.S. economy seems to be continuing near-record growth. Does this change your view of U.S. businesses?**

Hammer: The economic boom does not change my view. In fact, in some sectors of our economy, companies' reengineering of business practices in the last five years is the main reason for success. This is particularly true in key areas of manufacturing such as automotive.

Some companies may be doing well without making those changes, but that is not going to last. A new set of factors are creating new business problems that are putting a lot of pressure on companies. For example, we are seeing the rise of the super customer as many companies see the number of customers go down and the size of their remaining customers increase. The service and price demands of these more powerful customers are much more exigent. Manufacturers also face shorter product life cycles. There is the relentless drive of innovation among competitors. So even if a company has squeaked by until now, that doesn't mean it will be able to continue.

So I think some of the business pressures we talked about five years ago are still there and others have changed, but the name of the game remains improving performance.

you have to assume the worst and *stockpile* supplies

APICS: **You advocate reengineering of the supply chain as an important step for U.S. manufacturers. But the term supply chain means different things to different people. What is your definition of the main components of the supply chain for the purposes of reengineering?**

Hammer: To some companies, a supply chain is nothing but a euphemism for procurement and logistics, but I think that misses the point. To me supply chain really means everything that happens to fill the demands of the ultimate customer. That means all the work that is done by everybody who is contributing to the product and service that leads to the final customer. One of my favorite definitions is from a company in the tissues business that defines the supply chain as "from stump to rump."

Over the last five years we have made a lot of progress on the *intra*company order fulfillment process. The problem is the system breaks down. What makes supply chain a very different kind of process is that it does not exist within the walls of a single company. By its nature, supply chain is an *inter*company endeavor. It does not end with supplying the manufacturer's customer. It extends to the customer's customer and goes back to the supplier's suppliers.

It is a set of activities that are performed by a number of companies. They need to perform those activities coherently. Right now, different parts of the supply chain are done by different companies at arm's length from each other. We need everyone to work in synchrony. The goal is virtual integration. Companies should work together with no more overhead or difficulty than if they were part of the same enterprise. It should be no more difficult to get something from a supplier than from your own warehouse.

APICS: **Why should manufacturers reengineer their supply chains?**

Hammer: One reason is to improve financial performance by lowering costs. If you work synchronously with your customers and suppliers, you can eliminate a lot of redundant work to save money. But the more important reason is that you reduce asset utilization—raw materials, work in process, and finished goods in storage. And you can get better use of your production assets. If you do not know your supplier's schedule, you have to assume the worst and stockpile supplies in a warehouse. If your supplier does not know your production schedule, he has to assume the worst and stockpile supplies in his warehouse. If we reengineer to work together, we can eliminate most of that inventory and eliminate a great deal of waste and cost. That is probably the main reason companies reengineer their supply chains.

The second reason for reengineering the supply chain is to make it easier for customers to do business with you. In a world of increasing commoditization, how easy you are for your customers to do business with and how little overhead you add to your customers' costs can be critical differentiators.

In the long term, the most important reason for supply chain reengineering is to add more value to customers. If you really rethink your supply chain, you can end up adding more value to customers and even extending the nature of your product to deliver product bundled with service. This means you are doing more for the customer, which entitles you to higher margins and gives you greater market differentiation.

All of these goals are very important. Achieving them demands looking at the supply chain process from end to end and finding opportunities for eliminating redundancies and improving asset utilization throughout the process.

APICS: **What are some specific examples of how manufacturers achieved these goals through supply chain reengineering?**

Hammer: One example that is very current is IBM's answer to Dell Computer's new manufacturing model that allowed it to build PCs to order direct from the customer, with a short time to delivery. This gave Dell a major advantage over IBM in the PC marketplace. At the time, IBM had 12 weeks of PC inventory in the supply chain to its distributors. Twelve weeks of inventory in a system where product life is 12 to 18 months is a recipe for disaster.

IBM had to do something. But instead of just looking at its internal processes, it examined the entire fulfillment process from the time the customer places an order with the distributor until it is filled. [The reengineering team] asked themselves who should do each step of the process. One thing they found was that often distributors had to disassemble the PCs they received to modify them to meet the customer's requirements. So IBM started delivering components rather than assembled PCs to its distributors, saving both IBM and the distributors time and money. The assembly work IBM was doing is now being done by the distributor.

inventory is a *substitute* for information

On the other hand, the team discovered IBM was better at managing the distributor's inventory of components than the distributors were. Today, IBM manages its distributors' inventories.

So IBM does some of the work the distributor used to do, and the distributor does some work that IBM used to do. IBM and its distributors went from 12 weeks to two weeks of inventory in the system and eliminated a lot of errors, redundancies, and duplications. It is now cost competitive with Dell's direct build-to-order model.

APICS: **One major change that is often part of supply chain reengineering is choosing a single supplier for key raw materials or components. How does the manufac-**

turer ensure he doesn't end up paying inflated prices for those components once competition in the supply chain has been eliminated?

Hammer: The consolidation of suppliers is, in fact, a common aspect of supply chain reengineering. In theory, there is risk in being captive to that supplier, but that risk is more theoretical than real. The supplier with a single-source contract with a customer has a lot riding on that customer's success. Often, the supplier will succeed or fail depending on the success of that customer. If the supplier abuses that customer, the customer will terminate the relationship. So we have not seen that as a problem. I sometimes say this reminds me of mutually assured destruction. The two organizations are so dependent on each other that if either harms the other they end up killing both.

APICS: **Another major change is the much closer relationship between manufacturer and suppliers in many reengineered supply chains. Often this includes sharing sensitive information, such as designs for new products. Is the sharing information necessary for success of a reengineered supply chain?**

Hammer: Yes. Often, inventory is a substitute for information. If you are a customer, and I don't know what your demands will be, I have to assume the worst and pile up inventory. If you are the supplier and do not know my production plans, you have to assume the worst and pile up inventory. If you do not know my plans for a new product, you often will end up holding inventory that no longer has any value when the product changes. If we share with each other, we can both win.

Product life cycles are getting much shorter. If I share my new product plans with my suppliers, they can help design those products so they can produce higher quality components at lower cost. They can design and implement their component manufacturing processes in parallel with mine. As a result, when I am ready to start production of the new product, they're ready to provide the materials and components I need, eliminating huge amounts of delay and, often, redesign of products.

APICS: **How do manufacturers ensure that sensitive business information is adequately protected when shared with other companies in the supply chain who may have multiple commitments and divided loyalties?**

Hammer: Obviously, you have to put procedures in place to protect sensitive information, but it is in everybody's best interest to maintain that confidentiality. Any immediate benefit a supplier might realize from divulging secret information about a customer in a reengineered relationship would be far outweighed by what it would suffer through the termination of that relationship.

APICS: **How have manufacturers benefited from the creation of this close relationship?**

Hammer: We are really talking about the virtual enterprise or what Chrysler calls the "extended enterprise." Some industries, such as automotive, have adopted this concept already, and Chrysler has been a leader.

Chrysler and its suppliers try to work as one company. Chrysler realizes it needs to focus on product design and development, and on marketing. That means it must simplify manufacturing. The auto industry uses the concept of the "multi-tier supply chain." Some suppliers are designated as tier one, which means they produce whole subsystems like automobile seats. They deal with tier-two suppliers who provide springs, fabric, etc., for those seats. They, in turn, deal with tier-three suppliers who provide the raw materials. The tier one suppliers have the responsibility of bringing the supply chain together to deliver finished seats to the right Chrysler factory, ready to install, rather than springs, bolts, and fabric. The result is that the tier one suppliers concentrate on what they do best—producing specific car subsystems, freeing Chrysler to do what it most needs to do—design and sell cars.

APICS: **What part does information technology (IT) play in supply chain reengineering?**

Hammer: Information technology is the enabler for reengineering. The key to allowing companies to integrate across boundaries is sharing information, which is achieved by IT. Electronic Data Interchange (EDI) has been the primary mechanism for information sharing between partners in the supply chain until now, but we are starting to move past EDI. For example, as we speak, the automotive industry is going live with the Automotive Network Exchange (ANX) to allow sharing of a lot of information on the Internet along the entire manufacturing process.

APICS: **It's often advised that manufacturers should change their business practices first and then automate the new methods. However, IT often creates the opportunity to reengineer in ways that are impossible with paper-based methods. Which should come first—the installation of IT tools or reengineering?**

Hammer: You don't install the technology first, but you do have to understand it first. You cannot design your new business processes without a knowledge of what technology can allow you to do. Learning that spurs your imagination to design the process, and then you use technology to implement the design.

APICS: **You have said that a successful reengineering process needs a leader, a process owner, a reengineering team, and a steering committee. Who are the best candidates for leader and process owner for supply chain reengineering projects that, by their nature, involve two or more companies?**

Hammer: You really need a pair of people on each role because you are crossing enterprise boundaries. Typically, you need an executive leader and a process owner at both the customer and supplier. The leaders, in particular, need

How Reengineering Changes Jobs

Supply chain reengineering enormously affects the jobs of individuals within companies and their relationships with their counterparts among the company's suppliers and customers, says Hammer. As with internal reengineering efforts, supply chain reengineering shifts the focus of individual employee efforts from following the rules and pleasing the boss to improving corporate efficiency and meeting or exceeding customer expectations.

"Jobs become much bigger and broader," Hammer says. Responsibility moves down the corporate organization toward the people actually doing the work. As a result, people have much larger responsibilities for major chunks of the whole process rather than being confined to single tasks.

"Workers are expected to make their own decisions about the best way to accomplish complex pieces of the process as opposed to following orders and referring all issues up the chain of command," he points out.

To meet this responsibility, they need a greater understanding of customer requirements and customer operations. They need the authority to make the decisions that are now their responsibility and see those decisions carried through. "So we have moved from the narrow specialized jobs to big, broad and responsible jobs."

For instance, Hammer says, one manufacturing company he works with used to have a central group that created the production schedules everyone followed. The problem with this approach was its inflexibility, and the company could not respond quickly to customer requests.

To gain competitive advantage, it wanted to move to a build-to-order model with short production times between customer order and product delivery. To do this, it reorganized its manufacturing effort into production teams, each linked closely to customers. Every day, each team decided what it would build that day based on the customer orders it needed to fill and the raw materials available.

"The important concept for this model is the team," Hammer says. "The workers on the manufacturing floor work together as a team to decide not just how to produce the product but what to produce and when. So much more authority is pushed down to the front lines.

"Information about customer needs and the raw materials available are what lets these teams take on this broader authority," he says. By harnessing IT to provide direct links between the teams on its factory floor and its customers, it cuts through the normal chain of information from customer manufacturing engineers to customer supply managers to the manufacturer's sales force and through that to manufacturing schedulers and finally to the manufacturing floor.

Instead, the people who do the work hear directly and instantly from the key people in the customer's organization and can respond quickly to satisfy customer needs. The result is a major reduction both in the time it takes to deliver products and in the inevitable errors that happen as complex information on customer requirements are passed from hand to hand through the old information chain. —B.L.

to be reasonably senior people because you are expecting massive behavioral change in the organization, which never comes easily or lightly. You are asking people to change their attitudes and share information with other companies, which is very counter cultural.

Most important, they must be willing to share the benefits of reengineering with the other organization. A company that wants to hog all the benefits of reengineering will get slaughtered because no one will be willing to play with it. Everyone has to benefit for everyone to be willing to make the massive changes in operations that reengineering demands.

These are radical changes in traditional modes of operation. Unless someone at the very top is driving the process, these changes tend to be lost in the resistance of the organization to massive change, and the reengineering effort will fail.

Similarly, the process owner needs to be highly visible and respected person to demonstrate that reengineering is being taken seriously. A token person does not make a statement that the company is serious about cross-boundary change.

APICS: **Should the reengineering team include representatives of other organizations in the supply chain?**
Hammer: Yes, very much. Your suppliers and customers tell you what to do. Chrysler, for instance, has a program called Score in which their people work with suppliers to help the suppliers figure out better ways to do business.

APICS: **Do the people involved in reengineering have a personal stake in its success—what happens to those who succeed in reengineering their companies?**
Hammer: Success in reengineering can be a big career boost for the key people involved in it. At Texas Instruments (TI), for example, the process owner for one of the first reengineering efforts was Tom Engibous. At the time, he was vice president and general manager of a TI business unit. He had the authority and clout to drive fundamental change that lead to enormous improvement. Now, six years later, he is CEO of the company.

APICS: **In general, what advice do you have for manufacturers who are considering supply chain reengineering?**
Hammer: First, if you haven't already started, you're behind. Second, you must push the envelope. Merely replicating in 1999 what your competition did in 1996 will not get you far enough. You must go beyond, look for new ways to speed cycle times, cut costs, improve asset use, and add more value to the customer.

Bert Latamore is a freelance writer in Alexandria, Va.

Hurry Up and Wait

What would the country be like if every business valued its customers' time at $20 an hour? Very, very different.

BY KELLY BARRON

IF THERE WERE A CONTEST FOR DUBIOUS achievements in customer service, US West would win some kind of trophy. When Sally Moss, a retired high school Latin teacher, recently moved her mobile home a half-mile to another plot of land in Oakland, Ore, she asked US West for a new phone line. After a week, the installer was a no-show. When she complained, US West told her she wouldn't get phone service for two more months.

With help from the Oregon Public Utility Commission Moss got her phone service within a month. But she was one of the lucky ones. So many other Oregonians have found themselves in the same situation that the PUC ordered US West (now part of Qwest Communications) in March to refund consumers $270 million to compensate for installation delays and shoddy service. "They put profits well ahead of consumers," thunders PUC Chairman Ron L. Eachus.

Wait a minute. Shouldn't profits and customer service go hand in hand? How did we get to a point where a company thinks it can improve its prospects by wasting customers' time?

Regulated utilities aren't the only culprits. Think of the 50-yard check-in line at the airport; the cable guy who needs a four-hour window for an appointment, the doctor who has four busy patients waiting for every one that he is seeing, the insurance company with a call processor that saves a tad on labor costs but forces every customer to wade through a tedious telephone menu. In these cases and a million more like them, it seems that some cost-cutter has counted all the beans on the corporate side and none on the customer side. Despite all the new technology that was supposed to speed things up, many businesses have gone in the opposite direction in their dealings with customers.

"Customer time is not explicitly involved in a transaction," says Uday Karmarkar, director of the University of California, Los Angeles Center of Management in the Information Economy. "Businesses get this slowly. Banks have known for a century how to design more efficient queues. If your competitor isn't doing it, why be a missionary?"

Maybe we should blame the business schools. With the exception of the academic and somewhat pedantic study of queuing theory, there's little specifically taught about valuing customer time so much as exploiting it. Consider Las Vegas, where the rule of thumb is to place the room elevators as far from the hotel registration as possible, forcing guests to navigate the temptations of the casino along the way.

Businesses have had no trouble figuring out what their own time is worth ever since Frederick Winslow Taylor published his *Principles of Scientific Management* a century ago. The United Parcel Service has for decades followed Taylor's time-and-motion theories to make its internal operations highly efficient, to the point of measuring the paces between a double-parked truck and a customer's doorstep.

Where is the Frederick Taylor for the customer? Where is the time-and-fidgeting study?

Even when a business, breaking the pattern, attaches a value to its customers' wasted time, it's chintzy. The cable industry, for instance, has voluntarily promised since 1995 to give you $20 if the cable guy shows up late (and then sometimes only if you remember to ask). And what sophisticated theory went into equating that figure with your time?

"Well, it won't put us out too much, people are happy with it and $20 is $20," offers Eric Glick, a spokesman for the National Cable Television Association. He confesses that when consumers were later surveyed about

Reprinted by permission from *Forbes* magazine, October 16, 2000, pp. 158–164. © 2000 by Forbes, Inc.

HOW DID WE GET TO A POINT WHERE A COMPANY THINKS IT CAN IMPROVE BY WASTING CUSTOMER TIME?

the guarantee, they said the $20 was nice, but they'd rather just have the service on time.

Of course they would. Most Americans would rather have more time than money. Isn't that why union members strike rather than accept forced overtime at 150% of straight pay?

Now ask yourself how many minutes a day you spend waiting—for an elevator, a Web page, a customer service rep, a delivery person, a free cashier. If it's 30 minutes, and if all employed Americans have like experiences, and if time is worth $20 an hour, then we are wasting maybe half a trillion dollars a year. It doesn't seem that the people who plan call centers or design elevators have crunched the value of time into their equations. Congress couldn't have given more than fleeting thought to time when it added things like education credits and alternative minimum taxes to the tax code. We spend 1.3 billion hours a year tangling with 1040s.

As time wasters, though, the airlines are in a category by themselves. Facing the threat of yet more regulations by Congress last year, the industry adopted its own "Airline Customer Service Commitment" as a way of fending off the politicians. But anyone who had the misfortune to travel much this past summer probably already knows that the "commitment" hasn't exactly made things better.

"Airlines have a long way to go to restore customer confidence," Kenneth Mead, the Department of Transportation's inspector general, understated in scathing testimony to Congress in July. He cited the difference between what the airlines think will placate customers— prompt ticket refunds, quoting lowest available fares and retrieving lost luggage—and what's really annoying travelers: flight delays, long check-in lines and the 20-minute wait at the baggage carousel.

TIPS ON HOW TO NOT WASTE TIME

- Go to www.e-mps.org/en/ to get off spam e-mail lists.
- Cut lines, get baggage faster, by joining a frequent-flier program.
- Head left at tolls; slow-moving trucks usually move to the right.
- Go to the "telemarketing scum" Web page and others for tips on hanging up on time-wasting pests.
- Don't read time-management books or attend seminars on the topic.

Add Irvine, Calif. attorney Sheldon Fleming to the burgeoning list of ticked-off passengers. His recent American Airlines flight from Orange County, Calif. to San Francisco began with an hour's delay at the gate. Then the plane was rerouted to San Jose, forcing Fleming and his fellow passengers to endure a traffic-snarled bus ride to San Francisco's airport, where they arrived four hours behind schedule. Since Fleming charges an hourly fee of between $150 and $225, he figures that the delay cost him as much as $900.

"I could have billed the time and paid for my vacation," he deadpans. An American flack responds: "I'd be ticked, too,"and adds that the company is working to reduce flight delays.

Stanford University professor of economics Paul Romer, known for his theories about how knowledge and technology affect economic growth, is now thinking about how technology will make the hidden cost of wasted time less hidden. "We're taught not to waste things, but in the context of 'don't waste money,'" Romer says. "People aren't taught about wasting time." The Internet will teach them.

Take your aftertax salary—let's say it's $100,000 — and divide by 2,000 hours a year. Your time is worth $50 an hour. Say you want a John Grisham bestseller. If you get it by driving to Barnes & Noble, parking, asking inside the store for directions to the right aisle and waiting in line for a cashier, you might invest an hour in the acquisition. Then the novel really cost you $70, not $20. If the same purchase on barnesandnoble.com costs only 6 minutes plus a $4.50 shipping charge, the price falls to $29.50. A screaming bargain.

Why does it take six weeks to get a sofa after you have picked it out at the store? Because companies like Ethan Allen and Furniture Brands International know the value of their factory workers' time—something like $17 an hour, including benefits—and can save a bit of it by manufacturing in batches.

Robert Davidow is trying to teach them a lesson with his Benchmark BeHome Internet site and store in Kansas City, Mo. Davidow's 12-acre store stocks 37,000 items. If a customer likes one of the 400 sofas on Davidow's floor, he removes a tag from the item and scans it at a computer that can tell if it's in stock. Fifteen minutes later it's in the back of his Chevy Suburban, or, for a fee, delivered to his home the next day.

"Your time on this planet is precious," says Davidow. "Most industries just don't get it."

Yet old habits die hard. Some customers actually like browsing in book stores or wandering in supermarket aisles. If they didn't, George Shaheen would be a billionaire.

A STITCH IN TIME SAVES NINE

If it's true that time becomes our most precious commodity in a prosperous economy, then some companies will win by valuing their customers' time, while others will fall behind. Most winners on our list have developed new products or processes that value "the customer's life span as a crucially scarce resource," as technology pundit George Gilder has written. The losers may be running out of time themselves.

AIRLINES
WINNER: Virgin Atlantic
Speedy check-in for upper-class passengers from inside their chauffeured cars.
LOSER: United
Dubious honor of most flight delays of any airline for past 13 years has helped earn it a Web site, www.untied.com.

BANKS
WINNER: Wells Fargo
Internet account access with optional bill-paying service reduces banking chores.
LOSER: Citibank
Bails out of attempt at all-Internet banking service, Citi f/i.

FAST FOOD
WINNER: Wendy's
Serves up Big Bacon Classic within two-and-a-half minutes.
LOSER: Steak 'n Shake
More like Wait and Wait. Midwest chain takes almost six minutes for a steakburger.

HOTELS
WINNER: Omni Hotels
Tops among upscale hotels in J.D. Power survey. Services include fast Web access.
LOSER: Marriott International
Tumbles in American Customer Satisfaction Index.

LOCAL PHONE SERVICE
WINNER: BellSouth
Spares couch potatoes extra time of going to the phone by flashing caller ID numbers on TV screen.
LOSER: US West
New owner Qwest Communications has its hands full: Some US West customers can reach someone by mail faster than they can get a new phone line.

MAIL, SHIPPING
WINNER: United Parcel Service
Can download and print out merchant-return labels for speedy returns.
LOSER: U.S. Postal Service
Millennium digital clock promotion ticked off customers last year who saw life pass by while waiting in molasses-like lines.

ONLINE MERCHANTS
WINNER: Amazon.com
A faded darling on Wall Street, but still the best for one-click shopping, fast order processing.
LOSER: Value America
Seven-month delays for product refunds helped drive company into bankruptcy.

RENTAL CARS
WINNER: Enterprise
At-home customer pickup and tight relations with body shops speed up rentals.
LOSER: Alamo Rent A Car
Slow lines will leave it with only the most price-sensitive customers.

RETAIL
WINNER: J.C. Penney
Otherwise dowdy chain is a star on the Internet, with three-day delivery or in-store pickup of online orders.
LOSER: Fry's Electronics
Nighmarish service, snaking lines, make it the chain customers love to hate.

Shaheen quit his job running Andersen Consulting to take one running Webvan, the Foster City, Calif.-based Internet grocery store. For a $5 delivery fee (waived on orders of more than $50), Webvan comes to your door with your groceries within a 30-minute window, and even brings the bags into the kitchen. (No tipping allowed.) You are thereby spared the round-trip drive, the schlep from the cashier to the parking lot and from your driveway to the kitchen, the time spent wandering the aisles looking for the peanut butter, the tantrums of sticky-fingered kids in the candy aisle. Plus, the Web site remembers what brand of toilet paper you like.

Webvan doesn't take coupons, which probably saves you money. If that sounds paradoxical, do the arithmetic. If you take home $50 an hour, then a 75-cent coupon is a loser unless you can clip it out of the newspaper, save

it, find it on shopping day and hand it to the clerk in 54 seconds.

But Webvan, whose service is available in ten cities, has had a devil of a time getting people to sign up. It costs the company $137 to acquire each new shopper. Losses are climbing, and the stock is off from $34 last November to $3.

"The real clinker here is good old-fashioned human behavior," says Shaheen, who is sitting on 15 million underwater options. "People are reluctant change agents unless they have no other options."

Wells Fargo deserves a hesitant pat on the back for helping its depositors save time. An early adopter of Internet banking, Wells Fargo has persuaded 25% of its customers to bank online, a higher fraction than any other big bank can boast. But cynical customers may wonder:

"YOUR TIME IS PRECIOUS, MOST INDUSTRIES JUST DON'T GET IT."

Is all this aimed at saving my hours or saving teller hours? On a busy Friday before the Labor Day holiday, 25 customers were ensnared in a motionless line in a Wells Fargo branch in Santa Monica, Calif. At, say, an average $20 an hour, customer labor was being incinerated at a rate of $500 an hour. Where did this cost figure in the bank's branch budget? Nowhere, explicitly, but the bank says it is doing computer modeling to determine the busiest times at bank branches and how many tellers to schedule.

There's a whole discipline, called queuing theory, on scheduling service to cope with intermittent demand. The theory, which goes back to efforts by Danish engineer A.K. Erlang to predict phone traffic in 1909, gets pretty abstruse. Here's a mouthful from the *International Journal of Production Economics:* "A single-stage kanban system with Poisson demand arrivals and Erlang production times is addressed, and an optimizations of the number of kanbans when a change of load to the system is planned is studied."

FACEOFF: MORE TIME VS. MORE MONEY

Used to be that it was the company's way or the highway when it came to saving time. Thanks to the Internet, we now have a choice. It may cost you, whether it's in the form of fewer discounts and coupons for HomeGrocer.com, or processing fees to quickly get a passport. But it's worth it.

HOMEGROCER.COM DELIVERED TO LOS ANGELES HOME

TOTAL TIME TO SHOP: 19 minutes.
TOTAL TAB: $42
WEB PAGES TO NAVIGATE: Five.
PEOPLE WATCHING: Husband in boxer shorts.
PERKS: Avoiding L.A. traffic, time to clean bathroom and sit in the garden while awaiting delivery.
ANNOYANCES: Sending back bad fruit, organizing time to stay at home to wait for delivery, forgetting password to the Web site.
DRESS: Bathrobe and slippers.

TICKET FROM MOVIEFONE.COM

TOTAL TIME: 4 minutes.
COST: $9, no additional fee.
SITE CONTENT: Can see if show is sold out, saving time-wasting trip. Also includes directions to theater, maps, reviews.
SOCIAL INTERACTION ON LINE: Chat room, "Get Romantic" singles section to look for a date.
ANNOYANCES: Cheesy banner for Internet matchmaking service.

INSTANT PASSPORT INTERNET PASSPORT RENEWAL

TOTAL TIME: 20 minutes navigating Instantpassport.com site, getting passport photos, retrieving necessary documents.
TOTAL COST: $140 fees.
PHONE CALLS: One to Instant Passport's 24-hour hotline. Pleasant owner picked up, answered question immediately.
ANNOYANCES: Wish we knew about this private service before.

RALPHS SUPERMARKET IN WEST LOS ANGELES

TOTAL TIME TO SHOP: 35 minutes.
TOTAL TAB: $36 with discounts.
AISLES TO NAVIGATE: Eleven
PEOPLE WATCHING: Usual California oddities, including guy in flip-flops with German shepherd.
PERKS: In-store banking, 25-cent gumball machines, free samples.
ANNOYANCES: Grimy grocery cart, sticky floor at checkout, circling the lot for a parking space, pompous guy on cell phone.
DRESS: Work clothes.

TICKET FROM BOX OFFICE, AMC CENTURY CITY 14 IN LOS ANGELES

TOTAL TIME: 25 minutes.
COST: $9.
CONTENT OF LOS ANGELES TIMES
NEWSPAPER LISTING: Movie times, comics, daily bridge column.
SOCIAL INTERACTION IN LINE: Non-English-speaking family, obnoxious motor-mouthed teenagers.
ANNOYANCES: Dirty hands from newspaper, not knowing if tickets would be available.

COLLEAGUE'S RECENT EXPERIENCE RENEWING PASSPORT OLD WAY AT THE LAST MINUTE FOR TRIP TO SOUTH AFRICA

TOTAL TIME: 8 hours over several days, one day lost travel time.
TOTAL COST: $75 for fees, phone calls; $290 in wasted time.
PHONE CALLS: 30 into Kafkaesque government voice mail system.
ANNOYANCES: Scolded by bureaucrat, sending 73-year-old father on errands, panic, anxiety.

But there are ways that mathematics can be applied to the problem of allocating resources to serve customers. At IBM's research lab in Yorktown Heights, N.Y. computer scientist Baruch Schieber is using linear programming to help an IBM client schedule hours for 250 workers at a call center. The fluctuation in demand during the day, and the fact that workers want uninterrupted shifts, make the problem tricky. The computer has cut the number of wasted worker hours by 33%. The same math, of course, can rearrange a given number of labor hours to reduce customer waiting time.

Walt Disney Co. is sophisticated about solutions like this—and has to be, as anyone who has wilted in a theme park line knows. "We've made a big breakthrough," beams Bruce Laval, executive vice president of operations planning and development for Walt Disney Parks & Resorts. Laval's solution starts with the FastPass, a free ticket that entitles the holder to join a faster-moving line. FastPass is attached to a complicated data-gathering operation. Unbeknownst to most sunbaked tourists, the Happiest Place on Earth is an enclosed universe of monitoring systems that continually cull customer surveys and use computer modeling to predict everything from how many people will eat at any one time to passenger loads on the Jungle Cruise boats.

Taking his inspiration from the way a singles line speeds up lift lines on a ski slope, Laval reasoned that he could create something akin to a virtual singles line based on computer data that measure peak times on the rides. But instead of singles as the differentiating factor, Laval's FastPass line consists of real-time information about park conditions that predicts the best time for guests to return to the ride.

To keep the FastPass data current, a park manager monitors the time guests spend waiting in the regular standby line and punches it into a two-way pager connected to the ride's computer. At the Buzz Lightyear ride at Walt Disney World in Orlando, Laval ushers a visitor into a darkened, closet-size room designated for "cast members" only. He opens a metal cabinet exposing a humble Compaq PC. The waiting-time data goes into the computer, which helps decide how many FastPasses to distribute and adjusts the expected wait time on a neon sign (usually overstated, to trick tourists into thinking the line is moving more quickly). That computer is connected to a larger server housed at the park's headquarters, where FastPass rides throughout the park are monitored.

But none of the fancy technology can solve the bane of any complicated solution: the tourist who is flummoxed. For that reason a Disney worker hovers nearby to explain it and to catch cheaters. And what of those tourists chafing in the standby line when they see others skipping ahead of them?

"It's only a problem if they don't self-select," defends Laval. "The only challenge has been getting people to understand FastPass."

But despite Disney's relentless marketing of the new system, including letters about FastPass inserted into Walt Disney World reservation confirmations, there is still a learning curve. On Deb's Unofficial Walt Disney World Information Guide Web site, a recent anonymous FastPass user posted: "Be prepared for hostile stares from those who have waited in line and don't know what FastPass is."

Even so, Mickey Mouse might be able to teach corporate America a lesson about saving what is becoming their customers' most valuable possession. Technology pundit and FORBES contributor George Gilder has previously summed up the changing competitive mind-set on the topic: "The customer who grasps the possibilities of the new technologies of the speed of light is no longer going to put up with standing in unnecessary lines, filling out gratuitous forms, telling telemarketers whether he has had a nice day and waiting for bureaucrats to get around to his case."

Or, put another way: Time is money, but for whom?

Do **You** Have What It Takes to be **Lean?**

Everyone talks, talks, talks about lean manufacturing. Now, some guidelines for actually achieving success.

by William Feld, CPIM

Much has been written about lean manufacturing. Many in the field of manufacturing management have presented a multitude of approaches with similar sounding labels: cellular manufacturing, agile manufacturing, the Toyota production system (TPS), flow manufacturing, demand flow technology (DFT), and so on. All are very effective methodologies when implemented properly. All have generated substantial benefits to many organizations. And all have been used in some form or another across multiple industries.

So what is the difference between these approaches and this topic called lean manufacturing? To the seasoned practitioner, nothing. Besides semantics, there is no substantive difference. What is critically important however, is that few companies have ever actually deployed these approaches. Many talk a good story. Some point to the "showcase" cell they implemented on the shop floor two years ago. Several can provide computerized presentations of their plans for the year (often the same presentation they used last year with a revised date). In reality,

At-a-Glance

- After years of discussion about lean manufacturing, it's clear many companies remain unable to successfully use this vital tool to achieve improvement.

- Although early efforts may provide discouraging, lean manufacturing requires constant tweaking to avoid backsliding—or worse, "analysis paralysis."

- Labels aside, lean manufacturing requires a steady hand, a good road map, and a company-wide commitment to continuous improvement.

- Five primary elements form the foundation of lean manufacturing: manufacturing flow, organization, process control, metrics, and logistics.

few companies can demonstrate hard evidence of actual implementation across their production areas, let alone the entire company.

Why do so many companies struggle to achieve benefits that have been so well documented in publications and business periodicals? Why do so many manufacturers initiate improvement programs, but never bring them to completion? A common reason is not that they don't know what to do, but that they don't know how. This article provides a roadmap for implementing lean manufacturing, illustrating some basic fundamental steps used in preparing, planning, and deploying a lean manufacturing program.

More than redesigning the shop floor

LEAN MANUFACTURING INVOLVES A great deal more than just rearranging equipment into a U-shape, enacting a pull system, and pushing inventory back onto suppliers. In order to secure lasting benefits and continuous improvement, this initiative must be handled like a change program. Lean techniques and new ways of working are only part of the process.

A successful implementation requires people, partnerships, motivation, rewards, the understanding of fundamentals, and a consistent direction. Some of the topics that must be addressed as part of a lean manufacturing implementation include cross-functional teams, formal problem solving, line balance, continuous flow, customer/supplier relationships, reward and recognition, consistent performance, line-stop authority, defect

LEAN MANUFACTURING BENCHMARK	0	1	2	3	4
MANUFACTURING FLOW					
1. Does material flow one way throughout the plant?					
2. Is the manufacturing process designed to have operators touch material only one time?					
3. Are production areas aligned to end-customer products?					
4. Are workstations designed to meet daily customer demand?					
5. Is product passed between operators one piece at a time?					
ORGANIZATION					
1. Are cell/product line leaders held accountable for end-product performance results?					
2. Are cross-functional teams used on the shop floor?					
3. Are the roles/responsibilities for all team members defined?					
4. Do operators know all steps in the manufacturing process for their areas?					
5. Are support resources located on the shop floor?					
LOGISTICS					
1. Do production areas build to customer demand?					
2. Is material pulled between stations?					
3. Does the shop floor produce to a daily build schedule?					
4. Is material replenished to an A,B,C segregation?					
5. Are shop floor operations rules documented and understood?					
METRICS					
1. Are performance measures visible and current on the shop floor?					
2. Is schedule adherence 100 percent on time?					
3. Is manufacturing lead time less than one day?					
4. Is your shop floor targeted performance continually improving?					
5. Do your shop floor operators own and report their performance data?					
PROCESS CONTROL					
1. Are changeover times on bottleneck resources less than 10 minutes?					
2. Is there a formal continuous improvement program?					
3. Is response time to defects found in the production process less than 15 minutes?					
4. Do operators have the authority to stop the line when defects are discovered?					
5. Is the company philosophy "everything has a place and everything in its place"?					

Figure 2

prevention, and kanban signals. While not complete, this list provides some insight into the breadth of topics that must be addressed if lasting change is to be sustained.

In order for a lean manufacturing program to be completely successful, it must become institutionalized within the organization. When a company redesigns an area—and comes back 12 months later—the area should not have slipped backward to the old ways

of working. In addition, the lean program must focus on a wide array of topics that can be segregated into groups or elements. Figure 1 identifies the five primary elements used to categorize the focus for a lean manufacturing implementation.

Each of these primary elements has a sublisting of techniques or principles that must be deployed as part of a lean manufacturing program. A brief definition of each follows:

FIVE PRIMARY ELEMENTS OF LEAN MANUFACTURING

MANUFACTURING FLOW	ORGANIZATION	PROCESS CONTROL	METRICS	LOGISTICS
1. Product/quantity assessment (product group)	1. Product-focused multidisciplined team	1. Total preventive maintenance	1. On-time delivery	1. Forward plan
2. Process mapping	2. Cell manager development	2. Poka Yoke	2. Process lead time	2. Mix model manufacturing
3. Routing analysis (product, work content, volume)	3. Touch labor cross-training skill matrix	3. SMED	3. Total cost	3. Level loading
4. Takt calculations	4. Training (lean awareness, six elements, metrics, SPC, continuous improvement)	4. Graphical work instructions	4. Quality yield	4. Workable work
5. Workload balancing		5. Visual control	5. Inventory (turns)	5. Kanban pull signal
6. Kanban sizing		6. Continuous improvement	6. Space utilization	6. ABC parts handling
7. Cell layout	5. Communication plan	7. Line stop	7. Travel distance	7. Service cell agreements
8. Standard work	6. Roles and responsibility	8. SPC	8. Productivity	8. Customer/supplier alignment
9. One-piece flow		9. 5 S's		9. Operational rules

Figure 1

Figure 3

1. **Manufacturing flow**—the area addressing physical changes and the work standards deployed as part of the cell design.
2. **Organization**—the area focusing on the identification of people's roles/functions and training in the new ways of working and communication.
3. **Process control**—the area directed at monitoring, controlling, stabilizing, and pursuing ways to improve the process.
4. **Metrics**—the area addressing visible, results-based performance measures, targeted improvement, and team rewards/recognition.
5. **Logistics**—the area providing definition for operating rules and mechanisms for planning and controlling the flow of material.

Before getting too involved with how these elements are deployed, companies must understand why they are changing in the first place. Because many manufacturers are not currently in pain, they may be unmotivated to change their environment. What must take place is a recognized need for change. In other words, holding up a mirror to see reality. This can be accomplished by hiring a consultant to provide an outside perspective, hiring employees from the competition, or benchmarking against the best in the industry.

Figure 2 provides a template for conducting a self-assessment benchmark of organizations based on the five primary elements outlined above. Using this template may be just the ticket for awakening a sleeping giant, alerting an organization to the fact that to avoid future pain, something must change—and now.

The lean manufacturing road map described in Figure 3 provides a general guide, as well as a structure for the next steps in a lean manufacturing program. Organizations going through change often find the course to be difficult, loaded with land mines and uncertainty. This fear of the unknown

prerequisites required for difficult classes in school, the five primary elements of lean manufacturing must be deployed through a series of fundamental steps or stages. These stages are considered complete only when specific physical principles are in place and targeted performance levels are consistently achieved. Like building blocks, each stage has certain principles that must be in place before succeeding principles can be deployed.

Measuring performance is vital

MANUFACTURERS CANNOT EXPECT TO implement cross-training or set-up reduction unless they have identified the standard work content for a product or designed a cell to operate at the level of customer demand (*takt* time). Each stage contains a distinct set of performance measures and these measures can change as a company progresses through the different stages of an implementation. Figure 4 shows a set of lean manufacturing principles with different stages and various measures.

LEAN MANUFACTURING PRINCIPLES

STAGE 1	STAGE 2	STAGE 3
Cell Design (Takt)	SMED	Mix Model Manufacture
Standard Work	Poka Yoke	Make-to-Order
Pull (Intra-Cell)	Total Productive Maint.	Flex Fence
Team Role/Resp./Rules	Continuous Improvement	Finish Goods Variation
Kanban (ABC)	SPC	Back Flush
Level Production	Line Stop	1 Level BOM
Work Instructions (Graphic)	Cross Training	FMEA
5 S's	Material Plan/Control	Process Capability
Visual Controls	Pull (Inter-Cells)	DFMA
1 Piece Flow		

Measures:		**Measures:**		**Measures:**	
• Lead Time	• Density	• Productivity	• Process Yield	• Process DPPM	• Increase Work
• WIP	• Down Time	• Delivery	• Up Time	• Linearity	Volume
• Travel		• S/U Time		• Increase Work	• Pilot New
				Load	Product

Figure 4

causes most organizations to waffle. The lack of knowing "what's next" compounds the problem. By achieving a clear direction, an understanding of where to go next, and an insight as to what is coming, companies can go far in alleviating fear of change.

Once a company creates its lean roadmap, establishing implementation sequence and identifying fundamental building blocks comes next. As with the

When deploying these principles, not only is it important to satisfy the prerequisite steps, a company should mitigate risk and apply any lessons learned. This accomplished through the use of pilot implementation and gaining management buy-in. The first production area identified for implementation should be considered a pilot. Just like the flight test phase in an aircraft development program, ex-

IMPLEMENTATION METHOLOGY

	Stage 1	Stage 2	Stage 3
Pilot Cell	2 Month	2 Month	2 Month
Production Cell 1	2 Month	2 Month	2 Month
Production Cell 2		2 Month	2 Month

- 1 week Kaizen event
- 1 week adjustments
- 6 weeks stabilize production
- Conduct implementation audit

Lessons Learned & Management Report Out

Figure 5

pect some things to break. Then apply any lessons learned to the next area.

Above all, management expectations must be understood before deploying the pilot cell. Only after Stage One requirements have been satisfied can the company move on to Stage Two or begin with a second cell. Figure 5 shows a sequence of events and the path for a typical implementation. Notice that the second stage or the next cell is not started until management has approved the previous area.

Each stage is expected to take two months. This is a generic number depending on product complexity, cell size, receptivity for change, number of people involved, and so on. However, the checkpoints and the staggering of cells remain the same.

Four specific activities (kaizen event, adjustments, stabilization, and audit) are part of the implementation of each stage. These activities represent substeps in the process. The term kaizen, or continuous improvement, is used throughout the implementation. But it is not a loose, unstructured event. It is a "time-boxes" event with specific activities to be addressed and deployed during a particular stage. The training and knowledge transfer used with each kaizen is timely and spoon-fed for direct application. Knowledge is transferred first thing in the morning and deployed in the afternoon. Figure 6 depicts a template for conducting a Stage One kaizen event.

One of the philosophies used by those implementing lean manufacturing is that of RR/PW (roughly right/precisely wrong). The idea: a company can spend two weeks trying to be precisely right or spend a day to get close and do something. Companies often

process. After everything has been documented, communicated, and understood by all the people in the cell, the company must stabilize it and perform. By the end of six weeks of stabilizing and improving the performance of the process, it is time to audit the implementation to secure passage either to Stage Two or the deployment of the next cell. The idea is to get the ball moving and roll out the implementation across the rest of the factory floor.

Many companies have deployed several of these principles and received substantial operational benefits. Others have attempted to deploy some of these principles and not been successful. This loss in direction—and the inability to recognize what the next steps must be—hinders their progress. Using

KAIZEN EVENT

	2 HRS	2 HRS	2 HRS	2 HRS	2 HRS	1/2 HR
DAY 1 CELL DESIGN / STAND WORK	CELL DESIGN	Plan the week, Assign Responsibilities, Identify Parallel Activities		Review Detail Design	Generate First Layout	Wrap Report
DAY 2 PULL / 1 PIECE FLOW	PULL	Generate Second Layout	Move Preparation		Implement	Wrap Report
DAY 3 TEAM RRR / KANBAN ABC	TEAM RRR	Implement		Order Kanban Containers	50% Production	Wrap Report
	KANBAN ABC	Document Roles, Rules, Responsibilities / Establish Kanban Methodology				
DAY 4 LEVEL PRODUCTION / WORK INSTRUCTION	LEVEL PRODUCTION	Fill Kanban Containers / Graph. Work Inst.			50% Production	Wrap Report
	WORK INSTRUCTION	Level Production				
DAY 5 5 S's / VISUAL CONTROL	5 S's	5 S's		Visual Controls		Debrief

Figure 6

find that after rearranging the equipment, something was done incorrectly. It is common to adjust and then adjust again. A committed company continues to adjust and improve the area—this is not a one-time event.

Above all, an organization must avoid analysis paralysis. It must get close to the numbers in the design phase, and go with it. After the first week of the event is over, the implementation team must spend the next week tweaking and adjusting the

the information presented here may provide some insight as to how a company can plan and implement a successful lean manufacturing program.

William Feld, CPIM, is currently a lean manufacturing consultant working with Invensys plc. He can be reached at 314/422-9768, via e-mail at william.feld@worldnet.att.net, or at www.wmfeld.com.

RALLY OF THE DOLLS

It Worked for Toyota. Can It Work for Toys?

FOR THREE-QUARTERS OF A CENTURY, little girls have been unwrapping Madame Alexander dolls at Christmas. The collectible dolls, which cost from $40 to $600 apiece, are modeled on figures both fictional (Cinderella) and real (Elizabeth Taylor); with their hand-painted faces and elaborate costumes, they're charming artifacts of an age before Nintendos and Furbies. But the company that makes them has had to struggle to stay alive for its 75th Christmas. That the dolls are still around is due to an unusual group of manufacturing experts, who have adapted their experience in streamlining the assembly of fenders and crankshafts to the task of turning out wigs, shoes, and all the other tiny bits that go into a doll.

Alexander Doll Co. was founded in 1923 by "Madame" Beatrice Alexander, a daughter of Russian immigrants who was raised over her father's doll hospital in New York City. Her business prospered, and in the 1950s she moved it to a six-story building in Harlem. But after it was sold to two local investors for $20 million, the company faltered. It was headed into bankruptcy in 1995 when it was bought for $17.5 million by an investment group formed by TBM Consulting.

The partners of TBM, a North Carolina–based firm of manufacturing specialists, had studied Toyota's

SUZANNE OPTON (3)

At Alexander Doll Co. new managers have overhauled the factory in Harlem using Toyota techniques.

lean production system in Japan and had taught it to dozens of American manufacturers. TBM had assembled a buyout fund and was looking for underperforming companies where they could put their know-how to work. "We have a contrarian strategy," says TBM vice president Bill Schwartz. "Instead of moving production somewhere else, we want to make it lean and efficient at its current location."

Making dolls is easier than making, say, Lexus LS400s, but not as easy as you'd think. The costumes alone contain 20 or more separate items, which have to go through as many as 30 production steps. Accurate planning is essential because doll fabric is bought in tiny quantities that can't be reordered, and 75% of the styles change every year. As if that weren't difficult enough, before TBM arrived the factory was using archaic methods: It was organized according to old-fashioned principles of batch manufacturing, so boxes of costume material and vinyl doll parts were stacked to the ceiling. Since nothing was built to order, more than 90,000 dolls were stored in partly finished condition, and customers waited up to 16 weeks for delivery.

That began to change in August 1996 when TBM installed a new CEO: Herbert Brown, an earnest, fast-talking manufacturing expert who had run operations for Black & Decker and Johnson & Johnson. When Brown tried to fill a customer order for 300 dolls, only 117 could be completed because so many pieces were missing. So he went to work reorganizing the factory and, in true Toyota fashion, enlisted the aid of the 470 workers, mostly Dominican immigrants who speak limited English.

Instead of individually producing parts, the workers were organized in seven- or eight-person teams, each of which is responsible for completing about 300 doll or wardrobe assemblies a day. The amount of work in progress has been cut by 96%, and orders can now be filled in one or two weeks instead of two months. TBM also hired Bain & Co., a consulting firm, to help expand sales to collector doll shops and to create new marketing programs for home-shopping channels on cable television.

Gradually Alexander Doll is returning to health. Sales have risen from $23.8 million in 1995 to an estimated $32 million for 1998, though the company isn't expected to turn a profit until next year But the workers of Alexander Doll have a vivid incentive to apply Toyota's techniques, because the building itself is a constant reminder of what happens to companies that don't adapt to changing times. The doll factory's first occupant? Studebaker.

—Alex Taylor III

USING ERP DATA TO GET [CLOSE] TO CUSTOMERS

More manufacturers now make ERP data accessible to shop-floor personnel. By doing so, they are dramatically improving response to order changes, customer needs, and market conditions.

By G. Berton Latamore

Management

Sales & Marketing

Purchasing

Customer Service

Shop Floor

At-a-Glance

- Direct access to analysis data from ERP systems shows shop-floor personnel how their efforts contribute to meeting customer needs and gives them a feeling of working for the customer they never experienced before.

- Such access also increases and simplifies internal communications among departments, enabling purchasing to do a more accurate job, eliminate waste, and cut inventory.

- Companies become more agile by providing fast access to changes in orders in meaningful terms—changed supply needs for purchasing, changed work schedules for the shop floor, and so on.

From *APICS—The Performance Advantage,* September 2000, pp. 26-30. © 2000 by APICS and The Educational Society for Resource Management. Reprinted by permission.

"We have near real-time access to information on the state of every SKU, every production item, and highlights of every need to satisfy the customer," says Tim Chambers, director of business process consulting with Basic American Foods (BAF), Walnut Creek, Calif. "That has reduced the number of special efforts and saved customers considerable money."

Before BAF built its network, which consists of SCT's enterprise resources planning (ERP) system and its associated advanced planning and scheduling (APS) systems, coordination among plants to meet customer needs was difficult. Scheduling was a major problem because schedules are dependent on crop availability, and BAF often makes intermediary products that are shipped from one of its plants to another for inclusion in finished goods.

"We have always had very high customer service ratings, but it came at a high cost," says Chambers. "Our customer service folks spent a lot of time advocating internally for the customer—working with schedulers and production lines and transportation, etc., because up-to-date information wasn't available."

Today that situation has changed radically. "Having all that information available in a near real-time environment makes it possible for everyone to do their job better," Chambers says. "As a result, the customer service people can presume that the schedulers, shop floor personnel, and everyone else involved know what needs to be done to serve the customers. They can concentrate on working with our customers rather than with our internal staff."

The company used to work from a manually generated monthly plan that was outdated before it could be distributed. Now the entire company has access to a weekly production schedule, digested down to the individual production line level, generated by the APS engine attached to the corporate ERP system. Between APS runs, changes can be created manually based on ERP data and propagated through the network.

"This helps everyone in the organization align their efforts more toward serving the customer," Chambers says. "Today people on the shop floor can see how their efforts help meet customer needs. That's something new for employees who do not work directly with customers."

Switching from efficiency to goals

FOR MEDTRONIC SOFAMOR DANEK, a medical device manufacturer in Warsaw, Ind., this new customer consciousness at the shop-floor level has created a tremendous shift in emphasis, says Jay Feldman, director of information systems. "People on the shop floor have the same information as the director of production—what they have done and how well they are doing against their production goals by work center and shift. Instead of measuring themselves according to efficiency and effectiveness, today they concentrate on goals—how much quality product we got out, rather than how much equipment use we measured."

ERP Data Access Powers Continuous Improvement

Savage Arms, Westfield, Mass., is a small manufacturer of sporting rifles competing in a market dominated by much larger—and better known—companies such as Colt, Browning, and Smith and Wesson. To compete effectively, Savage Arms created its "Savage 2000" strategy to become a world-class manufacturer.

"We want to be the lowest cost, most accurate, highest quality rifle in the gun industry," says company chief financial officer and APICS member Albert Kasper. "We needed a tool to accomplish this, and we chose Ramco Systems."

The basic Savage Arms strategy is to create manufacturing teams working on specific improvement goals for six-month periods—a variation on continuous improvement. The company chose goals "where we believed we could hit home runs—shorter throughput, ergonomic design, etc."

Ramco's ERP system plays to important roles in this effort. First, nothing ever improves unless it is measured. The ERP system provides the teams with before-and-after performance measurements that enable them to see if they are going in the right direction.

At a more basic level, however, access to ERP data encourages employee involvement in the improvement by giving them the larger picture of how the company is performing and where and why it must improve. It tells employees their opinions count and that senior management respects them. It also encourages them to think about the larger problems of improving company performance. That, says Kasper, is just as important to a program's success as senior management buy-in.

Alone, the system has had a positive effect on daily operations. "We have eliminated all the intermediary reports that people used to get on green bar paper just to hand enter into their own spreadsheets. Now, we provide that final analysis directly on-screen from the central system," Kasper explains.

"Financial closings went from seven to five days almost immediately. We can e-mail purchase orders directly from the purchasing department to our suppliers. And we generate a daily dispatch to the shop floor that provides their priorities for that day, based on our orders."

—*G. B. L.*

> ## "They were competing on how fast they could get access to it because they saw how it would make their jobs easier."

Training is a key to success, he says. When this company rolled out its MAPICS ERP-based system onto the shop floor, the foremen and operators initially were concerned about using the system. After receiving training both in how it works and how to understand the information it provides, "they were competing on how fast they could get access to it because they saw how it would make their jobs easier."

Feldman picked the company's ERP vendor for two key reasons. First, "it works. MAPICS does not release a product until it is ready." Second, it is easy to administer. "I don't have a staff of 35 people devoted to our ERP system. We have two, actually, out of a total IT staff of four."

American Dairy Brands has carried the concept of ERP data access a step further by using it to directly control what takes place on the shop floor. The Columbus, Ohio-based firm is a three-year-old division of the Dairy Farmers of America. The national, 25,000 dairy farm cooperative—created to take over Borden's sliced, wrapped American cheese business—started with a directive to install an ERP system as quickly as possible. The thrust of the project from the start was to use the system to create lines of communication throughout the organization.

In 1998, a year after starting operations, the company installed SCT's ERP Package Adage, with its scheduling component, and a third-party shop floor management system from Wonderware. "The line operators scan materials identifications into the system as they are used," says Alan Turley, director of information services for American Dairy Brands. "Wonderware confirms that they have the right material and right plot numbers for the formula. It then checks the ERP system and posts quantities directly to the inventory module."

The company used its system to build communications from field sales through sales demand planning and master production scheduling and eventually through the materials requirement planning (MRP) system to procurement personnel. They place purchase orders based on the materials forecast generated from data directly from the orders placed by field sales.

"Before they had this information, purchasing had to work manually with a lot more guesswork," Turley says. "It was difficult to communicate accurate numbers between levels—sales to planners, schedulers, and procurement. We plan on significantly improving customer service and reducing inventories with this approach."

"As we speak, we are installing the supply chain planning piece of the system including scheduling, advanced planning, and demand planning. This will enable us to provide field sales with the data they need to know whether we can meet a new order on schedule, before that order is placed." He noted that sales then negotiates orders the company can meet profitably and provides real guarantees of delivery dates customers can count on.

"Our vision from the founding of the company has been to align the entire organization to fill customer needs. Our ERP system and its add-ons enable us to make that vision a reality."

Centralized analysis increases ERP data value

DESPITE THE BENEFITS ERP information brings to the entire organization, knowledgeable companies have learned that raw ERP data often are not enough. It can easily confuse rather than inform. The better approach often is to provide management and the shop floor with the results of analysis of that data. For instance, one major goal of ERP installations is to increase flexibility, a key corporate quality in an era of lightning-fast market changes and constant adjustments in customer orders.

Lilly Software, Hampton, N.H. took this need so seriously, it subordinated the MRP engine at the core of most ERP systems to its own APS engine. As a result, its ERP engine, which is popular particularly among automobile component manufacturers and other discrete manufacturing companies, can generate daily discrepancy reports that show trouble spots in filling specific orders. Management uses these to adjust production schedules to react to order changes as well as to resolve problems before they affect customers.

The system accepts orders and changes electronically, direct from customers, via both electronic data interchange and extensible markup language, eliminating the time lost and errors generated when changes have to be hand-entered into the system. This also enables fully automated billing, bringing the benefits of business process reengineering within reach of midsize manufacturers.

"Smaller companies may rely on a few customers for a high percentage of their business," explains Scott Rich, vice president of marketing for Lilly Software. "They need to provide excellent customer service without cre-

"Our vision from the founding of the company has been to align the entire organization to fill customer needs."

ating processes that are too costly to stay profitable. Our focus is on making that possible."

Salem, N.H.-based ProfitKey International recently introduced another approach, providing canned online analytical processing (OLAP) tools that work with data from its ERP system, based on technology developed for Fortune 1000 companies by PilotSoft, a sister company.

"For instance," says Mark Smith, ProfitKey's vice president of sales and marketing, "these pre-formatted business intelligence tools can identify what orders have shortages or work cells where we have overcapacity. They provide graphical representations that enable managers to identify trends early and respond to them appropriately. This lets second-tier and third-tier companies manage by exception, just like the first tier."

These tools have not been available long enough for ProfitKey customers to install and capture results. However, says Smith, the initial response from ProfitKey users has been overwhelming. "At our user conference, people were screaming for exactly this kind of capability.

"Because these tools work directly off the ERP data, information stays centralized, and everyone sees the same thing. That often doesn't happen when individuals feed raw ERP data into spreadsheets on their desktops to do their own analysis."

There is a danger in providing widespread access to raw ERP data through the corporation, he cautions. For instance, suppose that the CEO asks five executives to analyze the profitability the company realizes from its key customers. Each of these people could easily arrive at entirely different conclusions. First, each may well define profitability differently, depending on what costs, income, and long-term dynamics they include. Second, they may use different data extracted from the ERP system at different times.

OLAP enables the company to arrive at a single definition of profitability. Because the tools are centralized and attached to the ERP system, at any given moment everybody is looking at the same data. "The entire company has one place to go to see how it did with each customer."

G. Berton Latamore is a freelance writer based in Alexandria, VA.

Unit Selections

7. **Fool Proof Service: Poka-Yoke,** Richard B. Chase and Douglas M. Stewart
8. **A Conversation With Joseph Juran,** Thomas A. Stewart
9. **One More Time: Eight Things You Should Remember About Quality,** John P. Mello Jr.
10. **ISO 9000 Myth and Reality: A Reasonable Approach to ISO 9000,** Frank C. Barnes
11. **2-D or Not 2-D?** Srikumar S. Rao
12. **Jac Nasser's Biggest Test,** Alex Taylor III
13. **Cause of Tire Failures Still a Matter of Dispute,** Terril Yue Jones

Key Points to Consider

❖ How would you define and measure quality for a manufacturer? How would you define and measure quality for a service firm?

❖ What are the basic beliefs and principles of Total Quality Management (TQM)?

❖ Where do you believe blame lies in the Ford and Bridgestone/Firestone incidents?

 **Links**   **www.dushkin.com/online/**

15. **American Society for Quality (ASQ)**
    http://www.asq.org
16. **Concept Corner**
    http://members.tripod.co.uk/tomi/concepts.html
17. **International Organization for Standardization (ISO)**
    http://www.iso.ch/welcome.html
18. **John Grout's Poka-Yoke Page**
    http://www.campbell.berry.edu/faculty/jgrout/pokayoke.shtml
19. **Plan-Do-Check-Act**
    http://www.inform.umd.edu/CampusInfor/Departments/cqi/Outlook/Tech/pdca.html

These sites are annotated on pages 4 and 5.

Over the last two decades greater emphasis has been placed upon quality and TQM: Total Quality Management. After World War II, American manufacturing firms had little significant foreign competition. European and Japanese factories were destroyed to a great extent during the war. American firms were able to increase their volume of exports to the world and labor enjoyed demanding and receiving higher wages. By the 1970s, American firms recognized growing production capabilities abroad. Clearly, by the 1980s, American firms faced greater challenges from foreign competitors. The growing United States trade deficit provided evidence of increased imports into the United States and evidence of greater difficulty in exporting American products.

By the 1980s, American firms recognized that they could no longer compete in a global market on the basis of lowest cost per unit. With lower wages abroad, foreign competitors had an advantage in competing on low cost. Some American manufacturers sought to deal with this situation by pressuring labor unions to accept minimal wage gains in negotiations and others relocated production overseas. Even with these efforts, American firms continued to face a trade challenge.

One solution that emerged in the 1980s was for American firms to compete globally on the basis of quality. The late Dr. W. Edwards Deming, a pioneer in the quality movement, had taught Japanese firms how they could improve quality. His approach to quality improvement relied upon statistical process control and a focus upon manufacturing principles that emphasized continuous improvement. The growth of exports from Japanese firms after the 1950s provided evidence that total quality management was a desirable approach for company success.

The articles in this unit examine the evolution of quality and attempts by firms to implement TQM. A conversation with Joseph Juran reviews the beliefs of one of the pioneers in quality control. With ISO 9000 quality system standards required in Europe, firms see the necessity of improving and documenting quality systems.

Ford and Bridgestone/Firestone faced a major crisis in 2000 involving quality and defective tires. The last two articles in the unit review the challenges faced by Ford and Firestone.

Don't read this article unless you want to add the term "poka-yoke" to your vocabulary. In the hands of Richard Chase, the Japanese term for "foolproof" becomes the means to do all of the tantalizingly simple actions necessary to do it right the first time.

fool

PO•KA YO•KE

PROOF SERVICE

BY RICHARD B. CHASE The Justin Dart Term Professor of Operations Management and Director of the Center for Operations Management Education and Research & DOUGLAS M. STEWART PhD '95

We know of no book on quality that does not advocate the "first principle of quality"—Do It Right the First Time—in chapter one. Likewise, we know of no book that provides any detailed theory or specific actions for doing this for services. There remains, therefore, the monumental challenge of quality assurance where the goal is to achieve zero defects in the day-to-day provision of services. While we are in favor of creating quality cultures, continuous improvement processes, quality training in statistics and the like, managers are missing a good bet by not starting fail-safing early in parallel with traditional quality initiatives.

Mr. Improvement

The idea of fail-safing is to prevent the inevitable mistake from turning into a defect. This basic precept was articulated by the late Shigeo Shingo (known as "Mr. Improvement" in Japan). In his many writings, Shingo showed examples of how manufacturing companies have set up their equipment in manual processes to prevent errors, particularly where full-scale automation is too costly or is otherwise impractical.

Central to Shingo's approach is inspection and "poka-yoke." A poka-yoke is a simple, built-in step in a process which must be performed before the next stage can be performed. In a manufacturing context, this may mean that someone running a brick-cutting machine would be forced to push a button with each hand simultaneously before the blade will come down, assuring that there are no hands left to be injured in the machine. Service poka-yokes function in exactly the same manner, assuring that some important step is performed so that the server is literally forced to perform the service well.

Task Poka-Yokes

Errors in the service task are errors in the functional aspects of the service, such as doing the work incorrectly, doing work not requested, doing work in the wrong order or doing work too slowly. There are many examples of poka-yoke devices for the detection and avoidance of task errors, including computer prompts to aid in technical discussions, strategically placed microphones to assure server's and customer's voices are audible, placing bills on a tray on top of the cash register to avoid making errors in change and use of the appropriate types of measuring and weighing tools. The french-fry scoopers at McDonald's are a perfect example of such a measuring tool. Sewell Cadillac and other like facilities use color-coded tags or icons on the tops of cars to help identify customers who belong to a specific service adviser and to show the order of arrival; the adviser can then look out across the sea of cars and find the next car he or she should deal with.

Due to the extreme costs of errors, hospitals are heavy users of poka-yokes in their medical processes. Trays used to hold surgical instruments have indentations for each instrument, and all of the instruments needed for a given

From *USC Business*, Spring 1994, pp. 33-35. © 1994 by the University of Southern California. Reprinted by permission.

operation will be nested in the tray. In this manner, it is clearly evident if all instruments have not been removed from the patient before the incision is closed.

A *poka-yoke* is a simple, built-in step in a process which must be performed before the next stage can be performed.

Treatment Poka-Yokes

Treatment errors by the server are errors in interpersonal contact between the server and the customer, such as failure to acknowledge to the customer, failure to listen to the customer and failure to treat appropriately. Standard treatment poka-yokes include signals such as eye-contact to acknowledge the customer's presence in a restaurant and the sound of bells from the shop door.

A novel poka-yoke is used by a major hotel chain to fail-safe recognition and timely acknowledgment of a guest's repeat business. The way it works is that when the bellman greets the arriving guest to bring his luggage, he asks if it is her first visit. If the guest says she has been there before, the bellman will discreetly tug on his own ear to indicate this fact to the front desk. The clerk at the desk will then greet the guest with a hearty "Welcome back!"

Many service companies train their service personnel to read negative non-verbal clues given by the customer early in the service encounter. This inspection activity allows the employee to take timely action to prevent any communication mistake. One poka-yoke for this is used at a bank to ensure eye contact with the customer: tellers are required to check-off the customer's eye color on a checklist as they start the transaction. In a similar vein, some companies place mirrors next to customer-service reps phones to fail-safe a "smiling voice" to their unseen customers.

A fast-food restaurant listed "friendliness" as one aspect of front-line employee behavior they wished to fail-safe. Rather than mandating that employees smile all the time, the mentors provided four specific cues as to when to smile. These were: when greeting the customer, when taking the order, when telling the customer about the dessert special and when giving the customer change. Employees were encouraged to observe whether the customers smiled back—a natural reinforcer for smiling. While it is tempting to disparage such behavioral management as simply Skinnerian manipulation, the fact is that when properly executed, the approach has been shown to lead to positive results for both the server and the served.

Tangible Poka-Yokes

Tangible errors made by the server are errors in the physical elements involved in the service, such as dirty waiting rooms and incorrect or unclear bills. There are many examples of poka-yokes to prevent tangible errors. One action is to position a mirror so that the worker can automatically check his or her appearance before greeting the customer. The paper strips that are wrapped around towels in many hotels serve as a poke-yoke to the housekeeping staff. The strips identify the clean linen and show which towels should be replaced. Most software programs have built-in checks for spelling and arithmetic errors, some of which even prompt the user to use before printing. W. M. Mercer Inc., a leading consulting firm in benefits and healthcare, engages in "peer review"—systematic pre-auditing by pairs of its associates—of all consulting reports. And Motorola's legal department performs a similar double checking with its two lawyer rule: all aspects of the legal work, memorandums, oral presentations, contract drafts and so on are reviewed by a second lawyer.

The Customer Is Always Right

While "the customer is always right," he also is frequently error-prone. In fact, research done by TARP, a service research firm, indicates that one-third of all customer complaints are caused by the customers themselves. Because of the customers' integral part in the service, their actions must therefore be fail-safed in all three phases of a service encounter: the preparation, the encounter itself and the resolution to the encounter.

Preparation Poka-Yokes

Specific examples of preparation error include failure to bring necessary materials to the encounter, failure to understand and anticipate their role in the service transaction and failure to engage the correct service. Preparation poka-yokes we have all encountered are "dress code" requests on invitations, reminder calls about dental appointments and the use of bracelets inscribed with the wearer's special medical condition. Many doctors and dentists give patients a card with information about a follow-up appointment rather than trusting them to note it themselves.

Encounter Poka-Yokes

Customer errors during the encounter can be due to inattention, misunderstanding or simply a memory lapse. Such errors include failure to remember steps in the service process, failure to specify desires sufficiently and failure to follow instructions.

Examples of the poka-yoke devices and procedures to warn and control customer actions include chains to configure waiting lines, locks on airline lavatory doors which must be turned to switch on lights (and at the same time activate the "occupied" sign), height bars at amusement rides to assure that riders do not exceed size limitations, frames in airport check-in for passengers to gauge the allowable size of carry-on luggage and beepers to signal customers to remove their cards form the ATM. Even symbols worn by employees can be warning devices: trainee buttons, badges, and gold braids are standard signaling methods to shape expectations about service before any actions are taken.

> **One *poka-yoke* is used at a bank to ensure eye contact with the customer: tellers are required to check-off the customer's eye color on a checklist as they start the transaction.**

One example consistent with the low-cost solution philosophy underlying fail-safing is the use of pagers at the 300-seat Cove Restaurant in Deerfield Beach, FL. Since there is often a 45-minute wait for a table, the maitre-d' provides customers with small pagers that vibrate when activated from the master seating control board at the host stand. This has the advantage over a passive take-a-number system since it allows guests to roam outside without missing their table call. The system cost about $5,000. A dentist, whose office is in a mall, loans parents a similar pager so that they can shop while their child receives dental attention.

Many service encounters take place over the phone. The most common mistake facing cable-TV companies in their telephone troubleshooting occurs when people report a supposed reception problem when in fact they have inadvertently changed the channel setting on their TV. However, if a service representative asks the customer if his or her TV is "on the correct channel," the customer will often feel embarrassed or will automatically say "yes." A multi-step fail-safing process employed by one company is to instruct the customer to "turn the channel selector from channel 3 (the correct setting) to channel 5 and then back to 3." This assures that the check is performed, while preventing the customer from feeling inept.

Resolution Poka-Yokes

Customers may also make errors in the resolution stage of the service encounter. Following the encounter, the customer typically evaluates the experience, modifies expectations for subsequent encounters and, ideally, provides feedback to the service provider. A range of errors can occur in this process, including failure to signal dissatisfaction with the service, failure to learn from experience, failure to adjust expectations appropriately and failure to execute appropriate post-encounter actions.

As an example of a follow-up poka-yoke at hotel checkout, management may include a comment card plus a certificate for a small gift in the bill envelope to encourage the guest to spend the time to provide feedback. Childcare centers use such resolution poka-yokes as toy outlines on walls and floors to show where toys should be placed after use. (In fact, a childcare consultant advocates placing photographs by the door to show kids what a "clean room" looks like.) In fast-food restaurants, strategically located tray return stands and trash receptacles act as reminders for customers to bus their trays at the end of their meal.

A clever resolution poka-yoke of historical interest is found in the bathrooms at L'Hotel Louis XIV in Quebec. Because the bathrooms were shared by two rooms, problems would arise when a guest forgot to unlock the door leading to another's room. The hotel installed a poka-yoke to take the place of the locks on the bathroom doors. Since the doors, on opposite sides of the bathroom, opened out into the guest rooms, a leather strap was connected to the handles on each door. When a guest was in the bathroom, the straps would be hooked together, thus holding both doors shut. It would be impossible for the guest to leave the bathroom without unhooking the strap and "unlocking" both doors.

Your Own Poka-Yokes

While this article relied on examples or anecdotes, they are meant to provide the imagery for you to begin to design your own poka-yokes. Some of the examples herein may be directly applicable to your business; hopefully others will trigger solutions by inspiration.

Admittedly, coming up with poka-yokes is part science and part art. You have probably been performing dozens of self-imposed and subconscious poka-yokes for years, such as placing your keys in a certain dish in your room so they can always be found. The science comes in sharing and systematizing the actions to turn them from a trick to a technique.

About the Authors

Richard B. Chase, The Justin Dart Term Professor of Operations Management, serves as Director of the Center for Operations Management Education and Research (COMER). He is a specialist in the design of service systems and manufacturing management. He recently gained attention for offering a money-back guarantee of satisfaction for his course on service. He received his BS, MBA and PhD from UCLA.

Douglas M. Stewart is pursuing his PhD at USC. He received his BS and MS from the University of North Carolina.

—Adapted from "Make Your Service Failsafe," *Sloan Management Review,* Spring 1994.

TOWARD THE CENTURY OF QUALITY

A Conversation With Joseph Juran

BY THOMAS A. STEWART • *Joseph M. Juran turned 94 on Christmas Eve. He is now exactly twice the age he was when he published his Quality Control Handbook, as much a classic in its field as Paul Samuelson's Economics is in his. A few weeks before his birthday, Juran came to New York City to talk up the Juran Center for Leadership in Quality at the Carlson School of Management at the University of Minnesota. We talked in a meeting room at the Warwick Hotel; next door two score police officers were attending a seminar on interrogation techniques. Compared with the beefy cops, some with pistols strapped to their hips, Juran seemed slight and frail, his voice soft. But there was nothing soft about his thinking or frail in his energy level; our conversation, scheduled for an hour, went half again as long, and Juran was going strong at the end. We started by chatting about the other nonagenarian guru, Peter F. Drucker, then turned to the past, present, and future of the quality movement.*

I got interested in Drucker when I read *The Concept of the Corporation*, which I thought was wonderful stuff—a little wordy, but wonderful. I remember contacting Drucker on the way to visit my boys at summer camp. He was a professor at Bennington College in Vermont, which in those days was a girls' school. I asked him, "What in the world are you doing here?" He moved to Montclair, N.J., and made contact with the business school at NYU. Our paths continued to cross, and we've become good friends. Of course, he moved to Claremont, Calif. From Montclair to Claremont—no imagination, you see.

On why quality matters: Historians will define our century, as far as economics is concerned, as the Century of Productivity. One of its biggest events was Japan emerging as an economic superpower. That came about primarily because of the Japanese quality revolution. While our consumers loved Japanese imports, our manufacturers did not. We exported God knows how many millions of jobs; our trade balance was shattered. We were forced to undertake a counterrevolution. Competition in quality intensified enormously.

The next century has to be the Century of Quality. We've got a situation where we have locked ourselves in with the technological revolution. We have put ourselves at its mercy. I've given a name to that: "life behind the quality dikes." We are in a situation that resembles that of the Dutch, who have gained a great deal economically by pushing the sea back behind enormous walls. But there's a price: They have to maintain those dikes forever. In the same way we put ourselves at risk with our communications system, transport system, and other systems. They're wonderful while they work. Just-in-time manufacturing is wonderful while it works. But if something isn't delivered on time, the factory stops.

We've made dependence on the quality of our technology a part of life. When I was a child, I lived in an Eastern European village. We never had power failures—because we never had power! Washing machines never failed; we had no washing machines. A satellite went down six weeks ago; my Visa card suddenly wouldn't work in the gas pump. You've got a satellite, satellite manufacturer, the communications company that manages it, Visa, and the gas company, all of whom have to deliver in order for me to pump gas. The interlocking is such that any part of it that fails may shut down the whole system. Why are we so afraid of Y2K? Massive quality failure.

On why quality takes so long: Our effort is going to occupy us for decades to come. It started up in the 1980s. A huge number of companies undertook initiatives in quality, but only a tiny number of them succeeded and became quality leaders. We know what they did. How they did it provides us the lessons to scale up.

It's a slow process. One of the limitations is cultural resistance. There are all kinds of ways of dragging one's feet. It's so universal, each language has its own expression for it. Invariably each industry says, "Our business is different." Within the industry each company says, "We're different." And in each company managers are different. Of course there are real differences, but with respect to management and quality, they're identical. They don't know that; some of us who have worked in a lot of different industries and companies do know that.

Department heads in a company don't march forward simultaneously. They march in single file, the most adventuresome at the head. You've always got one or two willing to have their departments become test sites. So the thing takes time, because the test site may take a couple of years before results are achieved and demonstrated and propagated. Those results become the means of convincing neighbors. And then it starts to spread. The companies that ended up as role models, like Motorola and Xerox—both were clients of mine—none of them got there in less than six years.

On the cost of quality: There's a lot of confusion as to whether quality costs money or whether it saves money. In one sense, quality means the features of some product or service that make people willing to buy it. So it's income-oriented—has an effect on income. Now to produce features, ordinarily you have to invest money. In that sense, higher quality costs more. Quality also means freedom from trouble, freedom from failure. This is cost-oriented. If things fail internally, it costs the company. If they fail externally, it also costs the customer. In these cases, quality costs less.

I had a look around Xerox before I got to talk to David Kearns [then CEO] on grand strategy. I was just dismayed. The top guys had no scoreboard relevant to quality. I started talking with people who had field reports. I wanted a list of the ten most frequent field failures, because this was killing Xerox. Their field-failure rate was ever so

> "WE'RE AT THE MERCY OF TECHNOLOGY. WHY ARE WE AFRAID OF Y2K? MASSIVE QUALITY FAILURE."

much greater than that of the Japanese. Xerox was losing huge amounts of money during the warranty period.

So I get the ten top failures for the current models. I ask, Have you got the same information relative to the models preceding these? *Both lists are identical.* They knew these things were failing, and they didn't get rid of them. Well, it wasn't too difficult when I did sit with Kearns to point out to him, "You're putting out models you know are going to fail."

On control vs. creativity: Take this example: In finance we set a budget. The actual expenditure, month by month, varies—we bought enough stationery for three months, and that's going to be a miniblip in the figures. Now, the statistician goes a step further and says, "How do you know whether it's just a miniblip or there's a real change here?" The statistician says, "I'll draw you a pair of lines here. These lines are such that 95% of the time, you're going to get variations within them."

Now suppose something happens that's clearly outside the lines. The odds are something's amok. Ordinarily this is the result of something local, because the system is such that it operates in control. So supervision converges on the scene to restore the status quo.

Notice the distinction between what's chronic and what's sporadic. Sporadic events we handle by the control mechanism. Ordinarily sporadic problems are delegable because the origin and remedy are local. Changing something chronic requires creativity, because the purpose is to get rid of the status quo—to get rid of waste. Dealing with the chronic requires structured change, which has to originate pretty much with the top. You've got two totally different processes that have to work here: the control process, to maintain the status quo, and the improvement process, to get rid of it. You need both, and good managers engage in both.

On perfection: Bob Galvin of Motorola has come out over and over again with a big finding of his—"perfection is possible." Back in the '20s when I first came out of engineering school, nobody in industry would have said that. We had what we call "tolerable percent defective"—stuff that's one or two or several percent defective. That was part of life. We've developed quite a few means of achieving perfection when it comes to very critical things, like airplanes. You have redundancies, backups; you deliberately understress materials; you keep people's hands off to limit human error.

We have to dig deeper into the approach to perfection now, given that we're pushing the use of information technology so that we depend on it for transmission and communication and financial systems. I'm not sure where to dig. I can say that those of us who have been around a long time have never seen a limit to human ingenuity. Toyota makes over a million improvements a year. Human beings have no limit to their creativity. The problem is to make it possible for them to use that creativity.

One More Time: Eight Things You Should Remember About Quality

by John P. Mello Jr.

HOW DOES AN organization maintain its dedication to quality? Quality encompasses more than goals and numbers—it embraces the emotions as well. Once quality standards are in place and an organization has an intellectual commitment to quality, how does it turn that commitment into conviction? The experts and in particular two consultants, Patrick L. Townsend and Joan E. Gebhardt, authors of *Quality in Action*, have a few suggestions. Here are eight of them.

1
Nothing pumps up conviction like increased profits.

Surveys by the American Society for Quality Control (ASQC) show that consumers are willing to pay more for an item if it is guaranteed to meet their expectations when they buy it. In the ASQC study conducted in 1988 by the Gallup Organization,

when the item was a $12,000 automobile, 82% of the consumers surveyed said that they were willing to pay more for a quality automobile. How much more? On average, $2,518. Townsend and Gebhardt note, "People are willing to spend more in the hope that the extra money spent will bring them the peace of mind that comes with services and products that are trustworthy."

On the flip side, poor quality results in repair work, rework and scrap costs, returned goods, warranty costs, inspection costs, and lost sales—all told, some 30–35% of gross sales for most companies.

The executives in a company producing quality products are in a very attractive strategic position. If they cut prices, quality improvements will enable them to maintain their profit margins, while their lower prices will enable them to garner a larger market share. And once the company's reputation for quality spreads, it can cash in

on that reputation by raising prices and increasing profit margins.

2
Avoid future problems by aggressively seeking out customer opinions.

The adage "The squeaky wheel gets the grease" is anathema to the quality-conscious company, which strives to anticipate which wheels need greasing before they start to squeak. Townsend and Gebhardt cite the cautionary tale of the Tennant Company, a maker of floor-finishing equipment in Minneapolis, Minnesota. Soon after entering the Japanese market, Tennant began to receive complaints that their machines leaked. Managers were mystified—they had never heard this complaint from their American customers. The company really began to worry when it learned that Toyota was considering entering the market, so it started interviewing its American customers in earnest. Sure enough, the machines did leak. But the American customers didn't "squeak": they just wiped up the leak, silently suffering and waiting for a competitor to enter the market so they could shift their business to it. Tennant eventually fixed the problem, and Toyota never entered the market. But had it not been for the squeaky wheels in Japan, Tennant might not have found out about its quality problems until it was too late.

3
Guarantees + deep customer knowledge = 1 potent combination.

Anyone who has ever gagged on cafeteria food can appreciate the guarantee made by Daka, Inc., the food service contractor at Clark University in Worcester, Massachusetts: if you don't like the food, we'll give you your money back. The guarantee certainly pleased the customers, but the managers had a larger goal—a quality goal—in mind. They wanted to get past the general whining that comes with the territory and obtain specific criticisms that could be used to improve their operations. In addition to the guarantee, Daka stations a manager in each of the two campus dining halls every Wednesday to discuss food issues with students. A record of those discussions, in the form of questions and answers, is posted every week for the benefit of all.

During the first year of the program, only 28 refunds were made, but many more meals were adjusted to assuage students. Those adjustments could be thought of as part of the Daka's "service recovery plan"—originated by Ron Zemke, a well-known writer on quality issues. Such plans, says Zemke, are part of an intentional strategy for returning an aggrieved customer to a state of satisfaction after a service or product has failed to live up to expectations. When Daka launched the program, there was a flurry of activity, but by

the end of the first year, that activity had dwindled to the point that now the guarantee is invoked only once every two weeks or so.

4
Cast a net that catches both big and little ideas.

It's difficult for a culture weaned on the belief that size matters to accept the importance of small ideas. But as Masaaki Imai reveals in his seminal work *Kaizen: The Key to Japan's Competitive Success,* when trying to improve quality, the weight of the catch is more important than the size of the fish. Toyota has spent two decades building up a suggestion system that now produces 2.6 million ideas a year, or about 60 ideas per employee. What's even more amazing is the fact that 95% of them are implemented. Most of those ideas are small, but when they're taken together, their impact is huge.

Some companies offer their workers a cut of the savings that result from an idea. But this dampens idea generation because it encourages workers to look for the "big fish" so they can get the big payoff. By contrast, a company that encourages small ideas is playing the percentages. It's easier to find 100 people who can improve a process by 1% than it is to find a single wizard who can improve a process by 100%. When the wizard has a bad day, the process improves 0%; if 10 of the 100 workers have a bad day, the process still improves 90%.

5
In a quality shop, everybody has customers.

A commitment to continuous quality improvement requires that all workers know who their customers are. A customer can be the person into whose "In" box you dump your "Out" box— or just about anyone to whom you provide a product, service, or information. This maxim applies especially to top managers, whose customers include the people and organizations who

buy the company's services and products as well as the people who work for it. If the latter group isn't happy, there's a good chance the former won't be happy either. As Townsend and Gebhardt note, "To simply exhort employees to provide worry-free products and services without providing a worry-free work environment is folly."

6
Beware the disciples of complexity.

How can workers be responsible for the quality of their work if they're told the measurement of it is too complicated for them to understand? Firms should be wary of quality-control specialists who act as if their discipline is beyond the ken of mere mortals. If you want an effective quality-control program, design it so employees at every level can implement it. Having everyone participate in the design ensures that it will be implemented across your organization.

7
"Look out, Jim, that joke could rip a man in half!"

Humor helps create a sense of proportion in a shop. Without it, everything becomes a molar-gnashing crisis. With it, the management of a company that wants its workers to commit to quality can humanize itself and the quality process.

When the Mutual of Omaha Companies launched their 100% employee participation quality process in 1991, they had Jim Fowler, the host of the company-sponsored TV show "Wild Kingdom," introduce the process. Fowler brought along a 20-foot boa constrictor and, in an impromptu moment, invited company president Jack Weekly—known for his no-nonsense, bottom-line bent—to handle the snake. Gales of laughter erupted from the audience as Weekly tried to keep the snake from crawling into his trousers. What's an employee to think after watching that spectacle? Perhaps this: if the president of the company is willing to get off his high horse for this quality thing, maybe management's commitment to quality is as deep as it says it is.

Either that or: if Fowler had only brought a hamster instead, now that would have been funny.

8

If there are reasons to celebrate, do it. If not, look for them.

Companies large and small have found that appreciating employees through celebration helps build solidarity and loyalty—two qualities essential to the quality process. Fluoroware, Inc., in Chaska, Minnesota, celebrated ZD-Day (Zero Defects Day) by giving each employee a cooler with the label "Jazzed On Quality." Inside each cooler was an assortment of novelties carrying the same message. A recognition luncheon followed the giveaway.

Celebration of quality doesn't have to be an exclusively annual event. It works best if a company has recognition celebrations throughout the year. Indeed, without continuous recognition, annual awards can divide the company into the winning few and the many who finished last. At Paul Revere Insurance Group in Worcester, Massachusetts, the top managers recognize team efforts throughout the year. In the first four and a half years of its quality program, Paul Revere held more than 1,500 ceremonies. And when the Baldrige Award examiners were scheduled to pay a visit, the company kitchen baked 1,400 cookies in the shape of a Q, which were given out to workers by executives trailing the company snack cart when it made its morning run.

Paul Revere won a Baldrige Award that year.

If you want to learn more . . .

Commit to Quality by Patrick L. Townsend and Joan E. Gebhardt (1990, John Wiley & Sons. Inc., 208 pp., $12.95, Tel. 800-CALL-WILEY or 212-850-6000)

Gemba Kaizen: A Commonsense, Low-Cost Approach to Management by Masaaki Imai (1997, McGraw-Hill, 354 pp., $24.95, Tel. 800-722-4726 or 212-512-2000)

Kaizen: The Key to Japan's Competitive Success by Masaaki Imai (1986, McGraw-Hill, 259 pp., $43.12, Tel. 800-722-4726 or 212-512-2000)

Quality in Action: 93 Lessons in Leadership, Participation, and Measurement by Patrick L. Townsend and Joan E. Gebhardt (1992, John Wiley & Sons, Inc., 262 pp., $16.95, Tel. 800-CALL-WILEY or 212-850-6000)

Why TQM Fails and What to Do About It by Mark G. Brown and others (1994, Business One Irwin, 252 pp., $30.00, Tel. 630-789-4000)

ISO 9000 MYTH and REALITY: A Reasonable Approach to ISO 9000

Frank C. Barnes, *The Belk College of Business Administration, The University of North Carolina at Charlotte*

Is ISO 9000 just another imposing title on consultants' brochures or is it a system you must adopt to survive?

ISO 9000 quality systems standards have undoubtedly become more prevalent over the last decade. More than 90 countries have adopted the ISO 9000 series or its equivalent as national standards. Adherence to ISO 9000 standards has become mandatory for companies wanting to sell medical devices or telecommunications equipment in Europe, where more than 20,000 companies are registered. In the U.S., suppliers to the electrical, chemical, and nuclear industries are expecting certification to become mandatory. The number of ISO 9000 registrations is doubling every nine to 12 months in the U.S., from 100 in 1990 to 4000 in 1994.[1]

As more companies have gained first-hand knowledge, myths are giving way to reality. Success with ISO certification has not guaranteed success in business. The focus is often on paperwork, which may not directly benefit the firm. Registration can be expensive and has unfortunately become a vehicle to increase consulting revenues. Studies show that the majority of installations come from customer demands, maybe just a vendor qualification checklist, instead of from internal needs to improve quality. As a result, several groups around the world are reexamining the nature and role of ISO 9000 and certification.

What should a company do about ISO certification? We believe most companies should open up a moderate project on ISO 9000 but not give implementation any more time or money than is clearly justified. After providing a very brief overview of ISO 9000, we will examine more deeply the costs and benefits, the industries and size of companies where it is more relevant, the complaints about registration, and where ISO appears to be going. In the end, we will suggest a proactive but prudent course of action for any company.

ISO Background

ISO 9000 is "a series of international standards dealing with quality systems that can be used for external quality assurances purposes," according to the original 1987 bulletin from the International Organization for Standardization.[2] This group, founded in 1946, has become the focus of efforts to develop international quality standards to facilitate worldwide trade. The organization is a coordinating, consensual group with member bodies from more than 90 countries. The U.S. representative is the American National Standards Institute.

ISO 9000 sets standards for systems and paperwork, not products. It provides companies with a series of guidelines on how to establish systems for managing quality products or services. ISO 9000 requires organizations to document practices that affect the quality of their products or services. Organizations are then expected to follow these procedures to gain and maintain certification. Proponents see the key to quality as the creation of an internal auditing system whereby all company functions are constantly monitored.[3]

Reprinted with permission from *SAM Advanced Management Journal*, Spring 1998, pp. 23-30. © 1998 by the Society for Advancement of Management, Texas A&M University–Corpus Christi, College of Business, 6300 Ocean Drive, FC111, Corpus Christi, TX 78412.

Exhibit 1
"ISO 9000" systems

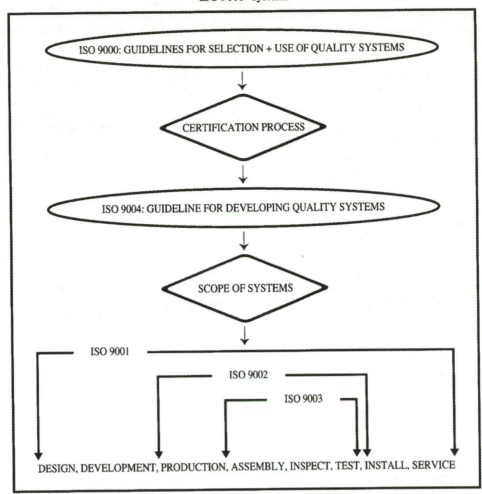

What is referred to as ISO 9000 is actually made up of five different subsets (Exhibit 1). ISO 9000 is the general guide to the others. ISO 9001 is the most comprehensive, covering research, design, building, shipping, and installing. ISO 9002 is for companies that only produce and supply existing products; ISO 9003 is for companies which do even less, such as assembly. ISO 9004 is a document to guide further internal quality development, and ISO 14000 is a new standard to address environmental issues.

Certification rests on an audit by an independent "registrar" after all the systems are in place. The original ISO technical committee envisioned a simpler system than what has developed. It saw ISO 9000 as a guide mainly for self-certification or certification by customer companies and did not anticipate the profusion of outside groups offering to guide, audit, and register companies.

Why do companies seek ISO certification? Well, why do people go after C.P.A., CPIM, or P.E. certification? External goals are first: customer expectations, market advantage, and competition are the major reasons half the companies seek certification. Reduced

costs and quality improvement were the reasons for less than a quarter of the companies. One in 10 was driven by international issues.[4] So, having the "ISO 9000 Certified" sticker on the box is an important driving force for ISO 9000.

Benefits

What benefits are reported? A survey by Lloyd's "Register of Quality Assurance" indicated that ISO 9000 increased net profit.[5] Some companies saw cost reduction of 5% to 30%.[6] A joint study by Deloitte-Touche and Quality Systems Update reported that companies claimed average annual savings of $175,000 from registration.[7] Another Deloitte-Touche survey reported that the costs of registration were recovered in three years.[8] But, in fact, ISO registration is a cost, and any savings are indirect, the result of using the ISO work to improve a company's practices.

Access to markets is the one possible direct ISO impact. While ISO 9000 is not a requirement for doing business in the United States, it can be one in other countries. The European Council of Ministers now requires certification for the producers of certain types of products, including commercial scales, construction products, gas appliances, industrial safety equipment, medical devices, and telecommunications terminal equipment.[9] In the European Community, any type of product that is potentially hazardous or involves personal safety is a candidate for ISO 9000 requirements.

However, most ISO requirements are not government mandated. Large certified corporations, mainly in Europe, are requiring ISO 9000 certification of their suppliers. ISO 9000 requires that certified companies qualify their vendors, and many companies fulfill this requirement by mandating that their suppliers become certified as well.

It is frequently stated that ISO 9000 certification will improve company standings in the important European Community. On January 1, 1993, the EC became the second most powerful economy in the world and the largest trading partner of the U.S.[10] The U.S. exports more than $100 billion to the EC annually. More than half of this amount is affected by ISO 9000 standards. In Europe, more than 70,000 sites are registered for the series, so ISO 9000 certificates are becoming like passports and visas.[11] Therefore, to international companies, certification provides the opportunity to do more business in Europe. Some other reasons include EC regulations requiring ISO 9000 compliance, EC companies preferring ISO 9000 standards, or suppliers voluntarily adopting ISO 9000 as a way to be more competitive.

Because ISO 9000 standards are intended to be uniform throughout the world, corporations should have the assurance that a certified company has had to demonstrate and document proper quality systems. Certification also provides credibility. It gives assurance to a corporation that its potential suppliers can provide products of a consistent quality. And ISO 9000 certification tends to cut down on the number of audits performed by customers on their suppliers.[12] If the supplier base, including first-, second-, and third-tier suppliers are ISO certified, then the final products, which may consist of thousands of parts and components from registered suppliers, should have superior quality, performance, and reliability. Also, ISO 9000 certification may allow the company to control risks and exposures associated with defective products. With extensive quality systems in place and operating properly, future failures and possibilities for defective product litigation should be minimized.[13]

• *Improved Communication*
Zuckerman claims that ISO 9000 serves not only as a quality tool but as a communication system. If implemented correctly, the ISO 9000 system:

• Builds communication between managers and employees.
• Helps resolve political conflicts, work procedure inconsistencies and conflict between formal and informal communication flows.
• Trains management and employees in communication skills, such as interviewing, writing and editing.
• Creates a documentation system and a system for disseminating information company-wide and to all customers.
• Provides the basis for a networked communications system.
• Lays a foundation for using employees as sophisticated information gatherers and sorters.[14]

• *Good Business Sense*
The system standards in the ISO 9000 series provide a comprehensive model for a quality management system that should make any company more competitive. The standards offer a solid foundation for establishing a total quality management philosophy and help companies establish the discipline, procedures, and methods to assure that all areas in the company are aligned with the principles set forth in the company's quality policy statement. So we see there are many potential benefits from the ISO 9000 program.

• *The ISO 9000 Process*
The ISO 9000 program is somewhat complex and has a number of requirements. Many books, such as Johnson's[15] and Zuckerman's[16] as well as articles suggest a step by step process to achieve certification. The Autumn 1995 issue of *SAM Advanced Management Journal* provided a "manager's guide" to understanding and implementing ISO 9000.[17] They all suggest the following five steps in some form:

1. *ISO 9000 Assessment.* The initial assessment is a detailed review of the company's quality systems and procedures compared with ISO 9000 requirements. This process defines the scope of the ISO 9000 project. It might take two or three days to complete.

2. *Quality Assurance Manual.* While ISO 9000 standards do not require a quality assurance and policy manual, they do require the company to document everything it does and every system that affects the quality of the finished product. The quality manual is often used because it is a good way to get all the necessary documentation together in one place.

3. *Training.* Everyone, from top to bottom, needs training in two areas. First, they need an overall understanding of ISO 9000 vocabulary, requirements, role of the quality manual, and benefits that will be derived from the system. Second, they need to be aware of the actual day-to-day process of upgrading and improving procedures.

4. *Documentation of work instructions.* Processes that have been improved will need new documentation. Once completed, this manual should outline every process a company undertakes that affects the quality of a finished product.

5. *Registration Audit.* The final step in the ISO 9000 program is an audit by a company-chosen registrar to see that the system is working as described in the quality manual and that the system meets ISO 9000 requirements. But, as we'll soon see, certification is now subject to some criticism.

● *Certification*

The length of the registration effort depends on many factors, including the firm's size and complexity, current level of quality, extent of current documentation, and the degree of management commitment. (See Table 2) Typically, a 6 to 12-month training and preparation period is followed by an intensive year-long effort to adapt one's procedures to the ISO standard. In 1992, about 35% of companies failed the assessment the first time around, but the success rate has now risen to more than 70%. About half of the failures are due to a lack of documentation.[18] A registered organization faces follow-up visits by auditors every six months to make sure the company follows its quality procedures. After three years, the organization must undergo another full assessment.

Cost

ISO 9000 certification can be expensive. "Quality Systems Update" reported that the average total cost was $245,200.[20] The factors influencing the cost are the size of the company, the number and type of products, and the existing state of the quality control system.

In a 1994 survey of equipment manufacturers, large corporations reported spending more than $1 million for certification, whereas smaller companies with about $25 million in annual sales spent an average of

$250,000 plus annual maintenance costs of more than $70,000. These costs include set registration fees of about $35,000 for a three-year cycle, employee time and, in some cases, additional employees.[21] See Table 3.

The level of documentation prior to implementing ISO 9000 is also a factor in the cost picture. In a survey conducted by Microwaves & R-F, companies that had already received ISO 9000 certification reported on average that they invested nearly $100,000 to prepare and achieve certification. In the same industry, Maxim Integrated Products spent only $25,000 because many systems were already in place.[23] Bethlehem Steel required about eight months to achieve certification in one of its plants, while a similar-sized company with no prior quality program took two and a half years.[24]

Colorado State University found 58% of ISO registered companies indicated that they did not keep track of costs, many because the decision to seek registration was strategic, customer-driven, or in the long-term business interest of the company. Ninety-three percent reported that they did not attempt to justify the cost of the ISO 9000 registration process.[25] Table 4 shows the breakdown of ISO costs.

Training for a single site may cost $4,000 to $5,000. A core group, consisting of the ISO coordinator, senior managers, and team leaders would receive a formal overview through a one-day introductory class typically costing under $500 per person. The coordinator should take about two advanced seminars, which take two days and cost about $1,000.[26] A major expense is the internal costs of preparing documents, document control, and retraining of employees.

Consultants are available to assist with any part of the process. For a fee ranging from $700 to $1,500 a day, consultants can provide a package to take a company from start to finish, promising quick, easy passing of the ISO audit.[27]

We believe this is an area for solid business decision-making. Each cost should be subject to cost-bene-

TABLE 2 Relevant Time Requirements	
Time Frame	**Existing Condition of Organization**
3 to 6 months	Company in full compliance to a military or nuclear standard.
6 to 10 months	Company has fairly current procedures, job descriptions, and a working quality organization.
10 to 16 months	Company has only sketchy procedures and its records are haphazard. The quality organization is still responsible for final inspection, and still takes the blame for the substandard product shipped if plant is very large.
16 to 24 months	Company has no commitment from senior management.

TABLE 3	Cost and Savings by Company Size	
Sales Volume of Companies	Avg. Annual Savings	Avg. Cost per Company(*)
Less than $11 million	$25,000	$62,300
$11 million–$25 million	$77,000	$131,000
$25 million–$50 million	$69,900	$149,700
$50 million–$100 million	$130,000	$180,800
$100 million–$200 million	$195,000	$208,700
$200 million–$500 million	$227,000	$321,700

(2)*

fit analysis. Some suggested activities are so logical they should have already been done. Some have no benefit except getting certified. A company should clearly understand where each proposal fits between these extremes. As we'll see, it may not be necessary, or desirable, to buy into the whole program.

• *Registration Fees*

In a survey of ISO 9000 registrars in North America, the National ISO 9000 Support Group tried to clarify the costs of assessment by asking a sample of registrars to submit a quote for a 250 employee automotive supplier with a single manufacturing site. The average estimate for registration fees was $11,300, ranging from $4,000 to $20,000. Half of the registrars said they had special pricing packages for businesses with fewer than 75 employees.[28] The fee for a large business site could reach $40,000. Surveillance costs over the three-year period can run another $3,000 to $4,000, plus travel. Bibby reported the base costs of registration may run over $50,000. However, fees paid to consultants, employee time, and documentation can drive costs over $200,000.[29] Gallagher suggested additional costs from ongoing biannual audits range from $5,000 to $10,000.[30] Doing business in Europe will cost more. Britain's BSI charges a 15-person facility about $25,000 for a three-year certification process.[31]

• *Problems With Certification*

The last step, registration or certification, is becoming the subject of a good deal of criticism. Many experts believe that ISO 9000 has become a pursuit of quality certificates rather than a pursuit of quality.[32] Jacques McMillan, chief of the senior standards group for Directorate-General III, Industry, a major force behind European standardization, stated "we just need to be sure that certification is used when it's necessary and isn't overused . . . to put certification back into perspective."[33]

ISO left the regulation and implementation of the standards up to the participating countries' standards organizations, which select the organizations that are qualified to issue ISO 9000 certificates. Once registrars become accredited, there is no single set of operating guidelines for them to follow, and the amount of work a company is required to perform varies according to the registrar. Therefore, not all companies or countries will acknowledge certification from all registrars. Perry Johnson referred to the international scene as a "bureaucratic Byzantium."[34] Furthermore, many companies in Europe only accept certification from European registrars. To eliminate this problem, the national standards organizations are in the process of creating operating guidelines. The U.S.'s Registrar Accreditation Board has signed Memorandums of Understanding with the Netherlands, U.K., Italy, Japan, and Australia to move these countries toward mutual Recognition of registrars.[35]

TABLE 4 Source of ISO Costs

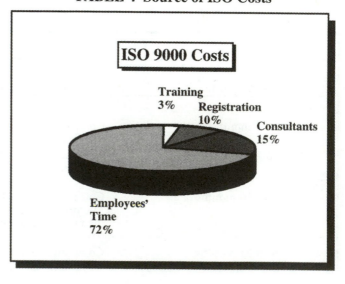

46

• *Compliance Versus Registration*

The ISO 9000 documents were written as two-party documents between buyers and sellers and did not address certification, which has largely been a commercial response to legal mandates in Europe and the competitive push to sell outside the US.

Brown, in *Machine Design,* stated, "While rooted in good intentions, once dissected, it is painfully obvious that ISO certifications are merely more expensive and elaborate schemes that promise high quality and a competitive edge . . . namely, certification costs are astronomical and growing, and an ISO registration in the U.S. means little in Europe. When the smoke clears, the only organizations guaranteed to profit from this experience will be those deemed qualified to do the audits and issue the certificates."[36] The Chicago Metal Working Consortium considers ISO 9000 a "cash cow" for consultants and the service sector.[37]

Computer giant, Hewlett-Packard, along with Motorola, Novell, Microsoft, and others, is leading a self-certification movement. This option provides greater flexibility to meet business objectives, reduce costs, and increase customer understanding the quality management systems.[38] Likewise, the National Tooling & Machining Association is asking its 3,000 members to conform with ISO 9000 rather than pursue actual certification. Self-paced compliance is clearly an option for domestic U.S. companies, and industry-specific programs have merit.

There is no law requiring ISO 9000 compliance for all products sold in Europe. Some now say that ISO 9000 is overrated, even counter productive. The Senior Officials Group for Standardization Policy of the EC's Directorate-General III for Industry, concerned that ISO 9000 has turned into a pursuit of certificates rather than quality, called for the creation of a Europe-wide quality program that could include a European quality award, like the Deming or Baldrige Awards.[39]

The ISO 9000 certification process requires a mountain of paperwork. Opponents claim that it is only for documentation, but proponents believe that if a company has documented its quality systems as it should, then most of the paperwork has already been completed.

Some say ISO 9000 discourages free thinking and employee empowerment. They claim that the ISO 9000 program is so structured that companies lose their power to develop creative solutions to problems or to think of new, better ways of doing things.

• *Other Problems*

It is charged that ISO 9000 focuses too much on the company involved and not enough on its customers. ISO 9000 is not directly connected to product quality but to the company systems. Many opponents believe that the program focuses on product consistency at the expense of product quality. (There is the often repeated claim, "One can manufacture cement life-preservers and still receive ISO 9000 certification").[40]

ISO 9000 is not industry-specific. Opponents claim ISO 9000 is too general and fails to address the problems and issues inherent in particular industries.

ISO is strongest worldwide in the transportation, oil, chemicals, electronics and computer industries. Tool manufacturers, automakers, steelmakers, and woodwork machine manufacturers are among those who tend to say that ISO 9000 is a program created by consultants primarily to benefit consultants.

The Big Three auto manufacturers have chosen their own system, QS-9000, which includes ISO 9000 as a baseline. Auto industry leaders say ISO 9000 is too immature to impose on their suppliers and they hope to save their suppliers the expense of ISO registration. QS-9000 "was created to reach beyond the limits of ISO 9000 by incorporating the powerful components of continuous improvement, a parts approval process, and manufacturing capabilities."[41] European officials are not pleased with this development, which they see as unnecessary duplication and fragmentation.[42]

There is not much enthusiasm for ISO 9000 in the steel industry, where leaders view ISO certification as a marketing tool. But Bethlehem Steel, the first integrated mill to be registered, views ISO 9000 as a means of cutting down on customer audits.

On the other hand, the chemical processing industry, which faces tough international competition, has openly embraced ISO 9000. In fact, DuPont has created its own ISO 9000 consulting service for use both inside and outside the chemical industry.

Although ISO 9000 certification is prevalent in the electronics industry, Motorola's quality chief dismisses the standard. AMP's director of supplier programs and performance comments that "We would not arbitrarily impose the additional costs on our suppliers."[43]

Recommendations

Over the years we've observed a pattern with new business practices; can we say "fad?" There is the period of euphoria and wild overpromise. It appears ISO 9000 is emerging from this phase and good business sense will be reinstated. Several trends are apparent. There will be a continued growth in U.S. firms registered, but there will be more attention to industry-specific standards, such as auto's QS-9000 or Motorola's self-certification. There will be reform. An editorial in *Quality Progress* called ISO 9000 Europe's "revenge" for years of American management fads.[44] Registrars will be subject to more regulations. Effort will be made to streamline the process and increase the effectiveness of registration in assuring quality products and services. There will be some deemphasis of ISO 9000 registration. The European Council is likely to back a proposal to deemphasize ISO 9000 registration and promote a European quality award like the Baldrige Award. There is a push for EC approval of a Europe-wide quality policy that will recommend ISO 9000 as only one quality tool that companies can use on the path to improvement.[45]

We recommend that a company use its own sales department and top management to determine clearly the role of ISO certification in its industry and markets. Is certification important to the marketing plans of the company?

We recommend that the company use the ISO 9000 model as a benchmark to assess the adequacy of its quality program. Those responsible for the quality function should become thoroughly familiar with ISO 9000. This might be a one-month or a 12-month goal, depending on company needs. During the ongoing operation of the quality function there should be routine and regular opportunities and advantages from aligning the company's systems with the ISO model. This should contribute to the systematic improvement of quality and profit. If it becomes important in your markets to have certification, the company could take that step with little disruption or costs. Good business sense is your guide to confronting ISO 9000.

With over 20 years of teaching experience and 10 in professional positions with leading corporations, Dr. Barnes has developed extensive expertise in problem solving and systems design to improve managerial and operational success, and has contributed case studies of successful corporations to a number of textbooks.

NOTES

1. Gallagher, M. (1995, April) ISO Expands; Most large companies have adopted ISO 9000 and new the standard is moving down all levels. *Chemical Marketing Reporter*, 247, 12.
2. International Standard (1987) Quality systems model for quality assurance in production installation.
3. Zuckerman, A. (1994, July). The Basics of ISO 9000. *Industrial Engineering*, 26, 13–14.
4. Rabbit, J.T., & Bergh, P.A. (1993). *The ISO 9000 book: A global competitor's guide to compliance & certification*. New York: Quality Resources.
5. Study finds that gains with ISO 9000 registration increase over time. (1994, May). *Quality Progress* 27, (5) 18.
6. Zanetti, R. (1993, January). ISO 9000: The benefits are boundless. *Chemical Engineering*.
7. Johns, V.H. (1994). Beyond the myths: The ISO 9000 certification process is still hampered by a number of misunderstandings. *Chemical Marketing Reporter*, 245 (15), 8–10
8. Murphy, P. (1996, March). Essay by Invitation. *LD+A* 19.
9. Johnson, P. (1997). *ISO 9000: Meeting the new international standards*. New York; McHill, Inc. 2nd Edition.
10. Craig, R.J. (1994). *The no-nonsense guide to achieving ISO 9000 registration*. New York; ASME Press.
11. Vasilash, G.S. (1995, August). Tooling up for better quality. *Production*, 107, 54–57.
12. Avery, S. (1994). ISO 9000 certification: Does it help or hinder? *Purchasing*, 116 (1), 102.
13. Hutchins, G. (1993). *ISO 9000: A comprehensive guide to registration. Audit guidelines and successful certification*. Vermont: Oliver Wright.
14. Zuckerman, A. (1996, July). How companies miss the boat on ISO 9000. *Quality Progress*, 23–24.
15. Johnson, Op. Sit.
16. Zuckerman, A. (1995). *ISO 9000 made easy: A Cost saving guide*, Amacon.
17. Hormozi, A.M. (1995). Understanding and implementing ISO 9000: A manager's guide. *SAM Advanced Management Journal*, 4–11.
18. Wingo, W. (1994, September 26). ISO 9000 certification snowball. *Design News*, 90–97.
19. Rabbit, & Bergh, Op. Sit.
20. Weston, F.C. (1995, October). What do managers really think of the ISO 9000 registration process? *Quality Progress*, 67–73.
21. Zuckerman, A. (1994). The high price of admission. *Appliance Manufacturer* 42(5), 8.
22. *Quality Systems Update*. (1997). Deloitte-Touche, Fairfax, VA.
23. Schneiderman, R. (1994, Jan.). ISO 9000 generates debate among industry companies. *Microwaves & R-F*, 42–46.
24. Zuckerman, A. (1994, Oct.). Second thoughts about ISO 9000. *Across the Board*, 51.
25. Weston, Op. Sit., pp 67–73.
26. Mancine, B.J. (1994, February). Succeed at ISO 9000 registration. *Chemical Engineering Progress*, 55–59.
27. Brown, R. (1994, June 6). Does America need ISO 9000? *Machine Design* 70–74.
28. Rubach, L. (1995, January). First-time ISO 9000 registration tops 70%. *Quality Progress*.
29. Bibby, T. (1995, July). ISO 9000, not a total quality solution, but a catalyst for continuous improvement. *Rubber World*, 212, 15–17.
30. Gallagher, M. (1995, April). ISO Expands: Most large companies have adopted ISO 9000 and new the standard is moving down all levels. *Chemical Marketing Reporter*, 247, 12.
31. Wingo, Op. Sit., p. 90–97.
32. Zuckerman, Op. Sit., p. 51.
33. Avery, S. (1996, Oct. 17). What's going on overseas could impact quality here. *Purchasing*, 50.
34. Johnson, Op. Sit., p. 137.
35. Murkami, R. (1994, March). How to implement TSO 9000. *CMA Magazine*, 18–21.
36. Brown, Op. Sit., p. 70–74.
37. Avery, S. (1994). What's wrong with ISO 9000? *Purchasing*, 116 (3), 49–52.
38. Morrow, M. (1994). Gauging the importance of ISO 9000. *Chemical Week*, (24) 38, 155.
39. Zuckerman, Op. Sit., p. 51.
40. Zuckerman, Op. Sit., p. 52.
41. Brown, J. (1997, Jan.). Achieving peak to peak performance using QS 9000. *IIE Solutions*, 34.
42. European officials have their say about QS 9000. (1996, Oct. 17) *Purchasing*, 52.
43. Avery, S. Op. Sit., p. 101–105.
44. O'Conner, P. (1995, March). ISO 9000 is Europe's revenge. *Quality Progress*, 8–10.
45. Zuckerman, A. (1996, September). European standards officials push reform of ISO 9000 and QS-9000 registration. *Quality Progress*, 131–134.

2-D or Not 2-D?

Something as humble as a bar code can save a nice pile of money for a factory. Especially in a world where paper remains king.

BY SRIKUMAR S. RAO

YOU MIGHT THINK THAT the bar code has little new to offer today, more than 20 years after it first greased the logistical wheels in factories. How many data can you cram on an ink blot, after all?

Quite a lot, it turns out, if you use not just one dimension—the across-the-stripes scan of yore—but two. A two-dimensional code can squeeze the Gettysburg Address on a postage stamp. That's far less than silicon can manage, of course, but bar-code stickers are much, much cheaper than chips.

The technology for the commonly used PDF417 bar-code format was invented by Symbol Technologies six years ago. It has finally started making life easier for a lot of different companies.

Example: Each consignment at a General Motors plant comes with bar codes describing quantity, reference number and so on, each of which has to be scanned individually. The formats frequently vary. "Sometimes there is very little space to put human-readable information on the label, so parts get shunted to the wrong place, and that's really expensive," says John Sakulich, logistics administrator for GM.

Starting next spring GM will require all its vendors to use a 2-D bar code—called, with a remarkable lack of marketing savvy, the PDF417—on all shipping labels. There will be a common global format and room for customization, and data will be captured in a single scan. And there is plenty of space for old-fashioned, printed information. Larry G. Graham, GM's global manager for automatic identification technologies, estimates that GM will save at least $100 million each year and perhaps as much as $300 million. This is worth the attention even of a manufacturing behemoth.

"A 2-D bar code is the only way in which you can put all of the information on a sheet of paper in a format readable by a computer and on the same sheet of paper," explains Jerome Swartz, founder and chief executive of Holtsville, N.Y.-

> **YOU CAN STORE THE ENTIRE GETTYSBURG ADDRESS ON A TWO-DIMENSIONAL BAR CODE THE SIZE OF A POSTAGE STAMP. THAT'S NOT WHAT SILICON CAN DO, BUT IT'S FAR CHEAPER.**

based Symbol. The information density of the bar code varies, but typically runs to 1,100 bytes without compression. You can shoot a bullet through it and still recover all the data, because of built-in redundancy. The code costs virtually nothing to produce, because you can generate it on any printer.

The state of Indiana put a PDF417 bar code containing all tax information on income tax forms and cut processing costs from 82.5 cents a form to 4.5 cents. "There are no errors, so we don't have to spend time fixing mistakes, and we have fewer irate taxpayers," says Kenneth Miller, commissioner of revenue for Indiana.

"About 3% of the more than 500,000 shipments we made each year contained errors resulting in rejected bills," says Terry J. Reuland, supply chain manager for Thomson Consumer Electronics. "It used to cost us $25 per document to fix the problem; we put 2-D codes on our bills of lading and our error rate is now zero."

You can put pictures or text into a 2-D code and encrypt it, for even greater security. NeoMedia Technologies of Fort Myers, Fla. is helping Mexico City avoid losses from doctored land tax bills by encoding the bills with tax data in the form of encrypted bar-code data. Laser Data Command, of Eden Prairie, Minn., uses a camera to photograph checked-in luggage and the passenger it belongs to, then compresses the image along with the identification data into the 2-D code on the boarding pass. That way, you can be sure that the guy who checks in is the one who boards, and not some terrorist.

Such applications, humble in themselves, are critical for integrating computers into daily life, where paper remains king. (That's why the fax machine remains a fixture, despite the availability of e-mail.) Paper will reign a long time, because, unlike silicon, it really does grow on trees.

Srikumar S. Rao *is Louis and Johanna Vorzimer Professor of Marketing at the C. W. Post campus of New York's Long Island University.*

Jac Nasser's BIGGEST TEST

Crisis-managing millions of potentially faulty tires will show how effective he's been at transforming Ford and define his tenure as CEO. One tip: Lose the clunky TV ads.

BY ALEX TAYLOR III

It is every CEO's worst nightmare—the crisis that strikes from nowhere, jolts customers as well as suppliers and employees, sends the stock reeling, and threatens a company's good name. How the boss reacts can define his or her tenure in the job and forever affect his or her reputation. James Burke of Johnson & Johnson became a business hero for sweeping Tylenol off America's drugstore shelves after a tampering scare. But Exxon's Lawrence Rawl was denounced as aloof and unresponsive for failing to rush to Alaska when the *Exxon Valdez* spilled its oil. More recently, Coke's Douglas Ivester appeared uncaring when he brushed off reports of contaminated soft drinks in Belgium, an incident that contributed to his premature retirement.

Ford CEO Jacques Nasser has seen the auto industry make more than its share of blunders in dealing with the public trust—a record that Nasser, 52, has vowed to improve since being named to the top job in late 1998. So when reports began to surface that the treads of Firestone tires on Ford Explorer sport utilities and Ranger pickup trucks were peeling off under pressure and causing fatal accidents, he seized on the crisis as an opportunity to show that Ford was, in his words, not "just another car company." The tires are now connected to more than 1,400 accidents and other mishaps in the U.S. involving 88 deaths, and the federal government has launched an investigation. In Venezuela, where Explorers have also crashed, the government has threatened to bring criminal charges against Firestone and Ford. Though the problems are not of Nasser's making, they are his responsibility. Says a Ford insider: "This is a test of character for Jac. He's been saying we're a consumer-focused company, and the way he handles this will determine his credibility going forward—both internally and externally."

Automakers are used to recalls, but speedily handling the return of 6.5 million Firestones is a monster challenge. It starts with the logistical conundrum of removing that many potentially defective hunks of rubber, nylon, and steel and replacing them with a like number of new ones. The recall is so big that even a simple task like finding enough service bays where the tires can be changed became an issue. In addition, Ford has had to collect and analyze accident data from four continents, coordinate a response with a Japanese-owned company that has a vastly different culture about public disclosure, obtain replacement tires from competing manufacturers, and manage it all under the scrutiny of federal regulators, Congress, safety advocates, plaintiffs lawyers, and journalists. In one of his most resounding actions, Nasser took the unprecedented step of closing three assembly plants so that Ford could raid its stockpile of 70,000 new tires and pass them on to consumers as replacements. Marveled a company official: "That's the most courageous decision I've seen since I've been at Ford."

Nasser has been a frequent presence in the tire-recall war room.

Ford has, by most accounts, managed the logistical end of the recall—finding replacement tires and getting them to Explorer and Ranger owners—partly by throwing hundreds of people at the task. But dealing with the public repercussions has been like trying to dampen a wildfire. Despite an exhaustive effort by Ford to assemble, analyze, and disseminate relevant information, it has faced a steady onslaught of negative stories in the media, especially on TV. "We are in the midst of a bloody nightmare," says an executive in the thick of the action.

Even as the recall got under way, opinion polls showed Ford's credibility was dropping. The company was hit with reports about tire failures outside the U.S. that suggested it should have known about the defects far earlier than it initially acknowledged, and that they may be far more widespread. Ford's response: The data were too sketchy. Nasser initially turned down invitations to testify before congressional committees, but public pressure soon forced him to accept. Meanwhile, the company tried to resist being drawn into a public dispute with Firestone, its supplier, while also trying to distance itself from the tire defects. Early on, Ford got

Nasser Speaks Out

Unlike many CEOs facing congressional hearings and lengthy litigation, Ford's chief talks openly about the crisis

At the end of August, Nasser talked with FORTUNE senior editor Sue Zesiger about the impact of the Firestone tire crisis on Ford and how he would have handled things differently.

When did you first hear rumblings about the tire problem?

It goes back a month and a half in the U.S. We knew there was an issue with tire failures in Venezuela and the Middle East. The incidents were looked at extremely carefully, and once we knew there was an issue here in the U.S., the important thing was to get as much data as we possibly could. This is a data-driven industry, but we're in an awkward position because in most cases we don't collect tire data. Tires are the only items on a vehicle where the vehicle manufacturer doesn't warrant the component.

Right from the start we said there were several things that we have to do. The first thing we wanted was to be open with the data we've collected. Much of it was raw, and we had to process it and put it into a form where it was statistically readable and understandable. But we wanted to share that data.

Second, we wanted to identify where the problem tires were and to get a supply of new tires out there as quickly as possible. Just because of its type of industry, Firestone is less connected with our customers than we are. Yes, these are Firestone tires, but our customers are driving on them.

Finally, we wanted to communicate with everyone—customers, dealers, the government, other suppliers—about where we stood and what we are doing. The one thing we didn't want was to quibble with Firestone or the government or anyone else on whose fault it is and who is going to pay for it Our primary concern was to get as quickly as possible to a point where we had a fence around what we considered the problem. We did everything we possibly could to facilitate that.

Did you bring in outside risk-management or crisis-management teams?

This is all in-house. We had our computers processing the data. We had some of our brightest Six Sigma statisticians and research engineers looking at the data by region, by product, by tire size—all to try to isolate the problem. It was like trying to boil the ocean.

Do you think you moved quickly enough?

I think we acted very quickly to understand the problem in a matter of 48 hours. We wanted to make sure our decisions were science-based, not I-think, you-think opinions. We crunched thousands of pieces of data. Once we understood the problem, we were out there with Firestone and the government recommending the replacement of the tires, and Firestone did it voluntarily. I don't see how we could have moved any more quickly, and I'm not the most patient guy in the world.

> **"My first piece of advice was to be open. Don't hold back any information."**

What is the magnitude of this, from the Ford perspective?

It has been literally night and day, seven days a week. We have 500 people directly involved, and indirectly, maybe tenfold that number. For example, we had call centers almost triple in size, and we increased our call center in Denver from 150 operators to 700 operators in four days, working around the clock. Ford went on Websites within 48 hours. We have a team that meets almost around the clock, and we have a daily meeting as well. It usually lasts an hour to an hour and a half, an update of all the key factors, and at every meeting the question is, What else can we do?

Are there any Firestone people here in Dearborn, or are they conducting their own effort at this point?

They are conducting their own effort. We have the group here, and we are in constant contact. We've had people visit with them as well. The communication is wide open. They probably talk to each other 20 times a day. In addition, I spoke to the leadership of Firestone here in the U.S. as well as President Yoichiro Kaizaki at Bridgestone in Japan, and we also had face-to-face meetings with them.

What was your first official involvement in the recall?

The first meeting we had was six or seven weeks ago with Tom Baughman, who is the lead technical person in charge of Explorer and other light trucks. He was taking me through some very early data on the tire-separation issue. My first piece of advice to him was to be open. Don't hold back any information. Share any data, statistics, or incidents with the government; share it with the supplier.

The second piece of advice was, Don't be constrained by what you believe to be product-liability issues. If you are mesmerized by that, you will not ultimately do what's right for the customer. The third thing is, Get the best scientific minds, particularly Six Sigma minds who are trained in statistical problem solving, involved as quickly as possible and offer their assistance to Firestone as well.

We immediately set up a room, a data-driven room for computer access and communication. We made sure that the team included our best engineers, technical people, research people, communications people, manufacturing people—just about everyone has been involved in it. You don't set it up off-site because it's very important that the chief executive officer be near the room. That way, even if you can't attend the meetings every day, guess what? You walk down the hall in the

(continued on next page)

morning or in the evening and you say, "Hey, what happened today?"

We used Tom Baughman and Helen Petrauskas, vice president of environmental and safety engineering, as the drivers of the task force. Tom is one of the best technical minds in the company, very experienced and extremely customer-focused. Helen is very familiar with the technical aspects, but she also knows the legislative process, which is important because we don't want to be forced into action by legislation.

They left you as the secret tactical weapon for the TV ad?

Yes, but we didn't want it to be a case of "roll out the CEO" [just] because that's what happened with Tylenol. The reason I did the television is because we felt that yes, the print ads were good and the print messages were good, but you almost had to have a face associated with them, and you could give a different message when you are speaking and connecting with people. The feedback from it has been very good. It's increased the demand for replacement tires, which is a positive.

The other thing we did was that we very quickly connected with the other tire manufacturers to ask them not only for help with supply and logistics but also for technical help. There is such a thing as nonpartisan behavior in this industry, and we got absolutely great support.

How damaged do you think your brand is from all of this?

Explorer or Ford?

Both.

It will depend on how customers perceive we have behaved. You don't wish for adversity, but this is testing us, and I think we'll come through with flying colors. My message to consumers is, if you don't think we have behaved in the way the world's leading consumer company should behave, then tell us, because we want to earn that loyalty and respect.

Given the importance of the relationship between tires and vehicle safety, and the importance of brand perception, how can you put Firestone tires on the new Explorer that comes out next January?

> ### "You don't wish for adversity, but I think we'll come through with flying colors."

When you look at the data, it's very clear that these failures are isolated around tires. So from a technical-quality statistical viewpoint, the answer is without any hesitation. However, then you get into the emotional elements. To me a more valid question at this point is to ask whether from a consumer viewpoint there's a compelling reason to want a Firestone tire. I think it's up to Firestone to provide that compelling reason.

How do you feel about the role of media?

Most of the reporting has been fairly balanced. One thing we worry about is hysteria about shortages that then would cause the problem tires not to be changed. But I'd say the media has been fair and, given the circumstances, reasonably straightforward.

What would you do differently, looking back over this experience so far?

I probably would have moved more quickly with competitive tire manufacturers to get more 15 inch replacement tires earlier. We probably waited two weeks before we did that. Also, we probably should have encouraged Firestone to expand the tire-replacement program to the other tire dealers earlier.

Historically, the automotive industry has entrusted the tire, and customer input on tires, to the tire manufacturers. If I were to rewrite history, 100 years of history, I would say that there should be much more involvement and much more data that is public and open and filter-free both to us and to the public about tire performance.

Also, for many different—and good—reasons, most manufacturers tend to select a single type of tire across a particular brand of car or truck. Again, with the value of hindsight, you'd want to perhaps hedge your bets by broadening the mix of tire availability on selected models.

What are your emotions about this?

Well, the first one is sorrow about the defective tires and the fact that we have had deaths attributed to these faulty tires. I think whenever there is a break in trust it pulls at our heartstrings. We don't want to let anyone down. And when something unintended like this happens, it really doesn't matter whose fault it is. We feel morally and emotionally connected to the people who buy our vehicles. If I could find a magic wand that would give me 6½ million 15-inch tires that I could personally hand carry to every customer, I'd do it.

---

caught up in an argument about whether the inflation pressure it recommends contributed to the failures, which it now concedes was a distraction.

Replacing the bad tires has been a massive logistical headache.

Merciless scrutiny and media coverage are part of what comes with being a big company that has a highly visible product today. Ford's response to the tire crisis is light-years ahead of its actions in the 1970s, when reports were published about engineering defects that caused the gas tanks in Ford Pintos to explode in rear-end collisions. "We stonewalled," recalls an executive who still works at the company. "We just kept denying, denying, denying. And we were guilty." When Ford finally recalled the Pintos to fix the tanks, it still refused to admit any problems with the car. All the same, the damage was done. "The thing was so badly handled that the public lost complete faith in the car, and its name was ruined," says the executive.

Ford has acknowledged that it became aware of tire failures on Explorers in Venezuela in late 1998, and that it replaced defective tires on vehicles in Saudi Arabia last year. But it says a coherent picture of problems with U.S. tires didn't start to emerge until this year. In March the company's public-affairs operatives began picking up reports of the overseas tire failures; in May they started holding weekly meetings to track the issue and opened discussions with the National Highway Traffic Safety Administration. Ford engineers reviewed accident data compiled by Firestone and struggled to identify the cause of the problem. They tested new and used tires at the company's Arizona track but couldn't find any evidence of tread separation. Ford still doesn't know what causes the treads to separate.

As reports of tire failures continued to mount, Nasser was briefed in early July, and the company created a war room (since expanded to three or four rooms) on the 11th floor of its world headquarters in Dearborn. Easily accessible to Nasser via an internal staircase from his office, the war room was the daily meeting place for a task force of manufacturing, engineering, finance, purchasing, legal, regulatory, and public-affairs executives. Nasser frequently participated in the meetings, in person during the week and by phone on weekends. On the tenth floor, Ford's public-affairs unit monitored media coverage of the issue and reviewed developments at 8:15 each morning during a global conference call.

As automotive recalls go, this tire recall is far from the biggest; in 1978, Firestone was forced to recall 14.5 million tires that were literally exploding on the road. But no company can afford to treat lightly public questions about the safety of its products and expect to stay in business. From the time of the recall announcement on Aug. 9, Ford officials say they realized they would have to shutter plants for up to a month to make replacement tires available. Assembly plants are the mainstay of the auto industry, and closing them is as financially calamitous as it is operationally complex. The flow of fresh parts to the plants must be halted, machinery mothballed, and partially assembled cars secured to prevent future manufacturing glitches. Revenues get hammered because of the lost production, yet there is little relief from costs. The 6,000 hourly workers at Ford's three plants continued to receive up to 95% of their base pay during the layoff, which lasted two weeks. Analysts figure that Ford lost up to $4,000 in pretax profit with each unbuilt Explorer, and that the shutdown cost $100 million.

Even as replacement tires are beginning to flow to Ford dealers and Firestone tire outlets, Ford faces tough questions about its actions. The big one is why it didn't act sooner to identify the defects. The company has since begun taking steps to collect data on tire failures directly from customers, the same as it does with other components. Privately, Ford executives complain about the cultural and language difficulties of communicating with Bridgestone/Firestone.

The automaker has also repeatedly been asked why it has not used Chairman Bill Ford Jr. as a spokesman in the crisis. Besides being the great-grandson of the company founder, Ford is also descended from the Firestone tire family on his mother's side, and he has presented the company's views effectively on environmental and safety issues. But Ford strategists say that Nasser was better qualified to speak in this crisis because of his operational responsibilities and his knowledge of Ford products.

Nasser's performance as a spokesman has been mixed. Critics have chided him for appearing too stiff and rehearsed on TV; with his formal syntax and thick Australian accent, the CEO does come across as a combination of Al Gore and Crocodile Dundee. More substantive is the complaint that Nasser may have repeated the mistake of Exxon's Rawl by not going to the scene of the crisis and demonstrating his concern for the individuals involved. Putting Nasser into the field to show him working with Ford dealers and talking to customers might have displayed a dynamic side of him that was invisible in the commercials taped at Ford headquarters. "This is a leadership moment, and he needs to be seen in action mode," says a senior public-relations executive who has been watching the press coverage.

Defective tires have been linked to hundreds of accidents and 88 deaths.

The heat on Nasser won't let up anytime soon. Congressional hearings set for early September will further stoke media coverage. So will litigation over safety issues totally unconnected to the tire problem, like faulty ignition switches on two million older cars. And Nasser is braced for complaints about a temporary shortage of replacement tires in mid-September as emergency stocks run dry before new supplies kick in. Says a Ford insider: "Jac realizes that the crown jewels are at stake, and once he decides on a course of action, he doesn't leave a lot of doubt about what needs to be done. He set the tone for the whole thing, and we are going to solve it." If he succeeds, he'll be worth every penny Ford pays him—and perhaps a little more.

REPORTER ASSOCIATE *Soo-Min Oh*
FEEDBACK: *ataylor@fortunemail.com*

Cause of Tire Failures Still a Matter of Dispute

■ **Autos:** Well into the recall, Bridgestone/Firestone and Ford can only point fingers at each other, and even at poor maintenance by consumers.

By TERRIL YUE JONES
TIMES STAFF WRITER

DETROIT

More than two months into the recall of 6.5 million tires linked to scores of fatal accidents, **Bridgestone/Firestone** Inc.'s investigation into the cause of the failures has zeroed in on fatigue cracks that form in the rubber between the steel belts and then spread throughout the tires.

But it's still anyone's guess what might be causing those cracks in the first place—manufacturing flaws, poor design or improper tire inflation and maintenance. The root cause of the sudden tread separations that are linked to 119 deaths in this country and dozens more overseas remains a source of mystery and controversy.

There is not even agreement whether the main culprit is the failing tires or the sport-utility vehicles that roll over after blowouts, often killing or injuring their occupants.

That's a worrisome thought, given the possibility that some SUVs equipped with certain tires not included in the recall might be, in effect, rolling time bombs.

Ford Motor Co. and Firestone have not reached any conclusion as to why the tires failed, prompting the Aug. 9 recall. They say they are working night and day to determine the reasons for the tire failures, most of which happened on Ford Explorers.

"We have not gotten to the point where there's anything definitive to report yet," Ford spokesman Jon Harmon said. Ford has stead-fastly maintained that whatever the cause is, it's a tire problem, not a vehicle problem.

The only word from Firestone came last week from Sanjay Govindjee, an associate professor in UC Berkeley's civil and environmental engineering department who was brought in by the tire company to conduct an independent investigation.

Govindjee said in a memo to Firestone that he is focusing on fatigue-induced internal cracks that spread between the two steel belts. "At some stage the cracks reach a critical size and the tires subsequently fail," Govindjee said.

The failure in this case is tread separation, or more correctly, belt separation. Tires tend to come apart between the two steel belts because that is the area subjected to the greatest stress.

Some tire experts say it is important not to rule out the most obvious cause: tire punctures from sharp objects in the road such as glass, rocks or pieces of metal. "The vast majority of tire failures are due to road hazards," said Harold Herzlich, an independent tire consultant based in Las Vegas. "You're dealing with a rubber object retaining air, holding up a 4,000-pound missile. These impacts are ballistic."

Encounters with sharp objects can leave a gash, causing instantaneous deflation of the tire or small lacerations or punctures that allow air or water under the tire's surface. There

Many Theories, No Answers

Two months into the recall of 6.5 million Firestone tires, investigators still don't know the cause of the blowouts. The theories that have been proposed fall into four main categories.

Design Flaws

- Poor rubber quality
- Composition (steel belts improperly spliced together)
- Tire treads too wide
- Low temperature resistance
- Lack of nylon overlay

Manufacturing Flaws

- Over- or under-vulcanized rubber
- Using overly dry rubber
- Misuse of solvent
- Humidity and moisture (water, rain, perspiration)
- Contaminants (dust, oil, bandages, cigarette butts, tobacco juice, candy wrappers, etc.)

Poor Maintenance

- Under-inflation
- Running tires at high speeds, temperatures for prolonged periods

Explorer Stability

- Center of gravity too high
- Track width too narrow
- Badly designed suspension

Source: Times research

Los Angeles Times

can be internal damage in the tire, causing a tiny area of separation that could continue to grow for 5,000 miles before the tire fails.

Although this accounts for a large number of highway tire failures, it nonetheless doesn't explain why treads have been coming off primarily on Ford Explorers equipped with certain Firestone tires.

John Lampe, chief executive of Nashville-based Bridgestone/Firestone, a subsidiary of Japan's **Bridgestone** Corp., made clear in testimony before Congress and in public statements that he believes Ford is partially responsible for the automotive industry's biggest liability crisis.

"In most cases a vehicle that experiences a tire failure can be brought safely under control," Lampe told Congress last month. "However, we have seen an alarming number of serious accidents from rollovers of the Explorer after a tire failure."

Experts say they think it's a combination of the two.

"It's definitely a tire and a vehicle issue. You've got the highly unstable vehicle and the tire that couldn't handle the endurance that the consumer was expecting out of it," said Keith Baumgardner, general manager of Tire Consultants in Georgia and a former retreader with Firestone.

Despite the lack of a conclusion, experts nonetheless have numerous theories as to what could be behind one of the biggest safety debacles in U.S. automotive history. The theories fall into four general categories: bad tire design, flaws in the manufacturing process, improper maintenance and design flaws in the Explorer itself.

Tire Design Flaws

Ford officials and plaintiff attorneys finger faulty tire design, whether in the tire's weight, chemical compounds used in the rubber, the strength and composition of the steel belts, the compounds that go into the tread, the circular wedges that fit between the belts to help keep them in place or even the tread design.

There could be defects in the knit of the steel belts themselves, which are woven steel strands encased in a layer of rubber known as a skim coat. The skim coat itself could have insufficient gauge, or thickness, to allow proper bonding.

Govindjee, Bridgestone/Firestone's outside investigator, wrote in his memo that he has found a slowly developing fatigue crack "that propagates through the belt wedge material and then subsequently into the belt skim between the steel belts." He did not suggest, however, that this was a blanket defect, saying he needed more time to study the failed tires.

Tire experts have suggested the treads on the recalled tires are too wide, providing more surface area that contributes to heat buildup, a factor known to promote tire failure.

High temperatures leading to belt separation could also result from the low tempera-

Firestone Tire Timeline

■ **March 12, 1999:** An internal Ford Motor Co. memo says "Firestone legal has some major reservations" about replacing tires in Saudi Arabia after numerous accidents involving Firestone tires, notably that the U.S. Department of Transportation might have to be notified since the same products were sold in the U.S.

■ **Aug. 17, 1999:** Ford begins replacing tires on Explorers in Saudi Arabia through what it calls a "customer notification enhancement action" and not a "recall."

■ **February 2000:** Ford offers free replacement tires for vehicles in Malaysia and Thailand.
■ KHOU-TV in Houston first reports on significant numbers of deaths and lawsuits involving Firestone tires on Ford Explorers.

■ **March 6, 2000:** The National Highway Traffic Safety Administration opens a preliminary inquiry after KHOU-TV programs prompt consumer complaints.

■ **May 2000:** Ford offers free replacement tires for vehicles in Colombia, Ecuador and Venezuela.

■ **May 2, 2000:** NHTSA opens a preliminary evaluation of the alleged failure of Firestone ATX, ATX II and Wilderness AT tires. Unknown to NHTSA, there are already lawsuits involving at least 35 fatalities and 130 injuries in the U.S.

■ **Aug. 2, 2000:** NHTSA says it is investigating 21 deaths in crashes of pickup trucks and sport-utility vehicles in which tire failure may have played a role.

■ **Aug. 7, 2000:** NHTSA raises to 46 the number of deaths associated with Firestone tires.

■ **Aug. 9, 2000:** Bridgestone/Firestone announces the recall of 14.4 million tires, including all 15-inch Firestone ATX and ATX II tires, and 15-inch Wilderness AT tires made at its Decatur, Ill., plant. About 6.5 million are believed still in use.

■ **Aug. 31, 2000:** Venezuela's consumer protection agency, Indecu, asks prosecutors to bring criminal charges against both Bridgestone/Firestone Inc. and Ford.
■ NHTSA raises to 88 the number of deaths associated with the Firestone tires.

■ **Sept. 1, 2000:** NHTSA issues a consumer advisory on an additional 1.4 million Firestone tires, saying some of them have "high tread separation rates." Firestone declines NHTSA's request to expand the recall voluntarily to include the 1.4 million.

■ **Sept. 6, 2000:** The Senate Appropriations Committee and the House subcommittee on consumer affairs conduct hearings on the tire recall. Bridgestone/Firestone executives claim for the first time in public that the Explorer has a tendency to roll over and is part of the problem.

■ **Oct. 10, 2000:** John Lampe replaces Masatoshi Ono as Bridgestone/Firestone chief executive and says the recall is likely to cost parent company Bridgestone Corp. $450 million over the year.

■ **Oct. 11, 2000:** Congress passes a sweeping auto safety bill that raises the maximum fines and adds criminal penalties for firms that deceive regulators about safety problems.

■ **Oct. 17, 2000:** Bridgestone/Firestone says it will shut three plants temporarily and lay off 450 workers indefinitely.

■ NHTSA raises to 119 the number of deaths in the U.S. associated with the Firestone tires.

■ **Oct. 18, 2000:** Ford says the recall cost the auto maker half a billion dollars in the third quarter.
Sources: National Highway Traffic Safety Administration, House Commerce Committee, Tab Turner, Public Citizen, Times reports

ture resistance of the recalled tires, which were rated "C," the lowest of three ratings, with "A" the most temperature-resistant. Each of the Explorer's top 10 competitors, from the Jeep Grand Cherokee and Chevrolet Blazer to the **Isuzu** Rodeo and **Mitsubishi** Montero Sport, comes equipped with B-rated tires. Only the **Toyota** 4Runner offers a tire with a C rating with its entry-level package—but it also offers three other tires rated B.

Some critics say Firestone could have avoided, or at least greatly reduced, the separations by adding a nylon layer known as an overlay to cover the steel belts. This is usually done for high-speed-rated tires but also occa-

sionally for puncture resistance, as the overlays stiffen the tire somewhat. Firestone's tire made to Ford specifications for use in Venezuela were supposed to have included nylon overlays (although when Ford examined tires sent back from Venezuela after accidents in that country it found that many lacked the layer).

But tire expert Herzlich says it is unlikely such a layer would have made a difference, in the U.S. or elsewhere. "Some say it would eliminate tread separations if you put them on all tires. That is simply not true," he said. "An overlay gives only a very slight—and I say very slight—protection from penetrating road hazards . . . and will not eliminate tread separation due to under-inflation."

Manufacturing Flaws

Defects can also be introduced in the manufacturing process through the use of substandard materials or ill-maintained workplaces; the introduction of contaminants, humidity or dryness; and improper vulcanization of the rubber.

The rubber in tires must be sticky enough to hold the pieces together until vulcanization welds the tire together. Under- and over-vulcanization are possible too; both weaken the tire's structure.

Several experts say over-tacked rubber, or rubber that is too dry and has lost its adhesive character, is likely to be a major culprit in tire separation. "That's the heart of the matter, the most damaging," said Max Nonnamaker, a tire consultant in Ohio who has worked for Firestone and **Mohawk Rubber** Co.

Workers have been known to overproduce the coated steel belts and then stock the excess; if they sit in inventory too long, the rubber gets too dry and stiff to bend and bond properly. Tire workers have been known to use chemical solvents to make them stickier, but solvent not allowed to dry properly becomes a contaminant that prevents proper adhesion.

Alan Hogan, a former worker in Firestone's Wilson, N.C., plant, testified in a deposition last year that he observed use of overly dry rubber "in the tire room the entire time between '91 and '94," as well as improper application of solvents that could lead to tire separation.

He testified that he found a variety of contaminants in the rubber mixtures used to make tires, including bandages, cigarette butts, chewing tobacco, pieces of wood, and metal nuts and bolts.

In depositions from another lawsuit, four former workers at Firestone's plant in Decatur, Ill., testified they used outdated, dried rubber; that solvents were not used properly, causing pockets of non-adhesion; that tires with defects commonly passed inspection; and that workers used awls to lance bubbles below the surface of tires.

"You should never, never awl anything," Nonnamaker said. "You make a hole and hope it knits back together, but it may not, and you're left with a hole in the tire."

Bridgestone/Firestone dismisses the allegations as charges by disgruntled ex-workers. Ford's Harmon said the auto maker is certainly "factoring in" what the former workers have to say.

Improper Maintenance

One theory given considerable credence by experts is that a low recommended tire inflation by Ford converged with something inherent in the tires and something inherent in the vehicle, effectively turning the recalled Firestones plus Ford Explorers into a deadly cocktail.

Running while under-inflated generates extremely high heat in tires, especially when they are carrying heavy loads, causing irreversible physical fatigue between the plies and deterioration in the tire's material.

Ford always recommended an inflation of 26 pounds per square inch, while Firestone's own recommendation was 30 psi. After the Aug. 9 tire recall, Ford recommended 26 to 30 psi, while Firestone held at 30.

In the end Firestone prevailed, persuading Ford to formally change its recommendation to a full 30 psi last month.

Generally, the industry considers inflation at 20% less than the recommended level to be dangerously low, said Ed Wagner, who runs the consultancy Tire Technical Services in Kentucky. Drivers, however, regularly reach that point.

"If it's supposed to be 30 psi, and we're riding at 24 psi with the same load, then you have gross under-inflation," Wagner said. He and other experts say that if Explorers left the factory with their tires at 26 psi, by the time they got into customers' driveways they were likely to be less than that, and given drivers' ignorance or neglect, tire pressures probably continued to decrease.

Clarence Ditlow, head of the National Center for Auto Safety in Washington, said Ford's 26-psi guidance was a "red flag," because from that point, the only direction for tire pressure to go is down. "Then you have more heat buildup and more failures," he said.

Both Ford and Firestone point to poor tire maintenance as a culprit in the accidents to date, pointing out that most Americans rarely check their tire pressure, though experts suggest tires be checked once a month. Woody McMillin, a senior Bridgestone/Firestone spokesman for consumer products, said the tire maker has seen two factors emerge from its examinations of failed tires at its technical center in Akron, Ohio: improper care and extended periods of under-inflation.

"By and large, and most people don't want to hear this, it's poor maintenance of tires," McMillin said. People basically don't understand how tires work, he said, and that improper air pressure will weaken the sidewalls, much the way a piece of metal, when twisted, breaks at the weakened stress point.

Tab Turner, a Little Rock, Ark., attorney and a veteran in bringing liability lawsuits against auto and tire makers, scoffs at the idea that drivers are to blame. "What evidence is there that only Explorer owners are sloppy with maintenance?" he said. "If you have sloppy maintenance on six cars, and one of them is killing 90% of the people because the tire's coming apart, that tells me there's something wrong with that tire and that car."

Explorer Stability

So there remains a vexing question: Why the Explorer? Critics charge that the Explorer, like many other SUVs, has a tendency to roll over, and they say that is why Ford recommended the lower inflation: A softer tire would keep the vehicle hugging the ground more.

Many suspect the Explorer is jinxed no matter how the tires are inflated: If too high, the vehicle has a propensity to tip over; if too low, the tires are prone to overheat and shred. "If someone has a flat tire on these Ford Explorers in the rear, I have seen them roll over," said tire expert Baumgardner. "So we have a problem with the Ford rolling over no matter whose tire's on it, but then we have the Firestone tire, which is designed for that vehicle and supplied for that vehicle that has exhibited these problems."

As previously reported by The Times, Ford documents show that the auto maker rejected

design changes twice in the last 10 years that would have made the Explorer more stable.

As the launch date for the truck drew near in 1989, designers declined to widen the Explorer's track width, which would have delayed the launch, and instead lowered the vehicle by half an inch and stiffened the front springs. For the Explorer's redesign in the 1995 model year, engineers considered lowering the center of gravity but chose not to, partly to save money and preserve high-profit margins, according to the documents.

Ford maintains those charges are based on only a few pages of technical opinions among tens of thousands of documents exchanged between engineers as they hashed out the design of a new vehicle.

"Then why don't they single out one that says it's safe?" said attorney Turner. "I haven't seen one where an engineer wrote in 1989, 'Oh, by the way, we don't need to change the design of this car; this is the best car we've ever made.' "

According to Ford, crash data show the Explorer is 20% less likely to be involved in a fatal accident for any cause, or a rollover, than comparable SUVs and therefore is one of the safest SUVs on the road.

Ford is understandably mortified at the prospect that the Explorer might be blamed in part for the tire separations. The No. 2 auto maker clears at least $5,000 on each Explorer sold, and Explorers account for 25% of Ford's profit.

Govindjee, the outside investigator, said the issue "is a quite complex interaction" of tire design and dynamics of the Explorer, though he stopped short of placing any blame on the vehicle.

He needs more time to inspect tires and field data, he wrote in his memo, but said he is confident he will be able to provide an explanation around the beginning of the year.

Unit 3

Unit Selections

14. **How Will Kawai's Hand-Built Grand Play Against Steinway?** Sonni Efron
15. **Less Stress, More Productivity,** Phillip M. Perry
16. **How Great Machines Are Born,** Stuart F. Brown
17. **Characteristics of the Manufacturing Environment That Influence Team Success,** Mark Pagell and Jeffrey A. LePine
18. **The Legal Limitations to Self-Directed Work Teams in Production Planning and Control,** Steven E. Abraham and Michael S. Spencer

Key Points to Consider

❖ Economists argue that jobs should be designed with job specialization to gain efficiency. Behavioral scientists argue that jobs should be designed with enrichment. What is your belief and why?

❖ Firms are moving to more technology use, automation, and replacement of workers with robotics. Given these trends, will human resources be of less importance in the future?

❖ European firms have had a longer history of having semiautonomous work units. What factors might hinder greater acceptance of semiautonomous work units in the United States?

DUSHKINONLINE **Links**   **www.dushkin.com/online/**

20. **Ergonomics, HCI, and Human Factors: Working Environments**
    http://www.workspace-resources.com/work00.htm
21. **Just-in-Time Manufacturing**
    http://dali.ece.curtin.edu.au/~clive/public_html/jit/jit.htm
22. **Quality Circles**
    http://www.nw.com.au/~jingde/homepa6.htm
23. **SDWT: Self-Directed Work Teams**
    http://users.ids.net/~brim/sdwtt.html
24. **TQM: Total Quality Management Diagnostics**
    http://www.skyenet.net/~leg/tqm.htm

These sites are annotated on pages 4 and 5.

Production and operations management involves not just equipment, raw materials, and capital; the field also involves workers. Whereas competitors can gain access to the same equipment, hardware, software, and raw materials, the human resources of a firm can provide for a strategic advantage. For a long period of time, many firms have used the phrase, "our employees are our greatest asset" in their recruitment brochures. In the past some employees questioned the sincerity of these firms. Now it appears that many firms actually believe this claim that their employees are a critical strategic asset.

Earlier schools of management thought, such as the scientific management school, placed less emphasis upon the worker's psychological needs and more emphasis on the procedures of a job. With the behavioral school of thought and evidence from research after the 1930s, there was a recognition of how psychological factors affect worker performance and productivity. Firms and managers needed to now consider leadership style, motivation techniques, design of rewards and incentives, and performance appraisal systems. There was an agreement that human resources management practices were linked to employee morale and employee productivity.

Classical economists such as Adam Smith back in the late 1700s and the scientific managers of the early 1900s favored job designs that limited the number of tasks and jobs that were highly specialized. Although efficiency could be gained from division of labor and job specialization, boredom and low worker morale could occur. The behavioral scientists recommended a change to job rotation, job enlargement (increasing the number of tasks performed), and job enrichment (increasing the depth of the tasks and responsibility given to the worker). Many firms today are moving toward concepts such as employee empowerment, job empowerment, the inverted pyramid (where frontline workers are given more empowerment because they are closer to the customers), and semiautonomous work teams.

The articles in this unit show examples of firms that see the importance of human resources management to overall operations and production management success. Firms should consider ways to reduce employee stress to increase productivity. Mark Pagell and Jeffrey LePine's article reviews factors that lead to team success. Steven Abraham and Michael Spencer's article identifies legal limitations to self-directed work teams in production planning and control.

Human Resources Management for Productivity

How Will Kawai's Hand-Built Grand Play Against Steinway?

By SONNI EFRON
TIMES STAFF WRITER

HAMAMATSU, Japan—Like stately ocean liners about to set sail, the grand pianos roll down an assembly line of craftsmen, black, elegant and silent. The instruments, a marriage of ancient wood and high-tech engineering, have a mission: Prove that Japan can make a world-class, luxury piano fine enough to challenge the gold standard of the music industry—the Steinway grand piano.

It is an audacious gambit for their maker, the Kawai Musical Instrument Manufacturing Co. Kawai has been building pianos for 72 years and boasts $870 million in total annual sales in 81 countries. But it has always been Japan's No. 2 piano company, mass-producing affordable family pianos in the shadow of its neighbor, Yamaha Corp.

Kawai's new pianos aim to change all that. Much as Toyota Corp. tried to dump its reliable-but-dull image by introducing the Lexus as a luxury car to equal the Mercedes-Benz but at a lower price, Kawai hopes that acclaim for its new Shigeru Kawai grand pianos will boost the value of the company's brand worldwide. The Shigeru Kawai pianos are produced like lithographs, in limited, numbered editions. Only about 80 have been sold in the United States since they hit the market in June. Quantities are limited because the soundboards inside are made of rare 200-year-old Ezo spruce trees from the northern island of Hokkaido. The soundboards are aged for five years, compared with one year of aging for an ordinary piano soundboard.

North American dealers have so far been shipped only 300 of the craftsman-built pianos. Prices range from $38,390 for a baby grand to $64,790 for a semi-concert model, said Brian Chung, general manager of Kawai's Los Angeles-based U.S. subsidiary.

Like the Lexus, the Shigeru Kawai piano is sold only through a special network of upscale dealers. The price includes a promise that a special technician will fly from Hamamatsu in central Japan to the buyer's home—anywhere in the United States or Canada—within one year and adjust the piano to perfection. "These people are pi-

ano doctors," explained Muneo Ishida, general manager of piano manufacturing for Kawai. "If you don't go to a real doctor, you might get a quack treatment."

Kawai's quest to produce a designer piano is driven in part by raw emotion. Before starting his own company, founder Koichi Kawai was a piano designer for Yamaha in Hamamatsu, a town famous for its delicious eel and for the dry, even climate that makes it a good place to manufacture musical instruments. The company's second-generation chairman, 78-year-old Shigeru Kawai, started out making radio cabinets and other furniture for U.S. occupation forces after his father's piano factory burned during World War II. But he says his dream has been to produce the world's best piano, fine enough to put his own name on it.

Trying to scale the top end of the piano market is also a strategy of necessity. Like many Japanese manufacturers, Kawai faces high production costs, and a weak economy means many domestic buyers are happy to snap up used pianos that formerly would have been exported to developing Asia. Abroad, the firm faces competition from cheaper piano and keyboard makers in South Korea and China, as well as from the better-known Yamaha.

Survival depends on producing high quality at a reasonable price. But in the subjective world of pianos, image is almost as important as sound. To promote its brand—and support a new generation of American pianists—Kawai has pledged to donate $1 million worth of musical instruments to U.S. schools over the next several years.

Millikan Middle School in Sherman Oaks is scheduled to receive a baby grand, a digital piano and three keyboards today. They are badly needed, said Sarah Kang, who chairs the school's music department and says her own classroom's piano is falling apart. "We're always struggling," said Kang, noting that the performing arts magnet school wants to offer after-school music enrichment classes but doesn't know where the money will come from. "I would never spend the money it takes to buy a baby grand piano," Kang said. "I'm just trying to buy a saxophone or two. It's a tremendous gift, and we're very, very grateful."

In addition to making friends at music schools with its lower-end pianos, Kawai is trying to reach out to the professional musicians, music teachers and critics on whom its reputation depends. According to Chung, American buyers fall into two major categories: musicians who appreciate the quality of the Shigeru Kawai and luxury piano buyers who are looking for something rare.

Glenn Treibitz, whose family owns the three Piano Factory stores in the Los Angeles area, carries the Shigeru Kawai together with the finest German pianos. So far, he has sold five. A Juilliard-trained pianist and composer, Treibitz insists that the Shigeru Kawai grand costs about $5,000 less than comparable pianos from Steinway & Sons, but sounds superior.

"The Shigeru Kawai is so much better it's not even funny," Treibitz said. "I wish I could put Steinways in my showroom next to the Shigeru Kawai, so people could understand." Most people who can afford it buy Steinways "because they want a trophy in their living room," said Treibitz, who says the first piano he bought was also a Steinway. "How many better brand names are there in the world than Steinway and Tiffany? It's a magical name, and for those who don't know, that's what they buy."

Treibitz and other fans concede that it may be a long time before Steinway is knocked off its pedestal—if ever. The vast majority of American concert pianists have always played the Steinway.

"They've got a tough row to hoe," one prominent California concert pianist and conductor said, asking not to be named. "If you called 100 concert pianists and said, 'Would you play a Kawai concert piano?' most of them would laugh. . . . I have rarely even seen a Kawai concert grand, and the pianos they make for mass use are mostly mediocre."

Kawai is well aware of this reputation and is aiming to change it. The Kawai factory in Hamamatsu is already turning out the "Boston" line of grand pianos under the Steinway name. While it has produced three Shigeru Kawai brand prototype concert pianos, specially built with Ezo soundboards aged for 20 years, Chairman Kawai said that version will not make its debut until top artists deem it worthy of performance. "We're not planning to sell it yet," Kawai said. "I want the world's top experts to evaluate it."

In the meantime, Kawai wants to boost production of the hand-built Shigeru Kawai pianos to 100 a month, up from 40. The Hamamatsu plant turns out 1,100 of the ordinary Kawai grands per month. The Shigerus are assembled in a designated area away from the main factory floor, where the plant's top workers fret over details. Under international law, ivory can no longer be exported, but politically correct acrylic keys offend the sensibilities of many pianists. The Shigeru's ebonies and ivories are made from a new material forged of plastic, cellulose and acetic acid. "The feel is almost exactly like ivory, and it absorbs sweat," said Ishida, who invented the material and patented it seven years ago.

In another high-tech improvement, the keyboard cover has been made slam-proof. It sinks gently down over the keys even in case of earthquakes or attacks of human pique. "Fingers are a pianist's life," explained Ishida.

When each Shigeru is finished, it is rolled into a private soundproof room—with the piano technician's nameplate mounted on the door—for the finishing touches. That means tuning, to adjust the pitch; voicing, to adjust the tone; and regulation, which means adjusting the weight, depth and feel of each key.

Ishida is a piano maker who does not call himself a pianist. But at the end of the assembly line, he sits down to test his work with a Chopin nocturne. The sound surfs atop the clean silence of the factory.

Researcher Makiko Inoue in The Times' Tokyo bureau contributed to this report.

Less Stress, More Productivity

Six workplace psychologists provide practicable suggestions for alleviating employee stress and thereby enhancing productivity.

By Phillip M. Perry

THE HEAT IS ON.

Gone are the days when businesses responded to increased workloads by hiring more people. Nowadays, faced with the need to wring more profits from limited resources, employers are demanding better performance from their already overburdened staffs. Today, everyone is expected to work smarter and faster.

But there's a downside to this mad rush to greater productivity. Workplace stress has become a costly business issue. Overworked personnel become uncooperative. They call in sick; they sabotage projects; they even jump ship for other employers where the atmosphere is more congenial.

The workers are not the only ones who suffer—customers who are ignored or even mistreated by a stressed-out staff start buying from competitors. "Stress creates a major negative impact on creativity, innovation, and business profits," asserts Dr. Richard Hagberg, president of Hagberg Consulting Group, Foster City, Calif. "That's counter to the traditional thinking of many managers. They have the idea that if they pour on the pressure, people perform better. In reality, stressed-out workers patch together short-term fixes to business problems, while costly, deep-rooted issues remain unaddressed and take their toll on the bottom line."

So what to do? Well, here's some help. In this article, six renowned workplace psychologists give solid, nuts-and-bolts techniques for reducing costly stress in your place of business. Let's see what they have to say.

Spot Signs of Stress

Before you can cure the disease, you have to spot the symptoms. "Supervisors can become attuned to signs of employees experiencing stress," confirms Dr. Rodney Lowman, a professor of organizational psychology at the San Diego campus of the California School of Professional Psychology. He points to the following common signs that the general stress level is on the rise:

- Absenteeism is increasing, whether from illness or for other reasons. Just when individuals are needed the most, they come down with the flu.
- People seem to need more vacation time.
- Everyone becomes more irritable and difficult to get along with.
- There's a general rise in comments such as, "We're really stressed out around here."
- People exhibit confusion and make mistakes at tasks they usually perform well.
- You yourself are feeling stress. "If the boss is stressed, the whole staff will be," says Dr. Lowman. "This is the trickle-down theory of management."

Bonus tip: Stimulate upward communication by regularly asking individuals, "What can we do to make your job less stressful"

Identify the Sources of Stress

Now that you've spotted stress in the workplace, how do you get at what's causing it? "Stressors can result from a variety of situations," Dr. Lowman continues. "These include downsizing, with fewer people left to do more work; a bad boss; a difficult match between a boss and a subordinate; and conflicts between people in the workplace who can't get along with each other."

To find out which specific stressors are causing grief, go right to the source: Get people to open up and tell you. In general, you should encourage people to speak up when they feel as though they are being overloaded with work, or when they are getting mixed signals about their work roles from managers.

But you can do even better, according to Dr. Peter Chang, a professor of organizational psychology who is at the Alameda, Calif., campus of the California School of Professional Psychology. He recommends scheduling regular meetings during which the staff can discuss what they like and don't like about their work environment. "It can make a world of difference to have meetings where people express what is on their minds, and the management does more listening than talking." The trick is to open up a valve to allow people to "let off steam."

Sounds good. But how do you keep these meetings from deteriorating into gripe sessions? Dr. Chang suggests that prior to each meeting, hand out a questionnaire to be filled out by each employee. Ask each participant to describe the five tasks they perform most often, the five things they like the best about their work, and the five things they like the least.

Dr. Chang points to a number of advantages to a questionnaire: "It saves time by keeping the forthcoming meeting focused on work-related issues in a productive manner. It also alerts the staff that management is interested in this topic, and gets everyone to start some real thinking before the meeting."

Once the meeting is over, don't let the issues drop. "It is vital to follow up on the employees' requests and suggestions," says Dr. Chang. "Ideally, you should hold a loosely structured initial meeting where employees say what is on their minds. Then for efficiency's sake there ought to be a subsequent meeting that is action-focused. This is where you provide responses to specific employee suggestions. List which recommendations seem reasonable and which are out of the question."

Bonus tip: Hold the meetings often enough to communicate ongoing concern, but not so often that they become redundant. A quarterly schedule may be just right.

Is There "Good Stress"?

Maybe too much stress is damaging. But can a little stress stimulate performance? It depends on your definition of stress.

"There's is a misconception that stress is motivational," says Dr. David C. Munuz, a professor of psychology at Saint Louis University, St. Louis, Mo. "But stress is really wear and tear on the individual, and there is no way that can motivate. What *is* motivational is the demand of a task—if we see the demand as a challenge. Rather than stress, workers need a challenging environment, a measure of control over their workday, and the tools to complete their tasks."

Dr. Munz states that while some people may use the term "good stress," they are really referring to an environmental in which the business demands that the individual perform at 100 percent of capabilities. "Most people do not want to be exhausted at the end of the day, but neither do want a boring job."

Encourage Humor in the Workplace

Humor can go a long way toward reducing workplace stress. "Maybe we can't control what happens in our workday, but we can control what goes on in our minds," notes

Smart Ways to Handle Stress

1. Pause to re-evaluate yourself and your workday. Look at your performance and come up with ways to feel successful.

2. If you are going through a dry spell, set small goals that you can meet to establish a success attitude.

3. Relax and take deep breaths, do some push-ups, or stretch.

4. Schedule more time to get a certain task done. Ask for another full day to put together a proposal.

5. Use techniques such as meditation, yoga, and positive self-talk.

David Granirer, a consultant based in Vancouver, Canada. "Studies show that being able to respond to a situation with humor gives people back their cognitive control: That's the ability to focus on their sphere of influence and to respond creatively to difficult situations."

Barring the hiring of a workplace jester, just how do you stimulate humor? One technique, says Granirer, is to have the staff make ridiculous statements that pretend bad

things are good. "Humor often involves an attitude reversal," he explains. "You often see a stand-up comic take something that's a negative and pretend it's great. For example, you often hear variations of the joke, 'It's great going bald because I have less hair to comb.'"

You can do the same in your workplace, says Granirer. Assign people to groups of four or five. Then have each group come up with three or four outrageous reasons why they love being overworked, dealing with bad clients, and other stressors. For example, one attitude reversal might be: "I love dealing with the so-and-so client. I really needed to have my self-esteem beaten down today."

"This approach allows people to say the things they are not supposed to say because they are doing it in a humorous way," Granirer observes. "When people laugh, the stressors become less threatening. Later, when they deal with the difficult client, they remember the humorous statement they had made and it's difficult to be so serious about it."

Bonus tip: Encourage your staff to compartmentalize each task and concentrate on it until it is completed. When the task is over they should take a deep breath and move on. Avoid being overwhelmed by thoughts of many tasks still to do.

Create a Positive Work Environment

"Groups of workers can create positive or negative cultures," observes Dr. David C. Munz, a professor of psychology at Saint Louis University, St. Louis, Mo. "When the language used by your staff is positive, affirmative thinking becomes contagious."

Dr. Munz suggests encouraging positive language when people communicate with one other. Recommend the empowering "I will" rather than the passive "I should." If an employee says something like "I don't have enough time," persuade him to change

his goal so he can state, "I have just enough time." Has a staff member not become computer-literate? Prompt the employee to say, "I will learn a program by the end of this month" rather than "I am not that good at computers."

Finally, influence your staff to avoid negative self-talk inside their head. Phrases such as "That won't work" and "That was stupid" need to make way for "To make this work, I will . . ." and "From this experience, I have learned to . . ."

Bonus tip: Establish a "What's Good" bulletin board, where the staff posts photos and notes about the positive aspects of the workplace.

Create Work Flexibility

Individuals feel less stress if they have the power to manage the time they spend on business and personal life. "People are having difficulty balancing their family and work lives," says Paul Gibson, an attorney and human resources analyst at CCH Human Resources Group, Chicago. "Our surveys show that a paid-leave bank is the most successful way to reduce the stress that results when people have too few hours to do too many tasks."

A "paid-leave bank" system lumps all time off—vacation, sick, and personal days—into one bank that the employee can use as appropriate. This reduces stress because it allows the employee to schedule time as needed. It benefits the employer as well; the person who needs to take care of a family task can now let the supervisor know about a necessary absence well in advance. This avoids the last-minute scrambling—and increased staff stress level—that occurs when employees call in sick.

Bonus tip: Simple things such as the ability to take breaks freely, to augment desk lighting, and select their own work apparel can also contribute to employees' sense of flexibility.

Tackle Stress the Right Way

The information age is bringing rapid change to the workplace. It will take time for people to develop coping mechanisms for the increase in stress that is the result of the need to achieve more productivity from limited resources.

One thing's for sure: We can't reverse the clock. "Today, everything is moving in technology time," Dr. Hagberg concludes. "People who want things to be the way they were will be frustrated over the next few years. Handling stress will continue to be a major challenge for every business."

HOW Great Machines ARE BORN

In the home or in industry, friendly machines based on "human factors" are a joy to use. They are more efficient too, and often safer.

BY STUART F. BROWN

THE PLEASING, "BUTTERY" FEEL of manual shifting that motor buffs crave in an agile car. The welcoming contours of a power-tool handle. The sensuous blend of fluidity and resistance in the focusing knob on a pair of binoculars. These and more are the details of machines that are great to use because they fall naturally to hand and feel right and logical.

Devices so inviting don't just spring into existence. They result from the patient work of largely unsung specialists known as human-factors engineers. Also called ergonomists, these experts know the sizes and shapes people come in, how they can and can't move, how they acquire and digest information, and how machines can be shaped to accommodate them. Human factors traces its origins to World War II, when the U.S. and British military wanted to figure out, among other things, how many sizes of gas masks were needed to fit the troops. Industry designers still rely on the military's "anthropometric" tables that tally human dimensions.

Smart companies have been cashing in on the latest human-factors wisdom with a wide array of machines:

• The sleek, accident-minimizing oil field equipment developed by a unit of Schlumberger.

• Forklift trucks from Crown Equipment Corp. whose comfortable, rounded shapes and lovely controls are popular with warehouse workers.

• Deere's 8000-series tractor, which gives farmers control-tower visibility and whose four-wheel-drive version turns on a dime.

• DaimlerChrysler's minivans, whose latest user-friendly features have helped the company hang on to the biggest slice of the U.S. mini-van market.

• A hot-selling, easy-to-load Maytag washer that boasts the same energy efficiency as other models that are more awkward to use.

In sorry contrast to these successes are the many products whose human-factors aspects are ignored or executed badly. Think of VCRs with hard-to-understand timers. Or elevator buttons labeled with convergent and divergent arrows that many passengers can't figure out fast enough to open the door for somebody. At the extreme end of the

failure spectrum are catastrophes: the reactor meltdown at Three Mile Island, caused in part by hard-to-interpret control-room displays.

There are lessons in the way well-designed machines are created. One is not to rely unduly on market research, since potential customers may not know what they really want or what is possible. Another is to bring in human-factors people at the very beginning of a product-development program, when they can do the most good. In the later stages, bad ideas have often gained too much momentum to be changed, says Steve Casey, president of Ergonomic Systems Design, a consulting firm in Santa Barbara that has worked with three of the companies cited in this story.

When Casey is called in to consult on a new product, he first learns how to use existing versions. "I've been on 300 farms around the world to learn about the machines and talk to the people who use them," he says. Listening to users' gripes and praises, a human-factors engineer begins to compile what's called a function analysis, which asks every

Reprinted from the March 1, 1999, issue of *Fortune*, pp. 164C-164F, by special permission. © 1999 by Time, Inc.

conceivable question about the purpose of the product under development. Once a product's purpose is clearly defined, the designers carry out a detailed "task analysis" charting the way people will interact with the device. Finally, different prototype components must be tested to find out which work best in the hands of users.

The happy results are products like these:

Schlumberger's new way to "complete" an oil well. Though human-factors engineering is most familiar in cars and consumer products, it is just as important in heavy machinery. The Dowell division of Schlumberger Ltd. in Sugar Land, Texas, provides services to oil and gas drilling companies around the world. Many of its jobs involve operating heavy equipment called a coil-tubing unit at well sites. A new version that Dowell has designed, called CT Express, takes a lot of the cost, complexity—and hazard—out of the work.

One job of a coil-tubing unit is to "complete" a well, as the roughnecks say. When a well is drilled, large-diameter steel casing is put in place as a liner, and cement is pumped in to fill the gap between the casing and the hole. Once this is done, a large volume of drilling "mud," the heavy fluid used to lubricate the bit and flush away cuttings, must be removed before the well can begin producing oil or gas. The coil-tubing machinery includes a 10,000-foot reel of flexible, narrow-diameter steel pipe that is stuffed down the hole by a device called an injector head. To drive the mud up and out of the hole, nitrogen gas is pumped down the pipe.

The scene at a traditional well completion has a Wild West flavor to it. Four major vehicles collectively worth nearly $3 million are involved: a truck carrying the big reel of tubing, a crane truck that suspends the five-ton injector head above the well, a liquid-nitrogen tank truck, and a pump truck. The four operators of these noisy machines and their supervisor communicate by walkie-talkie. Keeping a close watch on the injector head is critical. This mechanism has powerful hydraulically driven grippers that look like a pair of bulldozer treads facing each other. They shove the tubing into the well and pull it out when the job is done.

As the tubing goes farther and farther down, the weight the injector head must support keeps increasing. If the tension is wrong and the device loses its grip, the tubing can go shrieking down the hole, and per-

Setup time with Dowell's old system was three hours, and 75 hydraulic hoses had to be connected. The new system is up in half an hour.

haps rip the reel off the truck as well. When underground pressure is high, on the other hand, the tubing can come spitting out of the hole like satanic spaghetti, spraying corrosive acid propelled by pressurized nitrogen. "If this starts to happen, and your efforts to control it don't work, it is time to run like hell," says Dowell engineer Athar Ali. He's the designated "product champion" in charge of overseeing and tweaking two prototype CT Express units that are designed to improve on this situation.

Heading the team that developed CT Express is Terry McCafferty, Dowell's section manager for coil-tubing surface equipment and an electrical engineer who makes dulcimers in his spare time. One of the first things the designers looked at was the accident history of coil-tubing units. Statistics showed that 74% of lost-time injuries occurred during rig setup and breakdown at the job site, and that 57% of

these involved workers falling or having fingers crushed while working on the injector head.

"These numbers," McCafferty says, "led us to set goals of keeping the people on the ground and not having them work under something that's hanging in the air." Improved productivity was another goal. Setup time with the old system was more than three hours, as the crane pulled up near the well and hoisted the 10,000-pound injector head, upon which workers scrambled to thread the tubing into the grippers. And 75 hydraulic hoses had to be connected between various pieces of equipment, creating an opportunity for errors.

The system McCafferty's team came up with, which could be seen in operation in western Canada in January, costs $1.5 million. It fits on two stately orange Peterbilt trailer trucks, needs only three operators, and incorporates a lot of features designed to improve safety and efficiency. The system uses a self-erecting mast on the reel truck, which brings a pre-threaded injector into place above the well. No hydraulic connections need to be made.

Instead of having four operators, with each running some of the equipment, CT Express puts one person in charge of it all. Housed in a booth that is heated in winter and air-conditioned in summer, the operator sits in an ergonomically designed chair equipped with integrated keypads and fighter-plane-style control sticks. A pair of large flat-screen displays shows the functioning of various subsystems in an iconic fashion that's easy to grasp. The injector is largely controlled by sensors that automatically detect slippage by comparing pipe speed with gripper speed, making any needed correction and alerting the operator. Says McCafferty: "We want the operator to be able to focus more on the mission and not on the individual devices."

At a 5,000-foot-deep gas well in central Alberta owned by Canadian 88 Energy Resource Corp., McCafferty and Ali recently watched a small crew get a prototype CT Express unit up and ready to go to work in less than half an hour. Dowell plans to order about 25 more of the units from its equipment supplier, Hydra Rig of Fort Worth, as soon as all the feedback from early users has come in.

Cool lift trucks from Crown Equipment. The small town of New Bremen, Ohio, in farm country about 50 miles northwest of Dayton, is the sort of place a film crew would go to make a movie about the early career of the Wright Brothers. Many of the perfectly restored buildings there belong to Crown Equipment Corp., a billion-dollar, privately held maker of electric lift trucks that dominates the local economy. Used in warehouses, factories, and stores, Crown machines can raise loads weighing as much as 8,000 pounds as high as 45 feet.

At the start of a shift, it's widely said, warehouse workers sprint to be the one who gets to spend the day aboard a Crown machine instead of another make—that's how slick they are to use. The operator's perch on a Crown lift truck looks like a Milan designer's idea of the personal transportation device of the future, with soft, rounded shapes everywhere and color-keyed, contoured controls that welcome the hand. Over the years, the Industrial Designers Society of America and other groups have heaped awards on Crown's designers.

How did a hard-boiled industrial-equipment company get so far into squishy aesthetic and human-factors considerations? It happened, well, by design. In the early '60s, when Crown was a newcomer in the mature lift-truck market, Tom Bidwell, then the company's director of engineering and manufacturing, decided that combining quality with clean lines and easy-to-understand controls was the way to stand out. Crown attracted praise in the '70s with the introduction of a counterbalanced lift truck on which the op-

erator stands sideways instead of facing in the direction of travel, a change since adopted by most competitors. The inspiration came from paying attention to human factors. A designer observing the machines then in use was bothered to see operators driving down narrow warehouse aisles facing forward, and then reversing the journey by turning around so they could see where they were going and working the controls behind their backs. Crown's new "side stance" layout allowed an operator to see either way by simply turning his head.

While pondering how to lay out the controls for this unorthodox machine, the designers hit upon another idea: combining functions in a joystick. The new trucks captured a 40% share of their market segment within four years of their introduction.

A Crown tradition has evolved in which designers brainstorm, sketch, and construct mockups, unmolested at first by engineers and marketing types. Design director Michael Gallagher entered this supportive environment when he left the consumer-electronics industry in 1994 to join Crown. A lanky guy who likes fast cars, Gallagher brings a perfectionist's zeal to defining and refining the trucks. The designers spend a lot of time watching videotapes of how they are used. "Real lift-truck maestros are silky smooth, and they never stop moving," Gallagher says. "They just dance with the truck."

The studio builds a lot of models to see how new ideas look and feel. Lines of sight receive particular attention, because when operators pick up something with the weight of a car and put it into a spot 30 feet up on a rack, accidents can be serious.

For its latest generation of side-stance truck, the RR 5000S, Crown devised a flip-up seat and extra foot pedals that allow the operator to relieve body fatigue during the workday by varying his posture from sitting to leaning slightly back to standing. The controls are within easy, ergonomically sound reach to keep the operator's body stable,

with hands and feet firmly planted to minimize his chance of falling off while whipping around corners. As an extra safeguard, brake switches underneath spring-mounted floorboards prevent the trucks from moving if the operator doesn't have both feet in the proper position.

Crown puts extensive research and testing into its displays, which give the lift operator information in an uncluttered fashion. By switching to remote, electrical control of the lift's hydraulic valves, the company has been able to place switches and buttons near the operator's hands and feet. All the controls are "electroproportional" these days, which means that the farther you push, the more you get, be it travel speed, fork-raise rate, or whatever. The company has also invested a lot of development time in deciding how sensitive a control should be through its range of motion. It's akin to calibrating the response increments of a radio's volume knob.

Deere's big but nimble tractor. Deere & Co. is proud to hear farmers say they have "green blood" and won't consider buying another brand of tractor. "It's their life, working with these machines," says Bruce Newendorp, a human-factors staff engineer at Deere's product-engineering center in Waterloo, Iowa. Newendorp helped develop the powerful 8000 series of tractors that first went on sale in 1994. Built in both wheeled and tracked versions, the machines cost from $109,000 to $138,000, and you can see them working the fields wherever there are big-acre farms.

When it launched the 8000 tractor development program, Deere wanted to design in features that customers hadn't thought to ask for. At the top of the list was forward visibility from the operator's cab. "It's very valuable to be able to clearly see the front wheels and the rows of crops as you drive a tractor through a field," Newendorp explains. "So we did a lot of things, including finding other places to put the instruments that formerly narrowed the view."

Another goal was to give the four-wheel-drive versions a tight turning radius. The majority of wheeled-tractor customers these days order four-wheel drive. But the bigger wheels and fatter tires used on the front of these machines bump up against a traditional tractor frame, restricting the turning radius. Wide turns are not the farmer's friend. They can force him to leave land uncultivated at the ends of a field.

To fix the problem, Deere designers rethought the front layout of the machine. Now the tractor has a pinched waist when seen from above, which allows the front wheels to pivot under the frame during a tight turn. The company ran an ad showing its 8000 series four-wheel-drive model carving a figure eight inside a competitor's minimum turning circle.

Climbing up the steps and slipping behind the wheel of these tractors is a delight. The glass area is immense, almost like an airport control tower. The front portion of the cab floor slopes slightly downward to increase visibility by a few degrees, and there's a cup holder on the floor atop an air-conditioner vent to keep drinks cool. Deere's engineers grouped the primary controls, which include the throttle, 16-speed shifter, and implement controls, on an extension of the right armrest called the Command Arm module.

Interiors matter most in minivans: "It's a little cabin with a homey feeling, and the outside is just a wrapper."

That makes possible another nifty improvement. When the farmer looks over his shoulder to check a plow or other attachment through the back window, the seat of the tractor swivels and the Command Arm module moves too. Details like this mean a lot to farmers during harvest season, when they may spend 14-hour days in the driver's seat and work into the night with floodlights burning.

DaimlerChrysler's driver-friendly vehicles. A lot of human-factors thinking went into the original minivan, which when it hit the showrooms in 1983 rescued Chrysler Corp., now part of DaimlerChrysler, from looming extinction. The minivans have been through two redesigns since then, and engineers are toiling behind locked doors on a fourth generation. Though competing makes have crowded in, DaimlerChrysler has hung on to a 45% share of the U.S. market by drawing on a rich body of knowledge about drivers' preferences, as well as their dimensions, physical and cognitive capabilities, and lifestyles.

When planning was under way for the current generation, launched in 1996, Chrysler's human-factors staff reexamined critical dimensions such as the driver's seat height. "We tried different heights and found out that the one we had chosen in 1978 was truly the optimum for most people, so we left it there," says David Bostwick, director of corporate market research. "This is one of the details that makes owners feel like the vehicle was made for them, because they didn't have to climb up or plunk down into the driver's seat."

But there were changes too. Chrysler widened the vehicles, creating room for the driver to extend her or his legs straight to reach the brake and accelerator pedals. The company also added 40% more window-glass area, which improved the lines of sight through the top and bottom of the windshield, and put as many controls as possible within the driver's comfortable reach.

Access was improved. Market research had long indicated that people wanted two doors on each side of a minivan, but with past engineering methods that would have required adding excessive weight to strengthen the body. In the latest generation, computers came to the rescue. The CATIA computer-aided-design system from France's Dassault group of companies, which Chrysler has been using to develop all its vehicles, can run finite-element analyses that tell precisely where to add and delete metal to get the strongest, lightest body. The new four-door structure turned out to be stiffer than the old three-door one.

Perhaps more than on any other vehicle, the interior layout of the minivan is what can make or break a customer's purchase decision. In years of Chrysler research, exterior styling has never ranked among the top ten reasons for buying, which it almost always does with cars. Says Bostwick: "It's a little cabin that has a homey feeling to it, and the outside is just a wrapper for what's inside."

All of Chrysler's "cabins," be they for vans or sedans, are previewed and refined these days on a virtual reality system. An engineer working on an interior design sits down, straps on sensors that track his hand locations, and dons special goggles that display a virtual-interior model stored in the CATIA system. Looking around, he can check the lines of sight through the windshield, to the sides, and even out the back window. Grasping an authentic 7-Eleven Big Gulp cup, he can check the reach to a virtual cup holder. Other people in the room can see what he's seeing projected on a wall screen.

"Early in a development program," says advance vehicle engineering manager Kenric Socks, "we use virtual reality to evaluate a lot of visual and reach-oriented things. It has hugely cut down on the number of go-arounds with physical mockups."

One future product Socks is able to talk about is the 2000 model year Neon subcompact, which DaimlerChrysler has displayed in prototype on the auto show circuit. When designers of a new model like this one go to work on the interior at CAD terminals, Socks says, they are guided by anthropometric descriptions of the sizes people come in and how they sit in a vehicle. From this starting point, they can begin to block out the locations of primary controls such as the steering wheel, shifter, brakes, and throttle. Then they begin selecting the placement of secondary controls, including turn signals, light switches, radio and climate controls, and so forth.

As these decisions get firmed up through successive design reviews, what are known as the "first surfaces" of the interior become precisely defined. "The first surfaces of the interior are what you and I see as customers," says Socks. "From an ergonomic standpoint, you really want to lock them in early in a project, which is why we're a part of advance-vehicle engineering. If you want a small-car interior to feel big enough, you've got to get this stuff right. Then comes second-surface design, which is the car's structure underneath."

Some of the Neon's changes have been prompted by complaints. Shorter Neon owners groused about bumping their arms on the seat cushion while lowering the window with a manual crank. Engineers built a test jig with a movable window crank, and measured and plotted the preferences of people of widely varying stature. Now they know the crank-pivot point that will satisfy 95% of the population, which is more than two inches higher than in the current model.

Maytag's easy-loading washer. With gasoline selling for less than bottled water, it might seem that Americans no longer care about energy conservation. The strong demand for the high-efficiency Neptune clothes washer from Maytag Appliances of Newton, Iowa, indicates otherwise. The Neptune, which lists at a relatively high $1,099, was a hit from the moment it reached showrooms in June 1997. People like it because it's easy to use and can save as much as 38% on water usage and 56% on electric bills.

That combination of attributes is missing in the top-loading washers Americans have traditionally preferred. While easy to load and unload, these machines require an agitator mechanism and a relatively large amount of water to get the clothes clean. Front-loading machines, popular in Europe, have a horizontal-axis drum inside that uses gravity's natural assist to tumble away dirt while conserving water. But they're almost impossible to sell in the U.S. because people don't like bending or kneeling to reach the low door opening.

The Neptune's design is one of those happy compromises that seems obvious after someone else has thought of it. To achieve the efficiency of a front loader but improve access, the designers tilted the washer's drum axis upward 15 degrees from the horizontal. And they devised a door that runs up the machine's front and then slopes back along the top to create a large opening. The Neptune's user can load it without aggravating those creaky knees.

Government was the spark plug that ignited the $50 million Neptune development program. Back in the early '90s, the U.S. Department of Energy was making noises about issuing water- and electricity-efficiency standards, which sent appliance makers scrambling. Maytag formed a partnership with the Electric Power Research Institute, a Palo Alto utility-industry group with a mandate to help members minimize investments in the next big round of expensive generating equipment.

Maytag sequestered 30 specialists from all parts of the company in a "war room" for three weeks to hammer out a new strategy. In subsequent consumer testing, the company learned that Americans had little fondness for the high-efficiency front loaders built by Miele of Germany, which are well regarded by Europeans living in cramped quarters. Too little capacity, too long a wash cycle, and too much bending over, said the focus groups. Maytag even built sev-

eral front-loading prototypes with more capacity than the Mieles, but consumer panels rejected those too. "We were slow to learn on this, and the light bulb didn't just instantly come on," admits Dave Ellingson, Maytag's director of product design engineering.

Progress began when engineers studied the Brandt washers popular in France, which have a sideways horizontal drum for efficiency but load from the top. The prototypes the engineers built required two inner drums and a total of three doors, however, which made loading too complex. Then one engineer began experimenting with tilting a horizontal drum upward a bit. Colleagues rejected the idea at first. But he stuck to his guns, performing washability tests and loading trials that proved it was a good design.

Using cardboard, a wooden dowel, and other low-tech stuff, the engineers then rigged up a variable-angle drum mockup that could be tilted from five to 40 degrees and turned a focus group loose on it. The panelists preferred a 20-degree angle, but Maytag settled on 15 degrees to meet some engineering considerations. When this type of drum was housed in a mockup with a vertical front and a door that wrapped over the top edge, Maytag was startled by the handsome price people said they'd be willing to pay for it.

Then came news that the Energy Department wasn't going to issue a washer-efficiency standard after all. But it was a no-brainer to forge ahead with what promised to be a money-maker. One moral of the story, says Don Erickson, Maytag's manager of horizontal-axis washer design, is that "it's good to have conflict early on in design, to have people with different ideas. We want to take the time and effort to prove things right or wrong early, rather than later." The other moral, whether for Maytag washers or equipment used at lonely oil fields, is that if machines are designed around people, the customers will come.

CHARACTERISTICS OF THE MANUFACTURING ENVIRONMENT THAT INFLUENCE TEAM SUCCESS

MARK PAGELL

Department of Management, College of Business Administration, 101 Calvin Hall, Kansas State University, Manhattan, KS 66506-0507

JEFFREY A. LEPINE

Department of Management, University of Florida, 201 Business Building, P.O. Box 117165, Gainesville, FL 32611-7165

Operations management as a field has evolved greatly during the past 20–30 years. In that time organizations have adopted a vast number of innovations to improve the performance of operations and the overall organization. These innovations have ranged from the development of programmable forms of automation that allow companies to compete on economies of scope rather than scale, to the adoption of companywide philosophies such as time-based competition, total quality management (TQM), and Just-in-Time (JIT) management.

Many of these innovations, especially philosophies such as TQM and JIT, were recognized as part of the reason Japanese companies had a major competitive advantage over their North American counterparts in the 1970s and 80s. Additionally, many managers realized that part of this competitive advantage came from the organization of workers into teams. Team-based work can speed up innovation, increase the sharing of knowledge across the company, reduce the numbers (hence costs) of managers, and generally enhance competitiveness [1]. Therefore, it is no surprise that establishing teams is one of the most popular approaches to increasing manufacturing performance [12]. Teams are used in operations for a number of tasks, including quality circles, JIT, process improvement, and product and process design and often they include members of the supply chain from outside an organization's boundaries [3, 7, 9, 10].

Research has identified many factors that enable team success. A focus on team-based rewards, team composition, leadership, and other issues such as the size of the team has led to improvements in team performance [6, 11]. However, reviews of the research also suggest that there is much more to learn about team-based work and the factors that affect team success [5].

One area that has not been well addressed is the actual context in which teams are used. Our research specifically addresses the use of teams in a manufacturing context. Our study takes an in-depth look at how teams are—or are not—being used by organizations. In addi-tion, we examine why one plant can have a variety of outcomes from team-based work.

Our results suggest that many elements of a manufacturing environment affect the usefulness of teams. More important, from a managerial standpoint, many of these elements may be fixed. Therefore we present a model of environments in which teams are (or are not) likely to work. And we discuss the model with an aim of providing prescriptions to help ensure that reengineering efforts, process improvements, and other major changes in operational systems explicitly consider the applicability of teams. The result is a model that can help managers determine whether their operational environment is suited to teams as well as help them direct changes that would make team-based work a worthwhile investment.

METHOD

The goal of the research was to explore the operations-specific factors that might be related to manufacturing team success. We chose field-based data-collection methods to help ensure the level of detail necessary so that we could not only identify factors, but could also develop an understanding of why the identified factors might be important [2, 4, 8].

Thirty plants in eight industries (see table 1) were visited between March 1996 and January 1997. All but two of the industries had multiple representatives. In general, a single plant represents each company. In some cases, multiple plants from a company were included in the sample if they differed from each other in some significant way.

At all the plants we used a structured interview protocol that was updated and improved with each replication. In addition to detailed information on the use and outcomes from team-based work, the protocol included items on the plant's external environment, the type of labor relations the plant had, its human resource policies,

TABLE 1: Sample

Industry	Number of Plants
Auto parts	5
Diesel engines	5
Office furniture	2
Stamping dies	5
Molds	3
Machine tools	8
Consumer goods	1
Construction equipment	1
Totals	**30**

business and functional strategies, competitive priorities, and elements of the manufacturing environment.

Structured interviews at each plant generally involved the plant manager as well as the human resource manager for the operational employees. At many plants additional interviews were done. Company presidents or vice presidents and manufacturing engineers as well as programming staff, shop floor employees, or both were interviewed. At a few of the smaller plants, interviews were limited to a single respondent because that person was primarily responsible for both manufacturing and human resources.

The interview protocol included a plant tour—and all the facilities were toured. The primary researcher was accompanied on 27 of the 30 visits by a second researcher. Using multiple researchers and multiple interviews for almost every case helped to limit possible biases introduced by a single researcher/respondent.

Analysis

The data were collected to address teams of operational employees within a single plant. The protocol asked plant managers if they used teams in operational settings and how well these teams performed. However, one of the first things to come out of the data collection was the fact that even within a single plant, experience with teams could vary significantly. One of the first respondents initially had very positive perceptions of team-based work in the plant. However, upon reflection this respondent noted that the teams were not universally successful in the facility and that there were areas of the plant in which teams did not work well.

This observation led to a change in the level of analysis—from operational teams across the plant, to specific types of teams. For plants that used teams for various types of operational tasks, we had multiple data points. Examples included plants with both assembly and fabrication teams or plants with teams based on function and teams based on products. This level of analysis allowed us to explore various outcomes even when many of the elements of the environment (such as top management) are held constant.

For the data analysis we used tools such as pattern matching [8]. We collated all the managerial comments about team success, failure, or nonadoption. Then through a process of combination, renaming, and redefining we were able to reduce the data to three main factors directly related to the manufacturing environment that may inhibit or enable team-based work. The following sections describe each factor as well as how it relates to team success or failure.

Operational System

A recurring theme in the research was how employees were linked together, not by their tasks or rewards (factors previously identified as important for teams), but rather by the layout of the facility and the type of work they were doing. For example, tool and die makers often had functional teams and assembly teams. The functional teams were composed of people doing the same type of work, usually machining parts. The assembly teams were composed of all the different people needed to complete a single project. Individual employees were often on both types of teams.

The functional teams, however, generally did not succeed because the employees on these teams performed work that was not linked to the work of other team members. Regardless of the structure of the task or the types of outcomes, the structure of the work did not encourage or enable employees to interact. Problems for one team member did not interfere with individual outcomes for another team member. However, when the same employees were put on assembly teams the outcomes were very different, with teams being perceived as very valuable.

Assembly teams are formed around a specific project and disband when the project is complete. The work of each team member does affect the work of all other team members. A part that is late from fabrication will slow the entire team. And a problem in assembly is usually solved by the entire team, not just the assembler. Similar relationships were found in more traditional assembly line environments. Team members who have a clear linkage to the next team member share problems. When the work of one team member does not meet specifications, the rest of the team members are instantly affected.

The operational system also enabled or inhibited teams in other ways. Fabrication is often done in cells to increase efficiency. In some cells a small team of employees runs a number of machines, often rotating jobs and responsibility. In these situations the work of each team member is tightly linked to the other team members. A problem or opportunity for one team member is a problem or opportunity for the entire team. However, when a single employee runs an entire cell alone, or when a single employee runs a stand-alone piece of equipment, the work of any one team member is not tightly linked to other team members. When a single employee encounters a problem, the rest of the team can continue working and may not even be aware that a team member needs help.

For teams to be of value, the structure of the operational system has to encourage employees to work together. This factor could and did vary significantly across a single facility. The importance of other forms of interdependence has been stressed in previous research; however, it should be noted that the operational system is usually a major capital investment and may not be changeable in the short to medium term. Hence managers who have systems that do not tightly link their employees will probably not get the return they expected on their investment in teams.

Informal Modes of Communication

Another key issue is the ability to communicate informally throughout the day. For example, one of the auto parts makers had instituted teams plantwide. However, the teams in the machining and fabrication areas proved to be of little value. Management felt that this failure was at least partly due to an inability of these team members to communicate throughout the day.

All the teams in the plant met at the beginning of the shift to solve team problems and discuss opportunities for improvement, but the fabrication equipment's size and noise level physically isolated employees. The only way for team members in this section to communicate with each other was to stop working and leave their work area. Because of this isolation, team members often solved problems or made improvements on their own. Or if additional knowledge was required, management might help the individual employee, without the rest of the team. Regardless, the team members did not pool their capabilities and stores of learning. By the time the team met the issue was generally resolved and/or forgotten. Therefore the key reason for using teams—building a shared knowledge—was not leveraged.

Team members who work in an environment that allows them to communicate throughout the day had very different outcomes. Their ability to discuss problems in real time facilitated the sharing of knowledge and generally led to their solving problems and making improvements as a team rather than as individuals.

Like the operational system, this factor poses a problem for operations managers because their system may not facilitate easy and frequent communication. Employees who work in an isolated area cannot easily communicate with other team members. Large, noisy equipment often increases their isolation, and work rules and/or company strategies, such as a focus on efficiency, may discourage them from stopping their work. This is not an issue in an environment that allows team members to communicate while continuing to work, but team members who must stop to communicate may have more incentive to keep working than to have an un-scheduled team meeting. Finally, different parts of a plant may be more or less hospitable to communication, making this factor variable across some facilities.

Novel Problems to Solve

A final operational issue for many teams was what they had to do. Many managers noted that their team meetings were little more than gripe sessions. When the opportunity to solve a problem arose, these teams would solve it or work to improve processes, but for them chances to do so were rare. In these types of environments, the value of the team was hard to discern.

A diesel engine manufacturer is one example. Its management had instituted team-based work throughout the plant, and although managers were generally pleased with the overall outcome of the project, the outcome from teams varied significantly across the facility. In general, the teams were successful when the team did a variety of work or faced a number of novel problems.

One of the company's products had more than 200 different possible intake manifolds. A single cell made all of these manifolds, and because the part being made was constantly changing, the team had many unique problems and many opportunities to improve the process.

However, a cell in another part of the plant fabricated a single part continuously. Once the equipment was debugged, very little that was new or interesting occurred for years at a time. And because the process was fairly well optimized, the team for this cell did not have much to do and was viewed by management and employees as unnecessary.

This example suggests that plants or parts of a plant that are fairly well optimized may not offer enough opportunity for a team to feel useful. Companies making mature products may also find that there is little for a team to do. The bottom line for respondents was that when team members do not have much to do as a team, the team is seen as a waste of time. The meetings become counterproductive, especially if management had invested in training the employees in team-based problem solving and then had given them little to accomplish with their new skills.

DISCUSSION

Figure 1 displays the factors, identified by the research, that affect team usefulness in operational environments. For each factor, a list of items that help to determine where a company stands is also shown. The items are not an exhaustive list of issues management should consider when deciding on the usefulness of teams for a given purpose, but they are a useful first step. These issues should be considered as part of reengineering efforts and the like to determine if a new process is suited to team-based work.

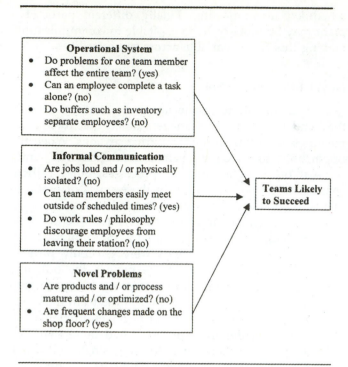

FIGURE 1:   Decision variables

All the successful teams have operational systems that encourage interdependence and high levels of informal communication. Teams that do not have these characteristics did not succeed because the team members spent most of their time working alone with no mechanism or incentive to share knowledge in real time. Having novel problems to solve was also very important to team success; however, a few companies without those types of problems were successful if their teams were tightly linked by the operational system.

Employees who work in isolated or noisy areas are not good candidates to be on teams unless they are free to leave their stations throughout the day. And employees who are making mature products and/or are using mature processes may not have many opportunities to use their team-based skills. Finally, decisions such as the use of buffers can significantly affect the usefulness of teams.

Inventory buffers provide a very good example. Assembly teams tend to work very well because the system puts employees in an interdependent state and in many assembly environments employees work near their team members, so they can communicate throughout the day. However, when buffers of inventory are used between the steps in assembly, the team is not as tightly linked and can lose some of its effectiveness.

The results give some direction to managers who are trying to improve the probability of team success. One of the key tasks for managers trying to make teams work is to design jobs in which workers are tightly linked and then to allow the team the freedom to communicate whenever necessary. Team-based work requires a culture in which employees feel free to move about the plant and talk to other team members. If management is serious about teams, managers must also be serious about giving employees the chance to communicate as well as something to talk about. In mature facilities with mature products teams should be considered only if employees are going to have something to do. Otherwise moving to teams will be counterproductive.

A culture that discourages communication, and tasks that don't give teams an opportunity to solve problems as a group are intellectual barriers that managers need to remove to make team-based work effective. There are also physical barriers that need to be removed. Inventory buffers provide a prime example. When team members are separated by safety stock, they have less incentive to work together. Removing the buffer not only lowers inventory costs, it also motivates the team to work together.

Because so many of the factors discussed are difficult to change, the results also have major implications for process improvement efforts such as reengineering. Team-based work has been shown to have a very large payoff, but results do vary [12]. To take advantage of teams, a company needs to explicitly consider its needs during the design or redesign of systems. When redesigning a facility's layout, management should move team members closer together to encourage more communication and interdependence. Rearranging work into cells that are run by semi-autonomous groups may enhance the ability of teams to help an organization. Similar cells that are staffed by a single person may be individually more efficient, but they may create a system that does not encourage the sharing of information and continuous improvement that comes from teams. Cells need to be designed with both efficient processing and effective teamwork in mind.

Results of this research are important to operations managers because they indicate that although team-based work can result in significant improvements, these improvements will not accrue in all environments or even all parts of a single facility. More important, many of the elements of the environment that affect team success or failure are at some level fixed and may be difficult to change.

CONCLUSIONS

Managers need to closely examine their manufacturing environment when deciding to institute teams. There is a large base of research on the human issues needed to make teams successful. However, our research indicates that even with very well formulated human resource policies, top management support for teams, and proper training in team-based work, the actual operational environment may inhibit teams. Major process changes and/or reengineering efforts tend to be infrequent; however, when these activities do occur management should explicitly consider whether the new process would be more or less hospitable to team-based work.

These findings are important as many of the facets of the operational context that have been identified are fixed because of capital investments. This suggests that some organizations will not be candidates for team-based work any time soon. It also suggests that change efforts on the shop floor should explicitly consider the ability to institute teams.

REFERENCES

1. Bursic, K.M. "Strategies and Benefits of the Successful Use of Teams in Manufacturing Organizations." *IEEE Transactions on Engineering Management* 39, no. 3 (1992): 277–289.
2. Eisenhardt, K.M. "Building theories from case studies." *Academy of Management Review* 14, no. 4 (1989): 532–550.
3. Ferras, L. "Continuous Improvements in Electronics Manufacturing." *Production and Inventory Management Journal* 35, no. 2 (1994): 1–5.
4. Glasser, B. G., and A. L. Strauss. *The Discovery of Grounded Theory: Strategies for Qualitative Research.* Chicago: Aldine, 1967.
5. Ilgen, D.R., D.A. Major, J.R. Hollenbeck, and D.J. Sego. "Team Research in the 1990s," in *Leadership Theory and Research: Perspectives and Directions*, ed. Chemers and Ayman. San Diego, Calif.: Academic Press Inc., 1993, 245–270.
6. LePine, J.A., J.R. Hollenbeck, D.R. Ilgen, and J. Hedlund. "Effects of Individual Differences on the Performance of Hierarchical Decision-Making Teams: Much More than g." *Journal of Applied Psychology* 82, no. 5 (1997): 803–811.
7. McLachlin, R. "Management Initiatives and Just-In-Time Manufacturing." *Journal of Operations Management* 15, no. 4 (1997): 271–292.
8. Miles, M.B., and A.M. Huberman. *Qualitative Data Analysis.* Thousand Oaks, Calif.: Sage Publications, 1994.
9. Minahan, T. "Platform Teams Pair With Suppliers to Drive Chrysler to Better Designs." *Purchasing* 124, no. 7 (1998): 44s3–44s7.
10. Tatikonda, L.U., and R.J. Tatikonda. "Top Ten Reasons Your TQM Effort Is Failing to Improve Profit." *Production and Inventory Management Journal* 36, no. 3 (1995): 5–9.
11. Weldon, E., K. A. Jehn, and P. Pradhan. "Processes that Mediate the Relationship Between a Group Goal and Improved Group Performance." *Journal of Personality and Social Psychology* 61, no. 4 (1991): 555–569.
12. Wharton, T. J., D. Reid, and E. M. White. "An Empirical Study of Manufacturing Approaches Over Time." *Production and Inventory Management Journal* 38, no. 4 (1997): 7–12.

About the Authors—

MARK PAGELL is an assistant professor of operations management in the Management Department at Kansas State University. He received his Ph.D. in operations management from Michigan State University in 1997. His current research interests include the interaction of human resource and operational decisions in manufacturing environments, manufacturing responses to the external environment, and supply chain management. His research has appeared in many journals including *The Journal of Operations Management, International Journal of Purchasing and Materials Management,* and *International Journal of Production Economics.*

JEFFREY A. LEPINE is an assistant professor in the Management Department at the University of Florida. He received his Ph.D. in organizational behavior from Michigan State University. His current research interests include the effects of team composition on team performance and adaptability, as well as extra-role behaviors and role development. His research has appeared in a number of journals including *Academy of Management Journal and Journal of Applied Psychology.*

THE LEGAL LIMITATIONS TO SELF-DIRECTED WORK TEAMS IN PRODUCTION PLANNING AND CONTROL

STEVEN E. ABRAHAM, PHD, JD
Department of Management, State University at New York—Oswego, Oswego, NY 13126

MICHAEL S. SPENCER, PHD, CFPIM
Department of Management, University of Northern Iowa, Cedar Falls, IA 50614

During the past ten years enormous changes have been observed throughout business organizations. Change has been especially profound in the production planning and control (PP&C) activities of both manufacturers and service providers. One specific change has been the rapid incorporation of Japanese management methods, such as Just-in-Time (JIT) and total quality management (TQM). One critical component of JIT is the use of employee-driven problem-solving teams [5, 8, 22], often called quality circles.

Change has been so rapid that often something relatively new, like quality circles, becomes the expectation. Entrants into the workplace begin to assume that current practices have always been the way things were done and, therefore, must be completely legal. After all, someone at headquarters must have reviewed and approved of quality circle teams. However, production management is somewhat isolated compared to the human resource management, accounting and marketing functions with respect to the legal environment of business. This may be the case with TQM, especially with the use of self-directed work teams. The fact that a team is in place does not necessarily mean that it fits correctly into the legal framework. In fact, the use of teams can expose the production management function to legal sanctions more rapidly than most of our other management aspects.

Most research into the implementation of TQM takes a positive stance towards, perhaps even advocating, employee empowerment [2, 23]. Personnel/human resource management problems that are discussed are usually the reward system, general supervision responsibilities, union-management relations, and overall change management [12, 21, 22]. Treatment of the legal implications of teams is found only in law journals. It is not discussed in the production management literature.

The purposes of this article are to examine the legal limitations of using employee teams in production planning and control and to provide a set of guidelines production managers can use in implementing employee teams.

BACKGROUND

Dumond [6] concluded that the use of employee teams is a key component to TQM success, finding that all companies in his study

From *Production and Inventory Management Journal,* First Quarter 1998, pp. 41-45. © 1998 by APICS, the American Production and Inventory Control Society. Reprinted by permission.

of successful companies reported using functional employee teams. Further, Tatikonda and Tatikonda concluded that "Flat organizations, empowerment, cross-disciplinary and cross-departmental efforts are essential for TQM success.... Quality improvements gained through empowered cross-functional teams can be 200% to 600% more effective than improvements obtained through functional teams." [26, pp. 7–8]. As organizations adopt the team approach, there appears to be a continuum of team structures used. The major determinant in the team structure continuum is the degree of employee empowerment [3]. Teams can range from a quality circle on one end to a self-directed work group on the other. A quality circle is defined as "[a] small group of people who normally work as a unit and meet frequently to uncover and solve problems concerning the quality of items produced, process capability, or process control [1]." A self-directed work team, on the other hand, is defined as "[g]enerally a small, independent, self-organized, and self-controlled group in which members flexibly plan, organize, determine and manage their duties and actions, as well as perform many other supportive functions. It may work without immediate supervision and can often have the authority to select, hire, promote, or discharge its members [1]."

What is clear from the definitions cited above is the blending of traditionally management-related activities with the activities assigned to the teams. Can an employee team be given the responsibility to find and solve production problems legally? What is management's reaction should the team fail? To what degree can the following common production planning and control activities be assigned legally to an employee team?

- Scheduling jobs to a specific piece of equipment
- Assigning jobs to specific employees
- Selecting or changing job priorities
- Scheduling overtime of individuals or the team
- Adding or deleting workers to the team
- Improving the process by changing methods or equipment
- Refusing additional jobs in a given time period.

The answers to the above questions are not as clear as some production managers might think. We will look first at the applicable laws and judicial findings, then establish a set of managerial guidelines.

EMPLOYEE TEAMS AND CASE LAW

One important legal pitfall for employee teams stems from the National Labor Relations Act (NLRA or the "Act"). Specifically, managers need to know that such teams might run afoul of §8(a)(2) of the Act. That section prohibits employers from "dominating, interfering with or supporting labor organizations." In a number of cases since the Act was passed in 1935, the United States Supreme Court and the National Labor Relations Board (NLRB or the "Board") have ruled that an employer violated this section by establishing a quality circle, self-directed work group, or similar program. In fact, a number of commentators have expressed the view that the current interpretation of §8(a)(2) would actually prohibit employers from establishing *any* type of employee participation program without violating the Act [15, 20, 24].

Others, however, find this interpretation to be mistaken, and argue that the NLRA does permit employers to establish teams and other employee groups without violating the Act [4, 14, 25]. Even William Gould, the current chairman of the NLRB, argues that employee teams and other employee participation programs are permissible under the NLRA [11]. Based on the relevant case law, we contend that an employer is able to establish a legitimate employee participation program without violating the NLRA, provided the employer avoids certain things likely to put the program in violation of the Act.

A potential complication with predicting what employers may and may not do stems from the fact that the Board and the courts have rendered arguably inconsistent opinions on the contours of the pertinent portions of the NLRA. Even under the most conservative approach, however, we contend that it would be possible for employers to establish employee teams without violating the Act.

Section 8(a)(2) of the NLRA states:

> (a) It shall be an unfair labor practice for an employer—(2) to dominate or interfere with the formation or administration of any labor organization or contribute financial support to it: *Provided,* ... an employer shall not be prohibited from permitting employees to confer with him during working hours without loss of time or pay (italics by authors).

"[L]abor organization" is defined by Section 2(5) as:

> any organization of any kind, or any agency or employee representation committee or plan, in which employees participate and which exists for the purpose, in whole or in part, of dealing with employers concerning grievances, labor disputes, wages, rates of pay, hours of employment or conditions of work.

Therefore, whether an employee participation program (quality circle, employee team) would violate the NLRA would depend on a two-part analysis: (1) would the team be considered a "labor organization" under §2(5) of the Act; and (2) if so, does the employer dominate that labor organization according to §8(a)(2)?

IS THE TEAM A LABOR ORGANIZATION

According to the NLRB's current interpretation, an organization will be considered a "labor organization" if the following four criteria are met: (1) employees participate, (2) the organization purports to represent others; (3) the organization exists, at least in part, for the purpose of dealing with employers, and (4) these dealings concern conditions of work or other statutory subjects such as grievances, labor disputes, wages, rates of pay, or hours of employment [13]. If any one of these elements is not met, the team will not be considered a labor organization and therefore would not violate the NLRA.

Employee Participation

It is possible that the members of a TQM team would not even be considered employees under the NLRA. The Act specifically defines the "employees" covered, and the definition of employee expressly excludes a "supervisor" from being an employee under the Act. According to section 2(11) of the Act:

> The term "supervisor" means any individual having authority, in the interest of the employer, to hire, transfer, suspend, lay off, recall, promote, discharge, assign, reward, or discipline other employees, or responsibly to direct them, or to adjust their grievances, or effectively to recommend such action, in connection with the foregoing the exercise of such authority is not of a merely routine or clerical nature, but requires the use of independent judgment.

Recent case law shows an ever-broadening view on the types of people the Supreme Court classifies as supervisors [18]. Hence, it is possible that all the members of a team would be treated as supervisors under the Act. If this were the case, §2(5) would not even apply and there would be no problem with the NLRA. Further, in [16], the Supreme Court held that "managerial" employees also were excluded from being employees under the NLRA by §2(11). Therefore, if the members of a team were treated as managers under the Act, §2(5) again would not apply and there would be no problem with the NLRA.

The Organization Purports to Represent Others

A TQM team would only be considered a labor organization if it purported to represent *other* employees (i.e., employees who were not part of the team). Hence, if all of a company's employees were organized into teams, or if there were one team with the members rotating on a regular basis, it is likely that the team would not constitute a labor organization under the Act, because it would not represent *other* employees. For example, in *General Foods* [10], the employer implemented a "job enrichment" program. All of the employees were divided into four teams, and each team: divided assignments, established rotations and scheduled overtime (among other things). Each team also periodically conferred with management on a variety of topics related to working conditions. The Board held that these teams were "nothing more nor less than work crews established by [the employer] as administrative subdivisions of the entire employee compliment." [10, p. 1234] The teams functioned as a "committee of the whole" rather than a "labor organization." The Board held that these teams were not §2(5) labor organizations. "If such a set of circumstances should give rise to the existence of a labor organization, no employer could ever have a staff conference without bringing forth a labor organization in its midst." [10, p. 1235]

Purpose of the Organization

The next question concerns whether the organization exists, at least in part, for the purpose of dealing with employers. The Supreme Court has defined the term "dealing with" in §2(5) quite broadly in *NLRB v. Cabot Carbon Co.* [17]. Anytime a group of employees discusses things with the employer, the "dealing with" re-

TABLE 1: Summary of Legal Team Actions

1. Overall Purpose
   If the purpose of using teams is to solve problems, then it is legal.
   If the purpose is to dissuade formation of a union, then it is illegal.
   If the purpose is to encourage the decertification of a union, then it is illegal.
2. Membership
   If team members are all supervisors or managers, then it is legal.
   If team members are all non-supervisors, then it is legal, subject to all points below.
   If the team is mixed then see point 5.
3. Labor Organization
   If the team is empowered to take actions rather than ask permission, then it is not a labor organization.
   If the team does not represent other employees, then it is not a labor organization.
   If the team deals with matters other than working conditions (i.e., wages, grievances, hours of employment etc.), then it is not a labor organization.
4. Specific Production Planning Activities
   If the team is empowered to:
   • Schedule jobs to a specific piece of equipment,
   • Assign jobs to specific employees,
   • Select or change job priorities,
   • Schedule overtime of individuals or the team,
   • Add or delete workers to the team,
   • Improve the process by changing methods or equipment,
   • Refuse additional jobs in a given time period
5. Team Organization
   If management takes any of the following actions:
   • Calling or scheduling the team's meeting,
   • Conducting the meeting,
   • Selecting which employees attended the meeting,
   • Setting the agenda for the meeting, then it is illegal.

quirement is likely to be satisfied. Nevertheless, there is one important exception. If the team has the authority to resolve employment-related problems on its own (i.e., without input from the employer), the "dealing with" element is likely to be absent. The critical issue appears to be: "Is the team able to take action with information provided to management, or is the team required to ask permission to take the action?" If the former is true, the team is likely *not* to be a labor organization.

Concerns of the Organization

The final issue concerns the subject matter of the TQM program. If the team deals solely with matters other than "conditions of work or other statutory subjects such as grievances, labor disputes, wages, rates of pay, or hours of employment," it is not likely to be a labor organization. While the Board and courts have found a wide variety of subjects to be encompassed by the phrase just quoted, if the team deals with matters apart from those subjects, it would not be considered a labor organization. In this regard, the Supreme Court's decision in *First National Maintenance Corp. v. NLRB* [9] would be relevant. In *First National Maintenance*, a case involving whether the employer was required by the Act to bargain over certain subjects, the Supreme Court held that subjects which "have only an indirect and attenuated impact on the employment relationship" were not considered "conditions of employment." Examples given by the Court were advertising and promotion, product type and design. Although *First National Maintenance* did not deal with the issue of labor organization status under §2(5), it is nevertheless relevant. Presumably, since an employer is not required to bargain over certain issues such as: scheduling work across machines, scheduling overtime or rearranging the job priorities in order to minimize setups, a group of employees could discuss these issues with the employer and not be considered a labor organization under §2(5).

DID THE EMPLOYER DOMINATE, INTERFERE WITH OR SUPPORT THE TEAM

Assuming the team is held to be a labor organization, the next question is whether the employer's dealings with the team are prohibited by §8(a)(2). That section has been held to prohibit the interference with or domination of the formation of a TQM team. In this regard, the following types of activities have been held to violate the section: formulating the idea for the organization, creating it, forming its structure, selecting the members, and retaining veto power over its decisions. In addition, the section has been held to prohibit the interference with or domination of the administration of a TQM team. In this regard, the following types of activities on the part of management have been held to violate the section:

- Calling or scheduling the team's meeting
- Conducting the meeting
- Selecting which employees attended the meeting
- Setting the agenda for the meeting.

According to the NLRB's most recent interpretation, "a labor organization that is the creation of management whose structure and function are essentially determined by management . . . and whose continued existence depends on the fiat of management" is unlawfully dominated [7]. In other words, the NLRB and many courts have treated §8(a)(2) as a blanket prohibition on any and all employer involvement with a group that is considered a labor organization under §2(5). In addition, it is clear that anti-union actions or a specific motive to interfere with employees' rights to organize is not necessary for a finding of unlawful domination [19]. Although several circuit courts have been less restrictive, allowing employers to establish labor organizations as long as no anti-union bias was involved, there is a potential that any employer "involvement" with an employee team that is a labor organization would be prohibited by §8(a)(2) even if there is no anti-union animus.

OBSERVATIONS AND CONCLUSIONS

Managers involved in production planning and control should be aware of the legal limitations on using quality circles or any other type of employee-driven work team presented by the various laws and cases. Some general guidelines now can be established (see Table 1).

First, the intent of the organization forming employee-driven teams is important. If the teams are formed to improve productivity or better use employee ideas, then they are likely to be legal. If, however, the teams are formed to dissuade the formation of a union or to encourage employees to decertify an existing union, the team will be illegal. Secondly, teams must not be dominated by the employer as defined in the previous section: no scheduling for the team's meetings, no establishing their agenda, no selecting specific employees to attend the meetings. It is not clear whether or not a supervisor can be part of a team if the supervisor's normal duties are management of the work group. The best approach is that, if a supervisor is on the team, he (she) should not be the team leader. Empowerment means empowerment; the team has the responsibility to make the changes by taking its own action rather than asking permission of management. The team may keep management informed of its actions, but management must not hold veto power over those actions. Finally, limit the scope of the team's responsibility to accepting the current working conditions, such as pay levels and hours of work at its inception. The conditions of work are for union negotiation, if a union exists.

Managers must also be aware that labor law is constantly evolving. While the concept of legal precedent is firmly part of our tradition, it does not guarantee that a court or the Board will interpret or apply the law to a changing business environment the same way every time, or that each situation will come out the same way. One key point is that managers must be able to prove their intent before the appropriate judicial bodies.

REFERENCES

1. *APICS Dictionary.* 8th ed. Edited by J. F. Cox III, J. H. Blackstone, and M. S. Spencer. Falls Church, VA: American Production and Inventory Control Society, 1995.

2. Baker, B. R. "The Empowered Employee in a Biotechnology Company: A Case Study." *Production and Inventory Management Journal* 34. no.1 (1993): 73–76.

3. Benson, J., S. Bruil, D. Coghill, R. H. Cleator, T. Keller, and D. Wolf. "Self-Directed Work Teams." *Production and Inventory Management Journal* 35, no. 1,(1994): 79–82.

4. Datz, H. J. "Employee Participation Programs and the NLRA—A Guide for the Perplexed." Daily Labor Report (BNA) No. 30 at E1 (Feb. 7, 1993).

5. Denton, D. K. "Creating High Performance Work Practices." *Production and Inventory Management Journal* 37, no. 3 (1996): 81–84.

6. Dumond, E. J. "Learning From the Quality Improvement Process: Experience From U.S. Manufacturing Firms." *Production and Inventory Management Journal* 36, no. 4 (1995): 7–13.

7. *Electromation, Inc.*, 309 N.L.R.B. 990 (1992).

8. Evans, J. R. "Quality Improvement and Creative Problem Solving." *Production and Inventory Management Journal* 31, no. 4 (1990): 29–32.

9. *First National Maintenance Corp. v. NLRB*, 452 U.S. 666 (1981).

10. *General Foods*, 231 N.L.R.B. 1232 (1977).

11. Gould, W. B. "Employee Participation and Labor Policy: Why the Team Act should be Defeated and the National Labor Relations Act Amended." *Creighton Law Review* 30 (1996): 3.

12. Hue, F. "Labor Issues in the Implementation of Group Technology Cellular Manufacturing." *Production and Inventory Management Journal* 33, no. 4 (1992): 15–19.

13. McLain, J. R. "Participative Management Under Sections 2(5) and 8(a)(2) of the National Labor Relations Act." *Michigan Law Review* 83 (1985): 1736.

14. Moberly, R. B. "The Worker Participation Conundrum: Does Prohibiting Employer-Assisted Labor Organizations Prevent Labor Management Cooperation?" *Washington University Law Review* 69 (1994): 331.

15. Moe, M. T. "Participatory Workplace Decisionmaking and the NLRA: Section 8(a)(2), Electromation and the Spector of the Company Union." *New York University Law Review* 68 (November 1993): 1127.

16. *NLRB v. Bell Aerospace Co.*, 416 U.S. 267 (1974).

17. *NLRB v. Cabot Carbon Co.*, 360 U.S. 203 (1959).

18. *NLRB v. Health Care Retirement Corp.*, 114 S. Ct. 1778 (1994).

19. *NLRB v. Newport News Shipbuilding Co.* 308 U.S. 241 (1939).

20. Price, K. "Tearing Down the Walls: The Need for Revision of NLRA §8(a)(2) to Permit Management–Labor Participation Committees to Function in the Workplace." *University of Cincinnati Law Review* 63 (Spring 1995): 1379.

21. Saraph, J. V., and R. J. Sebastain. "Human Resource Strategies for Effective Introduction of Advanced Manufacturing Technologies (AMT)." *Production and Inventory Management Journal* 33, no. 1 (1992): 64–69.

22. Sevier, A. J. "Managing Employee Resistance to JIT: Creating an Atmosphere that Facilitates Implementation." *Production and Inventory Management Journal* 33, no. 1(1992): 83–87.

23. Smith, P. A., W. D. Anderson, and S. A. Brooking. "Employee Empowerment: A Case Study." *Production and Inventory Management Journal* 34, no. 3 (1993): 45–49.

24. Stokes, M. L. "Quality Circles or Company Unions? A Look at Employee Involvement After Electromation and DuPont." *Ohio State Law Journal* 55 (Fall 1994): 897.

25. Summers, C. W. "Employee Voice and Employer Voice: A Structured Exception to Section 8(a)(2)." *Chicago Kent Law Review* 69 (1993): 129.

26. Tatikonda, L. U., and R. J. Tatikonda. "Top Ten Reasons Your TQM Effort is Failing to Improve Profit." *Production and Inventory Management Journal* 36, no. 3 (1995): 5–9.

About the Authors—

STEVEN F. ABRAHAM, PhD, JD, is an assistant professor in the Department of Management, School of Business, State University of New York—Oswego. He holds a PhD in industrial relations from the University of Wisconsin-Madison, a JD from New York University School of Law, and a BS from Cornell University. He is a member of the New York State Bar as well as the bars of the eastern and southern districts of New York. Dr. Abraham has practiced labor/employment law in New York City in two law firms and one corporation. He has also provided advice to law firms on several occasions in areas of labor/employment law.

MICHAEL S. SPENCER, PhD, CFPIM, is an assistant professor of management at the University of Northern Iowa. He received his PhD in operations management from the University of Georgia. Dr. Spencer previously held various materials management positions at the John Deere Engine Division where he implemented both MRP and JIT systems. Dr. Spencer has served on the APICS board of directors, and is currently the vice-president of the APICS Educational and Research Foundation.

Unit 4

Unit Selections

19. **Managing the New Product Development Process: Strategic Imperatives,** Melissa A. Schilling and Charles W. L. Hill
20. **BMW Drives New Web Strategy,** Dan Carmel
21. **Bringing Discipline to Project Management,** Jeffrey Elton and Justin Roe
22. **New Era About to Dawn for International Space Station,** Peter Pae
23. **Seven Keys to Better Forecasting,** Mark A. Moon, John T. Mentzer, Carlo D. Smith, and Michael S. Garver
24. **Vitamin Efficiency,** Amy Doan

Key Points to Consider

❖ Why is forecasting so central to operations/production management?

❖ Given the various techniques available for sales forecasting, how should a manager go about selecting the technique to use?

❖ Why do so many projects go over budget, end up delivered late, and/or face difficulty with quality and meeting specifications?

 **Links** | **www.dushkin.com/online/**

25. **New Product Development: Practice and Research**
http://www.eas.asu.edu/~kdooley/nsfnpd/practices.html
26. **Project Management Institute (PMI)**
http://www.pmi.org
27. **STORES June 1998: Editor's Choice**
http://www.stores.org/eng/archives/jun98edch.html

These sites are annotated on pages 4 and 5.

When examining the critical decisions and stages of operations/production management, the two initial areas of concern are forecasting and product design. A firm needs to have an accurate forecast of demand that will have an impact on capacity design, production scheduling, staffing, inventory, material requirements planning, and transportation. Even for service firms, an accurate forecast of demand is necessary to determine adequate staffing levels and requirements of supplies.

Various qualitative and quantitative techniques exist for sales forecasting. The major qualitative techniques rely upon opinions and include the sales force composite, jury of executive opinion, and buyer/user expectations. The sales force composite consists of pooling the next period sales forecast opinions of the sales representatives. The jury of executive opinion pools the opinions of managers instead of sales representatives. With both of these approaches there are potential biases to under-estimate (to have a lower quota/target, to look better when exceeding the low target) or to overestimate (to secure more resources, to secure a larger budget, or to ensure enough inventory on hand to avoid a customer cancellation of a sale due to stock-out). With the buyer/user expectations, care needs to be taken in unbiased sampling, getting credible responses from consumers, and recognizing that the buyer's stated intentions to buy do not always translate into actual sales in the marketplace.

There are also several quantitative techniques, such as the naive method, simple moving average, weighted moving average, exponential smoothing, simple regressions, and multiple regressions. These quantitative techniques rely upon extrapolation and analysis of historical data. The naive method assumes that sales for the next period will equal sales for the last known period. Simple and weighted moving averages involve an averaging of the last periods to forecast the next period's sales. Exponential smoothing, which is similar to a moving average, utilizes a formula involving an alpha factor (the weight placed upon the last period's sales) and smooths out prior period sales data. Regressions are causal models that assume that the dependent variable (sales) is a function of one or more of the independent variables (time, advertising, company price, interest rates, etc.).

Managers can determine which sales forecasting technique is best for use by their firms by considering factors such as data required, costs involved with the forecast, accuracy required, whether the forecast time horizon is long-term or short-term, and an examination of errors. Software packages for sales forecasting are widely available to assist firms with their sales computations.

Once a sales forecast has been developed, it is important to design the product. Although the marketing department is responsible for marketing research and initial product development, the operations/production area should be involved with technical support. With the use of techniques such as project management, new product launches can be kept on schedule and within budget. Project management techniques such as PERT (Program Evaluation and Review Technique) and CPM (Critical Path Method) can aid managers in developing a product more quickly and successfully.

The articles in this unit review forecasting approaches and provide illustrations from firms. A few articles on product development/project management are presented. In their article, Mark Moon et al. review seven key focus points that help a company to improve its forecasting performance.

Forecasting and Product Design

Managing the new product development process: Strategic imperatives

Melissa A. Schilling and Charles W. L. Hill

Executive Overview

For many industries, new product development is now the single most important factor driving firm success or failure. The emphasis on new products has spurred researchers from strategic management, engineering, marketing, and other disciplines to study the new product development process. Most conclude that in order to be successful at new product development, a firm must simultaneously meet two critical objectives: maximizing the fit with customer needs, and minimizing time to market. While these objectives often pose conflicting demands on the firm, there is a growing body of evidence that the firm may employ strategies to successfully meet these objectives. Successful firms are those that articulate their strategic intent and map their R&D portfolio to find a fit between their new product development goals and their current resources and competencies. Their success also rests on how well the technology areas they enter contribute to the long term direction of the firm by helping them build new core capabilities critical to the firm's long term goals. Strategic alliances to obtain enabling technologies may shorten the development process, but partners must be chosen and monitored carefully. When firms are choosing technologies to acquire externally, they must assess the importance of the learning that would be accrued through internal development of the project, and its impact on the firm's future success. Other imperatives include using a parallel (rather than sequential) development process to both reduce cycle time and to better incorporate customer and supplier requirements in the product and process design, and using executive champions to ensure that projects gain the resources and organizational commitment necessary to their completion. Development teams should include people from a diverse range of functions and should include suppliers and customers to improve the project's chances of maximizing the fit with customer requirements while reducing cycle time and potentially reducing costs. Tools such as Stage-Gate processes, Quality Function Deployment, Design for Manufacturing, and Computer Aided Design/Computer Aided Manufacturing may be useful on different projects.

The importance of new product development (NPD) has grown dramatically over the last few decades, and is now the dominant driver of competition in many industries. In industries such as automobiles, biotechnology, consumer and industrial electronics, computer software, and pharmaceuticals, companies often depend on products introduced within the last five years for more than 50 percent of their annual sales. However, new product failure rates are still very high. Many R&D projects never result in a commercial product, and between 33 percent and 60 percent of all new products that reach the market place fail to generate an economic return.[1]

These trends have prompted a great deal of research on how to optimize the new product development process. This research is both large and diverse, originating in disciplines as wide ranging as strategic management, engineering, and marketing. The purpose of this paper is to review the previous research on managing the NPD process, and make sense of it through a cohesive organizing framework. Through this synthesis, a number of strategic imperatives emerge for improving the management of new product development. Our focus is on how the firm may increase the likelihood of new product success, emphasizing the management of projects once the ideas have been proposed.

The strategic imperatives in this paper represent a synthesis of the best industrial practices in this area, and are the result of a high degree of consensus among various research efforts. Our objective is to provide a working guide for managers to identify opportunities for improving their NPD processes and a perceptual map for scholars to identify fruitful areas for research.

The Competitive Environment and Critical Objectives of New Product Development

The dramatic increase in emphasis on new product development as a competitive dimension can be traced back to the globalization of markets, and the fragmentation of markets into ever smaller niches.

The dramatic increase in emphasis on new product development as a competitive dimension can be traced back to the globalization of markets, and the fragmentation of markets into ever smaller niches.

The globalization of markets is a natural result of the steady decline in barriers to the free flow of goods, services, and capital that has occurred since the end of World War II. The result has been a substantial increase in foreign competition. The more competitive a market becomes, the more difficult it is for companies to differentiate their product offerings on the basis of cost and quality. As a result, new product development has become central to achieving meaningful differentiation. Product life cycles have been shortening as the innovations of others[2] make existing products obsolete. Schumpeter's "gale of creative destruction," blowing at full force, fosters shorter product life cycles and rapid product obsolescence.

While product life cycles have compressed, markets have also fragmented into smaller niches. Lean manufacturing technologies, developed in Japan, have enabled this fragmentation. By reducing set-up times for complex equipment, lean manufacturing makes shorter production runs economical and reduces the importance of production economies of scale.[3] As a result, it is now economical for manufacturing enterprises to customize their product offerings to the demands of fairly narrowly defined customer groups, thereby out-focusing their competitors. A prime example is Nike, which produces over 250 variants of its popular athletic shoes in twenty different sports categories, a portfolio of products that appeals to every conceivable market niche.[4] As a result, not only are product life cycles compressed, but the size of the potential market for each variant of a product declines because of the rise of niche marketing.

In order to recoup development costs and make an economic return in an environment characterized by rapid product obsolescence and market fragmentation, a company's new product development must meet two critical objectives: (1) minimize time-to-market, and (2) maximize the fit between customer requirements and product characteristics.

Minimize Time to Market

Minimizing time to market—or cycle time—is necessary for a number of reasons.[5] A company that is slow to market with a particular generation of technology is unlikely to fully amortize the costs of development before that generation becomes obsolete. This phenomenon is particularly vivid in dynamic industries such as electronics, where life cycles of personal computers and semiconductors can be twelve months. Indeed, companies that are slow to market may find that by the time they have introduced their products, market demand has already shifted to the next generation of products.

Companies with compressed cycle times are more likely to be the first to introduce products that embody new technologies. As such, they are better positioned to capture first mover advantages. The first mover in an industry can build brand loyalty,[6] reap experience curve economies ahead of potential competitors, preempt scarce assets, and create switching costs that tie consumers to the company.[7] Once achieved, first mover advantages can be the basis of a more sustained competitive advantage.

In many industries, issues of dominant design are paramount.[8] When a new technology is first introduced, competing variants of that technology are often based on different standards. Different companies will promote different technological standards, and the company that establishes its particular design as the dominant standard can reap enormous financial rewards, while those that fail may be locked out.[9] Some examples of this include Microsoft's Windows (which locked out Geowork's Ensemble 1.0, among others) and Intel's CPU platform. Companies with reduced cycle time have a greater probability of establishing their design as the dominant standard.[10]

Companies with short cycle times can continually upgrade their products, incorporating state of the art technology when it becomes available. This enables them to better serve consumer needs, outrun their slower competitors and, build brand loyalty. It also enables them to offer a wider range of new products to better serve niches.

Some researchers have pointed out problems with rushing new products to market. For example, Dhebar points out that rapid product introductions may cause adverse consumer reactions; consumers may regret past purchases and be wary of new purchases for fear of obsolescence.[11] Other researchers have suggested that speed of development may come at the expense of quality.[12] However, numerous studies have found a strong positive relationship between speed and the commercial success of new products.[13] The objective, then, is to minimize time to market by making the NPD process more efficient, without sacrificing product or service quality.

Maximize Fit with Customer Requirements

For a new product to achieve significant and rapid market penetration, it must match such customer requirements as new features, superior quality, and attractive pricing. Despite the obvious importance of this imperative, numerous studies have documented the lack of fit between new product attributes and customer requirements as a major cause of new product failure.[14] Illustrative anecdotes abound—for example, the failure of Lotus to establish Lotus 1-2-3 for Windows as the major spreadsheet for Windows, and the commensurate rise of Microsoft's Excel spreadsheet for Windows, can be attributed to the failure of Lotus 1-2-3 for Windows to satisfy customer requirements with regard to features (e.g., program speed) and quality. Similarly, Philips' CD-Interactive home entertainment system failed because of a lack of understanding of its customers' needs. The product was overly complex and expensive, and required almost an hour of training, and could not compete against the more straightforward game systems produced by Nintendo, Sega, and Sony.

Optimizing the New Product Development Process

Successful NPD requires attention to four strategic issues (see Figure 1). Strategic Issue 1 is the technology strategy, or the process by which the company constructs its new product development portfolio. Strategic Issue 2 is the organizational context within which a NPD project is embedded. Strategic Issue 3 involves the construction and use of teams, and Strategic Issue 4 addresses the use of tools for improving the NPD process.

Technology Strategy

A crucial step in optimizing the NPD process is to ensure that the company has a clear and consistent technology strategy. The purpose of technology strategy is to identify, develop, and nurture those technologies that will be crucial for the long run competitive position of the company. These technologies must have the potential to create value for customers. A coherent technological strategy, therefore, focuses explicitly on customer requirements as they are now, and as they are likely to become in the future.

Many companies lack a well-articulated technology strategy. A northwestern company that recently imple-

> *A crucial step in optimizing the NPD process is to ensure that the company has a clear and consistent technology strategy.*

mented a project tracking system found to its dismay that there were many more projects underway than the company could support. As one engineer put it, "We never saw a problem we didn't like." Because the company was attempting to support too many projects, employees were assigned to many project teams and had little commitment to any particular project. Furthermore, because development resources were stretched too thin, projects were delayed and several had been abandoned. One major project that was expected to take nine months in development had stretched to three and half years, and by the time the product was released, it was no longer clear that a market existed.

A company can focus its development efforts on projects that will create long-term advantage by defining its strategic intent.

Strategic Imperative 1: Articulate the company's strategic intent

An ambitious strategic intent should create a gap between a company's existing resources and capabilities and those required to achieve its intent.[15] At the same time, the company's strategic intent should build on existing core competencies. Once the strategic intent has been articulated, the company is able to identify the resources and capabilities required to close the gap between intent and reality. This includes identification of any technological gap and enables the company to focus its development efforts and choose the investments necessary to develop strategic technologies and incorporate them into the company's new products.[16]

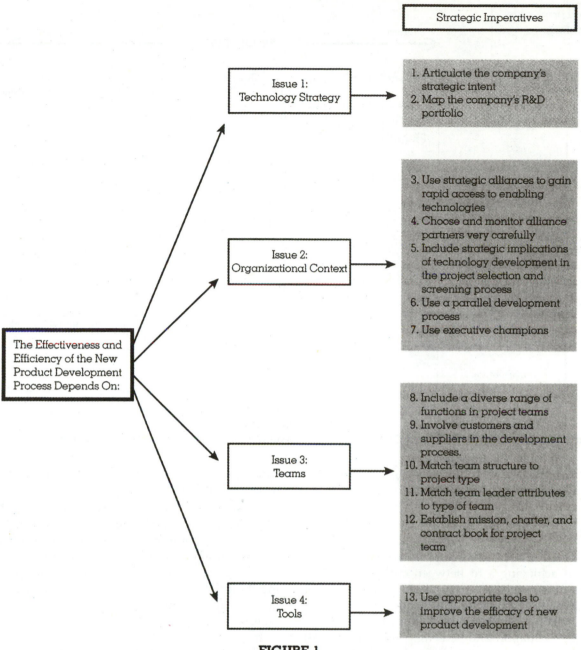

FIGURE 1
A Model of the New Product Development Process

Strategic Imperative 2: Map the company's R&D portfolio
New product development must be managed as a balanced portfolio of projects at different stages in development.[17] Companies may use a project map (similar to that depicted in Figure 2) to aid this process. Four types of development projects commonly appear on this map—pure R&D, breakthrough, platform, and derivative projects. Over time, a particular technology may migrate through these different types of projects. R&D projects are the precursor to commercial development projects and are necessary to develop cutting edge strategic technologies. Breakthrough projects involve development of products that incorporate revolutionary new product and process technologies. Platform projects typically offer fundamental improvements in the cost, quality, and performance of a technology over preceding generations. Derivative projects involve incremental changes in products and/or processes. A platform project is designed to serve a core group of consumers, whereas derivative projects represent modifications of the basic platform design to appeal to different niches within that core group.[18] Companies need to identify their desired mix of projects on a project map and then allocate resources accordingly. It is important that the mix of projects represented on such a map be consistent both with the company's resources, and with its expression of strategic intent.

Along with a coherent technology strategy, a company must establish an organizational environment that en-

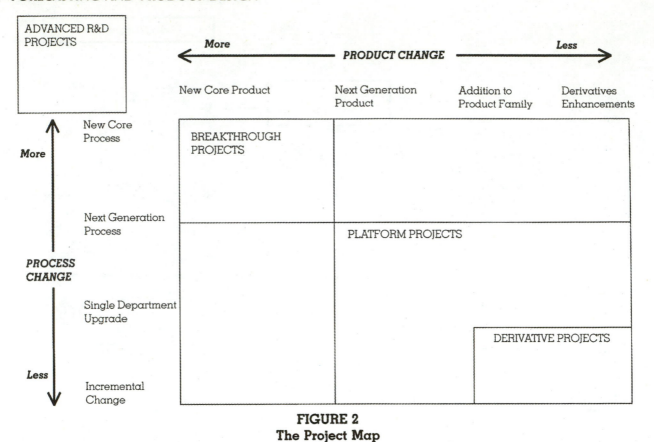

FIGURE 2
The Project Map
(adapted from Wheelwright, S. C. and Clark, K. B. 1992. *Revolutionizing Product Development*. New York: Free Press)

ables it to optimize its likelihood of new product development success.

Organizational Context

Organizational context factors important in reducing cycle time and achieving a fit between customer requirements and new product attributes are: (1) the use of strategic alliances, (2) the determination of how alliance partners are chosen and monitored, (3) the use of appropriate project valuation and screening mechanisms, (4) the development process scheme used by the firm (sequential process versus partly parallel process), and (5) the involvement of executive champions.

Strategic Imperative 3: Use strategic alliances to gain rapid access to enabling technologies

Developing new products often requires the joining together of complementary assets. Consider a company that has developed a body of technological knowledge with commercial possibilities, such as the pen-based computer company, GO Corp. To transform this knowledge into a viable product, the company had to assemble a set of assets that included complementary technological knowledge, market knowledge, manufacturing knowledge, and financial ability.[19] GO Corporation's product, a pen-based personal digital assistant (a palm-sized computer) lacked value without complementary

software, a powerful CPU, lightweight and long-lasting batteries, and adequate marketing and distribution channels. While the company was successful in developing its core product, the product did not integrate seamlessly with desktop environments because the software was not compatible. The product was also too heavy, slow, and too expensive. The company spent several years improving the product and trying to figure out the appropriate target markets, but eventually ran out of capital and failed.

It is not unusual for a company to lack some of the complementary assets required to transform a body of technological knowledge into a commercial product. The company can develop such assets internally, at the expense of cycle time. Alternatively, the company might gain rapid access to important complementary assets by entering into strategic alliances.[20] Consider Microsoft's strategic alliance with America Online (AOL). By the time Microsoft realized the importance of offering internet utilities such as a web server and a web browser, it had lost considerable ground to Netscape Communications Corp. Netscape's web browser, Netscape Navigator, beat Microsoft's Internet Explorer to market by almost a year. To rapidly deploy Internet Explorer and increase its exposure, Microsoft set up an exclusive contract with AOL, the largest online service provider in the US.[21] In this case, the asset gained was a distribution channel that encouraged rapid adoption of Microsoft's web browser. If Microsoft had taken the time to build a better online service itself, it might have never been able to catch up with the market lead attained by Netscape's Navigator.

Strategic Imperative 4: Choose and monitor alliance partners very carefully

Not all alliances for complementary technologies are beneficial.[22] It may be difficult to determine if the complementary assets provided by the alliance partner are a good fit, particularly when the asset gained through an alliance is something as difficult to assess as experience or knowledge. It is also possible that an alliance partner will exploit an alliance, expropriating knowledge while giving little in return. Furthermore, since managers can monitor and effectively manage only a limited number of alliances, the firm's effectiveness will decline with the number of alliances to which it is committed. This raises not only the possibility of diminishing returns to the number of alliances, but also negative returns as the number of alliances grows. These risks can be minimized if the company undertakes a detailed search of potential partners before entering an alliance, establishes appropriate monitoring and enforcement mechanisms to limit opportunism,[23] and limits the number of strategic alliances in which it engages.

Strategic Imperative 5: Include strategic implications of technology development in the project selection and screening process

Methods used to evaluate and choose investment projects range from informal to highly structured, and from entirely qualitative to strictly quantitative. Quantitative methods such as net present value (NPV) techniques provide concrete financial estimates that facilitate strategic planning and trade-off decisions. However, NPV may fail to capture the strategic importance of the investment decision. Failure to invest in a project that has a negative NPV may prevent a company from taking advantage of profitable future projects that build on the first development effort. For instance, NPV analysis may value platform projects or derivative projects much higher than advanced R&D or breakthrough projects (see Figure 2) because the former are more likely to result in immediate revenues from product sales. However, a firm that forgoes basic research or development of breakthrough projects may quickly find itself behind the technology frontier, unable to respond to technological change.

Some research has suggested that these problems might be addressed by treating new product development decisions as real options.[24] A venture capitalist who makes an initial investment in basic R&D or in breakthrough technologies is buying a real call option to implement that technology later should it prove to be valuable.[25] However, implicit in the value of options is the assumption that one can acquire or retain the option for a small price, and then wait for a signal to determine

if the option should be exercised.[26] In the case of a firm undertaking solo new product development, it may not be possible to secure this option at a small price, and in fact, it may require full investment in the technology before a firm can determine if the technology will be successful. Furthermore, while stock option holders can wait and exercise their option once its value is clear, a firm considering new product development may not have this luxury. By the time it becomes clear that the technology will be profitable, the firm may be locked out of the market by a competitor's dominant standard.[27]

Research has indicated that the support of an executive champion can improve a project's chances for success in a number of ways.

Although the use of option theory does not provide a problem-free solution to the development investment decision, it does provide a useful perspective for evaluating a firm's strategic alternatives. A firm may have either a project strategy of seeking direct venture gains from the immediate project at hand, or an option strategy that emphasizes development of new technologies. While these strategies are not mutually exclusive, they represent different perspectives on the opportunities available to the firm: the former emphasizes the short run gains of the project under consideration and does not consider other strategic implications of the investment; the latter seeks to evaluate and incorporate the less tangible and longer-term returns of the development project.

Strategic Imperative 6: Use a parallel development process

Until recently, most US companies used a sequential process for new product development, whereby development proceeds sequentially from one functional group to the next (see Figure 3, panel A). Embedded in the process are a number of gates, where decisions are made as to whether to proceed to the next stage, send the project back for further work, or kill the project. Typically, R&D and marketing provide input into the opportunity identification and concept development stages, R&D takes the lead in product design, and manufacturing takes the lead in process design. According to critics, one problem with such a system emerges at the product design stage, when R&D engineers fail to communicate directly with manufacturing engineers. As a result, product design proceeds without manufacturing requirements in mind. A sequential process has no early warning system to indicate that planned features are not manufacturable. Consequently, cycle time can lengthen as the project

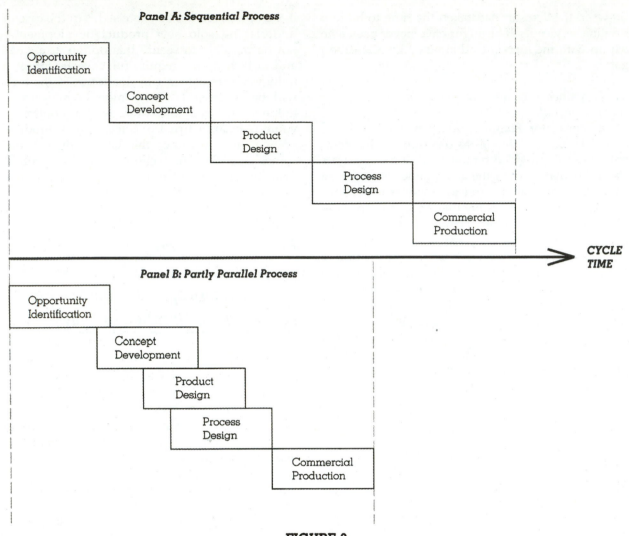

FIGURE 3
Sequential Versus Partly Parallel Process

iterates between the product design and process design stages.[28]

To rectify this problem, and compress cycle time, the firm should use a partly parallel process.[29] As shown in panel B of Figure 3, sequential execution of the NPD stages is replaced by partly parallel execution. Process design, for example, should start long before product design is finalized, thereby establishing closer coordination between these different stages and minimizing the chance that R&D will design products difficult or costly to manufacture. This should eliminate the need for lost time between the product and process design stages. The cycle time should be compressed.

Strategic Imperative 7: Use executive champions
An executive champion is a senior member of the company with the power and authority to support a project. Research has indicated that the support of an executive champion can improve a project's chances for success in a number of ways.[30] An executive champion can facilitate

the allocation of human and capital resources to the development effort. This ensures that cycle time is not limited by resource constraints. An executive champion can stimulate communication and cooperation between the different functional groups involved in the development process. Given that interfunctional communication and cooperation is necessary to both compress cycle time and achieve a good fit between product attributes and customer requirements, the use of executive sponsors should improve the effectiveness of the NPD process.

Teams

There has been a great deal of consensus that using crossfunctional project teams should increase the likelihood of project success. Research in this area has examined the advantages and difficulties of using crossfunctional teams, including suppliers and customers on the project team, types of team structures, team leadership, and the constitution and management of teams.

Table 1

Key Characteristics of Different Types of Teams

Characteristics	Functional Team	Lightweight Team	Heavyweight Team	Autonomous Team
Project Manager	No	Yes	Yes	Yes
Power of Project Manager		Low	High	Very High
Primary Orientation of Team Members	Function	Function	Team	Team
Location of Team Members	Functions	Functions	Co-Located with Project Manager	Co-Located with Project Manager
Evaluation of Team Members	Functional Heads	Functional Heads	Project Manager and Functional Heads	Project Manager
Incentives Skewed Towards	Functional Performance	Functional Performance	Team and Functional Performance	Team Performance
Potential for Conflict between Team and Functions	Low	Low	Moderate	High
Degree of Crossfunctional Integration	Low	Moderate	High	High
Degree of Fit with Existing Organizational Practices	High	High	High	Moderate-Low
Appropriate For:	Not Appropriate	Derivative Projects	Platform Projects/ Breakthrough Projects	Breakthrough Projects

Strategic Imperative 8: Include a diverse range of functions in project teams

A lack of communication between the marketing, R&D, and manufacturing functions of a company can be extremely detrimental to the NPD process. Crossfunctional miscommunication leads to a poor fit between product attributes and customer requirements. R&D cannot design products that fit customer requirements without input from marketing. By working closely with R&D, manufacturing can ensure that R&D designs products relatively easy to manufacture. Ease of manufacturing can lower both unit costs and product defects, which translates into a lower final price and higher quality. Similarly, as we noted earlier, a lack of crossfunctional communication can lead to longer cycle times.

The use of crossfunctional product development teams should minimize miscommunication.[31] For instance, in Chrysler's vehicle deployment platform teams, team members are drawn from design, engineering, purchasing, manufacturing, product-planning, finance, and marketing. Teams with diverse backgrounds have several advantages, over less diverse teams.[32] Their variety provides a broader knowledge base and increases the "crossfertilization of ideas."[33] The variety allows the project to draw on more information sources.[34] By combining members of different functional areas into one project team, a wide variety of information sources can be ensured.

Strategic Imperative 9: Involve customers and suppliers in the development process

Many products fail to produce an economic return because they fail to meet customer requirements. Financial considerations often take precedence over marketing criteria. This may lead to the development of incremental product updates that closely fit existing business activities (for example, the firm may overemphasize the derivative projects shown in Figure 2).[35] The screening decision should focus instead on the new product's advantage and superiority to the consumer, and the growth of its target market.[36]

One way of improving the fit between a new product and customer requirements is to include customers in the NPD process. This may be accomplished by including the customer in the actual development team, or by designing initial product versions and then encouraging user extensions.[37] By exchanging information effectively with customers, the company helps maximize the product's fit with customer needs.

The logic behind involving customers in the NPD process also applies to involving suppliers. By tapping into the knowledge base of its suppliers, a firm expands its information resources. Suppliers may be members of the product team or consulted as an alliance partner. In either case, suppliers contribute ideas for product improvement or increased development efficiency. For instance, a supplier may suggest an alternative input (or configuration of inputs) that would lower cost. Additionally, by coordinating with suppliers, managers can help ensure that inputs arrive on time and that necessary changes can be made quickly.[38] Consistent with this argument, research has shown that many firms using supplier interaction are able to produce new products in less time, at a lower cost, and with higher quality.[39] For example, during Boeing's development of the 777, United employees (including engineers, pilots and flight attendants) worked closely with Boeing's engineers to ensure that the airplane was designed for maximum functionality and comfort. Boeing also included General Electric and other parts suppliers on the project team, so that the

Table 2

Tools Appropriate for Different Types of Projects

Tools	Appropriate for:			
	Basic R&D	Breakthrough Research	Platform Projects	Derivative Projects
Stage-Gate Process	X	X	XXX	XX
QFD-House of Quality		X	XXX	XX
Design for Manufacturing			XXX	XXX
Computer Aided Design	XXX	XXX	XXX	XXX
Computer Aided Manufacturing			XXX	XXX

engines and the body of the airplane could be simultaneously designed for maximum compatibility.

Strategic Imperative 10: Match team structure to project type

There are a number of different ways to structure teams: functional, lightweight, heavyweight and autonomous.[40] In a functional team, members from different functional divisions of the firm meet periodically to discuss the project. The team members are located together, their rewards are not tied to the performance of the project, and the team may be temporary. Functional teams also lack a project manager and dedicated liaison personnel between the different functions. There is a general lack of coordination and communication between the different functions involved in the product development process. As a consequence, the dangers of long cycle time and a lack of fit between customer requirements and product attributes become particularly acute.

Lightweight teams have both project managers and dedicated liaison personnel who facilitate communication and coordination among functions. In lightweight teams, the key resources remain under the control of their respective functional managers. Lightweight team members often spend no more than 25 percent of their time on a single project. Because of these characteristics, lightweight teams, are often unable to overcome interfunctional coordination and communication problems. Consequently, lightweight teams may not improve the success of the product development process. While the lightweight team has deficiencies, it may be appropriate for derivative projects (see Figure 2), where high levels of coordination and communication are not required.

Heavyweight teams also have project managers and dedicated liaison personnel. A critical distinction, however, is the power and influence of the project manager. Heavyweight project managers are senior managers with substantial organizational influence. They have the power to reassign people and reallocate resources, and they tend to devote most of their time to the project. Often the core group of people in a heavyweight team is dedicated full time to the project and physically located along with the heavyweight project manager. Nev-

ertheless, within a heavyweight team the long-term career development of individual members continues to rest with their functional managers rather than the project manager. They are not assigned to the project team on a permanent basis and their functional heads still exert some control over them and participate in their performance evaluation. The heavyweight team is far more capable of breaking down interfunctional coordination and communication barriers, primarily because of the facilitating role of the project leader. Consequently, this type of team structure generally improves the performance of the NPD process, and would be appropriate for platform projects (see Figure 2).

The autonomous team also has a heavyweight team leader. The functional representatives are also formally removed from their functions, dedicated full time to the team, and located with other team members. A critical distinguishing feature of the autonomous team is that the project leader becomes the sole evaluator of the contributions made by individual team members. Also, autonomous teams are allowed to create their own policies and procedures, including their own reward systems, increasing the team members' commitment and involvement.[41] However, a problem with autonomous teams is that they can become too independent and get away from top management control. Moreover, once a project is complete it may prove difficult to fold the members of an autonomous team back into the organization since team members may have become accustomed to independence. Therefore, an autonomous team would be appropriate for breakthrough projects and some major platform projects. It is particularly appropriate when the existing routines and culture of the organization run counter to the objectives of the project, and the new project is likely to result in the development of a new business unit. Several of the business units of Quantum Corporation, a major disk drive manufacturer, were formed in this way. These business units are then integrated functionally in a matrix-like structure.

Table 1 summarizes a number of key dimensions across which the four teams vary. Note that the potential for conflict between the functions and the team, and particularly the project manager, rises as we move from

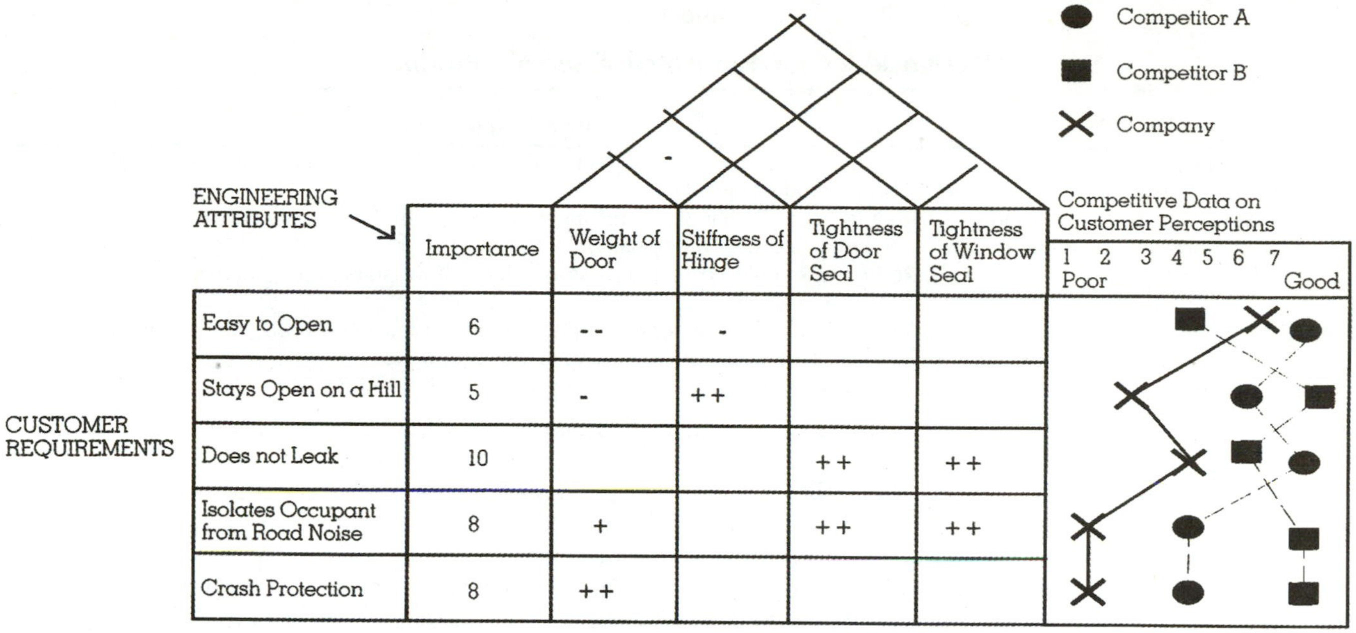

Competitor A
Competitor B
Company

ENGINEERING ATTRIBUTES

CUSTOMER REQUIREMENTS

Competitive Data on Customer Perceptions

Customer Requirements	Importance	Weight of Door	Stiffness of Hinge	Tightness of Door Seal	Tightness of Window Seal
Easy to Open	6	- -	-		
Stays Open on a Hill	5	-	+ +		
Does not Leak	10			+ +	+ +
Isolates Occupant from Road Noise	8	+		+ +	+ +
Crash Protection	8	+ +			

Competitive Data on Customer Perceptions: 1 2 3 4 5 6 7 — Poor ... Good

FIGURE 4
House of Quality

functional teams to autonomous teams. This occurs because the independence of heavyweight and autonomous teams may mean that they pursue goals counter to the interests of the functions. It is the task of senior managers to keep such conflict in check.

Strategic Imperative 11: Match team leader attributes to type of team

An important factor determining the effectiveness of project teams, particularly of heavyweight and autonomous teams, is the kind of leadership skills exerted by the project manager.[42] Project managers in heavyweight and autonomous teams must have high status within the organization, act as concept champions for the team within the organization, be good at conflict resolution, have multidiscipline skills (i.e., must be able to talk the language of marketing, engineering, and manufacturing), and be able to exert influence on the engineering, manufacturing, and marketing functions.[43] Other things being equal, teams whose project managers are deficient on one or more of these dimensions will have a lower probability of being successful.

Strategic Imperative 12: Establish mission, charter, and contract book for the project team

To ensure that the project team has a clear focus and commitment to the development project, the team should be involved in the development of its mission. The team's mission should be encapsulated in a clear and explicit project charter, whose purpose is to articulate the broad performance objectives of the team. Once the team charter is established, core team members and senior managers must negotiate a contract book that defines in detail the basic plan to achieve the goal laid out

in the project charter. Typically, the contract book will estimate the resources that will be required, the development time schedule, and the results that will be achieved. It is common practice following negotiation and acceptance of this contract for all parties to sign the contract book as an indication of their commitment to honor the plan and achieve the results. Establishing a mission, charter, and contract book for the team not only increases the team's awareness and commitment to the project's objectives, but provides a tool for monitoring and evaluating the team's performance in meeting its objectives.

Tools

Some of the most prominent of these are Stage-Gate processes, QFD—House of Quality, Design for Manufacturing, and Computer Aided Design/Computer Aided Manufacturing. Using the available tools for improving NPD processes can greatly expedite the NPD process and maximize the product's fit with customer requirements. Table 2 summarizes the usefulness of each tool to different types of projects.

Strategic Imperative 13: Use appropriate tools to improve the new product development process

Stage-Gate Processes. The Stage-Gate process is a method of managing the new product development process to increase the probability of launching new products quickly and successfully.[44] The process provides a blueprint to move projects through the different stages of development: 1) idea generation, 2) preliminary investment, 3) business case preparation, 4) product development, 5) product testing, and 6) product introduction.

Table 3

Design Rules for Fabricated Assembly Products

Design Rule	Impact Upon Performance
Minimize the number of parts	Simplify assembly; reduce direct labor; reduce material handling and inventory costs; boost product quality.
Minimize the number of part numbers (use common parts across product family)	Reduce material handling and inventory costs; improve economies of scale (increase volume through commonalty).
Eliminate adjustments	Reduce assembly errors (increase quality); allow automation; increase capacity and throughput.
Eliminate fasteners	Simplify assembly (increase quality); reduce direct labor costs; reduce squeaks and rattles; improves durability; allows for automation.
Eliminate jigs and fixtures	Reduce line changeover costs; lower required investment.

The process is used by such companies as IBM, Procter & Gamble, 3M, General Motors and Corning. In fact, Corning has made the process mandatory for all information system development projects, and Corning managers believe that the process enables them to better estimate the potential payback of any project under consideration. They also report that the Stage-Gate process has reduced development time, allows identification of projects which should be killed, and increases the ratio of internally developed products that result in commer-

The house of quality makes the relationship between product attributes and customer requirements clear, focuses on design tradeoffs, highlights the competitive shortcomings of the company's existing products, and helps identify what steps need to be taken to improve them.

cial projects.[45] The Stage-Gate process is primarily used for research projects that are aimed at developing a specific commercial product, and is more likely to be used for major platform projects than derivative projects. It could also be used, however, to assess the resources or advantages to be gained through development of a basic R&D or breakthrough research project.

QFD—The House of Quality. QFD (originally developed in Japan[46]) is a conceptual organizing framework for enhancing communication and coordination between engineering, marketing, and manufacturing personnel. It does this by taking managers through an instructional problem solving process in a very structured fashion. Advocates of QFD maintain that one of its most valuable characteristics is its positive effect on crossfunctional communication, and through that, on cycle time and the product/customer fit.[47]

The organizing framework for QFD is the concept known as the house of quality (see Figure 4), a matrix that maps customer requirements against product attributes. The starting point is to identify customer requirements. In the figure shown, market research has identified five attributes that customers want from a car door—that it be easy to open and close, that it stay open when the car is parked on a hill, that it does not leak in the rain, that it isolate the occupant from road noise, and that it afford some protection in side-on crashes.

The next step is to weight the requirements in terms of their relative importance from a customer's perspective. Once this has been done, the team needs to identify the engineering attributes that drive the performance of the product—in this case the car door. In the figure shown, four attributes are highlighted; the weight of the door, the stiffness of the door hinge (a stiff hinge helps the door stay open when parked on a hill), the tightness of the door seal, and the tightness of the window seal.

After identifying engineering attributes, the team fills in the body of the central matrix. Each cell in the matrix indicates the relationship between an engineering attribute and a customer requirement. This matrix should indicate both the direction and strength of the relationship. A fourth piece of information in the house of quality is contained in the roof of the house. The matrix here indicates the interaction between design parameters. Thus, the negative sign between door weight and hinge stiffness indicates that a heavy door reduces the stiffness of the hinge. The final piece of information in the house of quality is a summary of customer perceptions of the company's existing product compared with that of its competitors—in this case A and B.

The great strength of the house of quality is that it provides a common language and framework within which the members of a project team may fruitfully interact. The house of quality makes the relationship between product attributes and customer requirements clear, focuses on design tradeoffs, highlights the competitive shortcomings of the company's existing products, and helps identify what steps need to be taken to improve them.

Exploratory research has identified a number of project and implementation characteristics that distinguish successful attempts to apply QFD techniques from failed attempts.[48] QFD seems to work best for less complex product development projects, where QFD is seen as an investment that has the commitment of team members, where there is strong crossfunctional integration, where QFD is seen as a means of achieving an end, rather than a goal in its own right, and where the goals of the project stretch capabilities (note the fit with the concept of strategic intent discussed earlier). All of this would seem to suggest that QFD works best when used as a tool by a heavyweight project team pursuing a goal that is congruent with the strategic intent of the company, and when QFD is viewed for what it is—an aid to decision making rather than an end in itself.

Design For Manufacturing. To facilitate integration between engineering and manufacturing, and to bring issues of manufacturability into the design process as early as possible, many companies have implemented design for manufacturing methods (DFM). Like QFD, DFM represents nothing more than a way of structuring the NPD process. One way in which DFM finds expression is in the articulation of a number of design rules. A series of commonly used design rules are summarized in Table 3, along with their expected impact on performance.

As can be seen, the purpose of such design rules typically is to reduce costs and boost product quality by designing products that are easy to manufacture. This means reducing the number of parts in a product, eliminating any time-consuming adjustments that have to be made to the product during manufacturing, and eliminating as many fasteners as possible. The easier products are to manufacture, the fewer the assembly steps required, the higher labor productivity will be, and hence, the lower unit costs. Also, the easier products are to manufacture, the higher product quality tends to be.

The effect of adopting DFM rules can be dramatic. Taking manufacturing considerations into account at an early stage in the design process can compress cycle time. Also, because DFM tends to lower costs and increase product quality, DFM has a favorable impact on critical product attributes that customers normally require, such as high quality and an attractive price relative to the features of the product. When NCR used DFM techniques to redesign one of its electronic cash registers, it found it could reduce assembly time by 75 percent, reduce the parts required by 85 percent, utilize 65 percent fewer suppliers, and reduce direct labor time by 75 percent.[49]

Because DFM is oriented around improving the manufacturability of a product, it is more useful for platform and derivative projects than for basic R&D projects or breakthrough research.

Computer Aided Design/Computer Aided Manufacturing. Computer aided design (CAD) is another product development tool worthy of note. Rapid advances in computer technology have enabled the development of low priced and high powered graphics-based workstations. Using these workstations, it is now possible to achieve what at one time could only be done on a super-computer: construct a three-dimensional working image of a product or subassembly. The advantage of this technology is that prototypes can now be built and tested in virtual reality. The ability to quickly adjust prototype attributes by manipulating the 3-D model allows engineers to compare and contrast the characteristics of different variants of a product or subassembly. This can reduce cycle time and lower costs by reducing the need for physical model building. Visualization tools and 3-D software are used to allow nonengineering customers to see and make minor alterations to the design and materials. This has proven to be particularly valuable in architecture and construction.

By implementing machine-controlled processes as in computer aided manufacturing (CAM), manufacturing can operate faster, and accommodate more flexibility in the manufacturing process.[50] Computers can automate the change between different product variations, and allow for more variety and customization in the manufacturing process. Computer aided design is often used early in the development process, and may be implemented for basic R&D and breakthrough research projects, in addition to being used in the design of platform and derivative projects. Computer aided manufacturing is used in the later stages of those projects that become commercial projects, and therefore is more useful for improving platform and derivative projects.

Conclusion

Despite the rapidly increasing amount of attention that new product development has received over the last decade, the development project failure rate is still very high. Many companies develop interesting products—but only those firms that are effective in developing products that meet customer needs and efficient in allocating their development resources will succeed in the long run. Better new product development processes should translate into a higher completion rate of projects, more projects meeting their deadlines and budget requirements, and more new products meeting their sales objectives and earning a commercial return.

This article describes those strategies that have been shown to improve the process of new product development, and about which there is a great deal of consensus. This is not meant to imply that other, newly emerging processes will not also improve new product development processes. This is an area that is receiving a great deal of attention in both managerial and academic arenas. Just as innovation is rapidly producing new products from which we may choose, so too is the research into the NPD process producing new methods of configuring and managing development projects. Staying abreast of the work being done in this area is challenging. Being able to rapidly assimilate and implement strategies for maximizing the effectiveness of new product development may prove to be as important to a firm's competitiveness as the innovative products themselves.

Endnotes

[1] Booz, Allen, & Hamilton. 1982. *New products management for the 1980's.* Privately published research report. Mansfield, E. 1981. How economists see R&D, *Harvard Business Review,* November–December: 98–106. Page, A. L. 1991. PDMA's New product development practices survey: Performance and best practices, *PDMA 15th Annual International Conference,* Boston, MA, October 16.

[2] Qualls, W., 1981. Olshavsky, R. W., & Michaels, R. E. Shortening of the PLC—an empirical test, *Journal of Marketing,* 45: 76–80.

[3] Womack, J. P., Jones. D. T. & Boos, D. 1990. *The machine that changed the world.* New York: Rawson Associates.

[4] The automobile industry provides us with another example. In the mid 1960s the largest selling car in the US was the Chevrolet Impala. The platform on which it was based sold approximately 1.5 million units. In 1991 the largest selling car in the US was the Honda Accord, which sold about 400,000 units. Thus, in a market that is larger than it was in 1965, the volume per model has declined by a factor of four.

[5] Stalk, G. & Hout, T. M. 1990. *Competing against time.* New York: Free Press. Kessler, E. & Chakrabarti, A. 1996. Innovation Speed: A conceptual model of context, antecedents, and outcomes, *Academy of Management Review,* 21(4): 1143–1191.

[6] Note that brand loyalty may be important even in industries in which rapid technological change causes short product life cycles. In fact, when technological change is fast and the technology is complex, brand loyalty may reduce the uncertainty of customers who wish to stay on the technology frontier but who would be unable to adequately assess the quality of each successive technological generation.

[7] Lieberman, M. & Montgomery, D. 1988. First mover advantages: A survey, *Strategic Management Journal,* 9: 41–58.

[8] Abernathy, W. J. & Utterback, J. M. 1978. Patterns of industrial innovation, *Technology Review,* 80(7): 40–47.

[9] Schilling, M. A. 1998. Technological lock out: An integrative model of the economic and strategic factors driving success and failure. *Academy of Management Review,* 23; and, Arthur, W. B. 1994. *Increasing returns and path dependence in the economy.* Ann Arbor: The University of Michigan Press.

[10] Mahajan, V., Sharma, S. & Buzzell, R. 1993. Assessing the impact of competitive entry on market expansion and incumbent sales, *Journal of Marketing.* July: 39–52.

[11] Dhebar, A. 1996. Speeding high-tech producer, meet balking consumer, *Sloan Management Review.* Winter: 37–49.

[12] Crawford M. C. 1992. The hidden costs of accelerated product development, *Journal of Product Innovation Management,* September, 9(3): 188–200.

[13] Nijssen E. J., Arbouw, A. R. & Commandeur, H. R. 1995. Accelerating new product development: A preliminary empirical test of a hierarchy of implementation, *Journal of Product Innovation Management,* 12: 99–104, Schmenner, R. W. 1988. The merits of making things fast, *Sloan Management Review,* Fall: 11–17, Ali, A., Krapfel, B. & LaBahn, D. 1995. Product-innovativeness and entry strategy: Impact on cycle time and break-even time. *Journal of Product Innovation Management,* 12: 54–69; and, Bothwell, B. 1992. Successful industrial innovation: Critical factors for the 1990s, *R&D Management.* 22(3): 221–239.

[14] For example, Rothwell, R., Freeman, C., Horley, A., Jervis, P., Robertson, A. B. & Townsend, J. 1974. SAPPHO Updates—Project SAPPHO, PHASE II, *Research Policy.* 3: 258–291, Mansfield, E. 1981. How economists see R&D, *Harvard Business Review,* November–December: 98–106; and, Zirger, B. J. & Maidique, M. A. 1990. A model of

[15] Hamel, G. & Prahalad, C. K. 1991. Strategic Intent. *Harvard Business Review,* May–June: 63–76.

[16] Marino K. 1996. Developing consensus on firm competencies and capabilities, *Academy of Management Executive,* 10(3): 40–51.

[17] Wind, Y. & Mahajan, V. 1988. New product development process: A perspective for reexamination, *Journal of Product Innovation Management,* 5: 304–310.

[18] For an illustration, consider Intel's 486 microprocessor. This is a platform, but Intel also offers variations of the 486 platform along dimensions such as speed, cost, and performance, to appeal to different groups of consumers. These variations on the 486 theme (e.g. 486DX/30, 486SX/66) are derivative products.

[19] Teece, D. J. 1987. Profiting from technological innovation: Implications for integration, collaboration, licensing and public policy, *Research Policy,* 15: 285–305.

[20] Hamel, G., Doz, Y. L. & Prahalad, C. K. 1989. Collaborate with your competitors and win, *Harvard Business Review,* January–February: 133–139, Mitchell, W. & Singh, K. 1992. Incumbent's use of pre-entry alliances before expansion into new technical subfields of an industry, *Journal of Economic Behavior and Organization,* 18: 347-372, Shan, W. 1990. An empirical analysis of organizational strategies by entrepreneurial high-technology, *Strategic Management Journal,* 11: 129–39; and Pisano, G. P. 1990. The R&D boundaries of the firm: An empirical analysis, *Administrative Science Quarterly,* 35: 153–176.

[21] Rebello, K. 1996. Inside Microsoft, *Business Week,* July 15: 56–65.

[22] Hill, C. W. L. 1992. Strategies for exploiting technological innovations: When and when not to license, *Organization Science,* 3: 428–441, Shan, W. 1990. An empirical analysis of organizational strategies by entrepreneurial high-technology, *Strategic Management Journal,* 11: 129–39; and, Teece, D. J. 1987. Profiting from technological innovation: Implications for integration, collaboration, licensing and public policy, *Research Policy,* 15: 285–305.

[23] Williamson O. E. 1985. *The Economic Institutions of Capitalism,* New York: Free Press.

[24] Kogut B. 1991. Joint ventures and the option to expand and acquire, *Management Science,* 37(1): 19–33.

[25] Hurry D., Miller, A. T. & Bowman, E. H. 1992. Calls on high-technology: Japanese exploration of venture capital investments in the United States, *Strategic Management Journal,* Vol. 13: 85–101.

[26] Bowman, E. H. & Hurry, D. 1993. Strategy through the option lens: An integrated view of resource investments and the incremental-choice process, *Academy of Management Review,* Vol. 18: 760–782.

[27] Schilling, M. A. 1998. IBID.

[28] Griffin A. 1992. Evaluating QFD's use in US firms as a process for developing products, *Journal of Product Innovation Management,* 9:171–187; and, Kimzey, C. H. 1987. *Summary of the task force work shop on industrial based initiatives.* Washington DC: Office of the Assistant Secretary of Defense, Production and Logistics.

[29] De Meyer, A. & Van Hooland, B. 1990. The contribution of manufacturing to shortening design cycle times, *R&D Management,* 20(3): 229–239, Hayes, R., Wheelwright, S. G. & Clark, K. B. 1988. *Dynamic Manufacturing.* New York: The Free Press, Cooper, R. G. 1988. The new product process: A decision guide for managers, *Journal Marketing Management,* 3: 238–255; and, Takeuchi, H. & Nonaka, I. 1986. The new product development game, *Harvard Business Review,* 64: 137–146.

[30] Zirger, B. J. & Maidique, M. A. 1990. A model of new product development: An empirical test, *Management Science,* 36: 867–883, Rothwell, R., Freeman, C., Horley, A., Jervis, P., Robertson, A. B. & Townsend, J. 1974. SAPPHO Updates—Project SAPPHO, PHASE II, *Research Policy,* 3: 258–291, Rubenstein, A. H., Chakrabarti, A. K., O'Keffe, R. D., Souder, W. E. & Young, H. C. 1976. Factors influencing innovation success at the project level, *Research Management,* May: 15–20, Johne, F. A. & Snelson, P. A. 1989. Product development approaches in established firms, *Industrial Marketing Management.* 18: 113–124; and, Wind, Y. & Mahajan, V. 1988. New product development process: A perspective for reexamination, *Journal of Product Innovation Management,* 5: 304–310.

[31] Brown, S. & Eisenhardt, K. 1995. Product development: Past research, present findings, and future directions, *Academy of Management Review,* 20(2): 343–378.

[32] Rochford, L. & Rudelius, W. 1992. How involving more functional areas within a firm affects the new product process, *Journal of Product Innovation Management,* 9: 287–299.

new product development: An empirical test, *Management Science,* 36: 867–883.

[33] Kimberly, J. R. & Evanisko, M. 1981. Organizational Innovation: The influence of individual, organizational and contextual factors on hospital adoption of technological and administrative innovations, *Academy of Management Journal*, 24: 689–713, Damanpour, F. 1991. Organization innovation: A meta-analysis of effects of determinants and moderators, *Academy of Management Journal*, 34(3): 555–590; and, Aiken, M. & Hage, J. 1971. The organic organization and innovation. *Sociology*, 5: 63–82.

[34] Jervis, P. 1975. Innovation and technology transfer—the roles and characteristics of individuals, *IEEE Transaction on Engineering Management*, 22: 19–27; and, Miller, D. & Friesen, P. H. 1982. Innovation in conservative and entrepreneurial firms: Two models of strategic momentum, *Strategic Management Journal*, 3:1–25.

[35] Johne, F. A. & Snelson, P. A. 1988. Success factors in product innovation, *Journal of Product Innovation Management*, 5: 114–128; and, Gluck, F. W. & Foster, R. N. 1975. Managing technological change: A box of cigars for Brad, *Harvard Business Review*, 53: 139–150.

[36] Cooper, R. G. 1985. Selecting winning new product projects: Using the NewProd system, *Journal of Product Innovation Management*, 2: 34–44.

[37] Butler, J. E. 1988. Theories of technological innovation as useful tools for corporate strategy, *Strategic Management Journal*, 9: 15–29.

[38] Asmus, D. & Griffin, J. 1993. Harnessing the power of your suppliers, *McKinsey Quarterly*, Summer (3): 63–79; and Bonaccorsi, A. & Lipparini, A. 1994. *Journal of Product Innovation Management*, 11(2): 134–146.

[39] Birou, L. & Fawcett, S. 1994. Supplier involvement in new product development: A comparison of US and European practices, *Journal of Physical Distribution and Logistics Management*, 24(5): 4–15; and Ansari, A. & Modarress, B. 1994. Quality Function Deployment: The role of suppliers. *International Journal of Purchasing and Materials Management*, 30(4): 28-36.

[40] Wheelwright, S. C. & Clark, K. B. 1992. *Revolutionizing product development: Quantum leaps in speed, efficiency and quality*. New York: Free Press.

[41] Damanpour, F. 1991. Organization innovation: A metaanalysis of effects of determinants and moderators, *Academy of Management Journal*, 34(3): 555–590.

[42] Clark, K. B. & Wheelwright, S. C. 1993. *Managing new product and process development*. New York: Free Press, McDonough, E. F. & Barczak, G. 1991. Speeding up new product development: The effects of leadership style and source of technology, *Journal of Product Innovation Management* 8: 203–211; and, Barczak, G. & Wilemon, D. 1989. Leadership differences in new product development teams, *Journal of Production and Innovation Management*, 6: 259–267.

[43] Brown, S. & Eisenhardt, K. 1995. Product development: Past research, present findings, and future directions, *Academy of Management Review*, 20(2): 343–378.

[44] Cooper, R. & Kleinschmidt, E. J. 1991. New product processes at leading industrial firms, *Industrial-Marketing-Management*, May, 20(2): 137–148.

[45] LaPlante, A. & Alter, A. E. 1994. Corning, Inc: the stage-gate innovation process, *Computerworld*. 28(44): 81.

[46] The concept was pioneered in the early 1970s at Mitsubishi's Kobe shipyard. It was then picked up and refined by Toyota and its suppliers. Among other things, at Toyota the house of quality approach to new product development was credited with improving Toyota's rust prevention record from one of the worst in the world's automobile industry to one of the best.

[47] Clark, K. B. & Wheelwright, S. C. 1993. *Managing new product and process development*. New York: Free Press, Hauser, J. R. & Clausing, D. 1988. The house of quality, *Harvard Business Review*, May–June: 63–73, Griffin, A. 1992. Evaluating QFD's use in US firms as a process for developing products, *Journal of Product Innovation Management*, 9: 171–187; and, Griffin, A. & Hauser, J. R. 1992. Patterns of communication among marketing, engineering and manufacturing, *Management Science*, 38: 360–373.

[48] Griffin, A. 1992. Evaluating QFD's use in US firms as a process for developing products, *Journal of Product Innovation Management*, 9: 171–187.

[49] Clark, K. B. & Wheelwright, S. C. 1993. *Managing new product and process development*. New York: Free Press.

[50] Millson, M. R., Raj, S. P. & Wilemon, D. 1992. A survey of major approaches for accelerating new product development, *Journal of Product Innovation Management*, 9: 53–69.

About the Authors

Melissa A. Schilling is an assistant professor of management policy at the School of Management of Boston University. Professor Schilling received her PhD in strategic management from the University of Washington in 1997. She has published several articles in peer reviewed academic journals, including the *Academy of Management Review*, *Journal of Management History*, and *Public Productivity and Management Review*. Her current research interests include the strategic development and management of technology, stakeholder theory, and corporate governance.

Charles W. L. Hill is the Hughes M. Blake Endowed Professor of Strategic Management and International Business at the School of Business, University of Washington. Professor Hill received his PhD in industrial organization economics in 1983 from the University of Manchester's Institute of Science and Technology (UMIST) in Britain. He has published over 40 articles in peer reviewed academic journals, including the *Academy of Management Journal*, *Academy of Management Review*, *Academy of Management Executive*, *Strategic Management Journal*, and *Organization Science*. He has also published two best-selling college texts, one on strategic management and the other on international business.

BMW *Drives*
New Web Strategy

**By letting customers "build" their own cars online,
BMW learns what the market wants.**

by Dan Carmel

When your brand image is that of "The Ultimate Driving Machine," how do you create a related experience on the Web? BMW of North America needed to answer that question as an early participant in electronic commerce. Its Web site already had a car configurator, one that could enable prospects to see the exterior and interior color schemes available—but not nearly enough to show all the features that can be built into a BMW. So its marketing executives developed the BMW Virtual Center (www.bmwusa.com), an online showroom where customers may shop for and build their own BMW.

"In an industry as competitive as ours, BMW must be as performance-driven in its e-business efforts as it is on the assembly line," says Carol Burrows, the company's manager of e-business.

A key component of the Virtual Center is the "Build Your Own" section, where users may customize a BMW model to their exact specifications. "The design is simple; the user interface engaging; the performance fast and intuitive—reflective of BMW's own sense of design," says Jim McDowell, vice president of marketing. "We wanted to give the consumer the full range of options that they could have in terms of building their next BMW."

To help achieve these goals, BMW implemented the Internet Selling System from Selectica Inc., San Jose, Calif. Selectica teamed with BMW's advertising agency, Fallon, to design and deploy the Build Your Own section of the Virtual Center.

Customers who enter the Build Your Own section of the site are guided through the specification of colors, wheels, engines, option packages and individual add-ons. Every feature displayed—from color to options selected, to the manufacturer's suggested retail price and financing

payments—automatically update with each mouse click so that users know exactly how each selection has changed the appearance and price of their virtual BMW. Users may proceed through the process in any order and change features at any time.

To give them time to consider their choices, customers may save an unlimited number of virtual BMWs for up to 30 days. When users return to the Virtual Center and retrieve saved vehicles, they may pick up where they left off. Once they have settled on a specific model, consumers may print out a profile of their configured BMW, view financing information and even contact a nearby BMW center to schedule a test drive. At every step, the interface is designed to be intuitive, responsive and even fun—to mimic driving the real thing.

Visitors who built a virtual Z3 received e-mail introducing a new Z3.

Residing on four Hewlett-Packard servers running Windows NT, the Selectica ISS provides the core functionality of the Build Your Own experience. The ISS models BMW's products, pricing and selling processes, and saves them as well as pricing data and car configurations in a customized KnowledgeBase. BMW can also manage the NT servers and automatically update its KnowledgeBases.

Fast pace and constant change characterize BMW's business, and the launch of the Virtual Center and Build Your Own system was no exception, BMW executives say. The automaker put its popular 3-Series sedan online first, and used the lessons learned when expanding to its other

From *EC World*, October 2000, pp. 66-68. © 2000 by EC Media Group.

product lines. Using Selectica's ACE Studio modeling environment, BMW rolled out the 3 Series for the Virtual Center in 16 weeks. Subsequent product lines were rolled out even faster, the company says.

Leveraging Customer Data

Updating the Virtual Center for BMW's 2000 model year went off without a hitch, according to Burrows, who was the internal champion involved in the BMW Virtual Center site development. "Modifications to the product KnowledgeBase happened without server downtime," she says. "Our customers had timely access to 2000 model year pricing and product data."

The Build Your Own BMW feature is one of the Virtual Center's most heavily trafficked sections. But popularity has not affected the system's reliability, Burrows says. After almost two years of service and millions of visitors, the site has been dependable—even during the crunch of viewers driven there by BMW's Super Bowl TV spots, she adds.

The Virtual Center played a key role in BMW's record sales last year. While BMW sold almost 155,000 vehicles in 1999, customers and prospective customers "built" and saved 100,000 virtual vehicles. Burrows predicts that in 2000, prospects will build more BMWs in the Virtual Center than BMW builds in its factories. "The Virtual Center and Build Your Own feature are now a mainstream part of our business," she asserts. "One-hundred percent of the users we surveyed reported they would recommend it to others."

Car configurations saved on the Virtual Center have become a strategic tool for BMW's marketing staff, which is constantly looking for ways to offer cars that better match customer needs. By analyzing the configurations of virtual BMWs saved on its Web site, the automaker can discern the combinations of features, colors and options customers would most like to see. Armed with this data, BMW can then manufacture products with sets of features more closely matching user preferences.

The company is also using the data it captures to alert prospects of new product features and models. For example, all users who had once stored a virtual Z3 model later received a targeted e-mail message introducing a new Z3.

Since the launch of the Virtual Center, BMW has increased the duration of user sessions and strengthened its relationship with its target market. The average session time spent on the Virtual Center is now equal to the average time spent in the rest of the site.

Linking to Production

For all its success, BMW hasn't let up on the gas. The company is currently working with Selectica to expand the Virtual Center capabilities to include bike racks, spoilers, roof racks and other accessories.

Other potential add-ons to the Virtual Center include offering buyers the choice between European delivery or delivery to BMW's Performance Center located in Spartanburg, S.C., with enrollment in its high-performance driving school. BMW is also evaluating how the Internet Selling System might be deployed on the Owners' Circle area of BMW's site, in order to assist owners in evaluating financial and other considerations when they are ready to trade up from their existing BMWs.

McDowell says BMW is working toward the day when its production pipeline links directly to the Virtual Center. "This would offer the ultimate choice to visitors," he says. "Consider, for example, a customer who just ordered a blue 740iL sports package with heated seats. We can build that exact car for him in six weeks. But he could also consider a car on the next boat that is very close to that, except that it has one more feature that he didn't order, or a car that's exactly what the customer selected, except it's red, but it's at his BMW center today. This is the level of detail we want to be able to add to the Virtual Center."

E-mail comments to: **ecweditor@tfn.com**

Dan Carmel is vice president of marketing for Selectica Inc., San Jose, Calif.

BRINGING DISCIPLINE TO PROJECT MANAGEMENT

Eli Goldratt's first novel,
The Goal, *shook up the factory floor.*
Will Critical Chain *do the same for projects?*

BY JEFFREY ELTON AND JUSTIN ROE

Critical Chain
Eliyahu M. Goldratt
Great Barrington, Mass.
The North River Press, 1997

How many projects in your organization have come in on time and on budget? If you are like most senior managers, the answer is likely none. And that despite using a plethora of project-management software tools, management processes, data management systems, team-training programs, and assorted "best practices." Every manager has an excuse for why a given project comes out poorly, but attempts to plan ahead to allow for unexpected problems rarely succeed.

Are these difficulties inescapable? One business thinker who says no is Eli Goldratt, a pioneer, if not the originator, of the *theory of constraints.* As introduced in his widely read novel *The Goal,* this theory provided a persuasive solution for factories struggling with production delays and low revenues. In his third novel, *Critical Chain,* Goldratt applies the framework to managing the development of new products and other projects.

Project management is a mature area that has systemic problems similar to many found in manufacturing processes, and the theory of constraints works well when dealing with individual projects. The book falls short, however, in explaining how companies can best manage a portfolio of projects, so senior managers need to supplement it with other advice. Still, its focus on constraints may be useful for dealing with one of the most difficult and pressing of management challenges: developing highly innovative new products.

Focusing on the Constraints

The theory of constraints explains how to boost the performance of any process that involves a series of interdependent steps. Instead of breaking the process down and improving the efficiency of each step, the theory has managers focus on the bottlenecks, or constraints, that keep the process from increasing its output. Once managers identify the bottlenecks, they widen them by making them more efficient—which often means changing policies that may promote efficiency at other steps in the process but hamper effectiveness at the crucial bottlenecks. Next, they need to limit the volume of production coming from the nonbottleneck activities to the level the bottleneck can handle. Once the overall operation is as effective as it can be at a given capacity, managers can increase output by investing in extra capacity at the bottlenecks. These steps need to be repeated over time because constraints can emerge at other points in the process.

Of course, project management texts have long told managers to focus on constraints. For projects, the constraint is the *critical path,* the series of tasks that determines the minimum time needed for the project. No matter how quickly the other tasks are completed, the project cannot be finished any sooner unless the tasks on the critical path can be done faster. But Goldratt adds an important second constraint to this framework that managers often overlook: scarce resources needed by tasks not only on and off the critical path but by other projects. In the case of developing a new product, for example, a manager may schedule the different tasks according to the pace of the critical path but still face delays because the computer-assisted design machine needed for several of the tasks is bogged

Most managers tend to pay little attention to the needs of a project as a whole. Instead, they start off with a series of dysfunctional negotiations.

down with other jobs. The *critical chain* thus refers to a combination of the critical path and the scarce resources that together constitute the constraints that need to be managed.

To keep the critical chain flowing smoothly, the book advises managers to use safety buffers similar to the inventory buffers used in production lines to make sure that bottleneck machines always have material to work on. Because managers can't predict exactly when any task will be completed, they need to allow extra time for tasks that impinge directly on the critical path. By inserting a time buffer wherever the noncritical paths feed into the critical path, the tasks on the critical path will always have what they need to proceed. For the same reason, managers need to allow extra time for tasks not on the critical path that feed into the scarce resource. (No buffers are allowed within the critical path.) Once the buffers are in place, managers must tightly schedule the activities of the scarce resource to maximize its use. As the project proceeds, managers need to monitor closely the scarce resources and the expected completion times of tasks on the critical path.

Apart from warning managers about constrained resources, the book also adds a useful discipline to what in reality is often a chaotic process. As the book describes, most managers tend to pay little attention to the needs of a project as a whole. Instead, they start off with a series of dysfunctional negotiations to get the

project approved. Project managers pad their resource requirements to buy a margin of safety. At the same time, functional departments (such as information services) understate their resource requirements so their portion of the work can come in on budget. Then senior managers cut the overall requirements for the project and move deliverable dates up because they assume that estimates for time and resources are inflated.

Project managers generally create a project plan composed of all the interrelated activities of the project, one that ascribes responsibilities and estimates resource requirements. That project plan involves a *work-breakdown structure* that defines individual tasks and then aggregates them into a large plan. The plan is arranged so that items on the critical path can be completed in time to meet milestones. But managers typically make the plan in conjunction with their budget, and they design it to validate some core assumptions related to the project's fiscal requirements. In most organizations, the significance of the plan itself diminishes from that point forward. Project managers know that the plan is only advisory and suggestive of the project's true structure and requirements. They expect to manage the actual project in real time, relying on only a core group of team members and a set of resources for which they will constantly need to negotiate throughout the project's life. As a consequence, plans are almost always "wrong" in the sense that the resources used and the time actually taken to complete tasks rarely correspond to those projected in the original project plan.

To get a sense of how imperfectly this process works, imagine that we managed corporate finances as we do projects. Pro forma income statements would mix together expenses and revenues, results from one division would be inextricably intertwined with those of another, and the timing of specific events would be so unpredictable that cash flow projections would be little more than wall art.

The most successful organizations, fortunately, have begun to bring order to this chaos. Project teams at those companies are placing particular emphasis on coordination and communication. Advances in project management software that can function over extranets are making such an approach possible. And in many industries, continual communi-

cation and coordination are becoming mandatory as the time allocated for project development shrinks dramatically, the members of the development team

Measurements should induce the parts to do what is good for the whole.

become geographically displaced, and the projects increasingly involve external partners and resources.

To this emerging discipline of coordination made possible through technology, Goldratt essentially adds a discipline for understanding what drives project performance and therefore what the focus of a project manager's attention should be. Goldratt does not discourage the use of plans, but he implicitly warns managers that elaborate plans should not distract them from focusing on constraints. By his analogy to production bottlenecks, he indicates to managers that most projects have only one essential constraint—and at most two—and that what they should be doing, therefore, is looking for and addressing this primary constraint.

Part of the discipline Goldratt offers involves the proper use of measurements. He reminds managers of two criteria: measurements should induce the parts to do what is good for the whole, and measurements should direct managers to those parts that need their attention. Many managers rely on milestones to monitor a project's progress (and individuals' performance), but that practice violates both of the above principles. Following the maxim, How you measure people is how they'll behave, the book points out that management by milestone motivates members of project teams and their managers to insert safety time before each milestone. Once safety time has been added to each task, various mechanisms arise that waste that time. So, Goldratt concludes, the fewer the milestones, the fewer the delays. We have found such dysfunctional behavior occurring when the milestones are set as artificial review points tied to the end of a development phase or task stream.

Goldratt weaves these lessons into the story of an executive M.B.A. class at a business school struggling with declining enrollment. The class's professor, who is himself battling to get tenure, is teaching a course in project management

> Project managers should stay focused on a few critical areas and not divide their attention among all of a project's tasks and resources.

for which he seems woefully unprepared. Along the way, he hears about the theory of constraints, and he and his students feel their way through it by applying the theory to various problems that the students are having with their own projects at work. The novel displays a genuine understanding of the experiences of project managers across organizations in all industries.

As in *The Goal,* this fictional approach makes for easy reading. But while the factory setting in *The Goal* established a realistic context in which to develop and test the theory, *Critical Chain*'s academic environment does not sufficiently bind together the various real-world vignettes. As a consequence, the reader is presented with hearsay evidence rather than given the opportunity to work through a full application of the theory during the course of the book.

The book is valuable to two main audiences: project managers and senior managers. Project managers and their teams will appreciate its main message: remain focused on a few critical areas and do not divide your attention among all of a project's tasks and resources. Project phases do not matter, milestones are largely meaningless, and building large project plans out of streams of concurrent or sequential activities is not useful. Instead, the book suggests, we need to "design" a project in the same

way we design a product. The project design needs to identify the potential sources of failure—critical-path tasks and critical resources—and then insert resource and work buffers to ensure maximum throughput.

The book addresses the concerns of senior managers in a brief discussion at its conclusion. Those managers need to know how to juggle a portfolio of projects, and the book's only advice on that subject is to make sure to allocate resources carefully across projects to minimize the constraints on the shared resources. But in our experience, managing project portfolios is far more complicated—and many of the delays in individual projects arise from problems at the senior management level rather than from mistakes made by project managers. The book is both accurate and useful in discussing the theory of con-

> Many of the delays in individual projects arise from problems at the senior management level.

straints as it applies to individual projects, but it may not give senior managers enough insight to enable them to handle multiple projects. To attain substantial improvement there, senior managers will likely need to extend Goldratt's systematic perspective to the level of multiple, concurrent projects and add some elements that *Critical Chain* either ignores or gives short shrift.

Advice in this area is all the more important now, as the pace at which markets change in all industries quickens, the increased use of standard components and processes accelerates the rate of technological innovation, and expectations about customer service and product performance continue to rise. In response, companies are spending more time on projects and less time on routine activities. The number of books and articles on project management, especially for developing new products, is burgeoning. Most major consulting firms have significant practices in this area, and the number of M.B.A. courses on this topic is increasing. Yet the success stories are few and

often based on the same corporate examples, and the performance of project teams remains generally lackluster.

Managing Projects as a Portfolio

Focusing on individual projects allows Goldratt to give us useful and well-illustrated advice, but it does not allow him to examine some important drivers of project performance: namely, how well new initiatives align with strategy and how successfully an organization balances its overall capacity and capabilities with its portfolio of projects. Managers cannot isolate and control different projects as easily as they can handle different factory-production processes.

What senior managers need is the wider perspective of aggregate project planning, which Steven C. Wheelright and Kim B. Clark defined in "Creating Project Plans to Focus Product Development" (HBR March–April 1992). Too often, projects fall short of resources or lose direction because of a lack of agreement among senior business and functional managers. This misalignment of goals can lead executives to make a number of mistakes. They may slow a project down by failing to take necessary actions or by limiting the available resources. They may fail to kill a project (the "undead") in order to avoid disappointing another executive or project team. The net effect is that most organizations have too many projects relative to their available capacity, and those projects, when viewed as a set, only distantly resemble the company's strategic intent.

Even if the right projects are picked, the way the projects relate to one another, coupled with pressure to get the highest return from the investment in development, can easily lead to an excess demand on limited resources. And even when resources seem to be adequate, projects can still fall short because the company doesn't have adequate skills for some parts of the product development process. Rapidly shrinking product and technology cycles make it increasingly difficult for companies to excel at all aspects of a project, so many of them are allying with outsiders. Senior managers need to balance the requirements of their projects with their company's capabilities and those of their partners.

As a result, the progress of any individual project is limited by factors outside an individual manager's control. Goldratt would have presented a richer prescription for project management had he fully extended the theory of constraints to the portfolio level. He does so when he considers the issue of scheduling the resource bottleneck, but he does not address the issue of stagnation caused by running too many projects at the same

When the degree of change is great, managers need to approach projects differently.

time. Reducing the overall number of projects relieves constraints on common resources; companies can then give remaining projects the resources they need and stop managers from wasting their energy in negotiations aimed at overcoming the constraints.

Putting Flexibility Where It Counts

Goldratt's narrower focus, interestingly, may be ideal for certain kinds of new-product development. While many companies excel at understanding current customers' requirements and at integrating established technologies into their new products, they often do poorly when they tackle technologies that represent a fundamental change in a product's design or purpose—what Clayton Christensen called *discontinuous technologies* in *The Innovator's Dilemma* (Harvard Business School Press, 1997). When the degree of change involved is great, managers need to approach projects differently. Projects incorporating discontinuous technologies involve much more risk and require managers to apply stringent and individualized criteria for determining how to proceed.

Because it focuses on eliminating constraints, which are necessarily unique in every project, the book does not show managers how to establish a detailed

product-development process. But for projects involving discontinuous technology, the less managers try to lay out beforehand, the better. Projects incorporating discontinuous technologies by definition involve work outside a company's experience. In such cases, a detailed project plan would give managers a false sense of security, but if they pay attention to the constraints, they will be on their way to capturing and consistently managing the essential risks of their project. They need to rely on their intuitions about where the pressure points are likely to arise and focus on managing those sources of risk. The book's highly intuitive approach may help in this area. Nor can senior managers help the project managers much in such cases: discontinuous projects tend not to require the same kinds of resources that more conservative projects need.

Nevertheless, even innovative projects may require more structure than the book describes. Given the high degree of uncertainty involved, such projects usually need some milestones, not to act as arbitrary checkpoints but to serve as opportunities to reassess the project's viability. Fundamental to Goldratt's recommendation to eliminate milestones is the assumption that all projects that are begun should be completed. But in many industries, especially those in which most of the investment takes place at later stages of product development, companies may do well by starting many more projects than they expect to finish and then culling them along the way. And in some cases, milestones are not just self-imposed deadlines, they are hard stops. For instance, in the pharmaceutical and medical-products industry, the milestone may be the completion of a regulatory filing required for approval by the Federal Drug Administration, which must be obtained before the project can move forward. Between milestones, which are often years apart, managers can still run the projects by concentrating on the constraints.

The scheduling of milestones that mark the phases of a project may need to change, however. When it comes to products for the Internet and other fast-emerging technologies, customers' needs are changing so rapidly that traditional, sequential product-development processes run the risk of generating products that are already obsolete by the time they are released. As Marco Iansiti and Alan MacCormack pointed out in "Developing Products on Internet Time" (HBR,

September-October 1997), companies in those industries have responded by modifying the traditional sequential development process to allow changes in product design right up to the last possible moment. Their managers employ a rapidly iterative product-development process that involves successive rounds of customer feedback, development, and testing in order to integrate the latest knowledge of markets and technologies into their new products. Goldratt's flexible approach may be more easily applied to products that need to or can be frequently modified than to capital-intensive or mission-critical products, such as aircraft engines. For these latter products, milestones play a crucial role as checkpoints that guard against making changes that can cause great expense or may have possible catastrophic consequences.

Finding the Ultimate Constraint

Ultimately, the parallels between process and project management give way to a fundamental difference: process management seeks to eliminate variability, whereas project management must accept variability because each project is unique. That is especially true for new-product development, which involves taking a vague concept for a new service or product that a particular market or customer segment will find valuable and turning it into an actual ongoing business proposition. Multiple individuals, functions, and increasingly even separate companies contribute to the concept's realization.

Project performance is often less a matter of understanding constraints and more a function of personal skills.

A significant weakness of *Critical Chain*, therefore, is that it leads us to believe that project management can be successfully accomplished largely through the same rational approach that works for production management. But projects involve much higher levels of uncertainty than processes do and depend much more on the contributions of individuals. For example, the book advises managers to work with the different individuals and functional departments involved in a project to set estimates for lead times so that they meet the needs of the critical chain. But anyone who has worked on a project, been a manager of key personnel on a project, or been a senior manager mediating a resource conflict among a number of projects knows that it is a rare organizational culture indeed that is capable of such an impersonal, rational approach to setting lead times. Organizations with an open, team-oriented environment at all levels, that tie the way they compensate individuals and measure their performance to the realization of common goals, are the ones most capable of this form of collaborative management.

Essential to fostering the necessary collaboration are project managers who can handle the political, as well as the technical, aspects of their projects. But when we ask executives to give us the names of all the people in their companies who are qualified to serve as the manager for the next major project, we are fortunate to get a list of three. Project performance is often less a matter of understanding the constraints of the project and more a function of the personal skills and capabilities of the potential leaders available. The skill to lead a team through unknowns depends not just on acquired but on inherent capabilities. Managers of product development projects also need unique leadership skills, such as the ability to perceive customers' future requirements before customers themselves can articulate those as-yet-unrealized needs. In our experience, the potential number of such leaders in almost all organizations is limited, usually fewer than ten. Critical Chain starts with a set of talented and driven project managers and assumes the resource constraints are inside the work of the project, not in its leadership. In truth, leadership may be the larger constraint.

Jeffrey Elton is a principal and **Justin Roe** *a consultant at Integral, a management-consulting company based in Cambridge, Massachusetts.*

New Era About to Dawn for International Space Station

■ **Aerospace:** Having survived budget battles and the end of the Cold War, orbiter is set for its crew to dock this week.

By PETER PAE
TIMES STAFF WRITER

The International Space Station is already one of the brightest stars in the sky, a marvel of human engineering visible to the unaided eye on a clear night.

To some, its purpose and future are just as lucid. To others the most expensive man-made object in space is really nothing more than an eyesore, a $25-billion boondoggle whose cost is growing out of control.

This week, despite chronic delays, massive cost overruns and fierce debate over its usefulness, the space station will finally go online with its first long-term crew.

With the basic infrastructure in place, three astronauts—an American and two Russians—are to lift off Monday from Kazakhstan and become the first inhabitants of the orbiting craft. Space station commander and U.S. astronaut Bill Shepard, Russian Soyuz commander Yuri Gidzenko and flight engineer Sergei Krikalev are scheduled to dock with the Zvezda service module Thursday and begin a four-month stay.

This week's mission is "a watershed mark," said Joe Mills, deputy program manager for the space station at Boeing Co., the project's prime contractor. "Everything is moving really fast now, and we're ready to go."

The fact that the program is moving forward at all is a marvel in itself. Fourteen years behind schedule and at triple its original budget so far, the space station has encountered numerous operational problems, and its funding has been under constant threat. The project has survived 22 full votes in either the House or the Senate to have it scuttled.

The station has been resilient thanks to the way it has been able to evolve, from child of the Cold War designed to counteract Russia's own space station, Mir, to olive branch intended to improve foreign relations in the aftermath of the Soviet Union's collapse.

In the process, it quickly became one of the largest aerospace programs in the post-Cold War era, helping the aerospace industry—particularly in California—cushion itself from defense spending cuts that led companies to lay off thousands of employees.

Still, critics who want the project shut down deride it as pie in the sky, a waste of taxpayers' money that has sucked valuable funds from other worthy scientific endeavors.

"We are still proceeding with this monstrosity that even Machiavelli could not have spread out with as much pork barrel," said Rep. Tim J. Roemer (D-Ind.), one of the space station's harshest critics and someone who unsuccessfully pushed to kill the program eight times in as many years. "If this was a welfare project, it would have been canceled a long time ago."

Others hail the station as a jewel in space with a potential to yield yet unknown scientific discoveries with huge commercial potential.

Marshall Kaplan, president of Launchspace, a Potomac, Md.-based space consulting firm, said Roemer and other critics are shortsighted.

Taking advantage of long-term zero gravity research on the space station, for instance, new drugs could be discovered or new manufacturing techniques developed that would not have been possible on Earth, Kaplan said.

"It's in the early stages, it's evolving and it's going to take some time before you see the benefits," Kaplan said, noting that nothing like it has been built before. "There is a good chance it may be much more useful than how it appears today."

Supporters also say the station is a critical test of international cooperation in the post–Cold War era. With the U.S. leading the technical effort and providing most of the funding, the station is one of the largest international scientific efforts ever undertaken, involving 15 other countries: Russia, Canada, Japan, Brazil and 11 member nations of the European Space Agency.

Despite the delays and cost overruns, Rep. F. James Sensenbrenner Jr. (R-Wis.), chairman of the House Science Committee, said the station "should happen, has to happen."

"This is the first international cooperative effort since the end of the Cold War," he said. "Yes, it's expen-

Some Assembly Required

The International Space Station will finally go online this week as its first permanent residents dock with the Zvezda service module. The linkup comes 16 years after President Ronald Reagan announced that the U.S. was going to build the outpost to counter the Soviets' success with their space station. With the collapse of the Soviet Union, the station evolved into an international project involving 16 nations, including Russia. In the U.S., California has played a key role in the project's development.

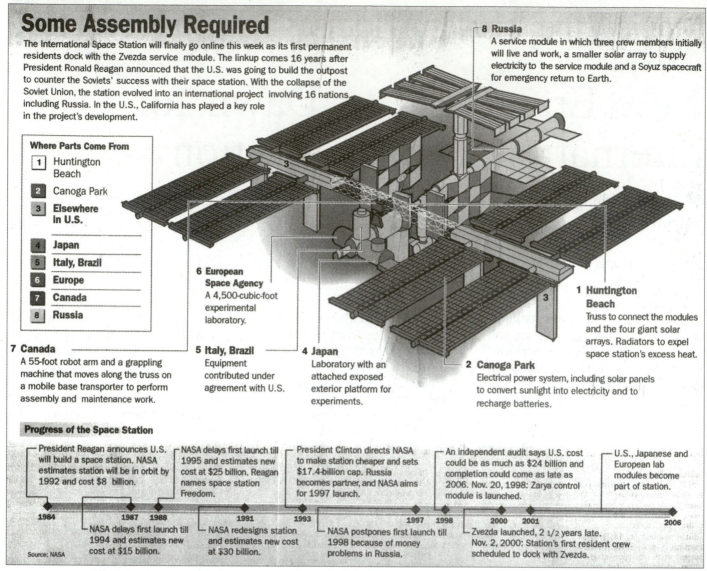

8 Russia
A service module in which three crew members initially will live and work, a smaller solar array to supply electricity to the service module and a Soyuz spacecraft for emergency return to Earth.

Where Parts Come From
1. Huntington Beach
2. Canoga Park
3. **Elsewhere in U.S.**
4. **Japan**
5. **Italy, Brazil**
6. **Europe**
7. **Canada**
8. **Russia**

6 European Space Agency
A 4,500-cubic-foot experimental laboratory.

1 Huntington Beach
Truss to connect the modules and the four giant solar arrays. Radiators to expel space station's excess heat.

7 Canada
A 55-foot robot arm and a grappling machine that moves along the truss on a mobile base transporter to perform assembly and maintenance work.

5 Italy, Brazil
Equipment contributed under agreement with U.S.

4 Japan
Laboratory with an attached exposed exterior platform for experiments.

2 Canoga Park
Electrical power system, including solar panels to convert sunlight into electricity and to recharge batteries.

Progress of the Space Station

- **1984** President Reagan announces U.S. will build a space station. NASA estimates station will be in orbit by 1992 and cost $8 billion.
- NASA delays first launch till 1994 and estimates new cost at $15 billion.
- **1987 1988** NASA delays first launch till 1995 and estimates new cost at $25 billion. Reagan names space station Freedom.
- **1991** NASA redesigns station and estimates new cost at $30 billion.
- **1993** President Clinton directs NASA to make station cheaper and sets $17.4-billion cap. Russia becomes partner, and NASA aims for 1997 launch.
- NASA postpones first launch till 1998 because of money problems in Russia.
- **1997 1998** An independent audit says U.S. cost could be as much as $24 billion and completion could come as late as 2006. Nov. 20, 1998: Zarya control module is launched.
- **2000 2001** Zvezda launched, 2 1/2 years late. Nov. 2, 2000: Station's first resident crew scheduled to dock with Zvezda.
- **2006** U.S., Japanese and European lab modules become part of station.

Source: NASA

REBECCA PERRY, MARK HAFER/Los Angeles Times

sive, but if this type of international cooperation fails, it will be a long time before we will be able to do another."

There are also foreign policy implications to the project. By being preoccupied with helping build the station, Sensenbrenner said, Russia may feel less need to develop weapons for Iraq, North Korea or other rogue nations.

While the debate has dragged on, the station has become an economic boon to California and other states, where it has helped offset a downturn in defense spending.

Boeing alone has about 4,500 employees working on the station across Southern California. In Huntington Beach, the company is build-

ing the structural backbone of the station, and in Canoga Park it makes and maintains the station's electrical power system.

Thousands more work for hundreds of subcontractors, most of them local. And Boeing, which has a $9.3-billion contract to help build the station, estimated that it has already paid at least $1 billion to suppliers from California.

So far, the National Aeronautics and Space Administration estimates that the project has provided jobs to more than 40,000 people in 30 states.

In all, the U.S. General Accounting Office projects that this country will have spent about $96 billion on the station by the end of its 20-year life span. The cost projections in-

clude shuttle launches to staff and resupply the outpost, making it perhaps the most expensive machine man has ever made.

"California will have had its share of the money," said Rep. Dana Rohrabacher (R-Huntington Beach), a supporter of the project. "The space station helped us at a time when the aerospace industry needed the boost."

Ironically, the station was supposed to be one of the more frugal space projects, costing about $8 billion. The budget concessions also meant that NASA could not pursue radical new technologies, as it did on the Apollo and space shuttle programs.

Still, critics argue that many of the experiments planned for the space station could have been done even more cheaply using satellites or other unmanned craft.

But President Ronald Reagan, smarting from the Soviet Union's success with its space station, wanted one for this country too and announced in 1984 that the United States was going to launch its version by 1992.

However, cost estimates on the station, dubbed Freedom by Reagan, kept rising—as high as $30 billion—and NASA twice delayed the first launch. In 1993, after the agency had spent $11 billion on the project, President Clinton directed NASA to re-engineer a cheaper and more efficient version that would involve the Russians. He also set a U.S. spending cap of $17.4 billion.

But the involvement of the Russians, planned as a cost-saving measure, turned out to be just the opposite. Money troubles held back the launch of the Russian-built Zvezda, the living quarters for the first crew, by 2 ½ years.

NASA now estimates that the current station will have cost U.S. taxpayers $24.1 billion to $26.4 billion by the time it is completely assembled in 2006, three times more than anticipated and 14 years behind schedule. And that doesn't include 43 rocket and shuttle launches still left to ferry crew and supplies at a cost of $15 billion to $20 billion. In addition, the estimated tab for maintenance and operations over the station's life span is about $40 billion.

Delays have also hurt Boeing's bottom line. Officials at the company said the project is running about 11% over budget, which could wipe out any profits, once expected to be about $200 million to $300 million. But the company could still receive a monetary award from the government if it meets certain targets at the end of the contract.

The cost overrun is "more than what we like but not unreasonable, based on past history of doing a project of this magnitude," Mills said.

For space buffs, the station will be an amazing sight. When fully assembled, it will span two football fields, weigh a million pounds and house six research laboratories—two operated by the U.S., two by the Russians, and one each by the Japanese and the European Space Agency.

From Earth, it is already one of the brightest celestial objects, clearly visible to the unaided eye as it moves across the night sky at 17,000 mph 250 miles above ground. When its four massive solar panels are in full bloom, the station will also be visible during the day.

The astronauts are to be ferried this week on a Russian Soyuz launched from the Baikonur Cosmodrome in Kazakhstan, the same launch pad that put the first man in space 39 years ago, setting off the space race. Much of the crew's work will involve flight testing and assembly.

The Expedition 1 crew, as the first inhabitants are called, will be picked up by the space shuttle Discovery in February as it drops off their replacements.

The workhorse for the station will be a Canadian-built 55-foot robotic arm, which will move along a central girder called the truss—built in Huntington Beach—and help connect the modules and four giant solar arrays.

Initially, NASA officials say, the station will be primarily involved in long-term scientific research, mostly related to taking advantage of the special conditions that space provides.

For instance, purer protein crystals can be grown in space, and they could help scientists develop new drugs to help treat cancer, diabetes and immune disorders. Such experiments have been conducted on the space shuttle but were limited due to the short duration of the flights.

In addition, conditions in space will give scientists the ability to develop new metal alloys or semiconductor chips as well as to study the long-term effects of reduced gravity on humans, which could be valuable for longer human space travel.

NASA officials say the benefit of a research lab in space is virtually impossible to quantify, although any development such as pharmaceutical research could result in drugs worth millions of dollars in potential sales.

"The future commercial markets for the [space station] are still too premature, and any market study would be wholly speculative," said a recent study completed by consulting firm KPMG, looking at commercial prospects of the space stations.

The report, commissioned by NASA, concluded that the station held strong potential for research and development of economically viable products or services in the long run but that in the near term the return-on-investment potential was limited to areas such as education, entertainment and advertising.

Indeed, three companies are vying to bring the space station into people's living rooms. They include Enermedia, a joint venture of Russian rocket company Energia and Washington-based Space Media. The venture hopes to eventually broadcast a space sitcom detailing the lives of astronauts living in a module.

And NASA is quietly conducting an internal study looking at the prospects of commercializing the space station, including the possibility of allowing companies to sponsor certain space station projects, similar to sponsorship of the Olympics by Visa or Samsung.

Last summer, NASA chief Daniel Goldin announced a deal in which Excite.com would pay $100 million to broadcast high-definition images from the space station. The Internet company would also gain access to the agency's huge trove of films and images.

In the end, NASA says private-public partnerships will free up billions of dollars of government money for new initiatives. Under a new policy enacted recently, 30% of America's physical space on the station will be set aside for commercial development.

"The only way we're going to break loose of Earth orbit is to turn over low Earth orbit to the entrepreneurs," Goldin said.

Seven Keys to Better Forecasting

Mark A. Moon, John T. Mentzer, Carlo D. Smith, and Michael S. Garver

Sales forecasting is a management function that companies often fail to recognize as a key contributor to corporate success. From a top-line perspective, accurate sales forecasts allow a company to provide high levels of customer service. When demand can be predicted accurately, it can be met in a timely and efficient manner, keeping both channel partners and final customers satisfied. Accurate forecasts help a company avoid lost sales or stock-out situations, and prevent customers from going to competitors.

At the bottom line, the effect of accurate forecasts can be profound. Raw materials and component parts can be purchased much more cost-effectively when last minute, spot market purchases can be avoided. Such expenses can be eliminated by accurately forecasting production needs. Similarly, logistical services can be obtained at a much lower cost through long-term contracts rather than through spot market arrangements. However, these contracts can only work when demand can be predicted accurately. Perhaps most important, accurate forecasting can have a profound impact on a company's inventory levels. In a sense, inventory exists to provide a buffer for inaccurate forecasts. Thus, the more accurate the forecasts, the less inventory that needs to be carried, with all the well-understood cost savings that brings.

The ultimate effects of sales forecasting excellence can be dramatic. Mentzer and Schroeter (1993) describe how Brake Parts, Inc., a manufacturer of automotive aftermarket parts, improved its bottom line by $6 million per month after launching a company-wide effort to improve sales forecasting effectiveness. Nevertheless, firms often fail to recognize the importance of this critical management function. Our objec-

> *Excellence in sales forecasting can boost a firm's financial health and gratify customers and employees alike.*

tive here is to take what we've learned about sales forecasting from working with hundreds of companies, and summarize that learning into seven key focus points (summarized in **Figure 1**) that will help any company improve its forecasting performance. Although no management function can be reduced to seven keys, or 70 keys for that matter, our hope is that the ideas presented here will inspire senior management to look closely at their own sales forecasting practices and recognize opportunities for improvement.

Key #1: Understand What Forecasting Is, and What It Is Not

The first and perhaps most important key to better forecasting is a complete understanding of what it actually is and—of equal importance—what it is not. Sales forecasting is a management process, not a computer program. This distinction is important because it affects so many areas across an organization. Regardless of whether a company sells goods

Figure 1
The Seven Keys to Better Forecasting

Keys	Issues and Symptoms	Actions	Results
Understand what forecasting is and is not.	• Computer system as focus, rather than management processes and controls • Blurring of the distinction between forecasts, plans, and goals	• Establish forecasting group • Implement management control systems before selecting forecasting software • Derive plans from forecasts • Distinguish between forecasts and goals	• An environment in which forecasting is acknowledged as a critical business function • Accuracy emphasized and game-playing minimized
Forecast demand, plan supply.	• Shipment history as the basis for forecasting demand • "Too accurate" forecasts	• Identify sources of information • Build systems to capture key demand data	• Improved capital planning and customer service
Communicate, cooperate, collaborate.	• Duplication of forecasting effort • Mistrust of the "official" forecast • Little understanding of the impact throughout the firm	• Establish cross-functional approach to forecasting • Establish independent forecast group that sponsors cross-functional collaboration	• All relevant information used to generate forecasts • Forecasts trusted by users • Islands of analysis eliminated • More accurate and relevant forecasts
Eliminate islands of analysis.	• Mistrust and inadequate information leading different users to create their own forecasts	• Build a single "forecasting infrastructure" • Provide training for both users and developers of forecasts	• More accurate, relevant, and credible forecasts • Optimized investments in information/communication systems.
Use tools wisely.	• Relying solely on qualitative or quantitative methods • Cost/benefit of additional information	• Integrate quantitative and qualitative methods • Identify sources of improved accuracy and increased error • Provide instruction	• Process improvement in efficiency and effectiveness
Make it important.	• No accountability for poor forecasts • Developers not understanding how forecasts are used	• Training developers to understand implications of poor forecasts • Include forecast performance in individual performance plans and reward systems	• Developers taking forecasts seriously • A striving for accuracy • More accuracy and credibility
Measure, measure, measure.	• Not knowing if the firm is getting better • Accuracy not measured at relevant levels of aggregation • Inability to isolate sources of forecast error	• Establish multidimensional metrics • Incorporate multilevel measures • Measure accuracy whenever and wherever forecasts are adjusted	• Forecast performance can be included in individual performance plans • Sources of errors can be isolated and targeted for improvement • Greater confidence in forecast process

or services, it must have a clear picture of how many of those goods or services it can sell, in both the short and long terms. That way, it can plan to have an adequate supply to meet customer demand.

Forecasting is critical to a company's production or operations department. Adequate materials must be obtained at the lowest possible price; adequate production facilities must be provided at the lowest possible cost; adequate labor must be hired and trained at the lowest possible cost; and adequate logistics services must be used to avoid bottlenecks in moving products from producers to consumers. None of these fundamental business functions can be performed effectively without accurate sales forecasts.

Many companies consider the most important decisions about forecasting to revolve around the selection or development of computer software for preparing the forecasts. They have adopted the overly simplistic belief that "If we've got good software, we'll have good forecasting." Our research team, however, has observed numerous instances of sophisticated computer systems put into place, costing enormous amounts of time and money, that have failed to deliver accurate forecasts. This is because system implementation has not been accompanied by effective management to monitor and control the forecasting process.

One company we worked with has an excellent computer system with impressive capabilities of performing sophisticated statistical modeling of seasonality and other trends. However, the salespeople, who are the originators of the forecast, use none of these tools because they do not understand them and have no confidence in the numbers generated. As a result, their forecasts are based solely on qualitative factors and are often very inaccurate. A similar case is a technology-based company that has created another highly sophisticated forecasting tool, yet the salespeople continue to underforecast significantly because their forecasts have a direct effect on their sales quotas. Both of these examples show how some companies focus on forecasting *systems* rather than forecasting *management*.

On the other hand, some companies have been more successful in their efforts by recognizing the importance of forecasting as a management process. Some have organized independent groups or departments that are responsible for the entire forecasting process, both short- and long-term. One large chemical company has formed a forecasting group not associated with either marketing or production. It has ownership and accountability for all aspects of forecasting management, with responsibility not only for the systems used to forecast but also for the numbers themselves. The group accomplishes its mission in several ways: providing training in the methods and processes throughout the company; designing compensation systems that reward forecast accuracy; and facilitating communication among sales, marketing, finance, and production departments, thereby improving overall forecasting effectiveness. Recognizing the importance of forecasting, this firm has put an organization in place to manage the process, not just to choose and manage a system.

Another way in which companies confuse what forecasts are and what they are not is by failing to understand the relationship between forecasting, planning, and goal setting. A sales forecast should be

viewed as an estimate of what future sales might be, given certain environmental conditions. A sales plan should be seen as a management decision or commitment to what the company will do during the planning period. A sales goal should be a target that everyone in the organization strives to attain and exceed.

Each of these numbers serves a different purpose. The primary purpose of the sales forecast is to help management formulate its sales plan and other related business plans—its commitment to future activity. The sales plan's purpose is to drive numerous tactical and strategic management decisions (raw material purchases, human resource planning, logistics planning, and so on), realistically factoring in the constraints of the firm's resources, procedures, and systems. The sales goal is primarily designed to provide motivation for people throughout the organization in meeting and exceeding corporate targets.

Whereas the sales forecast and the sales plan should be closely linked (the former should precede and influence the latter), the sales goal may be quite independent. The objective of those who receive a

THE RESEARCH

The ideas presented in this article are drawn from a program of research that has spanned more than 15 years. **Phase 1** began in 1982 with a mail survey of 157 companies that explored the techniques they used to forecast. Ten years later, under the sponsorship of AT&T Network Systems, the survey was replicated and expanded in **Phase 2** to explore not only techniques but also the systems and management processes used by 208 companies. **Phase 3,** conducted between 1994 and 1996, was sponsored by a consortium of companies consisting of AT&T Network Systems, Andersen Consulting, Anheuser-Busch, and Pillsbury. It took the form of a benchmarking study that consisted of in-depth analysis of 20 companies: Anheuser-Busch, Becton-Dickinson, Coca-Cola, Colgate-Palmolive, Federal Express, Kimberly Clark, Lykes Pasco, Nabisco, JCPenney, Pillsbury, ProSource, Reckitt Colman, Red Lobster, RJR Tobacco, Sandoz, Schering Plough, Sysco, Tropicana, Warner Lambert, and Westwood Squibb. Finally, **Phase 4** has been conducted since 1996 and consists of a series of forecast audits. The forecasting practices of seven companies— Allied Signal, Du Pont Agricultural Products Canada, Eastman Chemical, Hershey Foods USA, Lucent Technologies, Michelin North America, and Union Pacific Railroad—have been studied so far in this phase and compared to those of the 20 benchmarked companies. The references to this research are listed at the end of this article.

In addition to these formal studies, the learning presented here is augmented by more than 20 years of experience in consulting with a large number of major corporations on their forecasting systems and processes. Our ideas are drawn from firsthand observation of what actually works in sales forecasting in companies, large and small, that sell products and services and that are manufacturers, distributors, or retailers.

"In one company, the production scheduling department was so distrustful of the forecasts developed by marketing that it completely ignored them and created a whole 'black market' forecasting system."

sales goal should be to beat that goal. It can be developed based on a sales forecast, plan, and motivation levels. However, because forecasters should strive for accuracy, it is not appropriate for a forecast to be confused with the firm's motivational strategy.

It is particularly problematic when sales forecasts and sales goals are intertwined, because this mixture leads to considerable game playing, especially involving the sales force. If salespeople believe that long-term forecasts will affect the size of the next year's quota, they will be strongly motivated to underforecast, hoping to influence those quotas to be low and attainable. Alternatively, as one salesman at a parts supply company put it, "It would be suicide for me to submit a forecast that was under my targets." In both cases, because goals and forecasts are so intertwined, salespeople are motivated to "play games" with their forecasts. There is a built-in disincentive to strive for accuracy.

Some companies have expressed a reluctance to "manage to different numbers," suggesting that when the forecast and the goals differ, it creates confusion and lack of focus. The reaction to such perceived confusion is to develop inaccurate forecasts that can affect performance throughout the company. We believe the sales forecast and the sales goal must be distinct, because the behaviors they are meant to influence can conflict.

Key # 2: Forecast Demand, Plan Supply

One mistake many companies make is forecasting their ability to supply goods or services rather than actual customer demand. At the beginning of the forecast cycle, it is important to create predictions that are not constrained by the firm's capacity to produce. Consider the forecaster for a certain product who questions the company's sales force and learns they could sell 1,500 units per month. At the same time, current manufacturing capacity for that product is 1,000 units per month. If the forecaster takes that production capacity into account when creating initial forecasts, and predicts 1,000 units, there is no record of the unmet demand of 500 units per month, and the information on where to expand manufacturing capacity is lost.

This problem often occurs when historical shipments are used as the basis for generating forecasts. Forecasting shipments will only predict a company's previous ability to meet demand. Suppose demand for a particular product in the past had been 10,000 units per month, but the supplier could only ship 7,500. Corporate history would show shipments at 7,500 units per month, thus causing this amount to be projected and produced again the following month. The result is twofold: the impression of an accurate forecasting system, but an actually recurring unfulfilled monthly demand of 2,500 units. Forecasting based on shipping history only leads a company to repeat its former mistakes of not satisfying customer demand. Predicting actual demand allows measurement of the disparity between demand and supply so it can be reduced in future periods through plans for capacity expansion.

Often the symptom of this key is the attitude, "We do a great job of forecasting. We are very accurate, always selling close to what we forecast." Notice in the previous example that the forecast accuracy would appear very good because both the forecast and the actual sales were 7,500 units each month. The key, however, is the failure to realize the 2,500 units in sales lost each month because of an inability to meet demand. In fact, the "true" demand forecasting accuracy was not 100 percent, but only 75 percent. Forecasting by shipments and obtaining accurate results are often symptomatic of chronic underforecasting of demand.

Unfortunately, determining actual customer demand is more difficult than predicting a company's ability to supply. Systems and processes are needed to capture this elusive demand that was not fulfilled. Mechanisms are needed to allow salespeople to provide valuable information about customers who would order more if they could. In addition, records of orders accepted but not filled in the period demanded adds to the demand versus supply level of information. Finally, such electronic data interchange (EDI) information as point-of-sale (POS) demand, retail inventory levels, and retailer forecasts are all valuable sources of information that help a company move toward demand forecasting.

Although it is more difficult, forecasting true demand will help a company make sensible, long-term decisions that can profoundly affect its market position. By identifying where capacity does not meet demand forecasts, the company has valuable information on where to expand capacity through capital planning. Such a long-term program of matching capacity planning to forecasts will reduce the incidence of chronic underforecasting and result in higher levels of customer satisfaction.

Key # 3: Communicate, Cooperate, Collaborate

Companies that forecast most effectively consider it critical to obtain input from people in different functional areas, each of whom contributes relevant information and insights that can improve overall accuracy. But employees are often unable or unwilling to work across functions to achieve high levels of forecasting performance. To do so requires a great deal of communication across department boundaries, and not all communicating is equal; some companies are simply better at it than others.

When it comes to cross-functional forecasting, we distinguish among three levels: communication, cooperation, and collaboration. Companies at lower levels of sophistication merely *communicate*. This can take the form of one-way reports, in which one department responsible for forecasting informs other functional areas of the results of its efforts. With *coordination*, representatives from different functional groups meet to discuss the forecast. Often, however, one area—usually the one that "owns" the forecast—will dominate the discussions and work to persuade the other functions to accept the forecast it has created.

Coordination is superior to one-way communication, because at least there is opportunity for some dialogue. But it does not promote as effective a forecasting process as when different constituencies in a company *collaborate*. Here, the views of each functional area receive equal consideration, and no one department dominates. Such collaboration is most likely to occur when management of the forecasting process resides in an independent department instead of being part of marketing, finance, logistics, or production. Each area, with its unique biases and agendas, can contribute equally to a true consensus forecast.

In several companies we have worked with, the functional area responsible for generating forecasts—usually marketing—makes little effort to obtain input from other affected areas, such as production planning, operations, or logistics. A number of negative consequences result. First, critical information about production lead times or capacity constraints are not taken into account when the forecast is finalized. Because this information is missing, forecast users have little trust in projections they did not help develop. This lack of trust leads to duplicated forecasting efforts. In one company, the production scheduling department was so distrustful of the forecasts developed by marketing that it completely ignored them and created a whole "black market" forecasting system. Had

a consensus-based approach been used, such nonproductive duplication of efforts could have been avoided.

A further consequence of not working cross-functionally is a lack of understanding of the assumptions that go into forecasts, which leads to further distrust. In another company, a production scheduler would adjust the forecasts to take into account the seasonality she believed was present in the marketplace. However, she was not aware that the mar-

> *"The key is that both quantitative and qualitative tools are integral to effective sales forecasting."*

keting department had already accounted for that seasonality in the information they gave her. Had production planning been involved in a consensus-based forecasting process, the scheduler's adjustments—which skewed the forecasts—would not have been made.

It is most important in effective forecasting to establish a mechanism that brings people from multiple organizational areas together in a spirit of collaboration. Such a mechanism, often organized by an independent forecasting group, ensures that all relevant information is considered before forecasts are created. One such mechanism is in place at a national consumer products firm, in which the forecasting group organizes and holds regularly scheduled, half-day meetings that bring together representatives from National Accounts (sales), product management (marketing), production planning, logistics, and finance. Each participant comes to the meeting prepared to discuss upcoming issues that will affect sales and demand over the forecast period. Formal minutes are kept to document the reasons for making adjustments. The end product is a consensus forecast, with numbers that its users have helped develop. Duplicate forecasting efforts are eliminated and all the parties can trust the final result: a more accurate and relevant forecast.

Key # 4: Eliminate Islands of Analysis

Islands of analysis are distinct areas within a firm that perform similar functions. Each area maintains a separate process, thereby performing redundant tasks and often having the same responsibilities. Because islands of analysis are often supported by independent computer systems (which often are not electronically linked to other systems within the firm), information contained within the different islands is not shared between them.

In our research, we have identified forecasting islands in logistics, production planning, finance, and marketing. They have usually emerged because of a lack of interfunctional collaboration between units, which leads to a lack of credibility associated with the forecast. Because the "official" forecast generated in a particular department may not be credible to forecast users, the latter often take steps to implement processes and systems to create their own forecast.

Islands of analysis are detrimental to corporate performance. Forecasts developed in this manner are often inaccurate and inconsistent. Because each area maintains its own forecasting process and often its own computer system, data—if shared at all—are shared only through manual transfers, which are prone to human errors. When completely separate systems are used, the assumptions that underlie the forecasts, such as pricing levels and marketing programs, tend to differ from one system to the next. Moreover, each area forecasts with a unique bias, making separate predictions inconsistent and unusable by other areas. Redundancies generated by separate systems cost the firm both money and valuable personnel time and energy. Employee frustration builds up, along with an overall lack of confidence in the forecasting process.

To solve this problem, management must devote attention to eliminating the factors that encourage the development of islands of analysis. Such a goal can be reached by establishing a single process supported by a "forecasting infrastructure." This process should consist of software that communicates seamlessly with other information systems in the firm. Appropriate tools should include a suite of statistical techniques, graphical programs, and an ability to capture and report performance metrics over time. Historical sales data can be accessed from a centrally maintained "data warehouse" that is electronically available to all functional areas and provides real-time data.

Once this forecasting infrastructure is in place, effective training aimed at a common understanding of the process and its system should be implemented for both users and developers. Employees should be trained to comprehend the overall process, each individual's role in the process, and the importance of accurate forecasting. They must be able to use the system effectively and efficiently.

Once islands of analysis are eliminated, the company can expect improved forecasting performance and significant cost savings. Forecasts will be more precise, more credible, and better able to meet the needs of various departments. When systems are electronically linked, the errors that result from manual data transfers can be avoided, and the necessary information can be accessible to all functional areas. From a cost perspective, a single forecasting process elimi-

nates redundant efforts within the firm, thus saving valuable employee time and other resources. And because accuracy will be improved, all the well-documented cost savings in areas such as purchasing, inventory control, and logistics planning can be tracked and realized.

Key # 5: Use Tools Wisely

Many companies tend to rely solely on qualitative tools—the opinions of experienced managers and/or salespeople—to derive forecasts, ignoring such quantitative tools as regression and time-series analysis. Alternatively, many companies expect the application of quantitative tools, or the computer packages that make use of them, to "solve the forecasting problem." The key is that both quantitative and qualitative tools are integral to effective sales forecasting. To be effective, however, they must be understood and used wisely within the context of the firm's unique business environment. Without understanding where qualitative techniques, time series, and regression do and do not work effectively, it is impossible to analyze the costs and achieve the benefits of implementing new forecasting tools.

One common symptom of a failure to realize this key is the existence of detailed sales forecasting processes that, when examined, reveal the subjective judgments of managers or salespeople as the only input used in the forecast. In other words, the company has a quantitative sales forecasting process that supports only qualitative forecasts. It relies too much on the ability of experienced personnel to translate what they know into a forecast number, without taking into account the myriad of quantitative techniques and their ability to analyze patterns in the history of demand.

The opposite symptom is a sales forecasting process that performs intensive numerical analysis of demand history and the factors that relate statistically to changes in demand, but with no qualitative information on the nature of the market and what causes demand to change. The company depends too much on the ability of these techniques to determine estimates of future demand without taking experience into account.

A variation on these symptoms is relying on a "black box" forecasting system. This occurs when a company has a sales forecasting computer package, or "box," into which historical sales data are fed and the forecasts come out, but no one seems to know how it comes up with them, or even what techniques it uses. The company abrogates its responsibility by turning the important job of sales forecasting over to a computer package that nobody understands.

Using forecasting tools wisely requires knowing where each type of tool works well and where it does not, then putting together a process that uses the advantages of each in the unique context of the firm. Salespeople who do a poor job of turning their experience into an initial forecast may be good at taking an initial quantitative forecast and qualitatively adjusting it to improve overall accuracy. Time series models work well in companies that experience changing trends and seasonal patterns, but they are of no use in determining the relationship between demand and such external factors as price changes, economic activity, or marketing efforts by the company and its competitors. On the other hand, regression analysis is quite effective at assessing these relationships, but not very useful in forecasting changes in trend and seasonality.

To apply this key, a process should be implemented that uses time series to forecast trend and seasonality, regression analysis to forecast demand relationships with external factors, and qualitative input from salespeople, marketing, and general management to adjust these initial quantitative forecasts. This general recommendation must be refined for each individual company by finding the specific techniques that provide the most improved accuracy. Finally, key personnel involved in either the quantitative or the qualitative aspects of the forecasting process need training in using the techniques, determining where they work and do not work, and incorporating qualitative adjustments in the overall forecasting process.

Key # 6: Make It Important

What gets measured gets rewarded, and what gets rewarded gets done, say Mentzer and Bienstock (1998). This management truism is the driver behind our final two keys. Sales forecasting is often described by senior management as an important function. But although this assessment may be shared by individuals throughout the firm, few organizations institute policies and practices reinforcing the notion that forecasting is important for business success. There is often a gap between management's words and their actions. Companies frequently tell those who develop forecasts that "forecasting is important," but then fail to reward them for doing the job well or punish them for doing it poorly. Forecast users become frustrated by a perceived lack of interest and accountability for accuracy among forecasters. Such frustration often leads them to manipulate existing forecasts or, in the extreme case, develop islands of analysis that duplicate forecasting efforts and ignore valuable ideas.

One way to gauge how important forecasting is to a firm is to determine how familiar users and developers are with the entire process. Without such familiarity, individuals involved in forecasting throughout the

> "Salespeople, product managers, and other forecasters will see the importance of the task if salient rewards follow as a result of forecasting excellence."

firm have little appreciation of the impact of their inaccuracies and are therefore unlikely to spend the time and attention needed to do the job well. As a result, users perceive that forecasters are not taking the task seriously and thus discount the value of what they produce.

A number of actions can be taken to address this gap in forecasting importance. One way is to give all individuals involved adequate training. Forecast creators and users must know where and how forecasts are used throughout the firm. When forecasters become aware of all the downstream ramifications of sloppy work, the task takes on more relevance to them. Marketing and salespeople who typically are concerned about forecasting only at the product or product line level should understand that this does not provide the necessary detail for operations to plan stock-keeping unit (SKU) production or for logistics to make SKUL (by location) shipment plans. Similarly, forecast users should be more aware of the needs and capabilities of forecast developers.

Another action management can take is to incorporate forecasting performance measures into job performance evaluation criteria. Clearly, salespeople, product managers, and other forecasters will see the importance of the task if salient rewards follow as a result of forecasting excellence. Even senior managers become interested when the metrics of accuracy are worked into their personal performance evaluations and bonus plans.

But focusing on senior management is not enough. One company includes forecast accuracy as a meaningful part of the performance plans of its senior executives, but not of those on the "front line" who work with forecasts on a daily basis. The job has not been made to seem important to those who do it, with the effect that it is still not done very well.

This is particularly true of the people who are typically responsible for initial forecast input—the sales force. At nearly all the benchmark and audit companies, salespeople are critically important pieces of the forecasting puzzle. Yet in almost all cases, the ones who develop forecasts receive neither feedback on how well they forecast nor any type of reward for doing it well. Many agree with a salesman for a high-tech manufacturer, who said, "My job is to sell, not forecast." Similarly, product managers, who also provide critical input to the forecasting process at many companies, often consider forecasting an extra burden that takes them away from their "real jobs."

Key # 7: Measure, Measure, Measure

Obviously, before forecasters can be rewarded for excellence, a company must first develop systems for measuring performance, tools for providing feedback, and standards and targets for what constitutes forecasting excellence. Without the ability to effectively measure and track performance, there is little opportunity to identify whether changes in the development and application of forecasts are contributing to, or hindering, business success. This key may be intuitive for most business managers, yet our research has identified surprisingly few companies that systematically measure forecasting management performance. In cases where measures have been implemented, they are infrequently used for performance assessment or to identify opportunities for improvement.

A primary symptom indicating a lack of performance measurement can be gleaned from conversations with individuals involved in the forecasting process. Simply asking for a measure of forecasting accuracy typically elicits a response of "pretty good," "lousy," or other general descriptors. In some cases, the answer may include a number considered to be a measure of accuracy, such as "75 percent," or error, such as "25 percent." Further inquiry may indicate that the source of the measure is based on a general "feeling," estimate, or a second- or third-hand source of information, and the respondent is unsure of how such measures were calculated or what level of aggregation was used.

In cases where measures are collected and documented, there may still be insufficient detail or little realization as to how they can help identify opportunities for forecasting improvement. Generally we have found that even when accuracy has been measured over time, few individuals who contribute to forecast development review the history and can determine whether their performance has improved, remained constant, or deteriorated. This reflects a complacency toward performance measures when such measures are not used to evaluate a person's job performance, or do not provide support for identifying sources of forecasting error.

Effective measures evaluate accuracy at different levels of aggregation. Logistics operations are interested in forecast performance at the SKUL level; sales managers may be more interested in a forecast stated in dollars and at the territory or product line level of aggregation. Performance metrics should support these various units of measure as well as the aggregation of demand at different levels.

It is also important to track accuracy at each point at which forecasts may be adjusted. As an illustration, the forecasting task of the sales force of one company is to examine "machine-generated" forecasts for their customers and make adjustments. Those adjustments are then measured against actual sales to determine whether the salesperson's adjustment improved the forecast or not. Similarly, the product manager's job is to take the machine-generated forecast, which has been adjusted by the sales force, and make further adjustments based on a knowledge of market conditions or upcoming promotional events. Once again, these adjustments are measured against actual sales to determine whether they improved the forecast. In both cases, the salespeople and the product manager gain feedback that helps them improve their efforts.

Finally, companies should assess forecasting accuracy in terms of its impact on business performance. Accurate forecasts should not be an end in themselves, but rather a means to achieving the end, which is business success. Improvements in accuracy require expenditures of resources, both human and financial, and should be approached in a return-on-investment framework. For example, in a distribution environment, maintaining or improving customer service may be a worthy corporate objective. Investment in more accurate forecasts may be one way to achieve that objective. However, if the investment required to improve accuracy significantly is very high, then alternative approaches to improving customer service, such as carrying higher inventory levels, should be considered. The resulting strategy for improving customer service will then be based on sound business analysis.

Measuring and tracking accuracy will ultimately help build confidence in the forecasting process. As the users realize mechanisms are in place to identify and eliminate sources of error, they will probably use the primary forecast developed to support all operations in the company. Islands of analysis will begin to disappear, and the organization will be able to assess the financial return from forecasting management improvements.

As we work with companies, many of them come to realize what a profound impact these seven keys can have on their sales forecasting practices. As they improve those practices, they experience reductions in costs and increases in customer and employee satisfaction. Costs decline in inventory levels, raw materials, production, logistics, and transportation. Greater customer satisfaction accrues from more accurately anticipating demand and, subsequently, fulfilling that demand more often. Greater employee satisfaction comes from a more understandable process, easier information access and transfer, and explicit rewards tied to performance. But the first step any company must take before realizing these benefits is to recognize the importance of sales forecasting as a management function. With this recognition comes a willingness to commit the necessary resources to improving this critical process.

References

Kenneth B. Kahn and John T. Mentzer, "The Impact of Team-Based Forecasting," *Journal of Business Forecasting*, Summer 1994, pp. 18-21.

Kenneth B. Kahn and John T. Mentzer, "Forecasting in Consumer and Business Markets," *Journal of Business Forecasting*, Summer 1995, pp. 21-28.

John T. Mentzer and Carol C. Bienstock, *Sales Forecasting Management* (Thousand Oaks, CA: Sage Publications, 1998).

John T. Mentzer and James E. Cox, Jr., "A Model of the Determinants of Achieved Forecast Accuracy," *Journal of Business Logistics, 5*, 2 (1984a): 143-155.

John T. Mentzer and James E. Cox, Jr., "Familiarity, Application, and Performance of Sales Forecasting Techniques," *Journal of Forecasting, 3* (1984b): 27-36.

John T. Mentzer and Kenneth B. Kahn, "Forecasting Technique Familiarity, Satisfaction, Usage, and Application," *Journal of Forecasting, 14*, 5 (1995): 465-476.

John T. Mentzer and Kenneth B. Kahn, "The State of Sales Forecasting Systems in Corporate America," *Journal of Business Forecasting*, Spring 1997, pp. 6-13.

John T. Mentzer, Kenneth B. Kahn, and Carol C. Bienstock, "Sales Forecasting Benchmarking Study," Research Report No. 3560–ROI–1445-99-004-96, University of Tennessee, Knoxville, 1996.

John T. Mentzer and Jon Schroeter, "Multiple Forecasting System at Brake Parts, Inc.," *Journal of Business Forecasting*, Fall 1993, pp. 5-9.

Mark A. Moon is an assistant professor of marketing at the University of Tennessee, Knoxville, where **John T. Mentzer** holds the Harry J. and Vivienne R. Bruce Chair of Excellence in Business Policy and **Carlo D. Smith** is a research associate and doctoral candidate. **Michael S. Garver** is an assistant professor of marketing at Western Carolina University, Cullowhee, North Carolina.

Vitamin Efficiency

A demand forecasting system has helped Longs Drug Stores slash its inventory without running short.

BY AMY DOAN

WANDERING THE FLOOR OF THE 1995 Food Marketing Institute show in Chicago, Stephen Roath had plenty of worries and few expectations. The president of the $3.3 billion (sales) Longs Drug Stores chain had seen his margins raided by HMOs, insurance companies and Medicare. "We were all getting beat up," he says. Roath had attended the grocery industry's annual roundup for years. He thought he might return to his Walnut Creek, Calif. headquarters with a technology idea or, at least, some new ways to display Jell-O and spaghetti sauce.

To his surprise, he flew home with a plan that would save Longs $36 million a year.

At the Chicago show Roath, now 58, met Homer Dunn, also 58. Dunn, the founder of Nonstop Solutions, was pitching a service for cutting food distribution costs. Roath had heard about supply chain theory often enough; it's been around for decades and helps manufacturers plan factory schedules. Point-of-sale software crunches inventory numbers only after a sale has taken place. "Just-in-time inventory" had the right end in sight but was driven by manufacturers without much regard to customer behavior.

Dunn was pitching something more ambitious—"demand-chain science." It aims to cut costs by anticipating variations in customer behavior through statistical analysis. The goal is to produce a crystal ball of data showing the cheapest possible combination of how often to order stock,

how to ship it, and how much to carry on any day.

The computing power to analyze thousands of variables overnight was not available until the mid-1990s. Neither was Nonstop's secret sauce, a 46-page stack of formulas written by Hau Lee, the company's founding scientist and a Stanford University professor of business and engineering. Lee, 46, is a wizard of the "value chain"—the series of pit stops a product makes between the supplier and the buyer. He wrote the core algorithm in 1993, but refused to patent it so that competitors couldn't sneak a peek.

"It sees the future," he says. In a way, it does. Lee's black box incorporates more than 150 variables per product and can predict consumer demand out to 91 days with surprising accuracy. Its aim: free up some of the capital tied up in inventory and some of the labor tied up in restocking it.

Until recently, most drug chains combined educated guesswork with simpleminded purchasing software like Invision or IBM's Inforem. Longs used Invision in its distribution center and a custom inventory program in its stores but had to rely on dozens of manual order requests per store every day, which pulled pharmacists away from customers.

The old Longs system—not much different from the one set up in 1938 by the two founding brothers, Joseph and Thomas—encouraged pharmacists to spend lavishly on expensive drugs that collected dust. Their great-

est fear: empty shelves and unhappy patrons. "They all added zeros to orders to protect themselves," says Roath.

Pharmacists and buyers at the distribution center always had general knowledge about demand hills and valleys, like flu and allergy seasons, which they factored into orders to drugmakers. And they knew their top sellers. But they couldn't process all of the hundreds of variables at once, such as brand, dosage and bottle size, and often guessed wrong.

Dunn's counterintuitive suggestion was that Roath spend more money on shipping. By ordering drugs more frequently, Longs could more than earn back the higher transportation costs through inventory savings. Lowering inventory saves a retailer money two ways: in reduced demand for working capital and in reduced waste from stale inventory.

Roath was intrigued. In early 1996, he kicked in $100,000 for a $500,000 drug-channel study along with wholesalers McKesson HBOC and Bergen Brunswig. It suggested that if the Nonstop method were spread throughout the drug industry, nearly half of the $18 billion in capital tied up in the inventory demand chain would be liberated and put to better use.

In early 1997, Nonstop built secure Internet paths to pull data overnight from hundreds of Longs terminals in the western U.S. to 12 servers in Nonstop's cluttered San Francisco headquarters. Then analysts fed the algorithm two years of historical Longs inventory data. Included were things like seasonality, performance of different vendors, handling and transportation costs and order minimums.

The algorithms held out the hope that inventory could be cut without damaging Longs' enviable availability level—the 99% frequency with which shoppers walk out with exactly what they want. The Nonstop algorithm analyzed the sales patterns of each drug by retail location, and also the demand trends of all 362 retail stores. The hypothetical results were striking: Inventory at the distribution center in Ontario, Calif. could be reduced by 57% from an average 25 days; at the stores, a 37% cut from an average of 39 days. The potential savings was $56 million in working capital and several million in reduced financing and ordering costs, net of additional shipping costs.

Longs rolled out the program to the distribution center and retail stores beginning in the fourth quar-

Longs pharmacists lived in fear of empty shelves and unhappy patrons. "They were all adding zeros to orders to protect themselves."

ter of 1997 at an initial cost of about $200,000. But theorizing about the payoff was easier than telling 1,566 Longs employees—pharmacists, pharmacy technicians, cashiers, warehouse pickers and packers, the computer team—about how their jobs would be directly affected by the changes.

"We were scared," says replenishment buyer Susan Hunsinger, now in her tenth year with the chain. Her desk at the Ontario, Calif. warehouse is one of Longs' pressure points; she takes the heat when she can't fill store orders, and gets chewed out by management when she orders too much.

Hunsinger had been keeping a month's stock on hand and ordering from manufacturers twice a week. Lee's algorithm was asking her to pare down to only a week's supply but to order several times a week. Certain she'd run out of stock, she hunkered down for the worst.

Roath and Dunn rallied employee support by presenting the likely financial benefits of the system. It didn't hurt that 55% of Longs employees are shareholders. Still, Roath and Dunn rolled out the new system gradually.

In December 1997 Nonstop switched on its service at the warehouse. A few products from Upjohn made the transition first. Turnover of the antianxiety drug Xanax, which used to sit in the warehouse an average of 26 days, plunged to 6.7 days after seven weeks, and 100% of requests for the product were still met. Capital freed up: $15,210. Four months later every

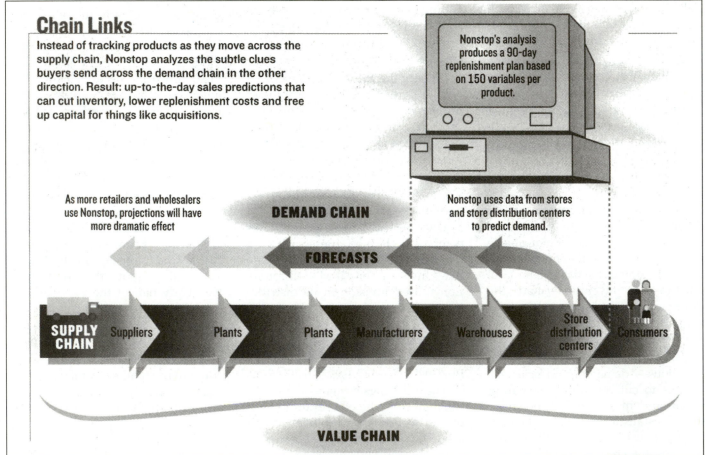

Chain Links

Instead of tracking products as they move across the supply chain, Nonstop analyzes the subtle clues buyers send across the demand chain in the other direction. Result: up-to-the-day sales predictions that can cut inventory, lower replenishment costs and free up capital for things like acquisitions.

Nonstop's analysis produces a 90-day replenishment plan based on 150 variables per product.

As more retailers and wholesalers use Nonstop, projections will have more dramatic effect

DEMAND CHAIN

Nonstop uses data from stores and store distribution centers to predict demand.

FORECASTS

SUPPLY CHAIN · Suppliers · Plants · Plants · Manufacturers · Warehouses · Store distribution centers · Consumers

VALUE CHAIN

LISA KNOUSE BRAIMAN

drug in the warehouse was running under the Nonstop program.

Today, you can see the changes at the 19,000-square-foot distribution center building. In the middle of a storage and shipping area protected by barbed wire, a U-shaped conveyer is used for picking and packing drugs. The 12-foot-high shelves surrounding the conveyer were once crammed to the rafters with extra inventory; now dozens are empty, and the company is working with Nonstop to determine which additional brands to carry in the extra space.

Dozens of boxes each day now go directly on the picking rack, meaning they're shipped to stores the same day they arrive from manufacturers. That rarely happened before—orders would sit on warehouse shelves for months, even a year, before being trucked to retail locations. Since they're not on the phone trying to predict demand all day, buyers have more time to haggle with suppliers like Merck and Pfizer, says the once-hesitant Hunsinger.

Retail stores were converted more slowly—from mid-1997 to late 1998—because more people were affected. Here, too, you can discern a big difference. Pharmacist Peter Kim, who once stalked the aisles with a clipboard for hours each day, now spends 15 minutes four times a week eyeballing the inventory that arrives auto-

matically. He rarely has to tweak orders; there have been no nasty surprises since the system was turned on. He has more time to devote to customers. "I got into pharmacy so I could explain side effects from Parkinson's scrips to a 70-year-old patient, not play small-business owner," he says.

Each morning, pharmacy managers get Nonstop's 90-day forecast and a detailed report on the day's stock levels and shipments. Every two weeks, they also get a top-ten list of how much money they can save by sending unneeded drugs back to the manufacturer.

For example, Kim's Fremont, Calif. store got a report in August that showed nobody had bought the birth control pill Tri-Levlen 21 in more than 180 days; returning 7 units would save the company $462. There were 19 extra Synarel Nasal Sprays; sending them back would save $700.

Kim is now working with other pharmacy managers on in-store cholesterol screenings. To implement the program before Nonstop, he would have had to hire more pharmacists. Now he has the time himself, because he isn't taking stock all day long.

The improvements at the stores are not yet as dramatic as at the warehouse level or the 37% reduc-

"I got into pharmacy so I could explain side effects from Parkinson's scrips, not play small-business owner."

tion Nonstop had projected; it's closer to 26%. Not everyone follows the top-ten lists, admits Dunn. But Roath isn't complaining. The stores have already saved $30 million, about half the projected total.

Longs says the Nonstop system has so far freed up $60 million in capital. It has put that money to good use, acquiring the 20-store Powell, Ohio-based Drug Emporium chain in July 1998 and 38 West Coast Rite Aid stores in September. They're due for a makeover via Nonstop since Rite Aid's inventory is among the most bloated in the industry, says Warburg Dillon Read analyst Steven Valiquette.

Roath recently signed a five-year contract with Dunn to continue the pharmacy service and spread it to nondrug items in the front of the store. Longs had been paying Nonstop a monthly fee of about $100,000; now the consulting firm gets paid only if it keeps cutting Longs' costs. The easy savings have been made, but the potential gains are not exhausted.

There are, of course, other software firms selling systems to handle inventory, and there is nothing to stop a drug chain from developing its own, as Walgreen Co. has done (FORBES, Oct. 18). Perhaps the ideal of a 50% reduction in the drugstore industry's inventory is not achievable, says Roath, but surely $7 billion can be stripped away if every drug chain and wholesaler uses a method like Nonstop's.

Roath is now Nonstop's best evangelist. He sent letters to rivals CVS, Eckerd and Walgreen, singing its praises. "They must think I get a referral, but I don't," he grins.

Taking Stock

Virtually any industry with a continuous flow of goods is tying up hundreds of billions of dollars every year by ordering and storing too much product too soon.

Industry	CURRENT		PROJECTED	
	Capital in finished goods ($bil)	Days of inventory	Days of inventory[1]	Capital freed up in first year ($bil)
Pharmaceutical	$18	70	42	$4.3
Packaged grocery	25	40	28	7.4
Auto parts	16	140	81	6.8

[1]End of 12 months with Nonstop.
Estimates for retail and wholesale goods.
Sources: National Wholesale Druggists' Association; Progressive Grocer Research/Trade Dimensions; Automotive Parts & Accessories Association; company annual reports; Nonstop Solutions analysis.

Unit 5

Unit Selections

25. **Not All Projections Bad for Overgrown Theater Chains,** Claudia Eller and James Bates
26. **State Declares First Stage 3 Power Alert,** Nancy Rivera Brooks and Nancy Vogel
27. **Changes in Performance Measures on the Factory Floor,** Robert F. Marsh and Jack R. Meredith
28. **Using Queueing Network Models to Set Lot-Sizing Policies for Printed Circuit Board Assembly Operations,** Maged M. Dessouky
29. **A New Route for Boeing's Latest Model,** Peter Pae

Key Points to Consider

❖ How are the decisions presented in this unit interrelated?

❖ If a firm is seeking to build a new factory in the United States, how should it select a location?

❖ What are the consequences of too little or too much capacity?

 **Links**   **www.dushkin.com/online/**

28. **Manufacturers Information Net**
   http://mfginfo.com/newhome2.htm
29. **Warwick Business School—Focus on Research**
   http://users.wbs.ac.uk/om/research/
30. **TWIGG's Operations Management Index (TOMI)**
   http://members.tripod.co.uk/tomi/index.html

These sites are annotated on pages 4 and 5.

Once a firm has identified its sales forecast and product design, it can turn its attention to other critical decisions in the operations/production area: capacity, location, logistics, and layout planning. These decisions are interrelated and require careful consideration.

Capacity planning involves an examination of the maximum output of a system in a given period. Economists recommend an analysis of short-run average cost curves for different levels of production. From these short-run average cost curves, a long-run average cost curve can be developed. The lowest point on the long-run average cost curve would indicate economies of scale and the most efficient quantity of production. Firms seek a high level of capacity utilization and face choices when capacity utilization is too low (selling equipment, subcontracting, reducing staffing) or when capacity utilization is too high (need for a subcontractor, expanding capacity, raising prices). In capacity planning, firms must also consider the seasonality of demand and attempt to level out production.

The location decision is important for both manufacturers and service organizations. Today firms have options to locate throughout the world. Most firms go through a sequence of deciding upon the country, deciding upon the region/community, and then an actual site decision. Factors such as proximity to markets, proximity to suppliers, labor productivity, exchange rates, costs, government incentives, and economic/political/social stability are among those that are considered.

The object of transportation planning is to have the right quantity of the right item, at the right place, at the right time, with minimum transportation cost. Various quantitative techniques have been developed to model transportation decisions. The major transportation techniques include the northwest-corner, the Vogel approximation, and the stepping-stone methods. These techniques aim at meeting customer requirements through minimal cost logistics. These techniques also permit analysis of situations where requirements exceed capacity or where requirements are below capacity.

The layout decision is also of great importance to a firm. Layout planning can aid with higher utilization of space, improved customer service, improved flow of information, materials, people, reduced time use, and reduced fatigue. The major

types of layout are fixed-position, process-oriented, product-oriented, or hybrid. With a fixed-position layout, the customer or item worked on stays in one fixed place (dentist's office or a ship). With a process-oriented layout, machines and workers are grouped together by process performed (i.e., receiving, assembly, finishing, administrative offices). With a product-oriented layout there is a grouping around products or families of similar high volume or low variety. For many firms, a combination, or hybrid, approach is used for layout.

The articles in this unit present illustrations of company approaches to capacity, location, logistics, and layout planning. As the articles point out, these decisions are often interrelated.

Capacity, Location, Logistics, and Layout Planning

Not All Projections Bad for Overgrown Theater Chains

By CLAUDIA ELLER and JAMES BATES

Movie theater chains have a lot more to worry about than whether patrons will buy stale popcorn, and that's not likely to change for at least a couple of years.

The continued shakeout gripping exhibitors caused largely by gross overbuilding will get worse before it gets better. The financial strains on the circuits could well lead to more bankruptcy filings. Already skittish lenders have tightened the spigot on funds.

This summer, **United Artists, Carmike Cinemas, Edwards Cinemas** and **Silver Cinemas**, which owns the Landmark art house theaters, have filed Chapter 11 bankruptcy petitions. A slew of other major circuits, including **Regal Cinemas, Sony** Corp.-controlled Loews Cineplex and **AMC** have seen widening losses. Movie theater stocks are about as popular with investors as "The Adventures of Rocky and Bullwinkle" was with summer moviegoers.

The result of the upheaval isn't all bad news, however. Industry leaders expect a much-needed consolidation to create a healthier business for the survivors.

Some major chains might merge, perhaps even the long-rumored combination of AMC and Loews. Expensive leases will be renegotiated, and obsolete, unprofitable theaters will be shuttered.

"All this turmoil is going to save the business," says Tom Sherak, chairman of 20th Century Fox's Domestic Film Group. "Exhibitors are not going out of business; they're looking for protection under the law to redesign their businesses."

Already, savvy investors such as Denver billionaire Philip Anschutz, whose investment group is taking control of the UA circuit; are seizing the opportunity.

Despite this summer's downturn in box-office revenues and attendance, people haven't stopped driving to theaters to see movies on the big screen.

"I think in the long term, exhibition is a very viable business because there is nothing

Too Many Theaters

Moviegoing has failed to keep up with the frenzied building of movie theaters across the nation. To survive, exhibitors are forced to close older, unprofitable theaters and increasingly run for bankruptcy cover.

WE ARE CLOSED

Robert Lachman/Los Angeles Times

An Edwards theater in Stanton the day that the bankruptcy filing was announced.

Since 1980, U.S. movie ticket sales have increased only 43% ...

Ticket sales in billions

1980: 1.02 billion tickets sold

1999: 1.47 billion tickets sold

'80 '81 '82 '83 '84 '85 '86 '87 '88 '89 '90 '91 '92 '93 '94 '95 '96 '97 '98 '99

... while the number of screens in the country has more than doubled.

1980: 17,675 U.S. screens

1999: 37,185 U.S. screens

'80 '81 '82 '83 '84 '85 '86 '87 '88 '89 '90 '91 '92 '93 '94 '95 '96 '97 '98 '99

Sources: National Assn. of Theater Owners, Motion Picture Assn. of America

more fundamental to the world of entertainment than going to the movies," says Shari Redstone, president of the closely held Boston-based circuit **National Amusements,** parent of Viacom Inc.

The rash of bankruptcy filings is in part a legal maneuver by exhibitors to break leases on unprofitable theaters they want to close. A spruced-up operation opens the door for suitors such as Anschutz to resurrect the company.

"He's the guy in white tie and tails at the fire sale," says Ted Shugrue, president of Loews Cineplex International.

Not all chains are on the ropes financially. National Amusements and Century Theatres in Northern California—both old-line, family-run businesses—say they are highly profitable, having avoided the pitfalls that tripped up many of their competitors.

These circuits were able to expand their businesses in the last five years without getting caught up in the megaplex building frenzy that began in the mid-1990s and left many theater operators saddled with massive debt and mounting losses.

"We have taken a very long-term strategic approach to the business," says Redstone, the 46-year-old daughter of Viacom's high-profile chief, Sumner Redstone. In 1936, her grandfather Michael Redstone founded the theater company, which today operates more than 1,350 screens in the United States, Britain and Latin America.

"When we looked at new markets, we always built in superior locations where we had access to all the product . . . and if it didn't make sense to build, we didn't build," Redstone says.

By building multiplexes too close together, aggressive exhibitors have cannibalized their own and one another's businesses. They also took on a lot of debt to build, putting themselves in precarious financial positions.

National Amusements, unlike most exhibitors, has the advantage of owning most of the real estate under its theaters, so it's not bound by burdensome leases. A lot of the troubled theater chains locked themselves into high rents in fancy new malls the last few years as landlords played competing exhibitors against each other.

This summer, admissions and box office were down from a year ago, largely because Hollywood didn't produce the same number of megahits it did during last summer's record-setting season.

And, even in the best of times, movie theaters are a slow-growth, mature business. There's only so much you can charge for a movie ticket or a box of Milk Duds. Studios get a bigger cut of the box office in the first weeks of a film's run. So, in an era when a lot of movies do the bulk of their business in the first two or three weeks and often don't have the "legs" to play longer, exhibitors get hurt.

So, what makes the movie theater business worth the risk?

Conservatively run, it's a cash cow. Century has doubled its business in the last five years, says Raymond Syufy, chief executive of the San Rafael-based company, which has more than 700 screens primarily concentrated in Northern California and other Western states.

Syufy declined to divulge the privately held company's margins, but noted, "I'd say 95% of our theaters are making money."

The exhibitors who got into trouble, suggests Syufy, are those who put all their efforts into building rather than operating and managing their existing theaters.

Syufy and Redstone concur that exhibition is fundamentally sound, and although it's a slow-growth business, it can be a cash cow.

"If you build the right number of theaters in the right locations for the right amount of money and operate them properly, you can make a lot of money," says Syufy.

Some exhibitors point a finger at Hollywood, blaming a lackluster box office and decreased attendance for their financial woes. Loews' Shugrue, a former studio executive himself, says Hollywood's strategy of releasing huge numbers of film prints to generate instant box-office results means more money for Hollywood and less for movie theaters.

But Syufy says that's a cop-out.

"Hollywood is not to blame. Over the last 15 years, the business has neither declined nor increased more than about 5%. If exhibitors cannot find a way to be profitable when the business is flat or down 5%, that is not Hollywood's problem. We need to look at our cost structures and balance sheet and have to protect our downside in a mature market."

State Declares First Stage 3 Power Alert

•Electricity: Exports are curtailed, other steps taken as reserves drop to just 1.5%. Officials expect further problems.

By NANCY RIVERA BROOKS and NANCY VOGEL
TIMES STAFF WRITERS

California's energy nightmare nearly came true Thursday as the strained electricity grid almost ran out of juice, threatening blackouts across the state.

Officials declared California's first-ever Stage 3 power emergency at 5:15 p.m. because the transmission grid serving about three-quarters of the state was projected to dip into its last 1.5% of reserves. The emergency order was lifted about two hours later.

But the California Independent System Operator, the Folsom-based nonprofit agency that balances supply and demand on the state's 12,500 miles of transmission wires, was able to avoid ordering rolling blackouts across the state.

That's because the Stage 3 emergency declaration permitted Cal-ISO to bring back some power that was being exported out of state and allowed two government-controlled power entities to free up enough electricity to help keep the lights on.

"There apparently won't be any blackouts," Steve Maviglio, a spokesman for Gov. Gray Davis, said late Thursday. "Over the next two weeks, it will be day by day, night by night. It's all hands on deck. We're doing the best we can."

Customers of the Los Angeles Department of Water and Power and many other, smaller municipal utilities around the state are largely unaffected by the electricity problems because they are not connected to the Cal-ISO grid.

This is just the latest extraordinary twist in the unfolding energy soap opera that has captured much of California as both the electricity and natural gas markets continue to behave in ways unforeseen when they were deregulated, producing threats of shortages and sky-high prices.

More Calls for Reform Expected

The day's events are sure to intensify calls for reform of both the electricity and natural gas businesses.

On Thursday:

• Electricity demand in California peaked at nearly 32,000 megawatts while power plants that could generate about a third of that sat idle for maintenance and other reasons. Frantic calls for conservation, including asking Californians to delay turning on holiday lights until after 8 p.m., were followed by voluntary

California on Alert

Thursday's first-ever Stage 3 alert stopped short of blackouts but represented the most dramatic development yet in California's continuing power crisis. The alert affected the 75% of the state served by the three big investor-owned utilities—Southern California Edison, Pacific Gas & Electric and San Diego Gas & Electric.

Three Main Utility Providers in California

Many municipalities, including Los Angeles, were unaffected Thursday, as they are served by their own utilities.

Sacramento

San Francisco

Pacific Gas & Electric Co.

Southern California Edison Co.

San Diego Gas & Electric Co.

Los Angeles

Sources: California Energy Commission, utility companies

Power Alerts

The California Independent System Operator, which runs the electricity grid for most of the state's power users, has declared 42 Stage 1 and 25 Stage 2 power emergencies this year. How the system works:

STAGE 1

Conservation. Declared when electricity operating reserves fall below 7%. The state's three big utilities are asked to urge businesses and consumers to conserve power by doing such things as turning off unneeded lights, machinery and appliances, setting thermostats at 68 degrees or even turning on holiday lights later in the evening.

STAGE 2

Voluntary power cuts. Declared when electricity reserves fall below 5%. Utilities ordered to cut power to residential air-conditioner customers and businesses that have agreed to voluntary power interruptions in exchange for discount rates.

STAGE 3

Rolling blackouts. Declared when electricity reserves fall below 1.5%. Utilities ordered to reduce power immediately, and rotating power outages become likely. Only essential power users—hospitals without backup generators, police and fire stations—are exempted from the blackouts, which would be scattered across the utilities' territories and typically last about an hour.

LORENA IÑIGUEZ/Los Angeles Times

power interruptions to thousands of large commercial electricity users and, finally, the Stage 3 emergency declaration.

- Natural gas prices in Southern California hit a record $50 per million British thermal units, the standard measure for large trades, and San Diego Gas & Electric asked federal regulators to cap pipeline transmission rates to the state, which are 21 times higher than normal.

- SDG&E requested that Gov. Davis declare an energy state of emergency to help increase electricity supplies in the state.

The San Diego utility, a unit of Sempra Energy, asked Davis to then lift air pollution limits on power plants so they can run when supplies are tightest, to require in-state generators to sell their electricity within the state, and to pledge the state's credit to back Cal-ISO's power purchases.

Although California avoided blackouts, the state is not out of the woods, said Jim Detmers, managing director of operations at Cal-ISO.

"Tomorrow will be just like what we dealt with today," he said Thursday night. Monday may be the worst day of all, he said.

For the last four days, California's power grid has teetered near the edge of collapse because growing demand has exceeded supply.

Power plants in the state representing more than 11,000 megawatts of generation were out of commission for maintenance, shutdowns caused by operational problems, or because the plants had reached their air pollution limits for the year. Pollution constraints alone accounted for about 2,700 megawatts of unavailable power, Cal-ISO said.

In addition, cold weather and low hydroelectric supplies in the Pacific Northwest sharply limited the kind of power imports that helped prevent blackouts during the summer, Cal-ISO said. Imports from the Northwest totaled only 800 megawatts Thursday, compared with a normal 3,000 or so.

A Stage 2 power emergency was declared at 4 a.m. Thursday, and Cal-ISO scrambled to find enough electricity to avoid rotating power outages. Thursday marked the 25th time this year that a Stage 2 emergency was declared, and hundreds of businesses were asked to shut off their power. These large electricity users had agreed in advance to cut power when supplies are tight in exchange for lower rates.

When a Stage 3 is declared, rolling blackouts might be ordered to keep the grid from collapsing.

Detmers said he worries about blackouts during evening rush hour because even traffic lights and street lights would be affected—adding that Cal-ISO employees took extraordinary measures to keep that from happening.

"That is the time when everyone is getting home from work. It's dark and foggy," he said. "The last thing I want is some bus going through an intersection and getting hit. How will I explain myself to parents?"

After the Stage 3 declaration, Davis ordered the California Department of Water Resources to free 1,000 megawatts of power by shifting the pumping of water through the massive state aqueduct system to daytime periods when electricity use is lower—but only 200 megawatts were needed Thursday. The state also took the symbolic step of keeping the lights off on the Christmas tree at the Capitol. In addition, the Western Area Power Administration, which markets hydroelectric power from 56 federal dams, was able to send 500 megawatts to bail out California because of the Stage 3 order. Cal-ISO wrung another 250 megawatts out of the system by blocking some power exports out of the state. (A megawatt is enough to serve about 1,000 homes.)

Consumer advocate Doug Heller of the Foundation for Taxpayer and Consumer Rights said the governor needs to step in and take over the state's privately operated power plants and get them running.

"This deregulated market is getting dangerously out of hand," Heller said.

Said Davis spokesman Maviglio: "The governor said California is not yet ready for deregulation. This is another example."

Complications in the Market

Cal-ISO's electron hunt was further complicated Wednesday and Thursday when Powerex, the electricity marketing subsidiary of BC Hydro, British Columbia's electricity utility, refused to sell power directly to Cal-ISO.

Powerex advised the agency that it had reached its credit limits with the relatively small power marketing company, according to a letter sent by Cal-ISO Chief Executive Terry Winter to Steve Frank, chief executive of Southern California Edison.

Powerex would sell power, at $1,000 per megawatt-hour, only if Cal-ISO were to obtain a letter of credit or if an investor-owned utility bought the power, Winter said. Cal-ISO's legal mandate is to maintain system reliability at any cost.

"This letter will confirm that the ISO believes that it is absolutely necessary that this power be secured from Powerex, at least for the next two days, that we do not believe that there are any other resources available that could satisfy this urgent need for power (this appears to be the last available resource that could meet the need), and that we see no other way to address the severe reliability need that we currently face, short of rotating blackouts," Winter wrote.

The $1,000-per-megawatt-hour price—four times the usual maximum price in the California market—was "the best price that we have been able to negotiate for this power," he said in the letter.

SCE agreed to buy the power for $10 million Wednesday and $13 million Thursday, spokesman Clarence Brown said.

"We elected to jump into the breach," Frank said. "Obviously, this is not the kind of thing we would want to do on a regular basis, but it is most indicative of what we have been saying for a long time: that having strong utilities to serve the needs of the state is a good thing."

SCE, the utility arm of Rosemead-based Edison International, has used that argument with the California Public Utilities Commission to push for an end to the current retail rate freeze. The utility further seeks rate increases to pay down its nearly $3-billion debt arising from six months of record high wholesale power costs that it cannot pass on to customers.

PUC President Loretta Lynch on Thursday turned aside those requests, and similar ones by Pacific Gas & Electric, calling them "premature."

Cal-ISO Chief Financial Officer Bill Regan said the Powerex situation did not indicate a fundamental problem with his agency's credit worthiness.

Instead, he said, it reflected Powerex's desire to limit its sales to one client, especially because it takes Cal-ISO about 10 weeks to pay its power bills after obtaining the funds from market participants, largely SCE, PG&E and SDG&E.

Powerex declined to comment on the matter.

PG&E was approached by Cal-ISO to buy electricity from Powerex but declined, spokesman Ron Low said.

"We are very concerned that the ISO, in an effort to keep the lights on, is paying ransom to the out-of-state generators," Low said. "The ISO needs to be more disciplined in its purchase of power because these outrageous wholesale costs will ultimately be paid by our customers."

The Procdures to Reduce Use

In a Stage 3, if blackouts are needed, Cal-ISO tells SCE and the other utilities how many megawatts of power each needs to dump off the system involuntarily through rolling outages to keep system reserves between 1.5% and 5%.

If this is not done, there is an immediate risk that large portions of the power grid could fail, which would be more widespread than the rolling outages and would take longer—probably hours—to bring back online.

Each block of customers selected would lose power for about an hour, and then their power would be restored while another block of customers would lose their power. The blackouts would continue until the crisis is over.

On June 14, voltage problems in the San Francisco Bay Area led to rotating blackouts of about 90,000 customers. The incident lasted about three hours.

In its Stage 3 plan, SCE has grouped customer circuits in such a way that the outages are scattered over a wide area. That way, no single community would be completely blacked out.

Only "nonessential" users would be blacked out. Considered essential are customers such as hospitals without backup power, police stations and fire stations. (Homes that are very near essential users, and therefore on the same circuit, also would avoid the blackouts.)

The utilities are given as little as 10 minutes to institute the blackouts, which does not allow time to notify customers individually. The only warning they would get would come from the media, particularly news radio stations.

Times staff writers Dan Morain and Liz Pulliam Weston contributed to this report.

CHANGES IN PERFORMANCE MEASURES ON THE FACTORY FLOOR

ROBERT F. MARSH

School of Business Administration, University of Wisconsin-Milwaukee, Milwaukee, WI 53201

JACK R. MEREDITH

Babcock Grad. School of Management, Wake Forest University, Winston-Salem, NC 27109

As a management method, cellular manufacturing (CM) continues to gain acceptance. The reasons are obvious; CM reduces work-in-process (WIP) inventory levels and correspondingly reduces lead times. Not coincidentally, many companies have recently shifted focus to compete on time-based parameters, like lead time. Also, the Just-in-Time (JIT) management philosophy of reducing waste (and thus WIP) is naturally complemented by CM practices on the floor.

Essentially, CM involves finding repetitive procedures in an otherwise random set and then performing that work in a more efficient manner. In terms more congenial to manufacturing, it is moving some production from a job shop to a line process design, or moving down the diagonal in Hayes and Wheelwright's product/process matrix [2] to gain efficiency. Customization is sacrificed, but only for a portion of the work load. And for many companies, the commitment to customization was never needed and was just another form of waste. Thus, CM often leads to lower costs and higher productivity than previously realized in job shops.

These two factors are the impetus for cells: lower costs and shorter lead times. If a company's management measures performance according to its objectives, cost and lead-time measures should be found in most cases of cell implementation. It might also be expected that data on these measures may have been kept prior to cells.

The objective of this study is to compare how management measures performance both before and after the move to cells. As the saying goes, "what gets measured gets done." On the other hand, in *The Goal* [1], we learn that activation and utilization are not synonymous. Therefore measuring something doesn't necessarily mean that it is important. This study also investigates what performance measures management is evaluated on both before and after cells. Finally, we examine the relationships between measures and methods. For example, does the use of JIT correlate with measures of lead time or WIP levels?

METHODOLOGY

To answer these questions, a survey was designed and administered to managers from 42 companies, all but three from the Midwest. All companies were involved in metal machining and held Standard Industrial Classifications (SIC) beginning with 34 or 35. All had operated cells for at least one year. Table 1 shows the year CM started and Table 2 classifies the size of the 42 companies. Most of these firms had assembly operations in the same plant as fabrication, but most of the part fabrication took place in cells (as indicated in Table 3).

When possible, surveys were conducted in conjunction with a plant trip. This improved the reliability of the responses and even led to some data modifications. It was occasionally found that rater bias factored into questions concerning the application of current management techniques and collection of data. For example, most managers considered their firm to be an advocate of JIT, yet the preponderance of evidence (inventory) suggested otherwise. Further questioning usually resolved such issues. Elsewhere, managers would indicate quality was maintained using control charts. If the manager could not show evidence of charts, the measure was not counted.

Measures varied greatly from plant to plant and some of that variation was attributable to the specific product or process. Quality, for example, was sometimes measured as amount of scrap, percentage of good pieces, number of rework hours, customer satisfaction, etc. For simplicity, performance measures were categorized into nine different types: productivity, quality, inventory, lead time, preventive maintenance, schedule performance, utilization, cell completeness, and other costs. This classification sufficiently covered the data collected from the 42 companies without creating discrepancies in the assignment of measures to categories. Managers from two firms mentioned a safety-based measure but the authors did not consider this related to manufacturing performance. Although important, some form of safety measure is required of all companies. An argument can be made that WIP levels (inventory) and lead time are inversely related [4] and therefore one of these

TABLE 1: Beginning of Implementation

Year Cells Started	Percentage
1994	5
1993	5
1992	7
1991	5
1990	10
1989	21
1988	17
1987	5
1986	17
1985	7
Pre-1985	2

categories is redundant, but since the managerial objective differs, i.e., cost versus time, the categories were not merged.

PERFORMANCE MEASURES VERSUS PLANT DEMOGRAPHICS

As companies grew in their experience with cells, performance measures generally became more refined. It often occurred that many measures were kept to validate the conversion to cells but some fell out of date as time went on. Three of the most experienced cell users only tracked one performance measure. The size of the plant (small, medium, large) didn't correlate with the number of performance measures kept, although it did relate to the progress toward converting to cells. Production at all five of the small plants in this study was between 91% to 100% in cells, while almost half of the large plants had less than 50% of production in cells. More than half of the plants in the study indicated that conversion to cells was ongoing. There was no significant correlation between plant size, CM experience, or percent of production in cells and the type of performance measure.

TABLE 2: Plant Size

Size of Plant (sales)	Percentage
Small (less than $50 million in annual sales)	12
Medium (between $50 and $250 million)	57
Large (greater than $250 million)	31

TABLE 3: Production Completed in Cells

Portion of Production in Cells	Percentage of Plants
91%–100%	50
81%–90%	14
50%–80%	14
Under 50%	21

PERFORMANCE MEASURES BEFORE AND AFTER CM

The first observation from the comparison of before and after CM was that the number of performance measures increased after the conversion to cells, from an average of 2.7 to 4.3. Table 4 summarizes how performance was measured in these 42 plants before and after the implementation of cells. The greatest beneficiary of this increase was in the quality area, with inventory and lead time close behind. The tremendous improvement in these latter two areas after the conversion to cells was definitely related to their measures. In many companies, the tracking of lead time led to improvements in the marketing of products. The shorter and more stable lead times meant increased sales and decreased delinquencies. A few companies even dropped schedule performance measures in lieu of tracking lead time.

The most common inventory measure was the number of times inventory was turned each year. In many cases, JIT and CM were undertaken simultaneously and the reduced WIP was used to justify the conversion expense. Tracking WIP or turns then became a gauge of how well the conversion went and a tool for continuously improving the velocity of material throughout the plant.

Similar to the schedule performance and lead-time relationship, a drop in the use of productivity-based measures coincided with the increase in measuring turns. The managers indicated a preference for the latter because it more accurately assessed costs. Most of the productivity measures centered on direct labor, a much smaller portion of total costs than materials (5% to 15% versus 40% to 60%). These same managers also felt more in control of inventory levels than work-force levels.

The increase in quality-related performance measures is not as easily explainable. Many companies did adopt quality improvement programs in conjunction with CM, but many others already had the programs in place. Anecdotal evidence from managers' comments indicates that tools to collect data on quality have become more affordable and understandable in recent years. The underlying issue here is the fundamental change in how management treated performance data. Fully 79% of these 42 companies posted results for all employees to see. No definitive data was collected to determine how this has changed over time but many managers implied that posting was relatively new and growing. The message from virtually every new manufacturing improvement program included more worker involvement in the process. Along with that, support functions like accounting and management information systems are using tools like activity-based costing (ABC) and the personal computer to improve the reliability and accessibility of performance data. Openness in the workplace and the ability to compress volumes of data probably explain the increased emphasis on tracking quality performance.

The other changes in measures are understandable. Total preventive maintenance (TPM) programs are frequently adopted by CM and JIT users. The reduction in WIP means less buffer inventory so machines must keep running. Maintenance measures like time spent on PM and downtime show an understanding of TPM significance and a commitment to practice it. Utilization was only tracked by one company that extensively used computer numerically controlled (CNC) equipment, and they mentioned it might be abandoned in the future. Cell completeness was a meaningless measure before cells. Some of the "other costs" measures concerned setup time, depreciation, and budget performance.

TABLE 4: Measuring Operating Performance

Type of Measure	Before Cells (%)	After Cells (%)
Productivity measures	93	79
Quality measures	33	93
Inventory measures	24	74
Lead-time measures	31	64
Preventive maintenance	5	24
Schedule performance	81	71
Utilization	2	2
Cell completeness	0	5
Other costs	7	21

PERFORMANCE OF MANAGEMENT MEASURES

As indicated, there was a new openness among managers to share performance data with all employees, and this might be partially responsible for the increase in measures kept. But do all of these measures reflect what is actually important to the company? Are managers evaluated on the same performance criteria they measure? Indirectly, the question being asked is: Have company objectives changed since the adoption of CM? This assumes that objectives have been communicated throughout the company and management understands it must operationalize these objectives into performance measures for feedback purposes.

Productivity and schedule performance were the most common measures upon which managers said they were evaluated, with no other measure coming close (Table 5). Little has changed here over time because these same two categories finished first and second before CM; in fact, 52% of managers indicated their evaluation criteria did not change. Interestingly, many companies still consider the comparison of standard to actual labor times (usually referred to as "efficiency") as the most important indicator of improvement even though labor may only be 5% of the cost of goods sold. As noted before when tracking general manufacturing performance, there was a slight drop-off in the significance of productivity and schedule performance with the conversion to cells, replaced by an increase in quality, inventory, and lead-time measures. This increase can logically be attributed to the 48% of companies that did change their management evaluation measures and probably indicates a strategic change in direction facilitated by shorter lead times and better quality.

Comparing the "after implementation" columns of Tables 4 and 5 gives the impression that many of the performance measures being tracked are of little significance in either evaluating the managers or steering the company toward its objectives. Although productivity and schedule performance measures held steady, the other categories appear to be kept for show by many companies. Quality and inventory measures drop significantly when it comes to evaluating managers. So why are they even tracked? A few managers said the measures started as part of the conversion and justification of JIT or CM and were never abandoned. Also stated was, "The employees like to see how they are doing in these areas so we keep it (data collection) up as a motivational factor."

Another possible explanation for the divergence on quality is based upon Terry Hill's [3] description of *order qualifiers,* a competence that customers assume exists. In this case, all managers are assumed to be delivering quality. Managerial performance is thus differentiated on *order winners* like productivity and schedule measures.

Table 6 summarizes what percentage of the 42 companies in the sample are using some of the newer management methods. Seven such methods gaining acceptance in industry were studied: JIT, TPM, statistical quality control (SQC), setup reduction, concurrent engineering, work teams, and ABC. Self-directed work teams, used by 62% of the surveyed companies, were often responsible for the bulletin board's content, including the display of performance measures. Some managers gave the workers authority to collect data as long as they seemed relevant and were obtained at a reasonable expense. In two firms, work teams actually created a business plan containing a mission statement and planned objectives, so tracking performance became a matter of pride rather than a management manifesto.

MANAGEMENT METHODS AND PERFORMANCE MEASURES

There should be some correlation between management methods and performance measurement. To gauge the impact of these improvement programs on the manufacturing setting, a performance measure may be opera-

TABLE 5: Evaluation of Operations Managers

Type of Measure	Before Cells (%)	After Cells (%)
Productivity measures	93	79
Quality measures	26	43
Inventory measures	10	26
Lead-time measure	28	40
Preventive maintenance	0	10
Schedule performance	81	71
Utilization	0	0
Cell completeness	0	0
Other costs	5	10

TABLE 6: Management Methods Currently in Use

Management Method	Plants Using (%)
Just-in-Time	71
Total Preventive Maintenance	64
Statistical or Total Quality Control	93
Setup Reduction	43
Concurrent Engineering or Design for Manufacture	48
Work Teams	62
Activity-Based Costing	29

tionalized. For example, tracking rework or warranty costs would be a natural measure of success in implementing SQC. And the correlation was perfect for the case of SQC and quality-related measures; all companies using SQC measured quality.

JIT success can be measured in a variety of ways including WIP levels, inventory turns, lead times, and worker productivity. Of the 30 companies claiming to be JIT, 27 used an inventory measure, 23 used a lead-time measure, and 28 used a productivity measure. TPM is claimed to be practiced by 27 firms, yet only ten of those 27 kept track of a measure like machine uptime or percentage of TPM completed. The success of TPM could show up indirectly from increased productivity or quality, but the implementation of TPM probably did not result in adding a measure in one of these categories. Some managers viewed TPM as a necessary burden for a JIT environment. Therefore justification of this policy didn't require additional proof.

Shorter setups could show up in productivity, inventory, or lead-times measures. Of the 18 firms practicing single minute exchange of die (SMED) or similar setup reduction methods, 17 also measured productivity, 15 measured inventory, and 17 measured lead times. Not all companies employed setup reduction to the same degree. Many would only look at setups to improve capacity at a bottleneck operation. Anecdotally, those companies using setup reduction appeared to be shifting to time-based objectives and it was very common for these same firms to be using concurrent engineering (17 out of 18). As expected, all but one of the 20 users of concurrent engineering also measured lead times.

Employee work teams of various levels of control were found in 26 of the companies including all but two of the firms with more than 90% of production in cells. Again, no direct measure of success can be attributed to teams, but productivity is the likely beneficiary with many secondary scenarios likely. Of these 26 companies, 24 measured productivity and all included at least one measure of performance. ABC was another method without logical correlation to one of the measure categories. This was also the method most difficult to verify. Nine of the 12 ABC users were classified as large companies. Based on the small number of firms using ABC, the significance of any relationships is difficult to determine.

CONCLUSIONS

Despite the moderate sample size of this research, enough evidence has been gathered at this time to suggest that performance measures in metal machining firms are increasing in number and variety. More emphasis has been placed on improving quality and lead-time performance since the adoption of cells. And posting performance results on the factory floor is now the rule rather than the exception, although this may be done more for worker motivation reasons than for measuring success toward corporate objectives. Managerial performance is still predominantly evaluated in terms of how well the plant achieves cost objectives and on-time deliveries. In other words, many items are measured for "show," but cost and schedule are tracked for "dough." This could, however, be changing in the future as a few managers indicated more significance is now being placed on quality and lead-time performance by their managers.

REFERENCES

1. Goldratt, E. M., and J. Cox. *The Goal.* 2nd rev. ed. New York: North River Press, 1992.

2. Hayes, R. H., and S. C. Wheelwright. "Link Manufacturing Process and Product Life Cycles." *Harvard Business Review* 57, no. 1 (1979): 133–144.

3. Hill, T. *Manufacturing Strategy: Text and Cases.* 2nd ed. Burr Ridge, IL: Richard D. Irwin, 1994.

4. Kekre, S. "Performance of a Manufacturing Cell with Increased Product Mix." *IIE Transactions* 19, no. 3 (1987): 320–339.

About the Authors—

ROBERT F. MARSH is an assistant professor of business at the University of Wisconsin—Milwaukee. He received his PhD in operations management from the University of Cincinnati. Prior to that he held positions at General Electric Aircraft Engines and Diebold. His recent articles have been published in Journal of Operations Management, International Journal of Technology Management, Omega, and this journal. His research interests include cellular manufacturing, enterprise resource planning, and lead-time compression.

JACK R. MEREDITH is professor of management and Broyhill Distinguished Scholar and Chair in Operations at the Babcock Graduate School of Management at Wake Forest University. He received his undergraduate degrees in engineering and mathematics from Oregon State University and his PhD and MBA from University of California, Berkeley. His current research interests are in the areas of research methodology and the strategic planning, justification, and implementation of advanced manufacturing technologies. His recent articles in these areas have been published in Decision Sciences, Management Science, Journal of Operations Management, Sloan Management Review, *and* Strategic Management Journal. *He has three textbooks that are currently popular for college classes:* The Management of Operations *(John Wiley & Sons),* Fundamentals of Management Science *(R. D. Irwin), and* Project Management *(John Wiley & Sons). He is the Editor-in-Chief of the* Journal of Operations Management, *an area editor for* Production and Operations Management, *was the founding editor of* Operations Management Review, *and was the production/operations management series editor for John Wiley & Sons, Inc.*

USING QUEUEING NETWORK MODELS TO SET LOT-SIZING POLICIES FOR PRINTED CIRCUIT BOARD ASSEMBLY OPERATIONS

MAGED M. DESSOUKY

Department of Industrial and Systems Engineering, University of Southern California, Los Angeles, CA 90089

The trend in today's manufacturing is to move towards a Just-in-Time (JIT) manufacturing environment. As outlined by numerous studies [11, 19, 23], successful implementation of JIT manufacturing principles may lead to reduced inventory costs, improved quality, and increased equipment utilization. A necessary requirement for successful implementation of JIT is the ability to run small lot sizes [5, 8, 17]. Numerous approaches have been developed to determine the appropriate lot size. For example, Hill and Raturi [9] propose an optimization model for determining the lot sizes, and Karmarkar et al. [12, 13] propose a queueing model.

Small lot sizes can reduce work-in-process (WIP) inventory and manufacturing lead time if the setup times are not much larger than the unit run times. A reduction in the lead time allows the manufacturer to respond quicker to new customer orders or any changes in demand and increases the likelihood of meeting the demand on time. Small lot sizes tend to reduce the WIP because a lot spends less time at a machining center, causing new arriving lots to wait less for the machines to become available. However, reducing the lot size too much can sometimes have the opposite effect by increasing WIP because machine utilization may increase significantly due to an increase in the setup times. Thus, the selection of an appropriate lot size needs to take the setup time into consideration. This consideration is especially important for automatic insertion machines used in printed circuit board (PCB) assembly where there is both a board and component setup time, and up to 35% of the theoretical assembly load of a PCB line is determined by the setup procedures [4].

Carlson, Yao, and Girouard [3] give an example where a PCB assembly manufacturer produced lots of 100 or more units because the setup time was on the order of three hours per production run. If the lot size is reduced to 5 boards, the setup time translates to around 36 minutes per board. Complicating the problem of determining the appropriate lot-sizing policy in PCB assembly is that the same line produces many different board types, each having its own unique setup time. These factors enhance the need for analytical tools to help determine how low the lot size can be without negatively impacting WIP.

In this article, a queueing network model is used to determine the lot size that minimizes WIP while considering setup time for a PCB assembly process. Although the focus of this article is on WIP reduction, not demand management, a reduction in the manufacturing lead time allows a manufacturer to respond faster to new customer orders, hence

From *Production and Inventory Management Journal,* Third Quarter 1998, pp. 38-42. © 1998 by APICS, the American Production and Inventory Control Society. Reprinted by permission.

increasing the likelihood of on-time delivery. Queueing network models represent the manufacturing process as a network of queues. Analytical formulas are developed to approximate steady-state performance measures of the manufacturing system such as average WIP, machine utilization, and average flow time (i.e., the average amount of time a part spends in the manufacturing process). The best lot size is determined by developing operating characteristic curves of the PCB assembly process. Operating characteristic curves of interest include WIP and machine utilization as a function of the lot size. We demonstrate our approach on a high product mix and medium production volume PCB assembly facility located on the West Coast.

A queueing network model is used rather than a simulation model because simulation may become tedious in the planning stage due to the numerous alternatives that need to be considered [22]. Suri [21] shows the robustness of analytical queueing network models for representation of real systems. The computation time required to solve a queueing network model is significantly less than the simulation run time, greatly facilitating the ability to consider numerous lot-sizing policies. Also, the queueing network models do not require any programming, making them simpler to develop than simulation models. Simulation also requires the analyst to have some knowledge in statistics.

Snowdon and Ammons [20] survey eight queueing network packages. Some of the queueing network software packages are public domain while others are commercially sold by a software vendor. MANUPLAN [16] is selected as the queueing software package because of its user-friendly interface, and it has been successfully used in the past in the design of PCB assembly lines. For example, Haider, Noller, and Robey [7] use MANUPLAN to help identify initial design alternatives for a PCB assembly facility at IBM. Other successful applications of MANUPLAN in the design of PCB assembly lines can be found in [1, 6].

PRINTED CIRCUIT BOARD ASSEMBLY PROCESS

The studied PCB assembly process is a high product mix and medium production volume facility. The product mix is approximately 300 board types and the daily production volume is around 600 boards. The assembly facility uses plated through hole (PTH) technology to insert components on a board. It is common to have both automatic and manual component insertions in PTH assembly lines. For an excellent review of the PTH process, the reader is referred to [14].

A diagram of the process flowchart of the studied PCB assembly facility is shown in Figure 1. The triangles represent inventory storage locations. This facility uses a mix of automatic and manual operations to insert components on a board. The boards and kits, where the components are stored, are withdrawn from inventory and are sent directly to the auto insertion process. There are two types of automatic insertion machines. One type is axial insertion using a variable center distance (VCD) machine. Sequencing is performed at this step to ensure the components are inserted on the board in the proper order. The other type of automatic insertion operation uses a dual in-line package (DIP) machine. The studied assembly facility has two VCD machines and one DIP machine. All board types do not necessarily have to be processed by both machine types. After the auto insertion process the boards and kits are stored in inventory. There is sufficient demand to justify maintaining a certain amount of inventory for each product type. Later, the boards and kits are withdrawn from inventory and put through a series of manual operations including loading and soldering. The last operation is a manual test and repair station. Since the boards go into inventory storage after the auto insertion process, the auto and manual processes are treated independently and modeled separately. In this article, the focus is on the auto insertion process since it comprises the majority of the setup time.

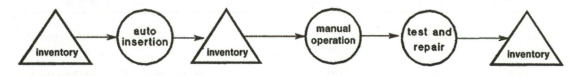

FIGURE 1: Printed circuit board assembly process flowchart

The total time to complete processing of a lot on an automatic insertion machine includes both a *setup time per lot* component and a *run time per board* component for each board in the lot. A setup is required whenever a changeover to a new product type is made. The setup time is incurred once at the beginning of processing of a new lot type. The setup time is independent of the lot size. The run time per board is incurred for each board in the lot.

Let S_{ik} be the setup time of board type i on machine type k ($k = 1$ refers to VCD and $k = 2$ refers to DIP). The setup time includes a fixed machine handling time and a time to prepare the components for insertion. The latter time is a function of the number of different component types to insert on the board. The setup time per lot of board type i at machine type k, S_{ik}, is

$$S_{ik} = a_k + m_k h_{ik}$$

where:

a_k = fixed prep time on machine k

h_{ik} = number of different component types to insert on board type i on machine k

m_k = component prep time on machine k.

Let B_{ik} be the run time per board of board type i on machine k. The run time includes a board handling time and a time to insert the components on the board. The latter time is a function of the number of components to insert on the board. Then, the run time per board type i at machine type k, B_{ik}, is

$$B_{ik} = f_k + r_k P_{ik}$$

where:

f_k = board handling time on machine k

P_{ik} = number of components to insert on board type i on machine k

r_k = insertion time per component on machine k.

Let the total time to process a lot of type i on machine k be T_{ik}. Then, $T_{ik}, = S_{ik} + q_i B_{ik}$, where q_i is the lot size. Note that the setup time is independent of the lot size.

Table 1 displays representative values for the setup and run times at both the VCD and DIP machines. The number of components inserted on a board (P_{ik} varied from a low of five to a high of 700 with the number of different types (h_{ik}) typically being two-thirds of that value.

MANUPLAN MODEL

MANUPLAN is a data-driven modeling tool. The input file contains data on board and machine characteristics. For each board type the demand rate, lot size, and route need to be specified. The route data contains the setup times and run times for each machine in the route. For each machine type, the capacity, the mean time between failure, and the mean repair time need to be specified.

The queue size in front of the machines is assumed to be unlimited, and the queue dispatching rule is first-come-first-serve (FCFS). Both the VCD and DIP machines are fairly reliable machines with 98% uptime. The material transfer in the auto insertion process is lot-for-lot. Since the material handling system is not capacity constrained and has negligible transfer time, the material handling system is not modeled.

The variability of the interarrival time of demand of each board type and the processing time in MANUPLAN are input as a percentage of the mean. Past experience in the facility has shown that the variability is typically 30% of the mean. The outputs of the MANUPLAN model are steady-state per-

TABLE 1: Representative Setup and Run Times in Minutes				
Machine	Lot Setup Time(a_k)	Component Setup Time (m_k)	Board Prep Time (f_k)	Insertion Time (r_k)
VCD ($k = 1$)	7.5/lot	0	.25/board	.008/insertion
DIP ($k = 2$)	8.5/lot	1/component type	.25/board	.024/insertion

formance measures of the manufacturing system including machine utilization, average WIP, and average flow time at each machining center. If all the demand cannot be met within the planning horizon, the output of the MANUPLAN model is an error message indicating that the demand cannot be met with the current machine capacity. The Appendix provides an overview on how the performance measures such as average WIP and flow time are determined in MANUPLAN.

AN APPLICATION

In this section, we demonstrate the use of queuing network models to help set manufacturing policy for an automatic insertion process of a West Coast printed circuit board assembly facility. Currently, the lot size for each board type is based on past experience. The purpose of this study is to identify a new lot-sizing policy that reduces WIP and the manufacturing lead time over using the historical lot sizes.

Demand data over a six-month planning horizon is used to perform the analysis. The demand is based on market forecasts. It is assumed that there are 125 working days during the six months. The automatic insertion line operates in two shifts with each shift having 6.5 hours available for manufacturing.

Using the current lot sizes, we first validate the MANUPLAN model by comparing its output to actual values from the assembly process. With the current lot sizes, MANUPLAN estimates the overall system WIP to be around 956 boards. This WIP includes boards in the queue and boards being processed, and is about 20% more than the levels experienced at the auto insertion process. To help identify the discrepancy between the results of the MANUPLAN model and the real system, a SLAM II simulation model [18] is developed to estimate the system performance measurements. Table 2 shows the machine utilization of each type and the average number of lots in the queue waiting for service.

The results show that the DIP machine is busy about 90% of the time while the VCD machine is busy only about 70% of the time. The percent busy time includes both the setup time and run time components of processing a lot. The DIP machine is heavily utilized because it spends about 35% of the time in the setup state while the VCD machine spends only about 8% of the time in the setup state.

TABLE 2: System Performance Measures

Machine Type	Percent Busy		Number in Queue	
	MANUPLAN	SLAM II	MANUPLAN	SLAM II
VCD	72.9	72.5	3.2	2.6
DIP	94.3	93.0	23.5	19.0

Due to high machine reliability, the machine utilization estimates from the MANUPLAN and simulation models are close to the static calculation. The estimates of the average number of lots in the queue differ by about 20% between the MANUPLAN and the simulation model. These results are consistent with the study by Huettner and Steudel [10], which showed that MANUPLAN tends to slightly overestimate the WIP levels. MANUPLAN is less accurate in estimating the WIP for the DIP machine in absolute terms because approximations for queueing networks are less accurate for heavily utilized machines [2]. Nevertheless, we are more concerned with making relative comparisons between different lot-sizing scenarios than with measuring the absolute value of the WIP. That is, typically one is not concerned with the absolute value of the WIP in determining the manufacturing strategy, but rather with how the WIP changes as a function of the strategy. Because MANUPLAN is data driven and solutions can be found quickly, a large number of scenarios can be compared in a small amount of computation time (roughly 30 CPU seconds per scenario on a Hewlett-Packard workstation).

Currently, each board type has a unique lot size and is set based on past experience. The lot sizes vary from a low of one board to a high of 747 boards. In order to move to more of a JIT environment, the PCB manufacturer wants to set a limit on the maximum lot size. In this manner, if any of the lot sizes based on historical experience are greater than the maximum limit, the lot size is reset to the maximum limit. Figure 2 plots the total average flow time in hours in the automatic insertion process as a function of the maximum lot-size limit. Setting a smaller limit reduces the overall average lot size and increases ma-

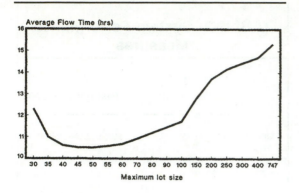

FIGURE 2: Average flow time vs. maximum lot size

chine utilization due to more setups. Figure 3 plots the equipment utilization as a function of the maximum lot-size limit. The results indicate that the best operating policy is a maximum lot size between 45 and 50. As the figure shows, bounding the lot size to a maximum of 50 reduces the average flow time (and subsequently the WIP) by 33%. A limit smaller than 45 increases the average flow time because the setup time starts to dominate. In fact, demand cannot be met with a limit smaller than 25 because the DIP machine utilization becomes greater than 100%. A limit greater than 50 increases the average flow time because a lot spends more time at a machining center due to the increased lot size, causing new arriving lots to wait more for the machines to become available.

The previous analysis helps determine an upper bound on the lot size. However, it still makes use of the historical lot-size values for board types below the limit. The company is interested in setting an overall lot-sizing policy in terms of a universal number of lots. For example, if the number of lots to run is set to five, the lot size for a particular board type is simply the demand over the planning horizon divided by five rounded up to the nearest integer. Note that, as the number of lots increases, the lot size decreases. In Figure 4, we plot the WIP (in terms of individual boards) as a function of the number of lots policy. Setting the number of lots for each board type to five is equivalent to the current lot sizes in

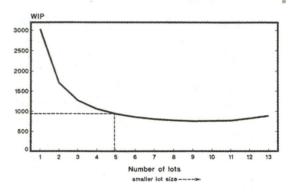

FIGURE 4: WIP vs. number of lots

terms of the resultant WIP because both lot-size policies yield a WIP level of around 950 boards. A number of lots policy of nine yields the smallest WIP levels of 756 boards which results in 21% less WIP than the current lot-size levels. Increasing the number of lots any further than nine will increase the WIP because the DIP machine incurs a lot of setups, causing high machine utilization.

CONCLUSION

As companies move towards a JIT environment, analytical tools are needed to guide factory managers on appropriate lot-sizing policies. Reducing the lot size too much may have a detrimental effect on WIP due to more setups. In this article, we demonstrate the use of queueing network models to develop operating characteristic curves on WIP for a studied PCB assembly process. The curves help identify appropriate lotsizing policies for WIP minimization. Historically, the facility sets the lot sizes based on past experience. The analysis using MANUPLAN shows that bounding the lot size to a maximum of 50 reduces the WIP by 32% with the same demand

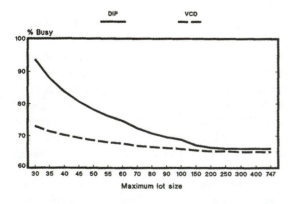

FIGURE 3: Machine utilization vs. maximum lot size

levels. The analysis also shows that the demand cannot be met with a bound smaller than 30 due to the frequent number of setups at this level, demonstrating that reducing the lot size will decrease the WIP up to a certain level. Future uses of MANUPLAN include determining an overall number of lots policy. Our initial analysis using the current demand levels shows that a policy of dividing the demand into nine production lots minimizes the WIP. Besides lowering inventory costs, reducing the WIP reduces the lead time which enables a manufacturer to be more responsive to new customer orders or any changes in demand.

Although the results are specific to the studied PCB assembly facility, the same type of analysis can be used to identify appropriate lot-sizing policies for other PCB assembly facilities. Previous to this study, the company had lot sizes, mentioned earlier, that varied between one and 747 boards. As a result of this study, the company set the maximum lot size to 50 for those products with lot sizes above this limit. Those products with lot sizes less than 50 were maintained at those figures. The advantage of using queueing network models for this type of analysis is that the models are simple to develop and many scenarios can be evaluated because of the fast computation time.

REFERENCES

1. Brown, E. "IBM Combines Rapid Modeling Technique and Simulation to Design PCB Factory-of-the-Future." *Industrial Engineering* 20 (1988): 23–36.

2. Buzacott, J. A., and J. G. Shanthikumar. *Stochastic Models of Manufacturing Systems.* Englewood Cliffs, NJ: Prentice-Hall, 1993.

3. Carlson, J. G., A, C. Yao, and W. F. Girouard. "The Role of Master Kits in Assembly Operations." *International Journal of Production Economics* 35 (1994): 253–258.

4. Feldmann, K., J. Franke, and A. Rothhaupt. "Optimization and Simulation of the Printed Circuit Assembly." *IEEE Transactions on Components, Packaging, and Manufacturing Technology—Part A* 17 (1994): 277–281.

5. Finch, B. I. "Japanese Management Techniques in Small Manufacturing Companies: A Strategy for Implementation." *Production and Inventory Management Journal* 27, no. 3 (1986): 30–38.

6. Garlid, S., C. Falkner, B. Fu, and R. Sun. "Evaluating Quality Strategies for CIM Systems." *Printed Circuit Assembly* (May 1988): 5–11.

7. Haider, S. W., D. G. Noller, and T. B. Robey. "Experiences with Analytic and Simulation Modeling for a Factory of the Future Project at IBM." In *Proceedings of the IEEE 1986 Winter Simulation Conference*, Piscataway, NJ, 1986: 641–648.

8. Handfield, R. "Distinguishing Features of Just-in-Time Systems in the Make-to-Order Assemble-to-Order Environment." *Decision Sciences* 24 (1993): 581–602.

9. Hill, A. V., and A. S. Raturi. "A Model for Determining Tactical Parameters for Materials Requirements Planning Systems." *Journal of the Operational Research Society* 43 (1992): 605–620.

10. Huettner, C. M., and H. J. Steudel. "Analysis of a Manufacturing System via Spreadsheet Analysis, Rapid Modelling, and Manufacturing Simulation." *International Journal of Production Research* 30 (1992): 1699–1714.

11. Im, J. H., and S. M. Lee. "Implementation of Just-in-Time Systems in U.S. Manufacturing Firms." *International Journal of Operations and Production Management* 9 (1989): 5–14.

12. Karmarkar, U. S., S. Kekre, and S. Kekre. "Lotsizing in Multi-item Multi-machine Job Shops." *IIE Transactions* 17(1985): 290– 298.

13. ———. "Multi-item Batch Heuristics for Minimization of Queueing Delays." *European Journal of Operational Research* 58 (1992): 99–111.

14. Kear, F. W. *Printed Circuit Assembly Manufacturing.* New York: Marcel Dekker, 1987.

15. Little, J. D. C. "A Proof of the Queueing Formula: L = SW." *Operations Research* 9 (1961): 383–387.

16. *MANUPLAN Users Manual.* Cambridge, MA: Network Dynamics, 1987.

17. Mehra, S., and R. A. Inman. "Determining the Critical Elements of Just-in-Time Implementation." *Decision Sciences* 23 (1992): 160–174.

18. Pritsker, A. A. B. *Introduction to Simulation and SLAM II.* New York: John Wiley & Sons, 1986.

19. Schonberger, R. J. *World Class Manufacturing: The Lessons of Simplicity Applied.* New York: The Free Press, 1986.

A New Route for Boeing's Latest Model

●**Aviation: In a first for the industry, the aircraft maker is manufacturing its 717 jet on a moving assembly line, hoping to improve the plane's prospects by speeding production and cutting costs.**

By PETER PAE, TIMES STAFF WRITER

In a cavernous building in Long Beach where 2,500 mechanics and engineers assemble the Boeing 717 aircraft, a 2-foot-tall bell sits silently atop a balcony. The bell, which sounds whenever a plane is sold, has tolled rarely, and instead has become a stark reminder of the airplane's uncertain future.

But this month, Boeing Co. launched an ambitious plan that could brighten the outlook on the factory floor.

With hopes of bolstering sales and improving the prospects of the struggling program by cutting production costs, Boeing has begun building the 106-passenger plane on a moving assembly line, a first for the industry.

Under the new process, Boeing hopes to churn out a plane every 20 days, a significant gain on the 65 days the old system required. The technique would also slash costs by more than half, making the plane's price more competitive and in turn boosting the viability of Southern California's last commercial airplane program.

How well the technique improves production and reduces costs could also be crucial to Boeing's decision to develop a smaller 85-passenger version of the 717, which would also be built in Long Beach, aerospace analysts said.

In addition, a successful outcome could prompt the world's largest airplane maker to employ the technique at other manufacturing plants. "The whole company is watching," said Fred Mitchell, executive vice president of operations for commercial airplanes at the Seattle-based company. "If we are successful down there, we will re-host it up here."

Boeing officials are already considering applying techniques learned in Long Beach at its new $400-million plant in Decatur, Ala., where it makes the next generation of Delta rockets. And in Renton, Wash., workers are in the early stages of putting together a similar moving assembly line to build the 737, the world's most popular commercial jetliner.

"It's going to be our model," Mitchell said of the 717 plant. Pierre Chao, an aerospace analyst with Credit Suisse First Boston, said successful implementation of the moving line is critical to the viability of the 717, which is about to enter a crucial period in its development. It's at about this point—two years after introduction—that airplanes either fly or flop.

"The real fork in the road will be the next two years," Chao said. "In other programs this is when sales really began to take off. If the moving line can lower the cost of manufacturing and be much more competitive on price, that would dovetail very nicely to when you also want to be hitting the marketplace very hard."

So far, it's been a struggle. Though Boeing received 149 orders—mostly during the plane's launch—it has not been able to sign up a major airline. In a recent filing with the Securities and Exchange Commission, Boeing suggested it would need to sell at least 200 to break even.

And Trans World Airlines Inc., one of the 717's biggest customers, is in financial trouble, putting future purchases in jeopardy. The airline, which recently posted another money-losing quarter, has a contract for 50 717s and so far has taken delivery of only nine. The other major order for 50 717s was placed by AirTran Airways, which is also trying to recover financially.

At the same time, competition is heating up. Brazilian jet maker Embraer struck a deal this month with a Russian research institute to develop a jet that can carry more than 100 passengers, in direct competition with the 717. The largest plane Embraer makes carries about 50 passengers.

And last year, Boeing lost a critical battle with its main rival, Airbus Industrie, when British Airways ordered 12 Airbus A318s with an option to buy 12 more. It was a major blow, because Airbus hasn't even built the airplane yet, and an order from the airline was seen as critical to garnering other customers.

The 717 is listed at $31 million to $34 million depending on the configuration, but it sells for about $25 million because of discounts based on volume and other factors, analysts said. Boeing won't say how much it hopes to reduce the cost. The Airbus A318, which will be launched in 2002, is listed at $36 million to $42 million.

"[The 717] has had a lot of headaches," said Adam Pilarski, an aviation consultant with Reston, Va.-based Avitas Inc. and former chief economist with McDonnell Douglas Corp. "It's a good plane, but there is lot of competition. They have their work cut out."

The 717's future has been tenuous from the beginning. Boeing inherited the plane—then called the MD-95—from McDonnell Douglas when the companies merged three years ago. Production of the MD-11, the MD-80 and the MD-90 was halted shortly after the merger.

Dropping the other McDonnell production lines, coupled with the slow start of the 717, left room for construction of the moving line without disrupting production. As planes were being assembled on one side of Building 80, construction of the line, which included digging a tunnel the length of the facility, began on the other.

Although the production technique has been a staple of the automobile industry for the more than 80 years since its invention by Henry Ford, it is a radical departure from the way planes have typically been made.

For as long as anyone can remember, commercial planes have been put together in discrete stages, mainly because of their complexity and low volume. For instance, Boeing's 747, the large commercial jetliner, has 125 miles of wiring and 3 million parts.

During World War II, military aircraft were briefly built on a moving assembly line, mainly to churn out planes as quickly as possible. But they were also far less complex than planes are today. When demand for airplanes slowed to a trickle at war's end, the industry quickly shifted back to the old way.

"We didn't think about it," Mitchell said. "'It was a cultural thing. That's just the way it was done."

At Boeing's Renton facility, a typical plane factory, much of the 737 is assembled as it is parked in a slant position, similar to the way parking spaces are arranged in shopping malls. Mechanics then surround the plane with equipment and tools and add parts to it.

About every two to eight days—depending on the work required—the plane is moved by means of an overhanging crane or a tow truck to another slanted position and more parts are added.

At the first position, for instance, insulation and wiring are installed in the fuselage. In the next position, the wings are joined to the plane's body, and in the final stage, passenger seats are added.

The plane is moved eight times before it leaves the Renton plant. Each move entails a crew of about 150 working the night shift removing equipment around the plane, shifting the plane to a new position and then setting up the next set of equipment and tools.

At Long Beach, the airplanes will now be hoisted onto a cradle pulled by a pair of chains under the factory floor. As it moves down the line, at about half an inch per minute, parts of the plane will be added.

This month the line moved under its own power for the first time, pulling three planes forward to the next station. The line will "pulse" forward about every six days and is expected to move continuously by summer.

The process, known as "lean manufacturing," also means a change in the way mechanics work on the airplanes. Mechanics will no longer have to run to the toolshed or the parts room, sometimes in another building, to get the necessary equipment.

Under the new process, the parts and tools will be brought to the mechanic "like a surgeon working on a patient," said Michael E. Graziano, director of Lean Enterprise for the Long Beach plant. He said that in the standard system, mechanics wasted a lot of time scurrying around for tools and parts.

"We want to treat the mechanic like a surgeon, and we don't want the surgeon to leave the operating room," Graziano said.

But not everyone is embracing the new production technique. Some Long Beach workers, bruised by years of layoffs, fear the moving line will mean more job cuts. About 5,000 of 7,500 commercial aircraft jobs in Long Beach have been slashed in the last three years.

Mike McQueen, a 20-year veteran who installs doors on the 717, said his co-workers are worried that automating the process is a way for Boeing to reduce the work force even more. But McQueen, a team leader and shop steward for the union, said he's been able to convince some that the new line is necessary to keep the program alive.

"It's hard teaching old dogs new tricks, but we need to do this, or we might be out of a job anyway," McQueen said.

Unit Selections

30. **Introducing JIT Manufacturing: It's Easier Than You Think,** Luciana Beard and Stephen A. Butler
31. **Tailored Just-In-Time and MRP Systems in Carpet Manufacturing,** Z. Kevin Weng
32. **The Critical Importance of Master Production Scheduling,** Steve Wilson and Chuck Davenport
33. **The Manager's Guide to Supply Chain Management,** F. Ian Stuart and David M. McCutcheon
34. **Squeezing the Most Out of Supply Chains,** Michael S. McGarr
35. **Saturn's Supply-Chain Innovation: High Value in After-Sales Service,** Morris A. Cohen, Carl Cull, Hau L. Lee, and Don Willen
36. **From Supply Chain to Value Net,** David Bovel and Joseph Martha

Key Points to Consider

❖ Should a firm place a high value and concern on shortage cost or should the firm assume that it is of little or no consequence?

❖ What is so different about supply chain management compared to how firms have always gone about supplier and distributor relations?

❖ What role have computers played in making supply chain management easier?

 **Links**

www.dushkin.com/online/

31. **System 21 Manufacturing**
   http://jbaworld.com/solutions/infosheets/masterprodsched.htm
32. **MAGI: Master Production Scheduling**
   http://www.magimfg.com/Master_Production_Scheduler.htm
33. **Informs: Institute for Operations Research and the Management Sciences**
   http://www.informs.org

These sites are annotated on pages 4 and 5.

Inventory and supply-chain management is very important for a firm. Inventories are found in raw materials, work-in-process, and finished goods. Inventories allow for meeting anticipated demand. The objective of inventory management is to satisfy customer requirements and to minimize total inventory cost. Inventory decisions rely upon an accurate sales forecast as an input and consideration of existing inventories, scheduled receipts, and production schedules. Inventory management is linked to both the MPS (Master Production Schedule) and MRP (Material Requirements Planning). Inventory management examines both dependent demand and independent demand. Dependent demand is the demand for raw materials, parts, and component items. Independent demand is the demand for finished goods.

Firms must analyze their inventory costs and determine the optimal reorder quantity. The major inventory costs are holding, reorder, and shortage costs. Holding costs are the costs associated with storing inventory and are measured in terms of the cost to keep one unit of inventory in storage for a year. The reorder costs are the costs associated with preparing and reordering inventory, and this is usually measured in terms of the cost per reorder. Shortage costs are the cost of having stock-out and not being able to satisfy customer requests for an item. Shortage costs are more intangible and tie in to the firm's marketing philosophy about maintaining adequate quantities to provide customer service. The EOQ (economic order quantity) formula examines the holding and reorder cost to determine the optimal reorder quantity. The formula needs as an input facts on annual demand, the reorder cost, and the holding cost. The EOQ quantity will minimize total inventory costs by balancing the holding and reorder costs. The EOQ formula assumes level demand throughout the year, ignores price breaks from quantity discounts, and ignores shortage costs.

Supply chain management involves a coordination of suppliers, manufacturers, and distributors to increase efficiency and effectiveness for all parties. From the earlier technique of EDI (Electronic Data Interchange), firms now utilize intranets to coordinate information flow through the supply chain. This new focus on coordinated management has received a great deal of attention by companies. This unit presents articles that review the historical roots of supply chain management, that explain the details of how to successfully implement supply chain management, and that offer case illustrations. As firms become more global, with both global suppliers and global distribution points to customers, there is a greater need to properly manage the supply chain.

Introducing JIT Manufacturing: It's Easier Than You Think

Luciana Beard and Stephen A. Butler

The practical difficulties arising from the implementation of a-Just-in-Time (JIT) inventory management approach have caused some managers to dismiss it as a passing fad. When asked to cite the inventory strategies that do and do not work for their companies, purchasing managers identified JIT as the most frequently mentioned failure. Their general sense was that "modified JIT works, pure JIT does not." The success of JIT implementation may also be a function of the size of the company, with smaller firms finding it more difficult.

If JIT is abandoned because it does not appear to work as described in articles and textbooks, the cost savings of an efficient, integrated manufacturing process will be lost. As documented here, the solutions of actual companies in response to the impediments of introducing JIT in its purest form may be instructive for other firms facing similar problems.

The popularity of JIT inventory methods has grown steadily over the last two decades. Officially introduced by Toyota in the 1970s, JIT methods have spread to manufacturing companies all over the world. The appeal lies mostly in an emphasis on simplicity and a cost-saving, "bare-bones" approach. Researchers generally agree about JIT on several points, one being that JIT methods, with some alteration, can be successfully adapted for use in American manufacturing plants of all sizes. Setting up a JIT system, however, involves the entire business, from suppliers to production to customers—even to administrative aspects such as accounting.

There may be significant disadvantages with the system, such as uncooperative suppliers, the distance between suppliers and manufacturers, and overstressed workers. On the other hand, the benefits to be realized include less need for maintaining safety stock, a lower lead time, higher quality, automated communication with customers, and cross training for workers.

A JIT approach has as its main goal the reduction of the levels of inventory and its associated carrying

> Several manufacturers have bypassed the obstacles and adapted JIT to fit their individual needs, deriving benefits along the way.

costs—or to reduce waste altogether. The less time a product is in process, the less inventory there is to finance, store, and manage. The objective is to push to zero the amount of time the product is waiting to be worked on, in transit, and/or being inspected.

Benefits that should result from the implementation of a JIT system include:

- lower inventory carrying costs;
- space and cost savings in the factory and warehouse;
- reduced risk of obsolescence; and
- reduced response time to customers' orders and delivery times.

To the extent that the JIT system can be put into practice without any impediments, a "theoretically correct" demand-pull system will be in place.

JIT in theory often differs greatly from JIT in practice. Not all companies can continuously feed inventory into work-in-process and manufacture their product without interruption. Different industries have different manufacturing processes that, for varying reasons, are not suited to JIT treatment. This does not completely rule out the possibility for the company to practice JIT; it just means it has to find a way to adapt or adjust its processes to incorporate as many JIT principles as possible.

To examine how different manufacturers have adapted JIT to fit the needs of their companies, we interviewed the production managers of five manufacturing companies. The sample was chosen to represent a variety of industries and manufacturing technologies available in the area, ranging from heavy manufacturing to food processing. We asked the managers to describe their general manufacturing environment, inventory and ordering practices, working arrangements with suppliers, and costs associated with switching to a JIT-type system (see Figure 1 for a list of the questions). Each company demonstrated a reason peculiar to its industry why it could not employ JIT in its theoretical form.

Electronics Manufacturer

This company had $7.4 billion in sales and $8.9 billion in total assets in 1994. Its lines of production include information systems and electronics, power systems, industrial systems, transportation, and consumer products. The inventory manager stated that the company has a special distributor system developed many years ago that is geared to work with its manufacturing process. Because of the nature of the complex electronic goods it produces, the company is restricted to ordering large quantities of parts from its suppliers, some of whom are located abroad.

These factors would preclude the company from practicing JIT in its theoretical form. However, some JIT principles have been incorporated into the distributor system. The company feeds the inventory directly into work-in-process, with no initial inspection. A minimum number of suppliers are kept for each category of parts: one for electrical parts and two for prefabricated parts. The distributor handles most of the requirement planning and delivery scheduling. According to the inventory manager, one of the main goals of this system is to decrease costs while increasing quality—a goal that coincides with one of the main principles of JIT.

Air Filter Manufacturer

This company manufactures air filters for use in air conditioning units, automobiles, and the like. It is a division of a corporation whose total assets in 1994 were $5.1 billion and whose sales were $6.6 billion. The division's main barrier to following theoretical JIT is that it must maintain a three- to four-week surplus of a critical part, one that is common to most of its manufactured products. According to the manufacturing manager, keeping a surplus is necessary because of the setup costs involved in production. It is cheaper overall to maintain this inventory than to manufacture a small number of these parts every time they are needed. Moreover, keeping inventory on hand reduces lead times.

Figure 1
Survey Questions

General Manufacturing Environment

1. Do you have a repetitive manufacturing environment, where the same product or type of product is manufactured or assembled again and again?
2. Is it a flow or process production, like an assembly line, where the product is manufactured or assembled in stages in different departments or in different parts of the line?
3. Do you have stable production rates so that you try to produce a given number of units of product for a certain time period (hour, day, week)?

Inventory and Ordering Practices

4. Do you have a program in place or are you implementing a program to reduce or eliminate inventories and work-in-process?
5. Do you have a "push" system, where you produce to inventory, or a "pull" system, where you produce to demand? In other words, do you produce as long as you have enough inventory to cover it, or do you feed inventory into production as it is demanded by the processes? What drives the production?
6. Is inventory delivered in frequent small batches, just enough to cover a few hours' or days' production?
7. Do you thoroughly inspect each incoming inventory order, or do you feed it directly into work-in-process?

Suppliers

8. What are the major parts you order from outside suppliers?
9. How many suppliers do you have for each of those parts?
10. Do your suppliers have a just-in-time or similar system, or do you encourage them to do so?
11. Are your suppliers' production and inventory methods similar to yours?
12. Do you have a "partnership" with your suppliers, working closely with them on production methods, quality control, and design specifications?
13. Are your suppliers located nearby?

Other

14. Have you had any problems or do you foresee any problems with your JIT system?
15. What were/are some of the costs the company incurred to switch to a JIT system?
16. If you do not have a JIT system, why not? What kind of inventory system do you have?

Figure 2
Comparison of Traditional, "Real World," and JIT Inventory Methods

Company	Traditional	"Read World"	Just-in-Time
Electronics	Batch or job lot processing	Hybrid of JIT and batch processing developed by company	Continuous feed—no batches
Air filter manufacturer	Inventory stockpiled	Only one part stockpiled due to setup costs	Little or no inventory held
Food processing	Raw materials inspected before being fed into work-in-process (WIP)	Raw food materials required by law to be inspected	Raw materials fed directly into WIP without inspection
Tire manufacturer	Inventory held in stock until needed	Certain materials, due to nature of material, must "age" before use	Materials ready for use upon arrival
Climate control equipment manufacturer	Supplier cooperation not necessary	Suppliers may not cooperate due to tax laws or other reasons	Close "partnership" with suppliers is key

Other than that, the company practices other components of JIT, such as holding little inventory, having a small number of certified suppliers, and reducing inspection of incoming inventory. The company has been using this system for several years. The manager mentioned the idea of driving down costs to remain competitive again, a central principle of JIT.

Food Processing

No financial information was available for this company, which produces food products and diet supplements from ingredients found all over the world. The manager said the company has been using a form of JIT since its birth in the 1950s. Its inventory system involves keeping only a few carefully screened vendors to supply inventory and working closely with them on quality control and product development. It also schedules deliveries of certain inventory items so that the materials arrive just when they are needed.

The barrier for this company in implementing theoretical JIT is the law mandating that deliveries of raw material food items such as flour and sugar must be inspected before they are put into production. The process takes about 12 days and the company incurs significant inspection costs. Moreover, because the ingredients required for the products come from many distant places, such events as natural disasters and political upheavals can affect delivery. If, for example, a certain ingredient comes only from Bangladesh and that country has experienced severe floods, production may be delayed. Other than these two difficulties, the company has applied JIT principles to other aspects of its manufacturing process with great success for years.

Tire Manufacturer

The fourth company, which also has no financial information available, has great variety in its product mix. It may produce 10 to 14 different types of just one size of a tire. The manager said the plant has been using a form of JIT since it opened in the 1970s. Inventory needs are forecast in three-month intervals with the aid of a computer. This three-month "view" is sent to the supplier, who delivers the order in small batches as needed. The manufacturer updates the supplier on changes in the material requirements as necessary. A *kanban* system is used as well, which signals when parts are needed, and incoming inventory is randomly selected for inspection. The plant sends its people to the suppliers' plants to work with them on improving production methods and quality control.

According to the manager, the plant runs its inventory system "as close to JIT as possible." The difficulty in achieving theoretical JIT lies in the nature of the raw materials themselves. Certain chemicals used in the tire-manufacturing process must be allowed to "age" a few days before being used in production. This means that once the chemicals have been delivered, they must be held on the shop floor as inventory for a while. Although traditional JIT theory aims to eliminate the need for holding any inventory at all, the tire manufacturer has benefited greatly from using as many JIT principles as possible.

Air Conditioning and Climate Control Equipment Manufacturer

A $1.6 billion corporation with net sales of $2.4 billion (as of 1994), the final firm in our sample makes large capacity cooling and heating equipment for commercial and residential use, as well as commercial and industrial refrigeration and gas compression equipment. It implemented a JIT system in the early 1990s. Of all the manufacturers interviewed, this company actually runs its plant closest to JIT in theory. Although it uses all the traditional principles and ideas, there is still some difficulty in getting cooperation from suppliers. The manager said that because of the state tax laws, some suppliers will not participate in the consignment program that is part of the company's JIT system. This makes it hard to find suppliers both willing to participate in such a program and able to meet the quality standards set forth by the manufacturer. Other than the problem of getting cooperation from suppliers, however, the JIT program has more than paid for itself in savings of carrying and freight costs, fewer stockouts, and more turns of inventory.

So far, these five companies have displayed five main practical difficulties in practicing JIT (see Figure 2). First, a company may already have its own system in place to handle special ordering requirements and does not see a need to change to JIT. Second, a company must hold inventory it manufactures itself due to the setup costs involved. Third, food manufacturers are required by law to inspect incoming raw food materials. Fourth, sometimes raw materials are not ready to be used in production immediately, thus requiring them to be held as inventory for a short time. Finally, there may be difficulties in working with suppliers.

There are, of course, other reasons why companies may not be able to practice JIT in its theoretical form, including:

1. Management may be unwilling to switch to JIT because of the initial costs involved.

2. Manufacturers in remote areas may not be able to arrange for frequent deliveries of inventory in small batches, as JIT theory dictates.

3. The manufacturing process itself may not be suited to JIT treatment, such as when some component of the finished product needs to be cured or dried between processes.

Although there are five actual and three speculative reasons mentioned here as to why companies may be unable to practice JIT in its theoretical form, the manufacturers interviewed have shown that it is still possible to work around these barriers and realize some savings by using as many JIT principles as possible. It may feel like a major effort to produce a seemingly insignificant amount of savings, but these savings can add up to provide a big competitive edge.

One final observation about JIT: In conducting this research, we found several articles hailing JIT as a major breakthrough and a new and exciting discovery that is just beginning to catch on in the United States. However, the interviews conducted with these companies seem to suggest just the opposite. Three of the five managers interviewed stated that their firm had been using a JIT-like system for many years, even before Toyota introduced it under the name "Just-in-Time." For these companies, the ideas in JIT are not new and have been saving manufacturers time, effort, and money for quite a while. One manager summed it up perfectly: "When all the hype came out about this new JIT stuff, we said, 'We've been doing that for years!'"

There are any number of techniques for improving quality that are described by "theoretical" conditions. With some careful thought, they can be implemented in practice.

References

M. Frank Barton, Surendra P. Agrawal, and L. Mason Rockwell, Jr., "Meeting the Challenge of Japanese Management Concepts," *Management Accounting*, September 1988, pp. 49–53.

Michael A. Cusumano, "The Limits of 'Lean,'" *Sloan Management Review*, Summer 1994, pp. 27–32.

Anne Millen Porter, "The Problem with JIT," *Purchasing*, September 18, 1997, pp. 18–19.

Arjan T. Sadhwani, M.H. Sarhan, and Dayal Kiringoda, "Just-in-Time: An Inventory System Whose Time Has Come," *Management Accounting*, December 1985, pp. 36–44.

Ragnor Seglund and Santiago Ibarreche, "Just-in-Time: The Accounting Implications," *Management Accounting*, August 1984, pp. 43–45.

Masaru Tanabe, "Making JIT Work at NCR Japan," *Long Range Planning*, October 1992, pp. 37–42.

Richard E. White, John N. Pearson, and Jeffery R. Wilson, "JIT Manufacturing: A Survey of Implementation in Small and Large U.S. Manufacturers," *Management Science* January 1999, pp. 1–15.

Luciana Beard is an accounting manager at webcasts.com, Oklahoma City, Oklahoma. **Stephen A. Butler** is an associate professor of accounting at the University of Oklahoma in Norman.

TAILORED JUST-IN-TIME AND MRP SYSTEMS IN CARPET MANUFACTURING

Z. KEVIN WENG, PHD

School of Business, University of Wisconsin–Madison, Madison, WI 53706

A great deal of attention has been focused in the literature on Just-in-Time (JIT) manufacturing since the last decade [1, 2, 3, 4, 8, 9, 10]. It is typical that JIT is applied and studied when the entire production process moves to JIT [6]. The purpose of this article is to show how, under certain circumstances, JIT can be applied to low-tech industries and can be used alongside a traditional MRP system. Of course, JIT in this form is a variation of the classical JIT manufacturing techniques [4, 6].

This article is a description of how a carpet manufacturer met standard orders within 24 hours by tailoring its JIT manufacturing techniques. In particular, the following managerial questions are addressed. How can a company compete on time with both customized and standard products? How can "mass customization" be achieved by managing standard products with JIT and customized products with MRP in one production facility?

PRODUCT, MANUFACTURING PROCESSES AND PROBLEMS

The firm under consideration for this new manufacturing process is a producer of high-end carpet tiles. Carpet tiles with a hard backing are installed much like traditional hard surface tiles. The company was the recent winner of the Malcolm Baldrige Outstanding Quality Award and is well known in the carpet industry for its capability to quickly respond to the market by developing new high-quality products. Along with quality, customer service is another selling point of the firm. Specifically, the firm was the first one to install "Quick Response," which guarantees shipment of products the following week. However, recent developments and competition in the carpet industry have led to some carpet manufacturers promising shipment of broadloom carpet in 24 hours. Note that while broadloom is not the same product as carpet tiles, its lower prices make it a competing product.

Two product lines are offered by this company. One line, representing approximately 65% of current total sales, is a series of standardized products called "standards," that sell through catalogs. The other line, representing approximately 35% of current total sales, provides customized products called "specials," in which new base colors and/or patterns are specified by customers and checked by the company's designers. While the fabrication of the products is identical for both product lines, the dyeing processes are different since special colors and/or designs are utilized for specials. Accordingly, a considerably higher markup is applied to specials due to the special attention given to these products and their customers during the whole production process.

The existing process encompasses two facilities located several miles apart. Materials are transferred between the two facilities several times a day. The company's marketing de-

From *Production and Inventory Management Journal,* First Quarter 1998, pp. 46–50. © 1998 by APICS, the American Production and Inventory Control Society. Reprinted by permission.

partment receives incoming orders and establishes due dates (see Figure 1). The average (total) manufacturing lead time is one week, or five working days. A traditional MRP system is employed to determine due dates and reorder quantities for raw materials. Basic raw materials are the same, and dye shades are made by combining a small number of primary colors.

The production flow and process are illustrated in Figure 2. The specific process can be characterized as follows. First, dyes are prepared to color the yarn that will be used for the base of the carpet tile. The yarn is then dyed. The dyed yarn is then either tufted or bonded into a broadloom form of carpet. Ordinary carpet would then be backed with a flexible backing. However, carpet tiles are given a hard backing instead. After the broadloom form of the carpet has been backed, it is then cut into squares (18" × 18"). For the standards product line, customers can choose between plain base carpet and geometric or a commonly designed carpet pattern. Specials are often made of standard base colors with special logos or colors dyed on the carpet tile. Products are then ready to ship after the dying process is completed.

A big part of the process involves setups

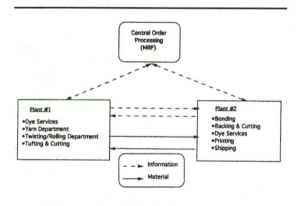

FIGURE 1: Business layout/information and material flow

and changeovers between the two product lines. In the last stage of the production process (tile pattern), patterns are dyed in what is called a colorway. A colorway is a set of five different dyes. The dyeing machines can produce any pattern using the current five dyes that are loaded on the machine. When products call for a different set of colors, a changeover must be made. The changeover takes approximately 45 minutes. When producing standards, production can start immediately after a changeover. When producing specials, a "strike" is required before production can begin after a changeover. A strike is a trial run of one yard of the product to test the shade of the dye and the detail of the pattern. A strike takes approximately 30 minutes. When the strike is off-shade, adjustments must be made on the machinery or the dye and then another strike must be run. When specials are run, it takes an average of 2.5 strikes before production can begin. Thus, an average changeover for specials takes two or more hours while an average changeover for standards takes only 45 minutes.

In the first process, yarn dyeing, a similar process occurs. The greige yarn is dyed a single color. In order to fulfill an order for a base, often two or three colors of yarn are combined in the twisting department. Thus, two or three vats must often be used in order to complete one order. Standards are again much easier to produce. The colors of standards are well established and do not require trial dyeing before the actual yarn dyeing can begin. Like in the tile pattern area, changeover for standards dyes are much quicker than specials. In both the yarn dyeing and pattern dyeing departments, standards dyes are also easier to make since the formulas have been well defined over a long period of time. The most frequently used standards dyes are made in large 500 and 1,000-gallon containers and are maintained at all times.

Efforts have been made to reduce both the lot sizes and lead times in the production process. Lot sizes have been reduced to the point where they currently equal the order size plus 5% for specials and 500 yards or more for standards. Manufacturing lead times are fairly consistent between production processes due to the company's low off-quality and smaller batch sizes resulting in less queueing time. It was also observed that work-in-process (WIP) spends the majority of its time in queue rather than actually in production.

JIT PHILOSOPHY APPLIED TO STANDARDIZED PRODUCTS

From the discussion in the previous sections, one can see that the line of standards seems to be an ideal candidate for consideration of JIT manufacturing. For the implementation of JIT to be successful, it is required that very few changes be made in the products themselves [3, 4, 6]. This implies that a firm

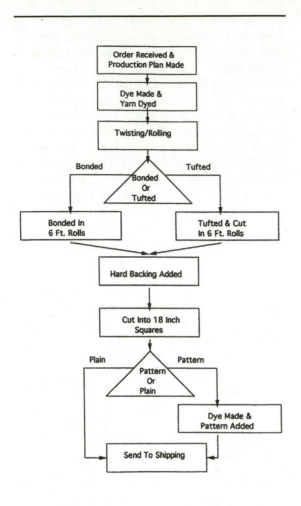

FIGURE 2: Current process flow

must already have high-quality production processes, steady demand, quick changeovers, short lead times, and low variability in the production process. In this company, efforts over many years have led to high-quality processes with low variation. The standards product lines are already established and require few changeovers per day for production. The standards product lines have been produced for years, and operators are accustomed to producing them with quick changeovers. The standards product lines are also well established in the marketplace and demand for them has remained steady for quite some time. For every point that can be made in favor of producing standards by JIT techniques, a counterargument can be made concerning specials that would make it impossible to manufacture them using JIT. For this reason a process must be established that allows standards to be produced using JIT and allow specials to be produced the same way they are currently being produced.

The production of carpet tiles, like most other textile products, utilizes multiple, slow-paced, and low-capital equipment. From the yarn dyeing though the pattern printing, this is a valid statement. The only process that is completed on only one machine is the backing process. The backing process, however, can change carpet shade and change from tufted to bonded instantaneously. The use of multiple machinery in each department will make it possible to dedicate machinery to the production of standards or specials and thus produce standards using JIT procedures and specials using the traditional MRP system.

THE NEW PRODUCTION PROCESS

Under the new system, raw materials are ordered using the existing procedures that utilize a reorder point. Since the raw materials are the same for both standards and specials and are used in the same proportion, this works efficiently without increasing the number of stockouts. The new system requires additional planning personnel to handle the standards orders. JIT manufacturing simplifies the production planning process so only one additional planner is necessary. Reduced work loads for specials production planners free up their time to help plan for the production of standards. Very few changes are needed in the com-

TABLE 1: Production Information for Standards Products

Department	Number of Machines	Standards Production Rate	Standards Changeover Time	Machines Needed To Produce 250 Yd/Hr
Yarn Dying	10 Vats	200 Yd/Hr	1 Hr	5 Vats
Yarn Rolling/Twisting	2 Rollers	400 Yd/Hr	.5 Hr	1 Roller
Tufting & Splicing	12 Tufting Machines	25 Yd/Hr	.5 Hr	6 Tufting
Bonding	8 Bonding Machines	40 Yd/Hr	.5 Hr	4 Bonding
Backing	1 Machine	530 Yd/Hr	0 Hr	Shared
Cutting	2 Cutters	450 Yd/Hr	.5 Hr	1 Cutter
Tile Pattern	2 Printers	250 Yd/Hr	1 Hr	1 Printer

pany's computerized production planning system since the JIT production process is self-regulating. The new planning personnel are responsible for ensuring that the daily, and often hourly, production plans are met in each department to ensure smooth-flowing production. This often requires working closely with those in charge of producing specials so that resources can be shared when needed. The lines between standards and specials should not be drawn stringently, but should be loose so that as demand for one type of product fluctuates, resources can be shared between the two production types.

The production of the standards products is done on machinery dedicated to them. One may recall that currently demand is split almost 65/35 between standards and specials. However, when looking at time to produce, standards require considerably less time. Thus, the split between standards and specials for machinery requirements is approximately 50/50 (see Table 1). The machinery that is dedicated to standards can be used for specials and vice versa when the current demand alters greatly from this 50/50 split. This flexibility is the key to the success of the newly established JIT production system. During some days, demand for standards is greater than what can be produced on the dedicated machinery. When this happens the other machinery, which has more flexibility in meeting its due dates, can be used for the production of standards. This should actually happen very rarely. Most often the opposite will occur, in that standards equipment will be used to help meet specials delivery due dates when the daily standards production has been met.

It should be pointed out that this new production system is not able to function as a typical JIT *pull* system. The reason for this is that the flexibility in the standards product line is established during its first and last processes. For this reason the system's individual departments cannot pull from each of their preceding processes like a typical JIT system. Instead, information needs to be shared between the first dyeing process and the last dyeing process/base order fulfillment. Working in this way, as an order begins in the last processes, work to replace the base inventory can begin in the first process. From the perspective of customer demand determining the work load, this can be viewed as JIT. Furthermore, the existing rule of 500-yard batches was changed for standards to match the size of customer orders exactly. Using these procedures requires WIP to be carried in substantial amounts to buffer the formation processes and the final dyeing and order fulfillment processes.

When this new production system was first installed, we recommended that a one-day inventory be carried between the formation processes and the final fulfillment processes for each base product. As the production system began to become refined and any problems that occurred were fixed, this quantity has been reduced greatly. After the new system had been fully implemented for a short time, we recommended that these levels be reduced to 12 hours' worth of WIP for common base patterns and fewer hours' worth of WIP for less popular base patterns. This represents a substantial reduction in total WIP from the previous production system which, at all times, had five full days of WIP on hand.

The installation of this JIT system was a gradual adjustment. Changes in the manufacturing process dictated the correct lot sizes and WIP inventory that should be carried. It was safe to discontinue WIP buffers between every process except the last pattern dyeing process. Lot sizes initially continued to be 500 yards or greater. However, these were quickly reduced or increased to exactly equal the periods' demand requirements for each base product. In the beginning, production periods were one day. That is, orders received today should be planned for tomorrow so that the first yarn dyeing process can set its day's production plan knowing what the final production process, tile pattern, is going to produce. As the new production process came on line, this one-period-per-day production was increased to two production periods a day. In this way, every 12 hours the first process, yarn dyeing, will know what the final process, tile pattern, is going to produce and can establish a 12-hour production plan. The remaining processes between yarn dying and tile pattern are captive to the production rates established by tile pattern. As a result, demand pulls inventory from base stock to tile pattern and sets the replenishment production in motion. The items will be replenished in 12 hours, just in time for demand to pull from them again.

RESULTS AND INSIGHTS

The obvious benefit to this new production system is the ability to gain market share by meeting orders for standards products in 24 hours. The current facilities have ample available space if capacity expansion becomes necessary in the long run. Since the majority of the textile machines being used are low-capital and easy-to-install items, capacity expansion is not a future concern. Even if there are no increases in market share, this new production system will allow the firm to maintain its current market share by meeting its competitor's new quick delivery programs in broadloom carpet. No other competitors producing carpet tiles are currently offering this type of quick response. One-time start-up costs were required for adjustments in the MRP system and the development of new system requirements; however, these were minimal. Savings that were realized in this new production process came from reductions in WIP inventory, based on a 12% annual holding cost. Calculations of these expenses and savings are summarized in Table 2.

While these annual savings are not very significant, cost savings are not the driving force behind the tailored application of JIT manufacturing techniques. This was and still is seen as a way to further meet customers' desires and thus improve the firm's overall profitability. Quick response as a key manufacturing strategy [5, 7] will continue to be emphasized in the carpet industry. The development of a production system of this type allows this firm to stay on the cutting edge of technology in the carpet market. Over time, additional savings can be realized in this system as lead times, lot sizes, and WIP are further reduced.

One area in which this firm is currently focused is in-depth research into the production flow. The production rates of each department are currently balanced. However, the exact timing between departments, and total production time from dyeing to receiving the tile into WIP inventory, would need to be investigated. The total production time should be targeted somewhere between 8 and 12 hours.

ACKNOWLEDGMENT

The author would like to thank Derik Davis, executive manager of a carpet manufacturer in Georgia, for his assistance in developing the ideas and data presented in this article. The author is also grateful to Scott Armstrong and Kathy Rye for their helpful comments on earlier versions of this article.

REFERENCES

1. Coleman, B. J., and M. R. Vaghefi. "Heijunka (?): A Key to the Toyota Production System." *Production and Inventory Management Journal* 35, no. 4 (1994): 31–35.

2. Merrills, R. "How Northern Telecom Competes on Time." *Harvard Business Review* 67, no. 4 (1989): 108–114.

3. Mishina, K. "Toyota Motor Manufacturing, USA., Inc." HBS Case N1-693-019, 1992.

4. Monden, Y. *Toyota Production System*. Norcross, GA: Institute of Industrial Engineers, 1983.

5. Peters, T. J. *Liberation Management: Necessary Disorganization for the Nanosecond Nineties*. New York: Ballantine, 1994.

6. Schniederjans, M. *Topics in Just-in-Time Management*. Boston, MA: Allyn and Bacon, 1993.

7. Stalk, G., Jr. "Time—the Next Source of Competitive Advantage." *Harvard Business Review* 66, no. 4 (1988): 41–51.

8. Webster, S., and Z. K. Weng. "Improving Repetitive Manufacturing Systems: Analysis and Insights." University of Wisconsin–Madison School of Business, 1996.

9. Weng, Z. K. "Manufacturing Lead Times, System Utilization Rates and Lead Time-Related Demand." *European Journal of Operational Research* 89, no. 2 (1996): 259–268.

10. Womack, J., D. Jones, and D. Roos. *The Machine that Changed the World*. New York: Harper Perennial, 1991.

TABLE 2: Cost/Savings of New Production System

One-Time Start-Up Expense	
Adjustment to existing production planning system	$100,000
Annual Operating Expense/(Savings) Adjustments	
Planning personnel salary	$50,000
Reduction in standards WIP (reduction of 52,000 yards)	$124,800
Net Expense/(Savings)	$74,800

About the Author—

Z. KEVIN WENG, PhD, is a faculty member at the University of Wisconsin–Madison School of Business. He received his PhD. in operations management from Purdue University Krannert Graduate School of Management. His current research interests center on global supply-chain coordination and management, robust manufacturing and distribution system design and improvement, and competitive lead-time management. His work has appeared in Management Science, IIE Transactions, Naval Research Logistics, European Journal of Operational Research, and International Journal of Production Research.

FUNDAMENTAL GROUNDING

The Critical Importance of
MASTER PRODUCTION SCHEDULING

Why MPS is one of the most CRITICAL POINTS needed to be addressed in order for MANUFACTURING COMPANIES to execute the CONCEPTS involved in the hottest trend SWEEPING THE INDUSTRY.

BY STEVE WILSON, CPIM, and CHUCK DAVENPORT

Manufacturing Control Supporting SCM

THERE ARE MANY new technological developments that are adding to management's excitement over actual or potential SCM arrangements: the advance of client/server technology; the expanding use of electronic commerce; enterprise resource planning (ERP) software utilizing real-time data; and advanced planning and scheduling applications balancing and optimizing supply and demand across the supply chain. After spending all this money on technology, CIOs see supply chain improvements as one of the primary payoffs and sources of competitive advantage.

It is indeed a fact that through technology investments, manufacturing companies are now not only better accessing real-time data to make internal decisions, but also are sharing this information across the enterprise among customers, suppliers and distributors. Information sharing of this type has essentially created any number of opportunities under the guise of SCM (see Figure 1).

Certainly critical to effective supply chain management alliances is timely, complete and correct data and information upon which to make decisions. But you must remember, technology is no panacea. It is a new and improved—and expensive—tool that you still must learn to use properly in order to make better decisions. But how do you know what decisions to make? For what customers? For what products? And when, how much and across what locations? Underneath the hood in any successful SCM arrangement is discipline in master scheduling skills and processes, ensuring that capacity, inventory and productive assets will be used and cost effective in serving and leveraging your SCM business relationships.

Master scheduling is defined by APICS as "the process where the anticipated build schedule is reviewed and adjustments are made to the master production schedule (MPS) to ensure inventory levels and customer service goals are maintained and proper capacity and material planning occurs." In an SCM environment, this process and its resulting MPS now involves your suppliers, distributors and customers. Your SCM partner's inventory, material plans, capacity schedule and order information is now information available to the master schedule to develop a more integrated picture of demand and supply. This insight allows the master scheduler to make better MPS decisions to optimize the entire supply chain and execute SCM.

So what are these decisions that need to be made to execute SCM? Given that the master scheduling role is to ensure customer service and balance demand with supply and stable production, Figure 2 provides an example of decisions that would need to be made through the master schedule in response to supply chain information. All of

THERE ARE ANY NUMBER OF IDEAS FLOATING AROUND THE BUSINESS world that espouse the virtues and possibilities of supply chain management (SCM). However, each of these definitions describes a top layer of information interaction. For any initiative using these philosophies to succeed, there must be an underlying infrastructure of capability in manufacturing supply and demand planning. Therefore, the critical link to success in a supply chain initiative, no matter what the level of information interaction, is the ability to plan and schedule production at each link in the chain so that the entire supply chain is synchronized. This link is the master production schedule.

From *APICS—The Performance Advantage*, October 1998, pp. 40-43. © 1998 by APICS, the American Production and Inventory Control Society. Reprinted by permission.

these decisions, and the range of potential consequences, are vital to servicing a SCM partner.

Critical to their success, SCM arrangements require effective sharing of information. But the larger question is: What do you now do with all this newfound information? For a manufacturing company, that responsibility falls primarily to the master scheduling process. Master scheduling is the fundamental manufacturing control process that allows you to leverage information to carry out supply chain planning and focuses management on optimizing operations—not just on expediting orders. Only with the kind of discipline and prioritization possible through the planning decisions made in developing a master schedule can a company anticipate and effectively balance customer service with supply chain costs and a stable, balanced production.

Where Has Master Scheduling Been?

MASTER SCHEDULING is not new. But in the dynamic world of SCM, it is changing—and becoming more critical. A robust master scheduling process is or should be a part of any disciplined operation and a standard part of a company's manufacturing control system. However, a master schedule in the more demanding SCM world must do more than just calculate finite loads and run MRP to generate dependent demand. The days are gone when the master scheduler could run weekly MRP/DRP batch applications and hide the inaccuracies and errors behind inventory or excess capacity. Inventory is low, capacity is short, and the range of events that can happen across a manufacturer's supply chain makes the manufacturer's master schedule the fulcrum for its entire supply chain.

A master scheduler in a lean, SCM environment where customers are demanding responsiveness and flexibility does not have the time or inventory to react slowly to orders or bottlenecks. Managing the master schedule and capacity requires dynamic responses to demand and supply events. Fortunately, with advances in computer processing power and the functionality existent in advanced planning systems, planning cycles have been cut and planning parameters can be changed as the environment dictates—not just in arbitrary weekly buckets. In SCM environments there is simply no longer the buffer and

slack that can hide slow decision-making and static master scheduling.

The following scenario illustrates the new MPS role where planners can—and must—react quickly to events throughout the supply chain:

Reduced productivity due to poor raw material quality in the most recent lot, and a series of unplanned maintenance downtime is impacting the week's manufacturing schedule. In addition, higher sales than forecasted for two key VMI customers generated a new set of replenishment orders this morning. Also, additional transportation capacity is available due to unanticipated back haul routes. Using APS (advanced planning and scheduling) applications, the planner must develop a new plan by evaluating a number of schedule and customer service alternatives. Instead of relying on the week's now outdated MRP run or running a full replan—or worse yet, just telling the people in the plant to figure it out and do the best they can, and not taking advantage of reduced transportation costs—the master scheduler in the SCM world must now react to these events. An event-driven master schedule must take event information available and in very short planning cycles evaluate the impact on resource availability, raw ma-

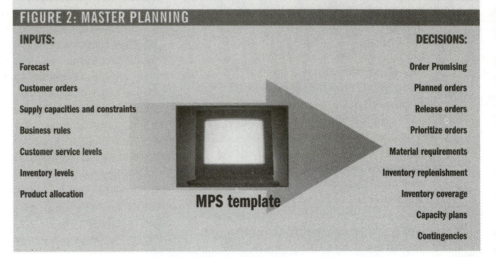

FIGURE 1: THE EVOLUTION OF SUPPLY CHAIN MANAGEMENT CONCEPTS

Level 1
Supporting
Functional Capabilities

- Develop internally focused total quality and process improvement programs
- Focus on stand-alone functional, i.e., inventory management, order fulfillment, purchasing
- Supplier quality programs based on internal measures

Level 2
Supply Chain
Processes

- Integrate company's internal processes and functions (i.e., customer service order promising with supply planning constraints)
- Develop supply chain capability by linking demand and supply through integrated forecasting, distribution planning and master planning processes

Level 3
Integrated Supply
Chain Channel

- Collaborative planning and decision-making (i.e., sharing schedule and demand information to conduct sales and operational planning)
- Integrated business processes, shared systems, and common goals across entire supply chain linking suppliers and customers
- Dynamic, customized processes used to support specific products and/or customer segments

FIGURE 2: MASTER PLANNING

INPUTS:

Forecast

Customer orders

Supply capacities and constraints

Business rules

Customer service levels

Inventory levels

Product allocation

MPS template

DECISIONS:

Order Promising

Planned orders

Release orders

Prioritize orders

Material requirements

Inventory replenishment

Inventory coverage

Capacity plans

Contingencies

CASE STUDY: THE POTENTIAL FOR PROBLEMS WITHOUT PROPER MPS

A manufacturing organization serving the retail grocery industry had a definite lack of MPS planning skills and a broken process for making MPS decisions. Its master schedule was essentially a finite load calculation, calculating open orders against manufacturing capacity at each of its plants. The lack of master scheduling taking place seemed at first a mild nuisance that the organization coped with well enough in times of excess capacity. But as capacity tightened in several of its plants and the industry began indicating interest in additional services in the name of supply chain management, the lack of good master scheduling became a direct cause for increasing customer service failures, high supply chain costs and a distinct competitive disadvantage.

Management and the process participants were quick to point to poor data and poor IT tools as the source of their problems; but as is often the case, there were process issues masquerading as systems issues.

Following are the characteristics of the company's master scheduling process:

• No process orientation or understanding of cause and effect throughout the process on customer service, capacity and plant scheduling.
• No established process roles and unclear responsibilities between customer service reps, sales reps, master scheduler, plant schedulers and shift supervisors. The different functions affecting the process had limited process perspective on the upstream and downstream activities.
• Inconsistent framework and criteria used for making decisions. Decisions made with insufficient information.
• Process relied on informal cross-functional interaction and limited flow of information.

The company's MPS policies also had the following problems:

• Lack of finite scheduling overloaded the MPS. This was the root cause for erosion of the process and high customer service failure rates.
• No business rules or use of time fences associated with the master schedule to stabilize production schedules.
• MPS was not linked with sales planning exercises or customer service reps order profiles, or integrated with plant scheduling systems.

• No systematic inventory practices and no formal guidelines within the MPS to support order promising and the order fulfillment process.
• Inconsistent tracking of inventory performance.
• No alignment of customer service guidelines, inventory practices and MPS time zone policies.

This lack of discipline in planning operations in an increasingly tight capacity situation created havoc across the company's manufacturing plants, resulting in a high number of expedited orders, stock outs and customer service failures. In addition, bad manufacturing controls kept them from having any confidence in inventory and manufacturing capacity numbers, therefore resulting in no integrity—or confidence—in their ability to make MPS decisions.

Because of all these shortcomings, most order decisions were relegated to the shop floor. This meant that important decisions such as what orders to run, what orders to move out and what stocks to replenish (essentially what customers to serve!) were being made, in some cases, by the shift supervisor who had just gotten off the phone with an irate sales rep. Thus, the company was in no position to promote and pursue SCM arrangements. Nonetheless, marketing and sales reps were in the marketplace developing a customer service strategy based on value-added SCM principles, such as vendor managed inventory and continuous replenishment of a variety of retail supply items.

This is just an example of how a company's operation and its supply chain capabilities did not match its avowed sales strategy. The fact is, their operational shortcomings and ineffective master scheduling processes prevented them from aggressively pursuing SCM opportunities with their key customers in the retail industry.

"They haven't proved they can manage our inventory turnover in these items better than we can," said one customer.

"We just can't be cost effective with our current operations," said one of the company's logistics managers. Therefore, the great potential for customer penetration and increased market share in a mature, commodity industry was lost.

---

terial availability, order priorities and distribution inventories to develop a superior recommendation that supports the entire supply chain.

These are obviously important decisions. For a manufacturing company living in an SCM world, they must be the right decisions. They also are the source for your company's ability to demonstrate the kind of SCM responsiveness that can differentiate it from its competitors.

Taking Strategy Towards Execution

SCM AS A STRATEGY is important. As discussed earlier, SCM concepts are well established in the marketplace, and manufacturing senior executives need to understand the

business opportunity and competitive advantages associated with SCM relationships. After years of focusing on manufacturing costs, executives are now recognizing the supply chain as the primary cost lever and competitive differentiator in many industry environments. In fact, as SCM evolves and expands, manufacturing companies will not compete solely on their product, but on the basis of their supply chain—how it collaborates and integrates with suppliers, distributors and customers to achieve its marketing and customer service strategies.

But when defining supply chain vision and direction, as with the concepts of reengineering and Six-Sigma quality, the topics are easily discussed and make good fodder for business conferences—but how many companies actually follow through and execute? Consumer retail is at the forefront in deploying SCM, but studies suggest that only about 20 percent of retailers have turned over their replenishment programs to vendors. The reason: A majority of customers did not believe that vendors could adequately support their continuous replenishment requirements.

So it comes back again to your people and the execution of business processes through management, systems, technology and skills. The execution process for a manufacturing company—promoting its ability to support and enable SCM business relationships—must also include an integrated master scheduling process using real-time data to make order promising, replenishment and capacity planning decisions.

Focus on Master Scheduling

ORGANIZATIONS GOING down this path should be very aware of what it takes. ERP transaction systems can provide data and information, but they must be incorporated into your processes to be an effective decision support tool. And don't forget that within a few short years there will be few, if any, of your major competitors without this kind of IT capability. It will be the companies that have leveraged technology to improve their master scheduling process and shorten their planning cycles—not just new systems and reliable data—that will be the industry leaders in SCM. They will be the companies that best plan and utilize their manufacturing, distribution and inventory resources to create competitive advantage in their supply chain capabilities.

So as you hear SCM discussed, proposed or expanded in your company, take account of how your master scheduling process works and how it acts as a decision support tool. Look at how it utilizes distribution and customer data; how it is used to broker customer service and plant scheduling; and how the master schedule supports order promising and the ability to optimize supply and demand decisions throughout your supply chain operations.

In many industries and for many companies, the SCM opportunity is well documented; for others it represents new opportunities and great potential. But execution and, more specifically, a robust master scheduling process remains the critical success factor. Don't simply confuse your new investment in an ERP system and running MRP with execution. Execution in the SCM environment depends on your company's ability to control its operation through the master scheduling function—the process, people, data and decision support tools that allow organizations to implement and meet the high expectations in their important SCM initiatives.

Steve Wilson, CPIM, is a manager with Pittiglio, Rabin Todd & McGrath, Inc. Chuck Davenport is a senior consultant with Deloitte & Touche.

The Manager's Guide to Supply Chain Management

F. Ian Stuart and David M. McCutcheon

"Competition makes the world go around. The only way to guarantee a supplier's attention to cost, service, and innovation is the ever-present threat of losing us as a customer."
—Vice President of Purchasing for a major steel company in Pennsylvania

"It's many times more advantageous to work with suppliers than to pitch them off and get new ones."
—David Nelson, former Senior Vice President of Purchasing for Honda of America

"They [suppliers] are in on the engineering meetings. They can drop in on the research guys. They know more about our requirements than some of our own people do and are instrumental for concurrent engineering of new products."
—Lance Dixon, former Director of Purchasing and Logistics for Bose Corporation

S upply management, the function of selecting sources for purchased goods and services and managing the flows of these inputs, has been growing in importance in North American firms. This trend stems from the steadily increasing reliance on outsourcing as a means to create added value. At the same time supply management comes into focus as a critical area, its practices are rapidly changing as companies experiment with different forms of supplier relationships.

Supply managers are to be forgiven if they are disappointed with the results of efforts to manage their supplier relationships better. Most efforts have failed to meet expectations. As with the above-quoted practitioners' advice, the academic and consulting communities have been equally inconsistent. Some have advised managers to be extremely cautious in forming supplier partnerships and alliances, and to continue to rely on competitive markets for their outsourcing needs. Conversely, partnership and alliance concepts have been touted as being universally applicable, sometimes with government encouragement, as with the U.K.'s Department of Trade and Industry's championing of "partnership sourcing." Overall, despite the occasional cautionary advice, the received wisdom—

The complexities of strategic outsourcing can be managed successfully only through rigorous technological forecasting.

which many practitioners are rigidly following—assumes that competitiveness in a global economy requires companies to:

1. focus on core competencies;
2. reduce their number of suppliers; and
3. develop strong partnership relationships built on shared information and trust with the remaining suppliers.

Our interviews with leading practitioners indicate that following this three-step approach, particularly blind adherence to the last step, trivializes the issue and may simply be bad medicine. As firms move toward even greater reliance on outsourcing, managers need clear guidelines for their outsourcing strategies and choosing the appropriate type of relationship with each supplier. In outlining three categories of supplier relationships, each of which makes sense for particular outsourcing needs, we provide a simple guideline for choosing the appropriate relationship for each supplier (see **Figure 1**).

SUPPLY MANAGEMENT OBJECTIVES: THE SIMPLE REALITY

T he strategic objectives in outsourcing an input are relatively straightforward. Basically, firms are interested in how they can either significantly *reduce product costs* or *add to what customers per-*

Figure 1
The Manager's Guide to Supply Management Objectives,
Relationship Choice, and Supporting Practices

Fundamental Objectives	Relationship Form	Critical Enablers	Benefits and Outcomes
Cost reduction	Competitive tension	*Competence trust* • Vendor certification to avoid evaluations • Commodity managers and supplier representatives • Direct-to-line shipment • Online demand information	Reduced cost Reduced transaction costs
	Cooperative partnership	• Problem-solving teams • Planning information • Consulting advice	Problem elimination Consistency Dependability
Value-added benefits/ Technology advancement	Strategic alliance	*Reciprocal goodwill trust* • Proprietary information • Technology forecasts • Engineering and technical exchanges	New products and processes Competitive advantage

ceive as value-added benefits. Naturally, firms hope that the value-added benefits can be achieved at lower cost, but in such cases the cost role is subordinate. Value-added benefits might include improved delivery speed, additional design features and options, or the ability to be customized. Some of these benefits are best achieved by using in-house product design and process management capabilities.

For most companies, however, the greatest opportunities for cutting costs and increasing value-added benefits lie with sourced materials, services, components, and technologies. Successful firms recognize and value their supply bases as critical sources of innovation and leverage. However, a firm can enhance any supplier's value by focusing the supplier's efforts on specific outcomes. The firm must choose and then communicate its fundamental objective for an input—whether it is primarily concerned with cost reduction or value-added benefits. Obviously, this choice has implications for the affected supplier and the firm's relationship with it.

Supply Cost Reduction Advantages

Typically, low cost is the primary requirement for most of a firm's purchased goods and services, with the strategic objective for the supplier relationship being cost reduction. This can be achieved by four primary mechanisms:

1. lower production costs of the supplies;
2. improved conformance quality (consistently meeting specifications);
3. material/location substitution; and

4. lower transaction costs, including the costs of incoming material inspections, vendor searches and evaluations, corrected supplier problems, and communications with suppliers.

Unfortunately, many cost reduction initiatives, especially those aimed at the first three mechanisms, suffer from diminishing returns or fail to yield sustainable competitive advantages. Most can be quickly imitated by competitors. Wal-Mart's initial cost-based competitive advantages were largely built on its supply chain's efficient performance (inventory management and control, direct-to-shelf delivery, on-line data access). But these advantages have gradually eroded as competitors have adopted similar customer-response practices. Astute competitors can seek out the same best-performing suppliers and attempt to duplicate their methods. Locating supply sources with low factor costs (such as selecting a Mexican supplier for a labor-intensive process) provides a cost reduction that may be short-lived (as exchange rates adjust) or rapidly duplicated by competitors. Likewise, cost reductions from material substitution, such as those developed using value-analysis practices, can be readily copied through reverse-engineering techniques. Even such practices as using active hedging to cut cost variability or "locking in" a reliable supply source are easily replicated and hardly represent a proprietary strategy.

In contrast, some transaction cost advantages can be sustained. Capability in *managing* suppliers and using specialized, dedicated inter-firm resources can greatly reduce transaction costs. Such a capability is more difficult to mimic because success depends heavily on how the buying firm interrelates with and manages a particular supplier. Biemans and Brand (1995) noted a significant difference in administrative costs between world-class supply management firms and the average firm. The difference amounted to sustained profit margin improvements of about 2.5 percent—a clear differentiating advantage.

Transaction-cost reduction approaches, whether tactical and readily duplicated or strategic and sustainable, encompass both supplier *selection* decisions and supply *management* practices. Some gains result from securing the best suppliers—those that continue to innovate, strive for high quality levels, and routinely drive out waste. Others come from the way the firm interrelates with the supplier and how the two companies interact. For example, a good supplier relationship may determine whether the firm gets to share in its supplier's cost reductions; one auto industry supplier confessed it had shown such preferential cost sharing with Ford and Chrysler but not with General Motors because of GM's history of adversarial supply management tactics.

Supply-Based Technology Advantages

The second strategic objective relates to technology. In most companies, this should apply to a limited segment of suppliers—those that provide critical inputs. Having proprietary access to a supplier's critical technological innovations can add customer value and improve competitive positioning, as well as cut costs. Now, more than ever; companies are relying on outsourcing rather than in-house development to secure their innovations.

Firms continue to identify core competencies, seeking the inherent benefits—such as improved knowledge depth and organizational learning—of greater focus. Other specific technologies may be essential for competitiveness but it may not be practical to maintain expertise for them in-house. The science base may be changing too rapidly, making it risky to be a player in that field. Or it may be too expensive to maintain technological competence. Or the product may be too complex for any firm to manage all aspects internally. In each case, outsourcing the technology becomes an alternative—but one that entails risks, especially if suppliers provide critical proprietary capabilities and technology integration skills. "Most companies I interact with," says Bob Drennan, Director of Corporate Materials at Tektronix, "are facing a fundamental issue as to the best use of money—invest in resources to design and manufacture products or invest in ways to grow faster without adding infrastructure."

Technology outsourcing leverages resources. To use it, however, firms must manage supplier relationships effectively to fully exploit suppliers' process and product design expertise while at the same time controlling the risk of relying on an outside source for critical inputs. For long-term advantage, a firm must not only manage its current critical technology suppliers but also look to future technology needs and possible impacts on current suppliers. Just as a firm might have an evolving R&D portfolio, it should also plan its technology sourcing portfolio with an eye to the future.

The *Economist* recently documented the technological barriers facing the magnetic-storage (computer disk) industry ("A Byte of the Action" 1998). Forecasts predict that this technology, which detects the polarity of a magnetized spot on a disk, will be dominated within five years by laser optics (although IBM researchers believe that the current technology will survive longer and ultimately be replaced by holographic cubes). Regardless of which new technology emerges, one thing is certain: Many new storage technologies are being advanced by firms that are new to the industry. Companies that source storage devices may face a radical supply-base upheaval as these emerging technologies force product design changes and render existing key processes obsolete. Supplier relations will be disrupted as new technology alliances are formed with emerging suppliers while some existing suppliers are dropped.

Even in industries in which discontinuities are unlikely, securing access to critical current technology remains a vital supply management role. Although the technology advantage objective has a much narrower focus than that of supply cost reduction, it may have a bigger impact on the firm.

RELATIONSHIPS TO MATCH OBJECTIVES: BEYOND THE RHETORIC

Clearly, fulfilling these two distinct strategic objectives requires quite different forms of supplier relationships. Once a firm understands its primary objectives for different types of inputs, it can develop distinctive and suitable supplier relationships. We classify the two basic types as *competitive tension* and *strategic alliance*. However, not every supplier targeted for either type is necessarily prepared for it, necessitating a special kind of transition relationship—the *cooperative partnership*—designed to prepare them. Each type has advantages in meeting specific objectives.

Competitive Tension Relationships

When seeking suppliers primarily for supply cost reductions, North American firms traditionally split purchases for a particular item among two or more competing suppliers—in effect, playing one off against the other(s). But such an approach reduces scale economies, drives up transaction costs, and tends to build suppliers' resentment rather than loyalty.

In contrast, competitive tension relationships use a single supplier—called "sole-sourcing"—for each item. Developed in the Japanese auto industry, this approach typically allocates all demand for a particular component over the product's life cycle to an individual supplier but concurrently ensures that similar parts are sourced from that supplier's competitors. This maintains the essence of competition yet provides the advantages of scale economies. Having potential alternative sources available ensures competitiveness and security of supply. Moreover, if the need arises to switch suppliers, the switching costs are lower. The higher-volume, stable market encourages the suppliers' investment in R&D and special services for the firm. Sole-sourcing also limits supply variance. Meanwhile, suppliers know that the business is not guaranteed. This competitive tension relationship ideally suits the supply cost reduction objective, because the firm can exploit its market power to achieve the advantages of inter-supplier competition while avoiding the problems of adversarial relationships.

Strategic Alliance Relationships

Companies may form a strategic alliance when the mutual objective is to use their complementary assets to gain long-term competitive advantage. In the supply context, alliances with suppliers are appropriate for securing technology advantages. A special relationship with a supplier can help ensure access to a critical technology that the firm must outsource. Bose Corporation, the high-performance audio manufacturer, has a strategic alliance for its integrated circuit design technology. Circuitry design is critical for the performance of Bose's high-end car stereo systems, but it is a competency that Bose has no long-term interest in developing internally.

Strategic supplier alliances seek to secure not just specified inputs but the technical expertise surrounding them. A firm may provide its allied supplier with only performance specifications (indicating what the input must do, rather than how it is to be designed). It may even rely on the supplier to provide the complete design, plus help in integrating it into the firm's products or processes, plus technical advice and technology forecasts. Defining such a broad relationship by contract is very difficult, especially when resource requirements and questions about the legal ownership of jointly developed ideas are hard to predict. For this reason, the strategic supplier alliance relationship needs to be nurtured and built up over time to be based on something other than ironclad contracts.

Supra Products, the leading U.S. manufacturer of real estate lock boxes, had seen its traditional technology, based on mechanical key locks, quickly give way to electronic-based systems. The firm had developed internal competency in the design, assembly, and logic programming for these electronic locking systems and had no desire to build expertise in manufacturing printed circuit boards. But Supra needed responsiveness; its products often required rapid modifications, and the company was expanding into new markets. So the supply management team was attempting to develop an alliance relationship with a small, local circuit board design firm that could handle its unique technical requirements.

Because these relationships must be developed for specific requirements, a firm's different divisions may maintain distinctly different relationships with the same supplier. We saw this with Applied Materials (AM), the semiconductor chip process equipment manufacturer, and CDS Leopold, a precision aluminum machining supplier. The Santa Clara, California facilities of both CDS Leopold and AM's product and process development division operated a technology alliance. Developing prototypes for new chip processing equipment requires considerable design latitude as well as an informal, rich exchange of critical information through guest engineers and frequent face-to-face meetings. However, the relationship stands in stark contrast to that developed between the two companies' commercial plants located in Austin, Texas, which we will describe a little later.

Establishing a strategic supplier alliance relationship absorbs considerable time and resources and may involve significant risks. It should be reserved for situations where it is warranted, such as one in which difficult-to-specify expertise is needed in conjunction with the purchased item, or the supplier provides unique, vital inputs.

Cooperative Partnership (Supplier Development)—An Interim Relationship

Recently, many companies have preferred to *help* their existing suppliers improve rather than locate, qualify, and switch to alternates. Often called *supplier development,* the merits of such a cooperative partnership as a long-term supply management approach may have been oversold. A cooperative partnership involves working closely with a supplier on problems the firms jointly face, principally over delivery and conformance quality. Such problems are often attacked through joint problem-solving teams that identify root causes, experiment to determine sources of variance, and implement incremental improvements. Benefits are shared equitably, consistent with the "partnership" terminology.

Companies choose this option for a variety of reasons. They may wish to avoid onerous switching costs, or they may see an underlying supply advantage masked by a supplier's current problems with delivery or quality conformance. However, the development effort should have a finite lifespan and the relationship should be targeted to assume another form eventually.

Applied Materials used this approach for supply contracts for its high-volume production components. Its Austin facilities source precision aluminum machined parts from CDS Leopold's local plant. When those plants were established in the early 1990s, the initial buyer-seller relationship resembled a cooperative partnership as the two firms worked together to overcome production startup problems. Once those problems were resolved, the relationship evolved into one of competitive tension. CDS Leopold representatives have privileged access to AM's plant and production information, but AM maintains a competitive source for the items it buys from this supplier.

The differences between the two divisions of AM and CDS Leopold—the Santa Clara facilities that operate in the technology alliance realm and the Austin facilities that have evolved from cooperative partnerships to competitive tension—stem from the very different supply management objectives for each division. Managing such diverse relationships between different divisions or for products at different stages of the life cycle adds to the supplier management challenges.

Allen Bradley Canada's supply management tactics in recent years provide another example. In the early 1990s, Allen Bradley (AB) was concerned about its suppliers' conformance quality problems. To communicate its dissatisfaction, the company introduced supplier evaluation reports and a "cost of nonconformance" assessment system. The suppliers' heightened awareness of these issues, coupled with AB's cooperative assistance to major suppliers, led to noticeable improvements. Within five years, the company's efforts helped reduce the nonconformance costs from $70 to $12 per $1,000 of material purchases. Subsequently, conformance issues largely disappeared and improvements became marginal. AB's concerns have since shifted to other issues. As the suppliers improved their own performance, the relationships, though cordial, ceased to resemble cooperative partnerships and drifted toward competitive tension. AB continues to sole-source from these suppliers but maintains ready access to alternative sources, and has in fact dropped at least one problematic supplier.

Competitive tension requires a pool of viable alternative sources for similar purchases; supplier development can be used to create the necessary alternative suppliers. John Goldberg, Procurement and Contracts Manager at Applied Materials, tells how in the 1980s Motorola complained bitterly that AM's products often failed to meet specifications or delivery times. However, there was considerable interest, both politically and from a general supply risk perspective, for

"Once it became a reliable supplier, the joint problem-solving teams were abandoned and the relationship between the two firms drifted toward competitive tension."

Motorola to help develop a domestic semiconductor equipment supplier. Rather than seek alternative suppliers, most of which were off-shore, Motorola chose to "micro-manage" the AM relationship continually over a two-year period to establish it as a reliable supplier. During this time, AM reduced its product cycle times from 16 to 12 weeks and conformance quality rose dramatically. Once it became a reliable supplier, the joint problem-solving teams were abandoned and the relationship between the two firms drifted toward competitive tension.

These situations were typical of the outcomes we saw with supplier development efforts. Although it wasn't always recognized, the strategic objectives usually reverted to either cost reduction or strategic technology development once the supplier had achieved a certain performance level. Improvements from the cooperative approach gradually diminished until they eventually ceased to warrant the associated high management and transaction costs. Our field interviews found that most reported partnerships and much-touted "close" supplier relations arose from less-than-acceptable supplier performance, which typically surfaced as the buying companies adopted lean production or just-in-time philosophies. Corrective action had to be taken to improve those suppliers seen as "weak links" in the value chain. Once those issues were resolved, the objective usually reverted to cost reduction.

Interestingly, in the technology-intensive computer chip manufacturing sector, we saw several cases in which the supplier development approach was the forerunner to the alternate strategic objective: the technology-based supplier alliance. Certain suppliers, despite their quality and delivery problems, were targeted for their valuable technological expertise. The manufacturers chose to assist them in overcoming these short-term performance weaknesses, viewing the costs of supplier development (much higher in the short term than simply switching suppliers) to be small compared to the benefits of maintaining the technology linkage. Once the problems had been overcome, the chip manufacturers could concentrate on exploiting the supplier's technological capabilities. In a similar vein, Bell Canada, the Canadian telecommunications service firm, has established alliance-like technology relationships, not only with its primary switching equipment supplier, Nortel, but also a host of small, specialized technology suppliers that offer the promise of future technological expertise.

The Relationship/Strategy Match

To use a firm's supply management resources most effectively, suppliers need to be segmented according to the strategic objectives they are to serve. Supplier selection and segmentation has even been called the "next best practice" in supply management. ICL, the U.K.-based computer company, learned of the need for segmentation the hard way. Initially, it treated all suppliers equally, attempting to form strategic alliances with each of them. But the transaction costs proved overwhelming. Interestingly, most of its suppliers did not feel that special relationships were warranted and complained about the excessive time and effort required. ICL has since segmented its supply base relationships for consistency with its different strategic objectives. Now, only 2 to 3 percent of its suppliers fall into the strategic alliance category, with the balance in the cost reduction category.

Thus, firms need to distinguish among the suppliers that are truly of strategic importance, those that are best managed for cost reduction, and those that require the special attention of supplier development. In this last category, the firm's supply managers should have a clear idea of which category the developed supplier is destined to fit—either as a strategic partner or as a low-cost supplier.

RELATIONSHIP ENABLERS: TRUST AND INFORMATION FLOWS

Having identified the strategic objectives and the appropriate matching relationship, the manager's task is to "make it so." Clearly, these different relationship types need to be implemented and managed using distinctly different practices. Although the approaches must differ in many ways, two aspects are of particular significance. First, the desired relationship must be matched by the types of information that flow between the firms. Second, each form demands that the two parties develop and maintain a particular level of trust.

Sako (1992) offers relevant definitions of *competency trust* and *goodwill trust.* Competency trust relies on confidence that a supplier can maintain delivery and quality standards without constant reminders or monitoring. A firm feels confident that it can curtail supplier scanning, competitive benchmarking, supplier evaluations, and audits, as well as reduce or eliminate inspections of incoming material. In short, competency trust is a critical enabler for reducing supply-related transaction costs.

In contrast, goodwill trust is one party's belief that the other party will always act in the first one's best interests, even when the second one could take advantage of it. Ideally, goodwill trust is reciprocal: the buyer must trust the supplier and vice versa. Either party can only verify that it has gained the other's trust by exposing itself to the other's possible opportunistic behavior and determining whether its trust was warranted. Mutual goodwill trust permits firms to share confidential and proprietary information and collaborate on new product and process designs without fear of opportunism. This *reciprocal* goodwill trust is viewed as a critical element in realizing technology-based competitive advantages.

Competitive Tension Enablers

Competitive tension relationships emphasize simplicity and transaction cost reduction, building on competency trust that enables streamlined communications and improved supplier response to deficiencies. As a first step, the firm must make a detailed assessment of each supplier's reliability, determined either through its track record in supplying the firm or through independent certification (such as ISO 9000). Next, it permits those suppliers with demonstrated reliability to ship products directly to the required point of use without inspection, providing an important signal that the buyer trusts the suppliers to conform consistently to specifications.

Ultimately, the firm may have some suppliers undertake activities traditionally managed in-house: self-monitoring their orders through electronic data interchange; administering their own accounts through automatic debit/payment systems; even supervising their use through in-plant supplier representatives. Key representatives may assume responsibility for a range of items, managing inventory and resolving any quality problems on behalf of the firm. Essentially, the supplier representative system can be used to outsource the entire part procurement responsibility. Bose (with what it terms "JIT II"), Allen Bradley Canada (through its commodity managers), and Applied Materials have all successfully implemented variants of the in-plant supplier representative approach.

Although all competitive tension relationships require competency trust, superior transaction cost reduction practices require *buyer-based goodwill trust.* Given sufficient goodwill trust in the supplier, the buyer might employ other cost-saving practices, such as the use of Kaiser purchase order drafts, whereby the payment process is handled on delivery by the supplier itself. (Yes, the supplier writes its own check!) This eliminates the need for duplicate accounting and verification activities. As another step made possible by buyer-based goodwill trust, some firms have implemented pricing models based on the supplier's direct-cost estimates—in essence, a "cost plus" pricing system based on the supplier's estimate of job processing time. The firm needs sufficient goodwill trust in these suppliers to be convinced that they won't take advantage of the arrangement. In return, the firm can eliminate the time and cost of bargaining and resolving disputes about contract pricing.

Along with the appropriate level of trust, cost reduction objectives also need appropriate information flows. At minimum, suppliers need clear performance specifications combined with a current and accurate demand forecast. Buyers need ways to advise suppliers of perceived problems and their priorities. A supplier evaluation and performance feedback system is critical. A "cost of supplier nonconformance" accounting report, like that used by Allen Bradley, can prove extremely valuable. Allen Bradley, Honda, and Warn Industries are just a few examples of firms that routinely provide suppliers with delivery and conformance quality feedback, highlighting areas of concern.

Cooperative Partnership Enablers

Information flows that facilitate joint problem-solving enable the cooperative partnership approach. Typical activities include training and education on problem identification and problem-solving techniques, as well as developing expertise in designing quality-related experiments. Like Toyota does as part of its supplier outreach program, the buyer can provide operations and quality consultants, free of charge, to help the supplier solve problems. Some firms, such as B.C. Tel, a regional telecommunications provider, use supplier benchmarking to inform the weaker suppliers about their comparative shortcomings.

The most effective cooperative partnerships we've seen have specific learning objectives for suppliers. They realize that, although they could intervene directly in a supplier's problem for fast results, there are long-term advantages in transferring broad management capabilities to the supplier and creating a philosophy of continual organizational learning—which does not necessarily occur when solutions are imposed.

Strategic Alliance Enablers

The strategic alliance relationship requires a very different set of enablers. A firm needs continued access to supplier technology and expertise to develop new processes and products. By relying heavily on key suppliers beyond their direct control, it seeks some techno-

logical integration between itself and allied suppliers while managing the risks of its dependence on them.

Usually, risk in inter-firm relationships is managed through contracts. However, developing a contract to handle all possible contingencies for a supplier alliance relationship would be difficult—and possibly counterproductive, since onerous contract terms could stifle both parties' creativity and commitment. If the relationship's purpose is joint technology development, it may be futile to specify precisely each party's required technological contribution, especially at the early stages. It may also be difficult to determine what each party's contribution has been throughout a close collaborative development, or to "fairly" allocate the resulting benefits. In place of contracts to cover these contingencies, both sides must rely on a high level of *reciprocal* goodwill trust to maximize each party's benefits from technological collaborations. The supplier's proprietary technology must be safeguarded, and the supplier must be compensated appropriately for its contributions. Reciprocal goodwill trust allows cooperative ventures not completely governed by contracts to be undertaken, since each party has little concern about the other's opportunistic behavior.

Developing goodwill trust takes time and management effort as well as risk. Firms can generate trust by exchanging critical technical resources, sharing confidential technology forecasts and drawings, collaborating on strategic plans and long-term product forecasts,

A Note About Our Study

We draw upon both previous supply management research and, perhaps more important, our ten years of field investigations of both successful and unsuccessful supplier partnerships and strategic alliances. We were particularly influenced by our assessment of what "best practice" companies—those frequently held out as exemplars of supply management practice—had done and where they appeared to be headed. In some cases, there were dramatic differences between reported practice and what we observed, underscoring the need for clarifying the situation. We are grateful to those managers who spared valuable time and shared their learning experiences.

For simplicity, we focus on the product level and the companies' relationships with their suppliers of component parts and materials. Our advice about supply management objectives and relationship choices are equally valid for purchased services, such as those for marketing consulting, information technology, financial auditing, and tax services. Finally, in our discussion, we assume that the firm has already decided to outsource the particular input rather than produce it in-house (recognizing that this decision to outsource may have to be revisited if purchasing proves incapable of meeting the strategic objective for the input).

or exchanging sensitive financial information. Both buying firms and suppliers must expose themselves to situations in which the other party might act opportunistically, thereby allowing the other party to demonstrate its trustworthiness by *not* taking advantage of such situations. For its part, the supplier can instill trust by, say, suggesting alternative sources that might better serve the buyer's needs, or voluntarily divulging cost savings it would be willing to share with the buyer, especially if the savings could otherwise be kept hidden. Both actions can add confidence that the supplier has the buyer's best interests at heart.

With sufficient mutual trust, firms have a host of actions available to them. They may use in-plant supplier representatives, as with the transaction cost reduction approach. Here, however, the buyer may choose to expand the representative's responsibilities and plant access, to include access to sensitive technical departments. These enablers ensure that, despite the inherent high risks of a strategic supplier alliance, the perceived probability of proprietary losses is extremely low and, hence, the overall expected value of such an event is maintained at acceptable levels.

While information flows with the other supplier relationship approaches are primarily one-way (from the firm to its suppliers), strategic supplier alliances thrive on two-way flows. The firm can provide its partners with channel market, production planning, and technical information; in turn, it should expect to receive technical advice, product design, and integration assistance and information from the supplier's environmental scanning. The firm must build multiple channels to capture the maximum benefit from these suppliers. Channels might include staff exchanges, regular forums to discuss areas of mutual concern, and relaxed procedures that encourage the easy flow of communication between the employees of the two partners.

Management Caveats

Some might argue that our assessment is too simplistic, claiming, for example, that the cooperative partnership offers much longer-lasting, sustainable gains. Our field interviews suggest otherwise, however. They provide considerable insight about these relationships, including how and why they formed, how they developed over time, and where they were headed. Going beyond the business press rhetoric, we found that many reported "partnerships" turned out to be little more than civil relations between firms—certainly an improvement over previous adversarial conditions but falling well short of being strategic alliances. Other relationships displayed alliance-type characteristics, but on closer inspection they were predominantly supplier development efforts initiated to correct supplier performance weaknesses. Most of them offered limited long-term strategic benefits beyond achieving cost reductions. Moreover, when pressed, the managers admitted that the future prospects for expanded interactions seemed limited.

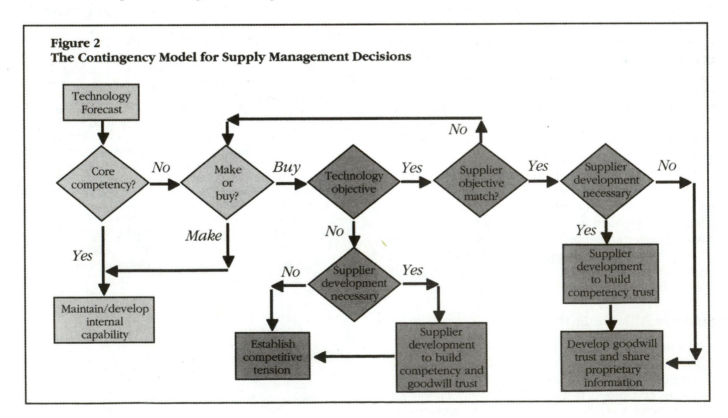

Figure 2
The Contingency Model for Supply Management Decisions

We do not pretend that our guide covers all contingencies. In particular, we point out three fundamental caveats to using this guide blindly. To make the manager's decision-making just a little less complicated, we incorporate these caveats into a contingency model, shown in **Figure 2**.

First, we have used the buyer's perspective in evaluating a relationship's value. Clearly, the supplier's perspective may be somewhat different. Suppliers have their own technology strategies and different views about the merits of a potential relationship. Quite rightly, the supplier may not want the buyer's envisioned relationship, or may even want to form an alliance with a different customer that demonstrates greater potential for long-term benefits. To offset this lack of supplier enthusiasm, a firm may have to adopt other tactics to secure access to the critical technology. We could easily see the case for taking more risks and making greater effort to establish goodwill trust in such circumstances.

Second, using any of these approaches will impose cultural adjustments and implementation difficulties, depending on how they differ from the firm's past supply management practices. GM's attempts to adopt modern supply management practices continue to be hindered by a long history and established culture of adversarial relationships with its supply community. If GM intended to adopt competitive tension in place of the traditional multisourcing adversarial approach, implementation would probably be more difficult than it would be for other firms without such a history. Once again, a firm may have to go to greater lengths over a longer period of time to overcome a similar historical legacy. Although we do not formally include this contingency in Figure 2, overcoming a prior history of adversarial relations should temper managers' expectations for implementing this three-approach system.

Third, our guide assumes that managers know where the company's products are headed technologically. Managers have to recognize what the firm's core competencies are and what its customers perceive as the product's future order-winning characteristics. Without rigorous work in this area, any outsourcing strategy will be a shot in the dark, with two fundamental risks. First, the firm may maintain some competencies that consume resources without adding value. It would be better off allocating its resources in areas where they could make a difference and relying on outsourcing where suppliers could provide the technologies more effectively.

On the other band, firms might outsource technologies that ultimately prove to be key areas of competitive advantage. This serious error results in a major loss of control and a weakened competitive position. In the laser printer industry, Canon has taken strategic advantage of its competitors' excessive technology outsourcing. By exploiting its optical electronics competency, Canon has amassed an 80 percent market share for laser printer engines, a critical technological component. Conversely, in a related industry, Kodak exited the camcorder business many years ago and later faced the daunting task of reacquiring digital photography capabilities, in which the technology architecture is based on electronic imaging rather than on chemical photographic systems.

Some key technologies, especially rapidly changing ones, should be retained in-house even if they are not currently viewed as vital. Core competencies and technologies will change over time. A non-strategic technology may become critical to the firm's order-winning criteria in the future, perhaps forcing the firm to reacquire previously outsourced knowledge, a potentially expensive and difficult process. The converse is also true. The supply manager may develop a strong alliance relationship with a supplier offering a critical technology only to find that radically different, alternative technologies are emerging from other sources. The buying firm may have to extract itself somehow from the alliance relationship, a potentially difficult action that may affect other supplier relationships.

Without a rigorous technological forecast, strategic outsourcing will be filled with many blind avenues and deeply regretted decisions. In all our visits, the firms with successful outsourcing strategies, complete with associated relationship-building strategies and implementation plans, began with well-developed and rigorous technological forecasts. Top management must understand the future technological requirements as an essential first step in the strategic outsourcing process and one that all but a select few of the "best practice" firms have yet to appreciate.

References

W.G. Biemans and M.J. Brand, "Reverse Marketing: A Synergy of Purchasing and Relationship Marketing," *International Journal of Purchasing and Materials Management* 31, 3 (1995): 28–37.

A.M. Brandenburger and B.J. Nalebuff, *Co-opetition* (New York: Doubleday, 1996).

J.A. Byrne, R. Brandt, and O. Port, "The Virtual Corporation," *Business Week*, February 8, 1993, pp. 98–102.

"A Byte of the Action," *Economist*, September 19, 1998, pp. 96–97.

K.B. Clark and T. Fujimoto, *Product Development Performance: Strategy, Organization and Management in the World Auto Industry* (Boston: Harvard Business School Press, 1991).

R.E. Corey, *Technology Fountainheads: The Management Challenge of R&D Consortia* (Boston: Harvard Business School Press, 1997).

W.G. Cutler, "Acquiring Technology from the Outside," *Research Technology Management*, May–June 1991, pp. 11–18.

M.A. Cusumano and A. Takeishi, "Supplier Relations and Management: A Survey of Japanese, Japanese-Transplant and U.S. Auto Plants," *Strategic Management Journal*, 12, 8 (1991): 563–588.

L. Dixon and A.M. Porter, *JIT II: Revolution in Buying and Selling* (Newton, MA: Cahners Publishing, 1994).

P.M. Doney and J.P. Cannon, "An Examination of the Nature of Trust in Buyer-seller Relationships," *Journal of Marketing*, April 1997, pp. 35–51.

J.H. Dyer, "Effective Interfirm Collaboration: How Firms Minimize Transaction Costs and Maximize Transaction Value," *Strategic Management Journal*, August 1997, pp. 535–556.

J.H. Dyer, D.S. Cho and W. Chu, "Strategic Supplier Segmentation: The Next 'Best Practice' in Supply Chain Management," *California Management Review*, Winter 1998, pp. 57–77.

J.H. Dyer and W.G. Ouchi, "Japanese Style Partnerships: Giving Companies a Competitive Edge," *Sloan Management Review*, Fall 1993, pp. 51–63.

Y.L. Doz and G. Hamel, *Alliance Advantage: The Art of Creating Value Through Partnering* (Boston: Harvard Business School Press, 1998).

G. Hamel and C.K. Prahalad, *Competing for the Future* (Boston: Harvard University Press, 1994).

M. Iansiti, *Technology Integration* (Boston: Harvard Business School Press, 1998).

V. Kapoor and A. Gupta, "Aggressive Sourcing: A Free Market Approach," *Sloan Management Review*, Fall 1997, pp. 21–31

J. Kluge, "Simply Superior Sourcing," 5th International Annual IPSERA Conference, Eindhoven, Netherlands, 1996.

A.A. Lado, N.G. Boyd, and S.C. Hanlon, "Competition, Cooperation and the Search for Economic Rents: A Syncretic Model," *Academy of Management Review*, 22, 3 (1997): 110–141.

R.C. Lamming, *Beyond Partnership: Strategies for Innovation and Lean Supply* (New York: Prentice-Hall, 1993).

B. Leavy, "Outsourcing Strategy and a Learning Dilemma," *Production and Inventory Management Journal*, Fourth Quarter 1996, pp. 50–54.

D. Lei and J.W. Slocum, Jr., "Global Strategy, Competence Building and Strategic Alliances," *California Management Review*, Fall 1992, pp. 81–97.

C.K. Prahalad and G. Hamel, "The Core Competency of the Corporation," *Harvard Business Review*, May–June 1990, pp. 79–91.

J.B. Quinn and F.G. Hilmer, "Strategic Outsourcing," *Sloan Management Review*, Summer 1994, pp. 43–55.

J. Ramsay, "The Case Against Purchasing Partnerships," *International Journal of Purchasing and Materials Management*, Fall 1996, pp. 2–12.

M. Sakakibara, "Co-operative Research and Development: Theory and Evidence on Japanese Practice," unpublished doctoral thesis, Harvard University, Cambridge, Massachusetts, 1994.

M. Sako, *Prices, Quality and Trust: Inter-firm Relations in Britain and Japan* (Cambridge: Cambridge University Press, 1992).

P. Senge, *The Fifth Discipline: The Art and Practice of the Learning Organization* (New York: Doubleday/Currency, 1990).

P. Senge, "The Leader's New Work: Building Learning Organizations," *Sloan Management Review*, Fall 1990, pp. 7–23.

M. Treacy and F. Wiersema, *The Discipline of Market Leaders. Choose Your Customers, Narrow Your Focus, Dominate Your Markets* (Reading, MA: Addison-Wesley, 1995).

R.J. Trent and R.M. Monczka, "Purchasing and Supply Management: Trends and Changes Throughout the 1990s," *International Journal of Purchasing and Materials Management*, Fall 1998, pp. 2–11.

R. Venkatesan, "Strategic Sourcing: To Make or Not to Make," *Harvard Business Review*, November–December 1992, pp. 98–107.

J.A. Welch and P.R. Nayak, "Strategic Sourcing: A Progressive Approach to the Make-or-Buy Decision," *Academy of Management Executive*, February 1992, pp. 23–31.

O. Williamson, *Markets and Hierarchies* (New York: The Free Press, 1975).

O. Williamson, *The Economic Institutions of Capitalism* (New York: The Free Press, 1985).

F. Ian Stuart is an associate professor of supply chain and quality management at the University of Victoria, Victoria, BC, Canada, where **David McCutcheon** is an associate professor of operations management.

Squeezing the Most Out of Supply Chains

By using software tools that leverage best practices, purchasers are improving the flow of goods.

by Michael S. McGarr

Purchasing more than 1,200 safety products from a dozen different suppliers, Eastman Chemical Co. was wasting time and money trying to manage its sourcing of everything from fire extinguishers to safety goggles.

The $4.6 billion manufacturer of plastics, chemicals and fibers realized it needed to reduce its number of safety equipment suppliers to one and establish a long-term partnership resulting in lower costs for both parties.

So the Kingsport, Tenn.-based company in June launched a plan to centralize the purchasing of safety equipment and, eventually, other indirect materials, which it had been conducting from four major U.S. purchasing sites. The sites worked independently and procurement decisions were based on each site's local requirements, two no-nos when it comes to best practices. Indeed, the company admits it should have known better, because it has been applying best practices techniques to other areas of its supply chain for eight years.

Eastman Chemical expects better procurement processes to save $15 million a year.

Eastman, which has 15,000 employees in more than 30 countries, established a five-person corporate service group in its indirect materials and services organization, with the goal of centralizing and standardizing procurement of certain indirect materials. The group's goal is to save the company $15 million annually.

Focusing on Strategy

"We needed to free people up to do more strategic things," says Debbie Davis-Waltermire, director of worldwide materials and services at Eastman. "We didn't have time to do anything but the manual sourcing work."

Traditional sourcing involves sending out requests for quotes, requests for proposals and requests for information to a number of potential suppliers, comparing and contrasting the results, before finally negotiating and contracting with the best supplier. Recently Internet-based collaboration tools have emerged to automate the process, replacing time-consuming, paper-based methods that do nothing to foster partnerships.

Eastman utilized a set of strategic sourcing tools from Webango Inc., Santa Clara, Calif. The hosted applications, which cost a minimum of $250,000 per year, are designed to select the best suppliers for complex commodities and services, negotiate and manage contracts, and develop long-term supply chain partnerships.

From *EC World,* December 2000, pp. 44-48. © 2000 by EC Media Group.

Seven Tips for Best Practices

Best practices are documented strategies and tactics employed by "the most admired, most profitable and keenest competitors in the business," according to Best Practices LLC, a Research Triangle, N.C.-based research and consulting firm specializing in benchmarking best practices.

While best practices vary from industry to industry, any company in a manufacturing supply chain can benefit by adhering to the seven best practices identified in a study conducted by Best Practices, "Best Practices in Supply Chain Management."

The two-year study, based on primary and secondary research, profiled more than 130 companies across 31 industries, including supply chain stalwarts Dell Computer Corp., Ford Motor Co., Texas Instruments Inc., Wal-Mart Stores Inc., Glaxo Wellcome Inc. and Eastman Chemical Co.

Best Practices:

- Align supply chain management systems with strategic initiatives and goals;
- Forge partnerships with suppliers;
- Certify supplier-partners;
- Employ technology to improve supplier partnerships;
- Refine and enhance the manufacturing process;
- Foster communication between partner organizations; and
- Emphasize the mutual benefits of partnership.

Source: Best Practices LLC

On average, Fortune 1000 companies spend $3.5 billion per year on external supplies, according to Webango's research. Strategically sourcing a commodity can yield savings of 10% to 30% relative to the price paid when buying on an ad hoc basis, Webango says.

Once a contract has been established, the terms of that contract must be managed. Typically if an invoice doesn't match a purchase order, for example, or goods don't arrive on time, people on both ends must step in and resolve the process, often erasing the profitability achieved by processing transactions over the Web.

Contract management products like Webango's record all of the negotiations and documents leading up to an agreement and simplify the process of resolving discrepancies. Using the Webango Network, Eastman's corporate sourcing team utilized tools for tabulating scores, analyzing results, and sharing information with team members over the Internet with only a browser.

"Typically we would mail out a 20-page request-for-information with 75 to 100 questions to our suppliers and wait for them to come back," says Davis-Waltermire.

Once the information was received, procurement employees would manually tabulate each RFI that con-

The winning supplier agreed to on-time delivery and inventory buy-back.

tained detailed information including suppliers' financial history for the past five years, quality initiatives, inventory management capabilities and payment terms.

Finally, after weeks of manual spreadsheet analysis, requests-for-proposals, the second step in the sourcing process, would be sent out to a subset of suppliers based on the information received.

"It was a very inefficient process that limited the number of contracts we could source," says Davis-Waltermire. "Corporate sourcing is not a lot of fun."

Picking the Winner

The entire process can take three to four months without automated tools, but in just six weeks Eastman was able to send out a total of 17 RFIs and quickly narrow the list to five strong candidates, which were subsequently trimmed to two using sensitivity analysis.

"Price was not the only factor we looked at," says Davis-Waltermire. "Sensitivity analysis lets us weight different factors depending on importance. We had five strong candidates [after the RFI analysis] but we were able to look at other factors besides price to narrow the list even further."

Davis-Waltermire says Eastman decided to offer a 3-year contract to a provider of safety supplies based on its willingness to work as a partner and cooperate on factors like on-time delivery and willingness to buy back excess inventory. As a result, she adds, Eastman will be able to transfer the management responsibility of 70% of its safety materials inventory to the supplier and achieve substantial long-term savings.

"Their willingness to work with us on inventory buy-back and adhere to best practices made them the obvious choice," Davis-Waltermire says, adding that, as its sole provider of safety commodities, the supplier will receive a volume of business formerly divided among 12 suppliers. (She was unable to name the supplier in time for publication, pending a formal signing of the contract.)

Eastman's strategic sourcing project reflected five facets of supply chain management best practices: supplier identification, technology utilization, process enhancement, relationship management and rewards and recognition.

It's no coincidence that adhering to industry best practices leads to higher profitability.

"If you look at the past winners of the Malcom Baldrige quality awards, which rely heavily on bench-

Supply Chain Partner Strategic Certification Process

Source: Best Practices, LLC

marking best practices, most of those companies have far exceeded the market as a whole when it comes to stock valuation," says Keith Symmers, vice president of consulting firm Best Practices LLC, Research Triangle, N.C., and a co-author of the firms' report on supply chain best practices (see "Seven Tips for Best Practices"). General Electric Co. and Eastman Chemical are both past winners of the annual award, which was established in 1988 by the U.S. government to promote total quality management practices.

Building Shareholder Value

Symmers cites GE and Motorola Inc. as two companies whose adherence to supply chain best practices and the Six Sigma quality initiative have resulted in huge cost savings and greater shareholder value.

Six Sigma, a quality program that originated at global electronics manufacturer Motorola, is a comprehensive quality philosophy that heavily relies on the use of statistical tools to measure and improve process quality based on customer requirements.

GE uses Six Sigma with its supply chain partners to reduce the number of defects in any process to 3.4 in one million. It's a corporate-side philosophy that GE applies to every facet of its business, from issuing loans through GE Capital to limiting the number of errors on its Web pages and reducing dropped calls at its call centers.

In the past five years best practices and Six Sigma techniques have helped GE achieve more than $5 billion in cost savings, says Symmers.

In support of its supply chain Six-Sigma efforts, Motorola uses a 400-page quality system review guideline to measure the processes of its suppliers. Partners that grade lower than 70% are required to develop and implement corrective action plans, while Motorola closely monitors their progress toward achieving world-class quality, according to the Best Practices report.

Certifying suppliers is another best practice that can lead to productive partnership and help companies achieve key performance results and strategic objectives (see chart, this page).

The winning supplier agreed to on-time delivery and inventory buy-back.

Steps for Managing Supply Chain Partnerships

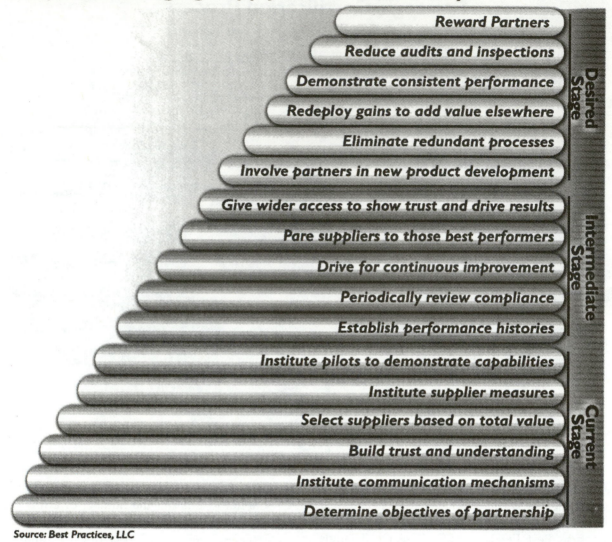

Reward Partners

Reduce audits and inspections

Demonstrate consistent performance

Redeploy gains to add value elsewhere

Eliminate redundant processes

Involve partners in new product development

Desired Stage

Give wider access to show trust and drive results

Pare suppliers to those best performers

Drive for continuous improvement

Periodically review compliance

Establish performance histories

Intermediate Stage

Institute pilots to demonstrate capabilities

Institute supplier measures

Select suppliers based on total value

Build trust and understanding

Institute communication mechanisms

Determine objectives of partnership

Current Stage

Source: Best Practices, LLC

"The mindset is how much of our quality systems and other processes can be born by the supplier," says Symmers. "It comes down to trust and how certain can I be that the right product in the right quantity will be there at the right time. If I certify key suppliers as true supply chain partners, I don't have to constantly look over my shoulder because they have proven themselves."

Certification and performance measurement criteria most often cover a multitude of areas including product quality, delivery speed, documentation, technical support, processing errors, value and customer service, according to the Best Practices report. On average, companies took two years implementing certification and partner programs.

While adhering to best practices can improve supply chain efficiencies, not all are feasible for every company. Symmers advises that companies implement best practices that attack the "lowest hanging fruit"—or those processes that can bring the greatest return through improvement.

Low-Hanging Fruit

Blue Circle Cement, a $5 billion Atlanta-based cement manufacturer and distributor, knew its lowest hanging fruit was its inefficient system of forecasting demand. Blue Circle implemented supply chain management planning and forecasting software from Rockville, Md.-based Manugistics Group Inc., which utilizes complex forecasting algorithms to help companies direct the flow of products from raw material stage through manufacturing, distribution and delivery.

Blue Circle owns and operates nine manufacturing plants, 22 distribution terminals, 500 rail cars and a num-

A matter of trust: Will your supplier deliver the right products on time?

ber of barges that sail on the Great Lakes and up and down the East Coast.

Prior to implementing its supply chain software, the cement company had little visibility to its supply chain, Blue Circle says.

Typically Blue Circle's customers would call at 9 in the morning and want cement delivered to a specific location by 1 in the afternoon, according to Vance Pool, business technology manager for Blue Circle. "And in the cement business, if our product doesn't show up when its supposed to, the project comes to a halt," he says.

Without forecasting tools, when capacity was low, they had two choices: "offer horrible customer service and deliver it late or not at all; or even worse, source it from a competitor," says Jeff Smith, vice president of chemical and energy for Manugistics.

Manugistics, which is mentioned in the Best Practices report as one type of supply chain technology that can foster relationships with suppliers and improve supply chain management, offers performance measuring features that allow companies like Blue Circle to identify and track key metrics like customer fill rates and on-time deliveries.

A survey conducted as part of the Best Practices study indicated that supply chain software can yield as much as 60% fewer days of inventory, translating into increased cash flow and working capital. Such software, the survey says, allows suppliers to meet customers' delivery schedules 96% of the time and frees up to 80% of functional staffing such as planning and scheduling.

Blue Circle is seeing similar improvements. "We are forecasting monthly demand at 90% accuracy and saving millions of dollars," says Pool.

With the new system, Blue Circle can see potential shortages up to six weeks early, which "allows us to divert product from plants Y and Z or import more from plant W if we need to," says Pool.

"I will go on the record as an IT manager and say that automated supply chain systems absolutely offer the greatest return on investment for your IT spending dollar," says Pool.

By applying best practices including implementing technology that improves forecasting ability and removes cost from the supply chain, Blue Circle appears to be on its way to joining Eastman Chemical and other leading manufacturers as a world-class company.

Please E-mail your comments to: **ecweditor@tfn.com**

Saturn's Supply-Chain Innovation: High Value in After-Sales Service

Few companies can match Saturn's after-sales service for efficient supply-chain management and satisfied customers. This case study details the thinking that turned supply-chain innovation into brand loyalty.

Morris A. Cohen ■ Carl Cull ■ Hau L. Lee ■ Don Willen

Can you have your cake and eat it too? When it comes to combining a high level of customer service with a lean and efficient supply chain, few companies can match Saturn Corporation's after-sales service business. Saturn's success in that area is a wake-up call; its approach should serve as a model for any industry trying to forge the critical link between after-sales service and customer loyalty.

What Saturn has done is adopt and continuously refine the concept of jointly managed inventory, a variant of vendor-managed inventory that involves sharing inventory risks with "retailers"—the name Saturn gives its dealers. In doing so, it has uncovered a precept with broad implications: Companies that match their parts-supply strategy to the criticality of the customer's need for the part can dramatically improve customer satisfaction in after-sales interactions.

Saturn's success in after-sales service has been well documented by industry watchdogs. Although its retailers' service-parts inventory turns over more than seven times a year, far exceeding major competitors' turnover, its retailers excel in off-the-shelf availability.

Such efficiency leads to both higher retailer profitability and satisfied, loyal customers. The spring 1999 survey from J.D. Power and Associates reported Saturn customers' high satisfaction with the availability of parts to support after-sales service—and the low incidence of out-of-stock parts resulting in the car not being repaired right the first time. Indeed, Saturn consistently ranks among the top 10 brands of automobile manufacturers for supply-chain service, comparing favorably with luxury automobiles such as Lexus, Infiniti and Acura.

Unsurprisingly, customers of Saturn return for repairs and scheduled maintenance for many more years than purchasers of other automobiles. As managers know, high levels of brand loyalty result in high levels of repeat purchases.

How did Saturn manage to achieve its impressive performance in after-sales service? Its secret is twofold. It designed a service-supply-chain strategy that matches the urgency, or criticality, of its customers' varying needs. And it effectively uses channel partners to execute the strategy.

All that didn't happen overnight. From 1985 to 1987, while we were studying General Motors Corporation and offering recommendations on GM's service support, the company coincidentally was forming Saturn. The ideas in our report greatly influenced the plans for Saturn. The GM team members working on our project also were involved in developing Saturn's service-support function. One of the team members was author Carl Cull, who left GM to join Saturn. Author Don Willen, a senior manager at GM at the time, was another member of that team.

With managers at the new company sold on the basic concept of matching supply-chain strategy to the criticality of the customers' needs, Saturn went about the task of implementing and refining that strategy. Saturn worked closely with its channel partners to de-

Saturn Is Best at Parts Availability...

Saturn has the highest off-the-shelf availability rate for parts of any car manufacturer, according to a leading industry publication.

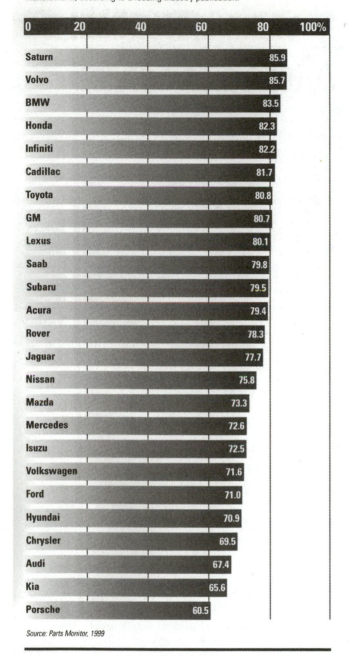

Manufacturer	Rate
Saturn	85.9
Volvo	85.7
BMW	83.5
Honda	82.3
Infiniti	82.2
Cadillac	81.7
Toyota	80.8
GM	80.7
Lexus	80.1
Saab	79.8
Subaru	79.5
Acura	79.4
Rover	78.3
Jaguar	77.7
Nissan	75.8
Mazda	73.3
Mercedes	72.6
Isuzu	72.5
Volkswagen	71.6
Ford	71.0
Hyundai	70.9
Chrysler	69.5
Audi	67.4
Kia	65.6
Porsche	60.5

Source: Parts Monitor, 1999

...and Wins Customer Loyalty for Repair Services

Saturn customers repair their cars at their retailers more often than customers of other carmakers.

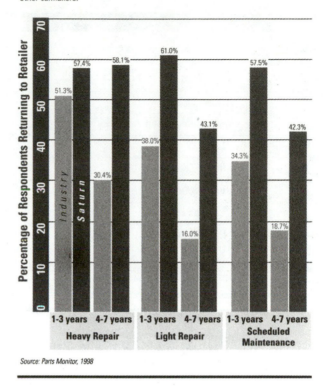

Percentage of Respondents Returning to Retailer

Heavy Repair: 1-3 years Industry 51.3% / Saturn 57.4%; 4-7 years 58.1% / 30.4%
Light Repair: 1-3 years 38.0% / 61.0%; 4-7 years 16.0% / 43.1%
Scheduled Maintenance: 1-3 years 34.3% / 57.5%; 4-7 years 18.7% / 42.3%

Source: Parts Monitor, 1998

sign a highly integrated distribution network that could meet the service requirements of the ultimate customers, the vehicle owners. The execution of the strategy requires tight coordination. In fact, the company uses an inventory-management process into which all retailers pour information, with Saturn making replenishment decisions for the channel. Proper incentives ensure that the risks and rewards of the collaboration are appropriately shared.

Saturn's approach is unusual. In most industries, it is rare to find successful implementation of a supply chain in which all participants are that closely linked. It is even less common to find it in the after-sales business.

The Saturn Service Parts Operations Story

In the mid-1980s, General Motors created Saturn as a new company with a strong customer-focused competitive strategy. The company started with a clean sheet. It had new products, a new service-supply chain and, perhaps most important, a new concept for the "retailership." Each retailer operates in a market region in which it is the only authorized Saturn retailer. Regions do not overlap, so retailers can put their energy into marketing the car against other brands, as opposed to competing with other Saturn retailers through "dealing." Particular emphasis is on removing stress from the automobile-purchase transaction.

Saturn's underlying competitive strategy is to give buyers life-cycle ownership value by providing a fair price (not necessarily the lowest price) and the highest level of after-sales service possible. It aims to create an intensely loyal group of customers, with a high level of repeat purchases and a high market share for after-sales service throughout the period of vehicle ownership.

Embracing the premise that the system must be oriented toward the welfare of the vehicle owner, Saturn managers designed the service operation from scratch.

Customers Give Saturn High Marks for Parts Availability...

Ranking	Model
1	Lexus SC 300/SC 400
2	Infiniti I30
3	Lexus ES 300
4	Saturn Coupe and Volvo 850
5	Lexus LS 400
6	Infiniti Q45
7	Volvo S90/V90
8	Cadillac Eldorado
9	Infiniti QX4
10	Saturn Sedan/Wagon

Source: J.D. Power and Associates, Customer Satisfaction Index, Spring 1999.

...And for Being the Car Most Likely To Be Fixed Right the First Time

Ranking	Model
1	Saturn
2	Honda
3	Volvo
4	Lexus
5	Saab
6	Acura
7	Infiniti
8	Subaru
9	Toyota
10	Lincoln

Source: J.D. Power and Associates, Customer Satisfaction Index, Spring 1999.

There were very few practices to emulate: Extensive benchmarking on after-sales service convinced Saturn that inventory management at the retailer level was at that time a "black art."

To make the new approach work, Saturn had to overcome four management challenges within the service-logistics systems connecting the various stakeholders in the industry. First, parts consumption tends to be intermittent, and therefore demand is hard to predict. Inventories of service parts typically move slowly and often have very low turnovers. (We have benchmarked annual turnover values as low as 0.5 in high-technology industries.) Second, there is enormous disparity in the cost of the parts that must be provided (from pennies to hundreds or thousands of dollars in computer- and technology-driven industries). Third, there can be great variety in models or platforms. Product proliferation leads to part-number proliferation. Most automobile manufacturers have to maintain hundreds of thousands of separate stockkeeping units (SKUs). Fourth, the value of the delivered service to the customer can vary considerably, according to the severity of the failure incident. Such factors lead to a wide range of requirements for parts-delivery responsiveness and availability.

With automotive parts, the total service supply chain can contain billions of dollars in inventory, stocked at thousands of locations, with high transportation costs when shipments must be expedited. And yet the service provided to vehicle owners is often dismal. Many automobile dealers do not have the competence or interest to become state-of-the-art inventory managers, nor do they see a direct connection be-

tween inventory management and improving car sales. So in many cases, even if an automobile manufacturer could improve the operational performance of its parts-supply chain, the ultimate consumer would still face poor service.

How the Supply Chain Works

Saturn uses a demand-based approach for triggering movement of parts down the supply chain, an approach that recognizes the probabilistic nature of the part-consumption process in the field.

The process starts at the factory level. Parts are produced at Saturn's factory in Spring Hill, Tennessee, or at vendor plants, which could be located anywhere in the world. The first actual decision to be made is where to stock the part and at what level—the "positioning" decision. Saturn stocks all parts at its central distribution center (DC) adjacent to its Tennessee factory. The retailers stock a subset of parts, and different retailers may stock different SKUs in different quantities.

Demands for parts might have their origin in a car crash or other repair incident, routine maintenance, a do-it-yourself project or the needs of a non-Saturn repair-service provider.

Repairs can occur at scheduled maintenance times or at random. Even if the repair time is scheduled in advance, the retailer will not know what parts are needed until the car is in the shop and the repair technician/mechanic can make a diagnosis.

The Origins of Saturn's Supply-Chain System

The design of the service operation by the Saturn Service Parts Operations (SSPO) was heavily influenced by an earlier study of the General Motors Service Parts Operations (GMSPO). In the mid-1980s, GMSPO invested in advanced information systems that enabled it to become more cost efficient and at the same time provide a high level of customer service to its direct customers (the dealers) from its internal warehouses and distribution centers. The GMSPO improvements, however, did not penetrate through to the level of the consumer. Vehicle owners generally were dissatisfied with the quality of the after-sales service. Unhappy customers led to reduced revenues and damage to the image and goodwill of GM.

A 1986 study conducted by the authors revealed that, if the dealers could use more scientifically based inventory systems and pool their inventories to support one another's out-of-stock situations, then the costs and service performance of both GM and the dealers could be significantly improved. The study led to a number of recommendations to GMSPO to help the dealers in managing their inventory. The basic idea was for GMSPO to provide its dealers with suggested parts-stocking lists in the short run and to provide them with a computerized, state-of-the-art inventory-management system in the long run. By linking such a system directly to GM, GMSPO would be able to see all the dealers' inventories and customer demands (total visibility) and be able to coordinate and encourage the pooling of dealers' parts inventories. We also recommended that GMSPO ultimately consider owning the parts inventories at the dealers in order to remove all barriers for dealers to pool their stock.

Because some people within GM had strong resistance and were concerned about possible negative reaction from the dealers, the recommendations were not adopted at that time. Managers at GMSPO believed that the recommendations were too risky and that GM was too large and complex to accommodate such drastic change. People in GM sales and marketing were nervous about asking dealers (their direct customers) to modify their internal management practices. The sales and marketing people were particularly concerned with any changes that could affect the service-parts sales-revenue stream to GM. In addition, those dealers who were consulted were skeptical that the predicted benefits could be realized. At the time, they could not identify any examples in the automotive industry or other industries where such radical supply-chain coordination mechanisms had been used successfully. Moreover, dealers traditionally paid little attention to service-parts-inventory management and were not inclined to invest senior managers' attention in something they considered a low-level, back-room process.

Saturn's strategy was set by the market-planning team, which consisted of GM dealers who wanted Saturn to be designed as a new company with primary emphasis on customer satisfaction and service. They embraced our ideas because they saw them as consistent with that goal and were well aware of the problems in the field that our recommendations addressed. GMSPO agreed to let Saturn adopt the recommendations and viewed the plan as an experiment that could ultimately influence its own operations—something that in fact did happen although it took some years.

The parts needed at the retailer's repair shop or another party's repair shop are ordered from the local retailer inventory. job-completion standards usually are same-day standards, except for major repairs and bodywork jobs. Customers do not want to wait more than one day to receive a car back in full operating condition.

In Stock and Out of Stock

If the part requested is in stock, the retailer will sell and, if necessary, ship the part to the location where it will be used. If the part is not in stock, the retailer will first ask members of its "pooling group"—a group of nearby Saturn retailers organized by Saturn for inventory pooling purposes—to see if it is available there. The search is facilitated by the information system Saturn maintains for all retailers. If the part is not available in the pooling group, then it can be ordered from the DC or from the supplier. It is possible to review all U.S. stocking locations in real time to determine the availability of a part. The retailer then orders the part and places the customer into a back-order position. The costs of such transfers are borne primarily by Saturn.

Retailers review Saturn's target-level recommendations at the end of each day, and then Saturn automatically replenishes to the agreed-on target level. Thus, retailers can say yea or nay and can set the target level higher or lower or at nothing.

Replenishment orders are received at the central distribution center and are shipped out according to a delivery schedule—leading to a three-day or shorter response time if the ordered part is in stock at the DC. Otherwise, the part is either put on back order or sourced from the production-inventory stock.

Note that a pull system such as Saturn's is based on target levels. Using one-for-one replenishment means that Saturn does not position inventory in advance based on forecast consumption. That is a key difference—one that is required by the highly unpredictable nature of the parts-demand process.

The financial arrangements include full reimbursement of costs to a retailer who supplies a part to another retailer as a result of a pooling-group request (rare because parts are usually in stock under the system). The shipped part also is replaced automatically within three days (assuming availability at the DC). Saturn essentially tells retailers what to stock. If a part does not sell after nine months, Saturn takes it back and repays the retailer for the cost of the part.

Each retailer's inventory system is linked directly to Saturn's management system. All transactions for all SKUs at the retailers are transmitted daily to Saturn via a satellite-based communication system. Upon receipt of the nightly updates, the central system at Saturn generates stocking decisions and replenishment quantities for each SKU for each retailer location. If an item is very high in cost and rarely demanded, Saturn sends fewer. Saturn initiates the process through which retailers buy parts, but it gives retailers the right to reject or modify the suggested replenishment decisions.

Overcoming Potential Obstacles

Saturn has innovated a variety of ways to leap over roadblocks.

People who keep things humming.   Saturn has material-flow coordinators—people positioned in the plant to facilitate coordination between manufacturing and service parts so that scheduling of parts production does not get overlooked. Material-flow coordinators represent a major innovation: They solve the classic problem that parts orders can be disrupted by the schedule established for assembling large numbers of new cars.

Performance measures.   Also important are appropriate performance measures that reinforce the right kind of behavior. Saturn realized that because it was managing inventory jointly with the retailers, it would not be sufficient to base its service-performance measures wholly on delivering parts to the retailers (as most supply chains still do). Instead, Saturn and the retailers together would have to be held accountable for the service performance the customers ultimately experienced. Hence, Saturn decided to use off-the-shelf parts availability (differentiated as crash-related, maintenance-related or consumable-related repair types)—at the retail level—as its performance metric for service delivery.

Avoiding the risk of excess inventory.   The Saturn service operation is designed to relieve retailers of the burden of inventory management. As described above, Saturn manages retailers' field inventory directly and shares the consequences of any over- or under-stock problems.

Implementation.   The heart of the matter is that the service-parts system is designed to support Saturn's customer orientation and to exceed the expectations of

Connecting Service Strategy With Criticality

When a customer needs a part quickly, it helps to have the part available from several places. When the need is not urgent, a central warehouse or distribution point makes more economic sense.

	Service Strategy	
	Centralized	**Distributed**
Low	Matched	Mismatched
High	Mismatched	Matched

Service Criticality

customers for quality in support and service. All decisions and incentives are set to support that central strategy objective, and all extra costs are borne by Saturn.

Convincing the doubters.   The decision to accept the recommendations was made jointly by the senior managers designing Saturn from the ground up and by the relevant GM managers, who were anxious to see an experiment carried out. The major concern within Saturn initially was from the financial managers. The provisions to cover retailer costs and to take back unsold parts worried them, but once it was demonstrated that the system worked—higher service with less inventory—there was uniform acceptance.

Aligning Supply-Chain Strategy With Criticality

Saturn's approach enabled it to meet customers' needs effectively and efficiently through alignment of its service-network strategy with the urgency, or criticality, of a customer's need. To assess that kind of alignment, managers can place their organizations on a matrix in which the vertical columns would indicate the structure of the service strategy and the associated level of coordination. At one extreme would be centralized supply chains (having essentially one central warehouse); at the other, distributed supply chains (with numerous, coordinated stocking points). The matrix's horizontal rows would represent high and low levels of criticality—how crucial it is to the customer to get product performance. Any company that analyzes its place on the matrix can gain insights to improve after-sales service.

Criticality

First, a company must look at the criticality of its products and services, asking, "What is the value of our product's performance (its uptime) to the end user? What is the cost to the customer if the product fails to function properly?"

A part in the computer system used by air traffic controllers would have high criticality. If it should fail, the cost could be catastrophic. Acceptable time to repair would be measured in seconds. Similarly, the manufacturing equipment used in a semiconductor fabrication plant could have high criticality. With a nonfunctioning piece of equipment, an entire manufacturing process line could grind to a halt. Lost profit: tens of thousands of dollars per hour. At the other extreme of the criticality spectrum might be a home hair dryer. if the dryer should cease to work, the cost perceived by most end users would probably be no more than a bad-hair day.

The definition of product failure for a car is more complex. If failure of an engine part renders the car undrivable, that would be perceived as serious, but for most drivers, failure of a radio part would have low criticality. Delivered value can vary, therefore, even for the same product.

Note that if product reliability could be increased to the point that downtime from product failure did not occur, then after-sales logistics support would be unnecessary. Product attributes, such as reliability, redundancy and the ability to self-diagnose a failure so that the product can "self-heal," can be critical components of a firm's service strategy. Upstream processes like product design and manufacturing can eliminate defects and make significant contributions to product service.

Centralized or Distributed?

In addition to looking at the criticality of its products and services, a company should examine the supply-chain service strategy that it uses for matching supply with demand (and for satisfying the customer's needs) to determine where it falls between a centralized strategy and a distributed or decentralized plan. Although there are many components of supply-chain strategy, it makes sense to focus on the critical elements in the Saturn case because of their relevance to after-sales service: performance targets, network structure, planning process and fulfillment process.

In weighing what kind of service strategy they have or want to have, managers may find it helpful to first assess their company's supply-chain performance targets—the targets established to meet customer needs. Different targets can be used for different products or situations, depending on the customer's attitude toward failure of a given product. Companies with a centralized supply-chain service strategy set their sights on cost reduction and efficiency. Their principal performance target is maximum inventory turnover. In a distributed strategy, companies emphasize such service metrics as availability and rapid response.

Next, managers should look at the structure of their distribution network—that is, the number of stocking and repair sites, the location of those sites and their interrelationship. The facility-network struc-

How Centralized and Distributed Service-Supply-Chain Strategies Differ

Attributes	Centralized	Distributed
Performance Targets	Achieving the highest level of inventory turnover at the lowest cost.	Ensuring that customers can rapidly obtain any critical part.
Network Structure	A small number of central warehouses and repair depots.	Inventory and repairs available from locations close to customers.
Planning Process	Visibility of demand at the point of sale.	Inventory and transaction visibility at all levels.
	Statistical forecasting of local demand and lead times.	Forecasting based on estimates of reliability of parts and installed base (customer region).
	Stocking decisions at retail locations made independently of network decisions.	Stocking decisions are made based on what products are required and where they are available for all locations.
Fulfillment Process	Drop-off or mail-in repairs are a viable alternative.	Parts are designed to be easily serviced by the service provider (the manufacturer).
	Little fulfillment coordination needed among stocking locations.	A high level of coordination exists among all stakeholders in the supply chain.
	Both planning of inventory levels and physical fulfillment may be outsourced.	Planning of supply-chain management is rarely outsourced.

How To Ensure Your Supply-Chain Strategy Keeps Your Customers Happy

1. Use performance metrics (such as uptime and overall response time for completion of repair jobs) to measure the value the supply chain delivers to the end customer throughout the life cycle of product ownership.

2. Set specific targets for that value consistent with the business strategy and reflective of the products' criticality to customers. For example, in the auto industry, a target might be a 95% job-completion rate within eight hours.

3. Communicate the goals to intermediate customers and suppliers: for example, dealers, parts vendors and auto-component plants.

4. Identify how the intermediate customers and suppliers contribute to the delivery of end-customer value. Delays and costs can be incurred at each step, but by coordinating supply-chain decisions and by pooling resources, it is possible to lower costs and increase service.

5. For all stages of the supply chain, set explicit cost-and-service performance goals consistent with or exceeding the end-customer value-delivery goal. In the auto industry, a company might set a goal such as: "No customer will have to wait more than 24 hours for arrival of parts to complete vehicle maintenance."

6. Adopt a service strategy that matches the criticality of the product to the customer.

7. Develop mechanisms (perhaps a Web-enabled central information system or collaborative planning- and forecasting-support tools) for sharing information, monitoring performance and coordinating decisions within the supply chain.

8. Develop explicit targets for continuous improvement: for example, a target of reducing response times at concurrent or high fill rates. At all stages of the service supply chain, use the shared information on current performance to promote the changes needed to meet the enhanced levels of performance.

9. Implement appropriate incentives to ensure equitable division of the costs, risks and benefits of the selected service strategy (for example, stock pooling and information sharing).

10. Understand the requirements for success and the pitfalls of implementation (for example, the need to get buy-in from all supply-chain stakeholders).

---

ture used in each supply-chain service strategy should be distinct. A centralized supply chain consists of a single stocking and repair point. In some cases, a small number of centralized stock and repair locations are organized into two distinct levels or echelons—central and retail. Distributed networks, however, are considerably more complex. Typically, the company will maintain multiple stock and repair sites organized into several echelons. Strategically positioning many facilities close to each customer location or "installed base" represents a considerable investment.

Managers also should weigh the supply-chain strategy's planning process—that is, the process the company uses to position inventory and manage the material that flows throughout the network. In a centralized strategy, planning is based primarily on visibility of point-of-sale (POS) transactions (at the retail part-consumption level) and utilizes statistically-based forecasting methods. Although central inventory resources can be shared, companies often make planning decisions for retail locations independently, looking at forecasts of local demand and lead times from the central depot or suppliers. In centralized environments, planning systems tend to be derivatives of the classic distribution-resource-planning systems that were developed to push finished goods through distribution channels.

Planning under a distributed strategy involves pull rather than push. The strategy is based on complete visibility of inventory and transactions at all locations. Forecasting is based on information such as the installed base of customer machines in each region and the underlying reliability aspects and other engineering characteristics of the products in the field. The stocking decisions are not based solely on projections of historical consumption patterns but also depend on the drivers of demand (installed base, national failure rates, market forecasts, and so on). The principal difference from a centralized strategy, however, lies in the provisioning process, where stock-level decisions for all SKUs and locations are linked and are interdependent.

Another aspect of a company's supply-chain service strategy, the "order-fulfillment process," is concerned with the physical processes of completing a service repair or delivering goods for a customer. In the centralized strategy, fulfillment requires little coordination among different stocking locations within the firm's supply-chain network. Centralized strategy fulfillment focuses on the central distribution facility, its linkage to suppliers, and its role as the sole source for emergency stock backup. Centralized systems are amenable to outsourcing to third-party logistics providers.

The fulfillment process in the distributed strategy, however, is characterized by a much higher level of coordination, both within the company and across company boundaries. All locations in the network act as emergency backup sources, and pooling of stock is promoted. In distributed environments, there also is more potential to link upstream processes like product design and manufacturing to after-sales service support. The linkages can be based on programs like "design for serviceability" and total quality management, which have the goal of increasing product reliability and/or decreasing the cost (and time) for defect diagnosis and repair.

Plotting one's own company on a strategy/criticality matrix is helpful for finding an appropriate match between a company's service strategy and the criticality of product uptime to customers. The supply-chain strategy Saturn adopted represented a significant move from GM's model to the distributed model. The strategy was accompanied by a market positioning of the product that promoted the quality of after-sales support to the vehicle owner. As a result, Saturn was able to obtain a match on the matrix that continues to provide the company with a clear competitive advantage. Saturn's more-coordinated and -integrated supply-chain strategy increases the value of product ownership to customers and lowers costs for all players in the supply chain. Saturn has fine-tuned a distributed service strategy that has let it go beyond automobile-industry standard practices to exceed its competitors in multiple performance measures. The result is that Saturn has gained a significant edge in the service dimension of the industry.

Much has been said about the potential for major change in supply-chain design and management as a consequence of the Internet. Automobile manufacturers are now involved in efforts to use the Web to sell directly to customers without using dealers as middlemen. Currently, such disintermediation efforts are proving difficult to pull off for a variety of legal and strategic reasons. Our case study of Saturn indicates that dealers remain important. A partnership between an automobile manufacturer and its dealers/retailers to provide maximum service quality to vehicle owners has significant value for all members of the supply chain. Such value-creating relationships make movement away from current industry-channel structures to an e-commerce basis even less likely in the near future.

Happy Customers

For most industries, matching the right supply-chain service strategy with the criticality of the product is a survival step. In the North American computer industry, for example, many companies face multiple market segments with very different perceptions of service criticality. At one extreme are corporate customers for whom computers are mission critical and who therefore demand same-day, on-site service and will pay for it. At the other extreme are consumers who are satisfied with three-day (or longer) service-response times and are not willing to pay a premium for same-day service.

Companies struggling with a single approach for all customers are following a route that leads to inefficiency and inappropriate levels of service. A better route to follow is a targeted service-supply-chain strategy. A competitively priced product, serviced in a way that meets or exceeds expectations, will lead to customer satisfaction.

Additional Resources

The 1999 videotape "Supply-Chain Management" is part of the Manufacturing Insight Series of the Society of Manufacturing Engineers. It contains a case study of Saturn and an interview with author Carl Cull.

M. Cohen and H. Lee, "Out of Touch with Customer Needs? Spare Parts and After Sales Service," Sloan Management Review, 1 (Winter 1990): 55–66.

M. Cohen and S. Zhang, "Benchmarking Service Parts Logistics: An In-Depth Analysis," project report (Philadelphia: Fishman-Davidson Center for Service and Operations Management, The Wharton School, University of Pennsylvania, 1997).

M. Cohen, V. Agrawal and Y.S. Zheng, "Service Parts Logistics: A Benchmark Analysis," IIE Transactions, 1997.

References

1. J. Ball, "Cutting In," Wall Street Journal, May 10, 2000, p. 1.
2. M.A. Cohen and V. Agrawal, "After Sales Service Supply Chains: A Benchmark Update of the North American Computer Industry," project report (Philadelphia: Fishman-Davidson Center for Service and Operations Management, the Wharton School, University of Pennsylvania, August 1999).

Morris A. Cohen is professor of operations and information management, the Wharton School. Carl Cull is benchmarking and operations research manager, Saturn Corporation. Hau L. Lee is professor of management science and engineering operations, Stanford University. Don Willen is former director of parts, plants and logistics, General Motors Service Parts Operations. Contact them at: cohen@opim.wharton.upenn.edu, carl.v.cull@gm.com, hau.lee@stanford.edu and dlwillen@cs.com.

FROM SUPPLY CHAIN TO VALUE NET

The supply chain can and should be a strategic differentiator, but too many companies are missing the strategic opportunities it offers.

David Bovel and Joseph Martha

CUSTOMER PRESSURE ON MANUFACTURERS and retailers is increasing relentlessly. Their appetite whetted by experiences with Dell and other fast and effective producers, a growing number of consumers—and business customers—want customized products, want them right away, and want them bundled with services they value. The Internet was supposed to have made this possible—indeed, "click it and get it" has encouraged these expectations with everything from online selections of prescription drugs, custom-built furniture, pick-your-tunes music, and home-delivered groceries.

But most shoppers find that the performance of Internet commerce has fallen far short of expectations. The wrong items are shipped. Items are slow in arriving, or fail to show entirely But Internet merchants are not the only sinners. Brick-and-mortar retailers have also failed to respond to customer desires for superior service and custom-tailored goods.

Why are so many companies—including business-to-business vendors—doing such a poor job of giving customers what they want? In many cases, the answer can be found in the supply chain—a part of the business to which senior executives have traditionally paid scant attention.

The traditional supply chain attempts to anticipate customer demand and satisfy it with standardized products and average service. Decades after the outlines of "demand-pull" manufacturing were first introduced, the standard supply chain pushes products down the line and out the door, hoping that someone will want them. Automobiles, home appliances, clothing, consumer electronics, business equipment, doors and windows, furni-

ture—just about all manufactured goods—are still handled in this way. Customized goods require a long wait and a tall bill. And customers often complain, "It's not what I *really* wanted."

Materials move sequentially down the traditional supply chain. Hand-offs, bottlenecks, and buffer stocks are commonplace, creating costly inventory. Information moves erratically, and customers are seldom in the loop. Speed and performance improvements are possible within this rigid system, but only at the margins.

Fortunately, there is a practical alternative to the unhappy mismatch of customer expectations and supplier performance, something we call a "value net." A value net is a dynamic network of customer/supplier partnerships and information flows. It is activated by real customer demand and is capable of responding rapidly and reliably to customer preferences.

Creating Value for All

A value net is so named because it creates value for all of its participants—company, component suppliers, and customers—and because the players operate within a collaborative, digitally linked network. A value net operates at a speed capable of satisfying real demand. It is reliable in delivering on promises made to customers. And it has the agility to change as customer preferences change.

A well-designed value net makes it possible for companies to:

From the *Journal of Business Strategy*, July/August 2000, pp. 24-28. © 2000 by Faulkner & Gray. Reprinted by permission.

Solve customer problems, rather than simply sell products.

Office furniture retailer Herman Miller recognized that the traditional process for specifying, ordering, and making office furniture was slow, cumbersome, and expensive. It was particularly frustrating for customers who needed custom-configured furniture on short order, or for small companies that needed furniture quickly. Once a deal was made and the buyer had selected from a confusing blizzard of material and color options, production stretched on for six to eight weeks. Change requests were costly and difficult to make, and added more time to schedules. Delivery dates were chronically unreliable.

So when Miller went after the growing small business furniture market, it rolled out an innovative new unit: SQA, for "Simple, Quick, Affordable." SQA is designed around a highly integrated, digitally linked supply network. A proprietary software tool, developed by Herman Miller, makes it possible to design, specify, price, and place an order at the customer's site from a salesperson's laptop computer. This eliminates the costly and time-consuming rendering of sketches and scale models. In seconds, a customer can see the furniture choices and a complete office arrangement in three dimensions and from any angle. Order changes are quick and easy to make, and are linked dynamically to pricing.

Each order on the salesperson's laptop represents a complete bill-of-material that can be ported electronically to the company's information system from anywhere in the country. All of Miller SQA's supply chain partners have access to this bill-of-materials, as well as to information on shipment schedules and inventories. Accurate and timely information reduce inventory costs and assure delivery when promised—with 99.6% reliability.

By solving a huge hassle for its customers, Miller SQA has generated 25% annual sales growth (versus 7% for its industry) and higher profit margins and inventory turns than the parent.

Respond rapidly to customer demands.

Zara, a Spanish clothing retailer, produces "fashion for the masses" of young, hip, urban consumers. Recognizing that what's in today may be out next month, Zara has organized a design and fulfillment network capable of meeting two key objectives: creating fashion ideas that resonate with its customers' fast-changing tastes, and moving those ideas from the drawing board to store shelves in 10 to 15 days—a lightning pace by the standards of its industry.

The company meets the first objective by getting its designers and store personnel out of their offices and into the plazas, discos, and universities where customers congregate. The designs that emerge from these customer contacts enter a fast-paced production and logistical system. Capital-intensive steps are executed in factories owned by Zara's parent company. Labor-intensive steps are outsourced to small shops with which Zara has col-

WHAT IS A VALUE NET?

During the second half of 1999, Mercer Management Consulting conducted research on 30 companies in the Americas, Europe, and Asia, identifying the best-practice examples of supply chain innovation. A number of these companies operated within our definition of value net, and we found that they shared, to a greater or lesser degree, five characteristics:

1. Customer aligned. Customer choice triggered sourcing, building, and delivery activities within the network.
2. Collaborative. Companies engaged suppliers and customers (and sometimes competitors) in networks of value-creating relationships. Each activity was assigned to the partner best able to perform it.
3. Agile and scalable. Responsiveness to change was assured through flexible production, distribution, and information flows. Brick-and-mortar restraints and capital requirements were minimized. In some cases, entire echelons of the traditional supply chain were eliminated. So the business can easily be scaled up to meet growing demand.
4. Fast flow. Order-to-delivery cycles were fast and compressed. Inventories were often entirely absent. Rapid delivery went hand-in-hand with reliable and convenient delivery.
5. Digital. E-commerce was a key enabler. Information flow and its intelligent use formed the neural system of the net, connecting customers, suppliers, and value-adding activities.

laborative arrangements that include assistance with technology and logistics.

Customers love the results of Zara's high-velocity operation. They queue up in long lines outside stores on designated delivery days—a phenomenon dubbed "Zaramania" by the Spanish press.

Build a strong brand based on valuable services.

Cemex, a cement company based in Mexico, has demonstrated how even a commodity product can become a powerful brand if it is bundled with services that customers value highly. Cemex's products are no different than those of its many competitors in Mexico and Latin America, with one exception: They are at the customer's site when they are needed, and often on very short notice. For the construction industry, reliable delivery is a cardinal virtue. Late deliveries of ready-mixed concrete wreak havoc with construction schedules. And since customers are unable to control their own schedules, keeping them happy isn't easy. Cancelled orders and reorders are commonplace. But Cemex's astute optimization of its plant and truck network, which incorporates satellite tracking, gives it the ability to deliver within a 20-minute window—guaranteed. Customers are willing to pay a premium for this level of reliability.

The Cemex guarantee, unique in the industry, has helped create a strong brand and, in turn, a high market valuation relative to competitors. Its focus on high-value services sets it apart from the typical supply chain, which aims to cut manufacturing costs and only incrementally speed up distribution.

Bake in barriers to competition.

Streamline.com is one of the new generation of online service companies that aim to simplify affluent families' lives by eliminating time-consuming chores. Using the Internet and digital "choiceboards" as their customer interfaces, these companies have placed many regular shopping items just a click away, with direct-to-the-door delivery—at least in theory. Actually fulfilling what's promised on the Web site is extremely difficult to execute, as many dot-com startups and their investors have discovered.

Streamline provides home delivery of groceries, heat-and-serve meals, dry cleaning, videos, and other items to affluent suburban families. Designing the customer interface was relatively easy compared to assembling and managing a supply network of food companies, local dry cleaners, bakers, and other vendors. The toughest part of all is the final mile—getting the goods from the distribution point and into customers' homes without either the ice cream or the profits melting away. The final mile entails lots of physical assets and labor-intensive tasks, such as driving delivery vans, and this is where many Internet companies stumble.

Home delivery has two major challenges. First, it takes a certain dollar volume of business to make drop-offs at individual households over wide geographic areas economically feasible. And second, those households must reorder on a regular basis in sufficient volume.

Streamline appears to have overcome this twin challenge thanks to the features of its value net design. One key feature is its system of regularly scheduled replenishment, which Streamline calls a "Don't Run Out" program. Don't Run Out puts every subscriber on a fixed weekly schedule that delivers the customer's choice of automatic replenishment items (a pound of coffee, a gallon of milk, a pound of sliced turkey, and so on) as well as special items selected by the customer, usually ordered on the Streamline Web site. Automatic replenishment helps assure that the size of most orders will support the cost of home delivery. As of November 1999, Streamline's average order was $104. Even better, the typical customer received 40 orders per year—far more than order levels reported by key competitors.

Another critical feature is unattended delivery, so that the customer does not have to stay home during a three-hour window to meet the delivery van and get the perishables into the refrigerator. Streamline solved this problem with "the Box"—a small refrigerator/freezer/cabinet unit installed in the customer's garage, and to which the route driver has a key. When a customer comes home, he or she finds that perishable items are in

the Box, and any recyclable items and clothes earmarked for the dry cleaner have been picked up.

The affluent households that subscribe to Streamline have plenty of options, but the convenience of the company's service, regular replenishment, and the Box, keep them hooked and competitors at bay. It's easier to stay with the Streamline service than to quit. As a result, Streamline enjoys high customer loyalty rates and more than twice as many repeat orders as its largest competitor:

- About 94% of current subscribers look to Streamline as their primary provider of groceries and household goods and services.
- Customer retention is over 90%.
- Streamline enjoys a 75% "share of wallet" among its Boston-area customers.

Given the cost of home delivery, one might ask why Streamline has built its business around a low-margin business such as groceries. In fact, only about 70% of items delivered by the company are groceries, with the rest being higher-margin items. The incremental cost of adding an item on the truck is nominal, and as of late 1999, Streamline claimed a blended gross margin of 29%. Mastery of home delivery could provide Streamline and similar firms with a direct pipeline through which clothing, birthday cards, gifts, flowers, liquor, and so forth can be sold to consumer households.

Bridging Operations and Strategy

Miller SQA, Zara, Cemex, and Streamline.com are representative of a small but growing number of enterprises for whom the supply chain is no longer just operations but rather a source of competitive advantage. Fast, effective, and digitally linked supply networks are the backbones of their business designs, which link customer needs and fulfillment capabilities holistically rather than

---

WHAT IS A SUPPLY CHAIN?

The *supply chain* is the set of inter- and intra-company processes that produce and deliver goods and services to customers. It includes materials sourcing, production scheduling, physical distribution, and the information flows that support them. Procurement, manufacturing, inventory management, and transportation are typically considered part of the supply chain organization. Marketing, sales, finance, and strategic planning are not. Product development, order entry, channel management, customer service, and accounts payable and receivable lie in a gray area; in theory, they are part of the supply chain process, but are seldom included within the supply chain organization.

THE STREAMLINE VALUE NET

The Streamline home replenishment service is built on a value net model that includes an Internet customer interface, an efficient service-area distribution center that stocks some 10,000 stock-keeping units, and relationships with many local and national suppliers, including Iams, Gillette, Procter & Gamble, Nabisco, and Blockbuster Video. The company retains direct control over all elements that directly touch its customers: customer service, Web site maintenance, marketing, and physical delivery to subscribers' homes. Everything else is outsourced, including distribution center management.

through a linear set of discrete activities. For these companies, innovation in making and delivering goods has been more important than the goods themselves.

Gateway and Dell, for example, make good personal computers, but so do Hewlett-Packard, IBM, Compaq, and other vendors. Since all are built from fairly standard components and loaded with identical software, it is difficult to say that one is better than another. What differentiates Gateway and Dell in the eyes of customers is the fact that they can build and deliver a customer-configured PC within five business days. What sets them apart in the eyes of shareholders is the fact that they can do this with almost no inventory, absolutely no working capital, and far fewer capital assets than most of their rivals. (Their asset intensity is one-fifth that of major competitors.) Their value net business designs make possible a very profitable business and high levels of customer loyalty.

Few businesses manage their supply chain activities strategically. For most CEOs and other senior executives, the supply chain is essentially off the radar, crowded out by people issues, the demands of new product development, acquisitions, technology strategy, and e-commerce initiatives. Supply functions are generally delegated to procurement and logistic specialists. These CEOs may be overlooking the most potent mechanism for gaining and sustaining a competitive advantage.

Lower your prices, and competitors will quickly match them. Cut operating costs, and competitors will soon find ways to do the same. Innovative new products provide a temporary edge, but within a year or two those new products will be replicated or surpassed. But reinvent your business around a value net supply model and you may be able to gain an edge over rivals that they will be unable to replicate for three to four years. That time can be used for improving the value net and then creating the next generation of supply chain innovation.

Questions for Managers

Is a value net design appropriate for your company—or for one of its units? What are the warning signs that change is necessary? Consider these indicators:

Value is migrating elsewhere. Value and profits migrate from outmoded business designs toward those that are better designed to satisfy customer priorities. This is true in all industries. Are your revenues per customer stagnating? Are profits moving away from your business to others with a more compelling value proposition and superior execution and delivery?

Your business is in danger of being "Amazoned." E-commerce is a disruptive technology, often loosening the grip of traditional leaders. Do you view e-commerce technology as opportunity or threat?

Your customers are defecting. The most profitable customers want their offerings customized, and shift their spending to companies whose business models meet their requirements. Are your most profitable customers being cherry-picked by rivals?

You are not meeting customer demands for speed, reliability, and convenience. Today, a good product is merely an admission ticket to the game. Customers are also demanding rapid fulfillment, on-time delivery, and convenience in doing business. Can you deliver on these three requirements?

Your managers treat suppliers as enemies. Traditional supplier relationships are often adversarial. Beating up suppliers, or playing one off against another, can drive down purchasing costs in the short run, but in the long run it gravely limits your ability to develop powerful new products and services. Could collaborative initiatives with your suppliers open up new opportunities?

Senior executives see the supply chain as an operational issue. Is your supply chain as the domain of purchasing and logistics specialists? Is cost-cutting your sole expectation of these specialists? A non-strategic perspective limits your opportunity to reshape the business.

If any of these indicators apply to your company, reinventing your business around a value net may be in order. And you don't have to be a dot-com start-up to do it.

David Bovet and Joseph Martha are vice presidents of Mercer Management Consulting based, respectively, in Boston and Cleveland. Their new book, Value Nets: Breaking the Supply Chain to Unlock Hidden Profits, *is published by John Wiley & Sons.*

Unit 7

Unit Selections

37. **Electronics Manufacturing: A Well-Integrated IT Approach,** Bruce Reinhart
38. **Are You Ready for the E-Supply Chain?** Jim Turcotte, Bob Silveri, Tom Jobson
39. **The Global Six,** *Business Week*
40. **Thinking Machines,** Otis Port
41. **One Giant Leap for Machinekind?** Usha Lee McFarling
42. **Environmental Management: New Challenges for Production and Inventory Managers,** R. Anthony Inman

Key Points to Consider

❖ How has information technology had an impact upon the job of an operations/production manager?

❖ Why are some consumers hesitant to use the Internet for electronic shopping? Why are some firms slow to establish their presence on the World Wide Web?

❖ What challenges and opportunities are created for firms from increased environmental concern in society?

 **Links**   **www.dushkin.com/online/**

34. **Centre for Intelligent Machines**
    http://www.cim.mcgill.ca/index_nf.html

35. **International Center for Research on the Management of Technology (ICRMOT)**
    http://web.mit.edu/icrmot/www/

36. **Information Technology Association of America**
    http://www.itaa.org

37. **KPMG United States**
    http://www.us.kpmg.com/cm/article-archives/actual-articles/global.html

These sites are annotated on pages 4 and 5.

The field of operations and production management has evolved over time and continues to evolve today. There are emerging trends that require careful examination by firms and managers. This unit examines three emerging trends: use of information technology concern for the environment, and globalization of business.

The first few articles examine the growth of information technology and the growth of the Internet and electronic commerce. The articles discuss the impact that information technology has today on supply chain management and on forecasts for the future.

There has been growing concern by manufacturers for environmental management. Green marketing and ISO 14000 provide evidence of how managers must incorporate environmental planning into their firms. The article by R. Anthony Inman reviews environmental management challenges for production and inventory managers.

In looking at the future of operations and production management, one can develop either a pessimistic scenario or an optimistic one. The pessimist could argue that current theories and concepts for managing are applicable for manufacturers and that they are inadequate for managing services and information-based firms. The pessimistic view would see the challenges as too great for managers and would think that American firms will face major difficulties when competing on a global basis. The optimistic scenario is that newer managerial concepts have emerged and have proven to be successful. This scenario holds that firms that are flexible in adapting to new market demands by remaining customer-focused should do well. Technology provides managers with new tools to support their decision making. American firms through their own competitive advantages and strategic alliances with other global firms should not fear their future in a global market.

ELECTRONICS MANUFACTURING

A WELL-INTEGRATED IT APPROACH

"What-if" scenario modeling, the **ubiquitous** best-practices tool and **first choice** of accountants and R&D groups in **virtually every** business, is **winning over** new proponents in the manufacturing planning and **scheduling arenas.** What prevented **more frequent** use of modeling for manufacturing/planning sooner were **the simple,** but **sizable tasks** of pumping information into the system and front-ending the data with a **practical user interface.**

BY BRUCE REINHART, CPIM

MAKING SUPPLY CHAIN PLANNING an everyday tool in the company's enterprise resource planning (ERP) system is one of those things that manufacturing planners at the Kimball Electronics Group (KEG) had as a priority on their radar scope. Specifically, they envisioned supply chain integration affording a critically needed ability to quickly validate customers' delivery schedules and understand how subsequent change orders would affect delivery. Yet, while early attempts proved problematic, the company remained watchful for the new elements that brought integration of supply chain tools and what-if modeling within range.

Thirty years ago, KEG'S product line featured electronic keyboard instruments. Today, the product line is vastly different and far more diverse. From three facilities—based in Jasper, Ind.; Burbank, Calif.; and Renosa, Mexico—KEG produces a range of complex electronic components including circuit boards, multi-chip modules and semiconductor components that are shipped worldwide. KEG also

contracts services to customers in the automotive, defense, aerospace, telecommunications, data communication, computer and medical industries.

At the Jasper facility, a single order alone can comprise over 300 components, and at any given time there may be 500 open orders in various stages of production. While the complexity of the individual products has obviously increased, so have manufacturing standards (KEG achieved QS9000 registration for its automotive customer base), complicating ERP and supply chain solutions.

In such dynamic environments, the industry relies heavily on information systems simply for survival. For example, it's not unusual for a top-50 customer with a current order for 20,000 circuit boards to decide one week before production is scheduled that the order must be doubled. On top of this, a minor configuration change must be made to these additional boards. In these cases, KEG also must be able to quickly confirm the feasibility of the change order and describe the impact on the initial de-

> Cost INCREASES, SHIPMENT schedules and other IMPACTS NEED TO be reported, timely and ACCURATELY, IN ORDER to keep that CUSTOMER. Not LONG ago, performing ALL THESE FUNCTIONS would have SEEMED unreasonable, but IT HAS SINCE BECOME a part of EVERYDAY manufacturing.

livery date. Cost increases, shipment schedules and other impacts need to be reported, timely and accurately, in order to keep that customer. Not long ago, performing all these functions would have seemed unreasonable, but it has since become a part of everyday manufacturing.

At KEG, we turned to the current generation of MRP II and supply chain planning software to handle increasing flexibility while supporting product quality standards. Our current system, which has evolved over the past four years, addresses inevitable, yet unforeseen and potentially disruptive changes to production schedules.

Higher customer expectations

DEVELOPING AN **IT** SYSTEM capable of addressing change order requests, along with the ability to answer the numerous questions that accompany such change orders, has enhanced our overall competitiveness. Meeting expectations hinges upon the ability to diagnose exactly what is happening on the shop floor at any given moment, along with the ability to determine how change orders alter the current production schedule. In short, an electronic manufacturing service requires applications to enable what-if scenario modeling for open orders and for accurately predicting the outcomes.

KEG's legacy system centered around IBM's COPICS MRP application, which the company had been running for some 20 years. It was a loosely integrated system which had grown with the addition of numerous in-house programs. The system had been customized with our own scripts for performing such tasks as order entry, master scheduling and shipping.

Initial use of what-if simulations at KEG began in 1992 with the creation of two separate instances of the MRP application on the mainframe for testing the impact of change orders. It was a cumbersome process, however. For each what-if scenario, it was necessary to refresh the test system with production data, return to the test system and enter customer changes to simulate the new scenario. Since this was a batch MRP system, the simulation could not be run until evening. KEG's service representatives

needed at least 24 hours before they'd have preliminary feedback for a customer. Material planners, too, needed three to five days to process test data, in addition to their production MRP, in order to spot any problems that might arise on their end.

That slow turn-around time kills lucrative contracting relationships. Improving upon this picture required a dramatically transformed and improved IT solution.

Opening the Door

KEG WAS PLANNING TO UPGRADE to a new MRP II system in the early 1990s, but with constant pressure from change orders, the company's supply chain capability needed to be implemented immediately. Since KEG had already purchased i2 Technology's Rhythm software for scheduling shop floor operations, the company elected to leverage whatever capabilities were possible from the existing MRP system by interfacing it with Rhythm's supply chain components.

Despite very distinct architectures of these systems (COPICS and Rhythm), interfacing was relatively straightforward since the software interfaces needed only to extract data.

This early experience proved a good foundation for a subsequent upgrade to the current MRP II system based on the CIIM application from Avalon Software (integrated with Rhythm). The new MRP II application runs on one HP 9000 Model K450 server that was configured, or sized, to meet users' response time demands with dual processors. Several additional servers were added to the network, ranging from the HP Model E- to K-Servers for network, application, and Oracle database support, as well as several HP 9000 workstations that support CAD applications. Platform standardization is aimed at minimizing administration and support costs.

Besides the standard reports that the supply chain component provides, KEG users extract manufacturing and supply chain data files and download these to off-the-shelf applications—Microsoft Excel and Access as well as Impromptu for ad hoc reporting. In this fashion, the planning

> . . . PERSONNEL can easily create AD HOC REPORTS CONTAINING basic information WITHIN MINUTES AFTER KEYING in the SPECIFICS of a CHANGE ORDER. Customers can also be PRESENTED with the NUMBERS INVOLVED in their RESPECTIVE CHANGE ORDERS.

system was made easy to use and provides immediate access to data for a variety of plant processes. This includes the order fulfillment group, master scheduler, production planners and material planners for assessing the impact of customer change order requests.

Integrated Supply Chain Planning Tools

THE FIRST SUPPLY CHAIN planning interfaces established a positive trend for KEG'S other IT environments. We are planning to implement similar systems in our facilities at Burbank and Renosa. Currently, MRP II systems at the three facilities stand alone from each other. However, while the respective MRP II systems are autonomous, there is an exchange of information and mutual support among the three sites. (Kimball International, our parent company, provides the wide area network which connects the corporation's U.S. and Mexico locations via T1 frame relay links.)

At the KEG Jasper facilities, the payoffs from the MRP II system were seen immediately. Our ability to respond more rapidly to virtually any customer request has increased dramatically. For one, personnel can easily create ad hoc reports containing basic information within minutes after keying in the specifics of a change order. Customers can also be presented with the numbers involved in their respective change orders.

Other payoffs of this IT solution include: reduction of stress on the shop floor (and everywhere else in the company) with such abilities as extracting daily runtimes and improving throughput significantly; in the warehouse, inventory has been cut by 59 percent; and KEG sales have doubled.

Bruce Reinhart, CPIM, is the materials manager for the Kimball Electronics Group.

The "E" Transformation

Are You Ready For the
E-SUPPLY CHAIN?

The Internet has become the fastest accepted communications medium ever, with 50 million people connected in five years. It took radio 38 years to reach that milestone and 13 years for television. Obviously, a technological groundswell like this is bound to affect every facet of our lives—personal and business. In this article, we will explore the impact the Net will have on one of today's most pressing business initiatives—how we manage the supply chain.

BY JIM TURCOTTE, CPIM, BOB SILVERI, C.P.M., AND TOM JOBSON

Undoubtedly, you have already heard about e-business. E-business can be described as the business transformation that occurs by exploiting the benefits of enterprise integration and global network connectivity. Think of e-business as the umbrella for any business process implemented using network technology. Under this umbrella fall many types of business processes including e-commerce, which is the transactional business process of selling and buying via the Net.

The type of e-business we want to focus on is aptly called e-supply chain. It refers to the management of the supply chain using Internet technologies. Currently, this is a tall order, but the concepts are sound and the technologies are proven. Most of us have used Internet technology to surf the Net, send e-mail to a friend or even do a little shopping. In fact 80 percent of businesses use the Web today, although less than 7 percent use it in support of supply chain management. So, while the technology is readily available and the applications are very pervasive, the use of the Net for supply chain management remains in its infancy.

The Net comes in Three flavors

BEFORE GOING ANY FURTHER, an explanation is required for the three types of "nets" that are used to support e-supply chain operations. (see Figure 1). Think of these as various types of information highways used to connect different parts of the supply chain. Each of these information highways is used for different reasons and therefore tend to support different business processes within the supply chain.

An intranet is an internal net that is normally used within the boundaries of a company. It may stretch across many manufacturing sites or even countries for that matter. Much of the data found in an intranet environment is considered sensitive, and therefore access is usually limited to people within the company. Companies are linking their ERP systems, or at least making information available from their ERP systems, to the intranet. Intranets are protected from outside access by a "firewall."

BUSINESS NETWORK VARIATIONS

FIREWALL

FIREWALL

Company "A" Intranet

SECURED LINK
Company A & B

Company "B" Intranet

SHARED DATA EXTRANET

INTERNET BACKBONE

PUBLIC ACCESS INTERNET

Figure 1

Think of an extranet as an external intranet shared by two or more companies. Each participating company moves certain data outside of its private intranet to the extranet, making the data available only to the companies sharing the extranet. An example of this use would be providing inventory data to your supplier to help support an automatic replenishment process.

Last but not least, is the Internet with which we are most familiar. This form is open to the general public. The Internet tends to be used more for e-commerce today, but has some emerging uses in supply chain management, such as advertising surplus inventory to outside brokers. In summary, think of the intranet as a private net, an extranet as a shared net and the Internet as a public net.

Making the Link!

BY NOW, YOU ARE WONDERING how an e-supply chain might operate. Let's start by creating a simple e-supply chain example (see Figure 2). Imagine that you are a toothpaste manufacturing company called TastyPaste. Not just any toothpaste, but the new flavored types that all the kids want. Yes, you have 99 flavors from bubble gum to apple-flavored toothpaste. You sell it to 250 retail chains throughout the world, which translates to thousands of retail stores and millions of consumers. You purchase the flavor additives, tubes and other materials from 50 suppliers. The question is: Given the complexity of this supply-demand environment, how can you manage the supply chain to achieve the right balance of customer responsiveness and low inventory levels with an aggressive cycle time.

Now imagine for a moment that TastyPaste's direct customers, the retail chains, have provided access to their inventory data through a shared data extranet. As consumer purchases occur, the data is fed to the retail chain's ERP system. The retail chain then moves the updated demand data to the extranet. At this time, the critical data is automatically fed to the TastyPaste ERP system. This system runs and makes the appropriate quantity and schedule adjustments. The key output is copied to the extranet set up between TastyPaste and its 50 suppliers. This data might include updated inventory snapshots as well as updated, forecasted demands and orders for additives, etc. Based on the data the suppliers see in the extranet, they automatically replenish TastyPaste's inventory and adjust their own ERP gross requirements to meet demands. The end result is the real-time update of demands from the consumer to the raw material suppliers.

The TastyPaste company has created what amounts to a seamless environment that stretches from customers right through to suppliers. Customer demand flows to those

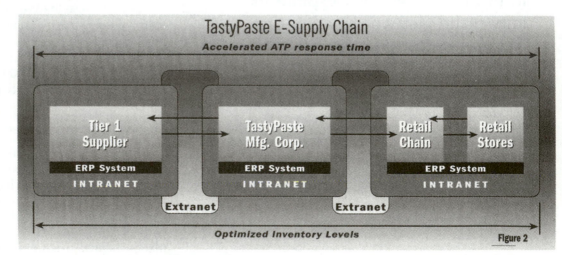

TastyPaste E-Supply Chain

Accelerated ATP response time

Tier 1 Supplier | TastyPaste Mfg. Corp. | Retail Chain | Retail Stores

ERP System | ERP System | ERP System

INTRANET | INTRANET | INTRANET

Extranet | Extranet

Optimized Inventory Levels

Figure 2

who need it, when they need it. And this supply chain capability is not limited to a single tier of customer or supplier, but can extend to multiple tiers of both. The bottom line is that they have created an integrated enterprise through the global connectivity of the Net.

The Benefits

So just how does e-supply chain benefit us? The objectives of any company are to reduce costs, reduce cycle time and grow revenue. E-supply chain supports these objectives by doing everything from improving the effectiveness of customer- supplier relationships to enabling faster customer response. Let's take a closer look at some of these below.

Companies are finding that enterprise integration is leading to a new level of supplier-customer working relationships never before imagined. Customers can literally check on their order status through access to a joint extranet, or a supplier can have access to your inventory levels in order to know when to replenish your stock. Data is able to move more easily and quickly between the links; but more importantly, the sharing of data is taking place like never before.

This is leading to significant business advantages for members of the supply chain. While strong relationships might have been considered an intangible item in earlier times, it is not so today. World-class competitiveness demands a closer relationship with our supply chain partners and the building of "value-based" relationships.

The benefits of reduced cycle time are a different matter, for they provide measurable, competitive advantages of both cost and performance. When we talk cycle time here, we are talking about the time it takes to react to a new demand statement from our customers. The quicker we can move critical data through the pipeline, the quicker we can react and hence, deliver the end product to our customer. We all know this leads to improved customer satisfaction and promotes a fertile environment for revenue growth.

Information Technology Implications

As discussed in the earlier example, Net technologies can dramati-

cally extend the value of supply chain management systems. This is accomplished by shrinking the cycle time in the movement of information up and down the supply chain. However, there are other positive features of using the net.

One of the benefits IT (information technology) folks especially like is the ability of the Net to support the thin client paradigm. Basically, the less software we need on the client workstation, the "thinner" the client becomes. Since the net is a server-centric environment, we can keep the majority of the software on the server and less on the client. A user (client) can access his key applications/data through a browser such as Netscape.

COMPANIES ARE FINDING that enterprise integration is leading to a new level of supplier-customer working relationships never before imagined.

Why do we care about how thin a client is? Two key reasons. One is that it's easier to upgrade a few centralized servers to a new software release than it is to upgrade several hundred widely dispersed client workstations. Second, the thinner the client, the less computing power required, reducing capital spending and ongoing maintenance costs for companies moving to Net-based technologies. In fact, some companies have moved to what is known as an NC (network computer), which is the equivalent of a stripped down personal computer optimized for Net use.

Another big IT expense-related benefit is the ease of installation and low costs of connectivity. This is where the net really enables enterprise integration. If you are a new supplier joining a supply chain, one of the requirements may be that you connect to an extranet. All you would need are three items. An NC system as previously noted, an ISP connection (Internet service provider) and a Web browser. This ease of connectivity also makes it easier for your own employees to access critical data while traveling. In fact, a sales person can have the ability to view the latest available-to-promise (ATP) data to make commitments and place orders while in a customer's office. The order is then fed directly to the sales person's company ERP system and immediately scheduled. In addition, transportation software is even being linked to ERP systems to allow

WHAT IS JAVA?

Developed in 1995 by SUN Microsystems, JAVA is an object-oriented programming language. This characteristic enables software engineers to achieve high levels of application productivity by virtue of the reusability of the code. Significant applications written in JAVA have been developed for the Internet and make use of the language's inherent capability to work on multiple software platforms. All major software product developers today have significant efforts in place writing JAVA-based versions of their platform products. Further, the advent of JAVA-compatible browsers is enabling the end-user to experience the same look and feel for all company applications written in JAVA which reside on its intranet. The combination of all these advantages is thrusting JAVA into a leading role in the development of e-commerce applications.

for the delivery information to be supplied along with the delivery date. The customer ends up placing a real-time order, is given a real-time delivery commitment, and is even told how it will ship—all done in the customer's office.

FOR AN E-SUPPLY CHAIN TO BE SUCCESSFUL,
you need to undergo both business process and technological transformations in order to maximize the benefits.

Application software direction

A SURE SIGN that Internet applications are being taken seriously is the massive amount of R&D dollars being spent. Key areas of expenditure include the development of software, hardware and services to support e-business by all the major software developers. More specific to e-supply chain are the moves of software industry heavyweights to make their applications Web-enabled. Major ERP providers, as well as major supply chain management players have comparable efforts. Many other companies, developing products from transportation logistics software to ERP tools, are racing to make their products Web-enabled.

On the technology side, one of the most promising avenues of Internet application software development is the explosive growth of the JAVA programming language. This is allowing companies to develop software that is portable across different operating system platforms and has high reuse capability (see sidebar). These benefits are particularly important as companies reengineer their applications for e-business opportunities.

Key items

WHILE WE TALKED A LOT ABOUT how great the Net will be when moving forward with e-supply chain uses, there are, however, a few items you need to be aware of. First and foremost, for an e-supply chain to be successful, you need to undergo both business process and technological transformations in order to maximize the benefits.

The other major items are security, scalability, integration and reliability. None of these are insurmountable, one just needs to address them to avoid problems. Security speaks for itself. No company wants sensitive data to get into the wrong hands or be corrupted. A properly set up intranet or extranet can be quite secure with today's technology. Scalability allows for long-term growth as well as seasonal spikes. The last thing a major retailer wants is for the system to get bogged down during the holidays when high net traffic is likely. Integration is the ability to use many of a company's existing applications together with future applications. A company's challenge is to migrate smoothly from its legacy systems to an e-supply chain environment. And finally there is reliability. Make sure you build a network that is robust and has sufficient redundancy, especially if you are talking about running mission-critical applications.

The Net of It All

IT'S NO LONGER A QUESTION of whether the e-supply chain is going to occur, it's now a question of when you will operate in an e-supply chain mode. While the "e" in e-supply chain stands for "electronic," it can also stand for "evolving," because that is what we are doing in the area of supply chain management. We are engaged in a continuous, business process and technological evolution!

Jim Turcotte, CPIM, has been with IBM for 17 years and is currently involved with advanced planning and scheduling tool development at IBM Corp. Logistics. Robert A. Silveri, C.P.M., is a consultant with Analysts International Corp. Tom Jobson is a senior IT architect at IBM.

THE GLOBAL SIX

Here's how the world auto industry will likely shake out: New economies of scale beef up the big boys, which gobble up less efficient parochial players. So who will be left?

It was a whirlwind first week on the job for Ford Motor Co.'s new CEO, Jacques Nasser. It began Sunday, Jan. 3, with rumors swirling in snowbound Detroit that cash-flush Ford was about to gobble up one of the world's big auto makers. By Tuesday morning, reporters were calling Nasser at home at 6 a.m. to inquire about a tantalizing but erroneous French radio report that Ford was taking over Honda Motor Co. "By Tuesday evening, we were supposed to be acquiring BMW, Honda, Volvo, Nissan—and there was someone else that I can't remember," quips Nasser.

By week's end, Nasser's every move was being scrutinized for hints as to how he might spend Ford's staggering $23 billion in cash. When he called a press conference for Friday evening's black-tie gala at the Detroit auto show, speculation was rife that he would announce a megadeal to rival last November's $35 billion DaimlerChrysler merger. "I'm not sure if I should be speaking to you in German, Swedish, or Japa-nese, the way the rumors have been flying," Nasser told a packed audience of Detroit swells. "I'm really pleased we're so popular." Nasser's only news was that Ford was bringing the Three Tenors to Detroit this summer. No big deal—yet.

But the green flag is flying for motor merger mania, and a dramatic shakeout is at hand. The top players are awash in cash and eager to buy, while the weakest are drowning in debt and glutted with factory capacity: The industry can make 20 million more cars and trucks a year than it sells, while global auto sales could hit a cyclical downturn within three years. What's more, consumers are demanding lower prices and more high-tech gizmos on their cars, forcing carmakers to squeeze costs. The result: Only a quarter of the world's 40 auto makers are profitable. "You're going to see a much more consolidated industry within the next five years," says Schroder & Co. analyst John Casesa. "The faster the global economy turns down, the faster it will happen."

Speeding the auto industry down the road to megamergers is a group of hard-driving bosses with expansive egos and big appetites for acquisition. Volkswagen's Ferdinand Piëch has snapped up European boutique players Rolls Royce and Lamborghini and is believed to have eyes for BMW. Denials aside, Ford's Nasser has at least investigated acquiring Honda and Volvo, and wouldn't mind picking off BMW, too.

MATING DANCE. Toyota's President Hiroshi Okuda, a black belt in judo, is particularly aggressive for a Japanese business leader and has started picking up bargains among Japan's struggling second-tier auto makers. And DaimlerChrysler Co-Chairman Jürgen Schrempp, having engineered a big German-American merger, now says he might be interested in hooking up with Japan's troubled No. 2 carmaker, Nissan. "Who knows, eh?" a smiling Schrempp said, following a Jan. 10 speech in Detroit. "We do not exclude the possibility of equity participation" in Nissan's car business.

Insiders expect the giants to pick up healthy, small brands in Europe, as well as bargains in Asia

He's already talking to Nissan about its heavy-truck business, and a deal could happen by the end of January.

This automotive mating dance is being triggered by cost pressures and cutthroat pricing on top of the overcapacity problem. "The industry lately has been a giant cotillion, with everybody looking for the best partner," says DaimlerChrysler Co-Chairman Robert J. Eaton, who predicts a big European deal this winter, although not involving his company. "Companies will have to rethink their ability to survive alone," he says.

Indeed, it was the stunning merger of Daimler-Benz and Chrysler Corp. that changed the rules of the road. The two prosperous companies saw that by combining they would have a better chance of growing in each other's home markets as well as in Asia. To make it in the high-cost, tech-intense global auto business, carmakers need vast resources and reach. And old national identities are becoming obsolete in a brave new auto world where size matters above all. "The industry landscape will need to change," says Nasser. "For global players to be really competitive, their sales volumes will have to be over 5 million a year." Predicts Toyota's Okuda: "In the next century, there will be only five or six auto makers."

Who will make it into the elite five-million-plus club? So far, only General Motors Corp. and Ford make that mark. But others are knocking on the door. Many industry leaders believe it will only take a decade for the world's 40 auto makers to collapse into the Global Big Six. To be sure, the shakeout will occur in stages, with profitable players such as Porsche or national champions like Renault holding out the longest. But by 2010, the thinking goes, each major auto market will be left with two large home-based companies—GM and Ford in the U.S., Daimler-Chrysler and Volkswagen in Europe, and Toyota and Honda in Japan. Players such as Nissan or Volvo may keep their brand names but won't be running the show.

As the industry reshapes itself, insiders expect the giants to head in two directions: They will seek out healthy but small brands in Europe, while picking up distressed merchandise in Asia. For the top companies, the goal is to establish an all-encompassing global footprint. No auto maker in the world has that now. The Americans and Europeans are mostly minor players in Asia, while the Japanese need a stronger presence in Europe. "The key is finding the right partner, who has

---

GENERAL MOTORS

1998 EARNINGS $2.8 billion*
1998 REVENUE $140 billion
WORLDWIDE VEHICLE SALES
 7.5 million
CASH $16.6 billion
STRATEGY GM is getting its own house in order. But it has found time to take a 49% stake in Japan's Isuzu and a 10% stake in Suzuki. Some speculate GM will rescue South Korea's Daewoo.

FORD MOTOR

1998 EARNINGS $6.7 billion
1998 REVENUE $118 billion
WORLDWIDE VEHICLE SALES
 6.8 million
CASH $23 billion
STRATEGY With a mountain of cash to spend, Ford is the hottest suitor on the global automotive scene. Predicted targets: Volvo, Honda, BMW.

DAIMLERCHRYSLER

1998 EARNINGS $6.47 billion**
1998 REVENUE $147.3 billion**
WORLDWIDE VEHICLE SALES
 4 million
CASH $25 billion
STRATEGY By merging, Daimler-Benz and Chrysler have created a global powerhouse. But it needs a presence in Asia and is already talking to Nissan about a deal.

VOLKSWAGEN

1998 EARNINGS $1.3 billion
1998 REVENUE $75 billion
WORLDWIDE VEHICLE SALES
 4.58 million
CASH $12.4 billion
STRATEGY VW has already acquired Rolls Royce, Bugatti, and Lamborghini. Hard-driving Piëch is often rumored to be eyeing BMW and Volvo, which itself is in talks with Fiat.

TOYOTA MOTOR

1998 EARNINGS $4 billion
1998 REVENUE $106 billion
WORLDWIDE VEHICLE SALES
 4.45 million
CASH $23 billion
STRATEGY Toyota wants to strengthen its hold on Japanese auto maker Daihatsu Motor, truckmaker Hino Motors, and affiliated parts suppliers like Denso.

HONDA MOTOR

1998 EARNINGS $2.4 billion
1998 REVENUE $54 billion
WORLDWIDE VEHICLE SALES
 2.34 million
CASH $3 billion
STRATEGY Honda must grow bigger if it is to make it into the Big Six. Honda insists it wants to go it alone. But joining forces with luxury carmaker BMW could result in a dream team.

---

*Includes one-time charges for restructuring
**Estimates of Daimler-Benz and Chrysler combined results.
DATA: MERRILL LYNCH & CO., SCHRODER & CO., SALOMON SMITH BARNEY, J.P. MORGAN, WASSERSTEIN PERLLA, COMPANY REPORTS

complementary products, geography, and a similar philosophy," says auto consultant Christopher Cedergren of Nextrend Inc. in Thousand Oaks, Calif.

Volvo could be the next company to be scooped up. It put itself in play on Jan. 6 by hiring J. P. Morgan to shop its car business. Fiat admits it's talking to Volvo; analysts say the two Europeans could make a good fit. Fiat would gain access to the luxury trade and the U.S. market, while Volvo, which sells less than 400,000 cars a year, would broaden its small base. Fiat needs a boost. With car sales down in its big markets, Italy and Brazil, the Italian company's auto division lost $38 million in the third quarter of 1998, vs. earnings of $245 million the year before.

But even a Fiat-Volvo combination might not be strong enough to survive longer-term, analysts say. Eventually, smaller players would need a big brother. Ford insiders say they are talking to Volvo, too, but they scoff at the $6 billion price tag Volvo's bankers are suggesting. Says one Ford insider: "Their car business is worth $3.5 billion, tops."

ASIAN SALES. Alongside Volvo, Nissan tops the list of rumored takeover targets these days. Japan's once mighty No. 2 player is on the brink because sales have plunged, thanks to lackluster models and economic distress in Japan. Nissan has been playing catch-up to Toyota and Honda since the mid-1980s and now is so debilitated it can no longer afford the same level of investments as its competitors. The auto maker is expected to lose as much as $626 million for the fiscal year ending in March, and is burdened with $22 billion in debt. Rivals says Nissan could be had for about $30 billion.

Nissan's neighbor, Mitsubishi Motors Corp., is in even worse shape. Struggling with $18.5 billion in debt, a bland product line, and recession in its home market, Mitsubishi, like Nissan, needs a white knight. Mitsubishi Motors President Katsuhiko Kawasoe admits he's talking to po-

---

FORCES BEHIND THE RACE TO MERGE

OVERCAPACITY More than 20 million units of manufacturing overcapacity, plus downward pressure on prices are forcing auto makers to slash costs and swallow rivals.

TECHNOLOGY Auto giants want to amortize heavy research and development investment in new high-tech features over a greater number of cars.

CASH The industry's biggest players have more than $100 billion in cash for deals, while smaller, less profitable players are seeking suitors. Europeans and Americans also have lofty share prices that allow them to swallow up smaller companies.

CULTURE Nationalism is declining in Europe as the new single currency spurs companies to compete, while in Asia economic crisis is compelling companies to consider foreign partnerships as never before.

DATA: BUSINESS WEEK

---

tential foreign partners, although he declines to discuss them. All the big global players are seen as prospective suitors for Mitsubishi. Daimler-Chrysler heads the list because Chrysler once had a 24% stake in the company and still buys from it.

Others likely to fall quickly include the remaining smaller players in Asia. GM recently increased its sake in Isuzu from 37.5% to 49% and took a bigger chunk of Suzuki—up from 3.3% to 10%. In Korea, meanwhile, Ford attempted to acquire bankrupt Kia Motors Corp. last year but was outbid by Hyundai Motor Co. Now, Hyundai, which piled Kia's $8 billion in debt on top of its own imposing $6.6 billion, is looking to launch discussions with foreign partners. But Ford isn't interested in bailing out Hyundai. "We're not going to do that," comments Henry D. G. Wallace, Ford's group vice-president for Asia-Pacific operations.

Over time, the biggest predators in Asia are likely to be Japanese giants. With $23 billion in cash, Toyota has as much money to spend as Ford. For now, the company is preoccupied with restructuring at home. It is considering creating a holding company that would make it far easier to streamline its vast operations—as well as merge with other

auto makers. Toyota already owns stakes in Daihatsu and Hino.

While Honda lacks Toyota's cash, it is blessed with strong growth—particularly in the U.S., where its 1998 sales topped 1 million vehicles for the first time ever. To make it into the Big Six, Honda needs to double its worldwide sales. Japan's No. 3 auto maker wants to go it alone. But with strong profits, the company is positioned to chart an independent future.

Compared to Asian players, Europe's smaller auto makers are likely to hold on more fiercely to their independence. So while the industry remake may be just as profound, the drama is not likely to unfold overnight. That's partly because of government stakes in companies such as Renault, and the opposition to job cutbacks that could accompany mergers. "You would have to see Europe facing economic recession or crisis before it merges volume-car manufacturers," says John Lawson, auto analyst at Salomon Smith Barney in London.

Indeed, analysts believe Fiat can prolong its independence if it can acquire Volvo without taking on too much debt. And Renault is developing breakthrough products such as the Mégane Scenic compact minivan, which was a hot seller in

Western Europe in 1998. CEO Louis Schweitzer aims to double Renault's sales over the next decade—a goal that could allow it to survive on its own.

TARGET: BMW. But a reckoning in Europe could be not far down the road. The emergence of a single currency is changing the rules of competition. Under European Union plans to liberalize its markets, foreign auto makers will gain unfettered access to Europe at yearend. An expected onslaught of Japanese competition could highlight the inefficiencies of Europe's smaller players. "Europe will become a battleground," predicts Furman Selz auto analyst Maryann Keller. "The Japanese are getting themselves ready to do in Europe what they did in the United States." Eventually, many observers believe, the battle will force Europe's smaller players to succumb.

The juiciest European target for the likes of Volkswagen or Ford would be BMW. The profitable brand would help these mass marketers move upscale. BMW made $624 million last year, but sells only 1.2 million cars worldwide. The Munich maker of luxury sedans is struggling to profit from its $1.3 billion acquisition of Britain's Rover Group Ltd. in 1994. Since then, the German company has invested $3.5 billion in Rover. Now, it must decide between investing the billions needed to develop a new line of front-wheel-drive cars for Rover, or seeking a partner to help.

Such a partnership—perhaps with Ford—could open the door to acquisition, but only if the Quandt family, which owns 47% of BMW, would give way to new ownership. For now, there's no sign of that. On Jan. 11, Heinrich Heitmann, BMW's North America chairman, declared in Detroit that his company will still be standing alone in five years.

But going it alone will get more expensive. The biggest wheels in the auto industry have already begun playing by the costly new rules. Advances in computer-aided design now allow them to develop vastly different models from one basic chassis. Consider three of Ford's newest models—the sexy $45,000 Jaguar S-type luxury car, the $30,000 Lincoln LS sedan, and the retro, rein-vented Ford Thunderbird, which is expected to sell for $35,000. Each is built off the same roughly $3 billion platform, code-named DEW98, but they couldn't look more different. Thanks to breakthroughs in manufacturing technology, hot models race to market in 14½ months—one-third of what it took a few years ago.

For the strongest and richest auto makers, these are giddy times. Amid the feeding frenzy of rumors at the Detroit auto show, Ford's Nasser couldn't help but sound like a man intent on building a global empire. "We already have a Japanese brand and two very British brands," said the Lebanese-born Nasser, who was raised in Australia and speaks four languages. "We've got the ability to absorb and really be quite comfortable with a lot of different cultures." No doubt. But the question is: Who will Ford, and the industry's other big wheels, absorb next?

By Keith Naughton with Karen Lowry Miller and Joann Muller in Detroit, Emily Thornton in Tokyo, Gail Edmondson in Paris, and bureau reports

THINKING MACHINES

After years of hype and letdowns, computers are starting to acquire real factory smarts

BY OTIS PORT

The trouble with engineers, says Andrew J. Keane, a mechanical engineer at Britain's University of Southampton, "is that we are trained to think with regular geometry—straight lines, circles, and 45-degree angles. But take a look at nature. How many bones in the human body have straight edges?"

Answer: none. And when it comes to manufacturing, it pays to take a cue from Mother Nature. That's why Keane has joined a growing band of evangelists for so-called evolutionary computation. This refers to a potful of biologically inspired techniques for creating new products, more efficient factories, and better business processes.

What you are really looking at, though, is artificial intelligence dressed up in fancy new garb. Many researchers would rather not mention AI. It conjures up shattered dreams of machines as smart as people. But AI is back, with all its mysterious and nonlinear edges. And it is delivering impressive results in manufacturing. "AI was really overhyped 15 years ago," notes William S. Mark, vice-president for computer science at SRI International, Silicon Valley's venerable think tank. Some of the early pioneers disappeared, he says, "but not the technology. It's far better than ever, and more prevalent."

QUICK STUDY. In fact, peek under the wraps of new software tools for manufacturing, and you'll often find AI,

probably sporting some other name. At Honeywell International Inc., a leading maker of factory control systems, it's called automated reasoning. Industry watcher AMR Research Inc. in Boston estimates that up to 40% of all new manufacturing-related software now incorporates some form of AI.

Unlike traditional AI, which tried to imbue computers with top-down intelligence, the new approaches let systems develop their own smarts, from the bottom up. The field has some colorful characters, such as intelligent

LET THERE BE MORE LIGHT

Evolutionary design helped GE's Raj Israel engineer a light bulb 48% brighter than standard halogen bulbs

100-WATT HALOGEN BULB	LUMENS PER WATT OF ELECTRICITY
STANDARD	14.0
G.E. HALOGEN IR	20.7

SOURCE: GENERAL ELECTRIC CO.

A QUICK PRIMER

EVOLUTIONARY COMPUTATION
A catch-all term for biologically inspired AI technology, including genetic algorithms and neural networks.

EXPERT SYSTEM A group of rules that prescribe a cause-and-effect reasoning process. Typically the rules cover some narrow specialty, such as operating a piece of industrial equipment.

GENETIC ALGORITHM A formula for using Darwinian principles of mutation to breed solutions. The problem is divided into two or more segments, or genes, and these are linked together in different ways, breeding new "child" solutions. After many generations, GA may produce results superior to anything devised by humans.

INTELLIGENT AGENT Autonomous software entities programmed to perform a specific task. Today's Webbots seek out prices or bid in Web auctions. Tomorrow, multiagent systems may handle most manufacturing-related chores.

NEURAL NETWORK An electronic circuit, usually simulated, modeled on the massively parallel structure of neurons in the brain. It learns by looking at examples, such as images of labels or collections of operating data on factory equipment. It can spot relationships that have escaped human notice.

---

agents, brain-like neural networks, and Darwinian genetic algorithms. Sometimes, evolutionary techniques can find answers that elude conventional problem-solving methods. General Electric Co.'s energy-efficient halogen light bulb is a good example. Other times, the new software can generate startling results that open the eyes of engineers.

Southampton's Keane, for example, used a genetic algorithm to design a support arm on satellites, called a truss. It produced a novel shape that human engineers might never consider. "When we found what the final designs looked like, we rethought how these things work, and now we see the logic," says Keane. The main goal he set: prevent vibrations from being transmitted along the truss so ultrasensitive instruments mounted at the far end would not be affected by vibrations from, say, the satellite's navigational rockets. The software discovered on its own that by changing the angles at every joint between crossbars and edge beams, vibrations could be progressively reduced to next to nothing.

While AI technology has made substantial progress, everything isn't hunky-dory yet. For example, engineers complain that they have trouble using some of the genetic tools aimed at optimizing manufacturing processes. One hitch with them is that the number of calculations required increases geometrically with each additional variable. Finding the best combination of just six variables would require analyzing 720 possible combinations. But with 12 variables, the possibilities explode to 479 million. Industrial problems may involve scores of variables, so even supercomputers can chug away for days, weeks, or years before coming up with the optimum answer.

The aerospace industry is notorious for the complexity of its optimization puzzles. Only recently has it become feasible to refine a plane's design by repetitively simulating the air flowing around an entire airframe. Before, that took so long it was done just as a final check. And at least a month was needed even for many a seemingly simple jobs, like simulating the firing of the braking jets on the Space Shuttle as it comes in to dock with the Space Station, says John Jian Dong, head of multidisciplinary optimization at Boeing Co.'s Reusable Space Systems unit.

PLANT MANAGER IN A BOX

When it comes to management foisting new technology on factories, "the plant-floor guys normally look at each other and roll their eyes," says Andrew J. Weiner, chief information officer at Myers Industries Inc. in Akron. But not last year, when he visited the Dawson Springs (Ky.) plant of Myers' Buckhorn Inc. unit. "Five minutes into the meeting," he recalls, "they all started asking questions about what else it can do."

"It" is, in this case, BizWorks, new software from the interBiz Solutions Div. of Computer Associates International Inc. It harnesses intelligent agents, neural networks, and expert systems to tackle thorny problems, such as making sense of all the data gathered by factory sensors. The first application involves predicting when big injection-molding machines at Dawson Springs are about to turn out defective products. After training neural-network watchdogs with past production data, the engineers put BizWorks to work early this year. It monitors data coming from the machines, looking for conditions similar to those that resulted in bad parts.

PAGER ALERT. Buckhorn is also testing a link to customer service and sales. When BizWorks spots a looming problem, it checks to see which customers ordered the products that machine is scheduled to make. If the problem threatens delivery to a key customer, the sales and customer-service managers get a pager alert.

Eventually, Weiner sees BizWorks uniting the different computer systems at Myers' 65 branches. "It can really create new business opportunities by putting management back on top of the technology horse. We'll be able to decide what information we want, and tailor BizWorks to provide it, instead of tailoring management practices to the software." That was just a dream yesterday, Weiner says.

By Otis Port

SOFTWARE THAT PLOWS THROUGH POSSIBILITIES

Evolutionary design was a revolutionary notion when Rajasingh S. Israel first heard about it back in the late 1980s. But Israel, an engineer with General Electric Co.'s Lighting Technology Div. in Cleveland, decided to give it a whirl. After all, the new software had been created at GE's research and development center. And Israel needed something radical: His task was to dramatically improve the energy efficiency of the halogen light bulbs popular in retail stores.

"Ordinary halogen bulbs are extremely inefficient," says Israel. "Only about 10% of the energy you put in comes out as light. The other 90% comes out as heat." For commercial users, that can mean tens of thousands of dollars are squandered every year.

What Israel wanted was a transparent coating on the bulb that would reflect the infrared rays, or heat, back into the bulb—without interfering with the visible-light rays. That would help keep the filament hot and glowing, so less electricity would be needed to produce light. Designing such a coating was only half the job, though. Israel also had to develop a method for applying it cheaply. And the interplay between coating formulation and the manufacturing process made the task complicated. Every tweak of the coating would require a change in the manufacturing process—and vice versa. "The coating has a very complex structure," Israel explains. "It's about one-twentieth as thin as a hair, and within that thickness we have multiple layers of different materials."

A BETTER WAY. Israel slaved for several years with no luck. Then he cranked up GE's new evolutionary-design software, dubbed Engineous. In a few months, Israel had his answer. GE unveiled its Halogen energy-saving bulb in 1991.

Engineous is basically a framework for finding optimum solutions. Using genetic algorithms and neural networks, it takes various elements of good solutions, then reshuffles them in myriad ways to "breed" thousands of alternative solutions—until it finds the best answer. Renamed iSight, the software has been available outside GE since 1995, after GE researchers founded Engineous Software Inc. in Morrisville, N.C.

Now, evolutionary design is getting hot. Genetic algorithms and neural nets are helping to create better designs for all kinds of products, from silicon chips to robots and bridges. At the University of Wisconsin in Madison, researchers recently "bred" a new diesel engine that promises to slash emissions of nitrous oxides and soot by 50% or more. It also consumes 15% less fuel.

Sometimes the evolutionary approach yields novel and surprising designs—like the satellite truss, or support boom, developed by researcher Andy J. Keane at Britain's University of Southampton. Typically such trusses have straight sides, like the tall TV-antenna towers common in rural areas. But when genetic algorithms were told to minimize the transmission of vibrations along the truss, they surprised everyone. After evolving progressively better solutions over 18 generations, Keane ended up, two weeks later, with a truss worthy of a sculpture garden. Its geometry is so counterintuitive that he built a scale model of one side to double-check the computer. Sure enough, the odd-looking shape reduces vibrations to almost zero.

No doubt more surprises are in store, as engineers launch evolutionary-design techniques into still unexplored realms.

By Otis Port

But evolutionary computing has some magic up its sleeve. Because the weak solutions from each generation aren't permitted to procreate, not every possible combination gets evaluated. So the problem shrinks dramatically, as does the execution time. Now, Dong gets his Shuttle-braking optimizations back in a couple of days.

Of course, as the technology grows more powerful, expectations rise, and people like Ren-Jye Yang end up feeling impatient. He's a Ford Motor Co. engineer who uses optimization to hunt for ways to improve vehicle safety, and his computer models of crash tests generally have 10 to 20 variables. Yang says each simulation takes an hour on a Cray supercomputer or a week on a high-end computer from Silicon Graphics Inc.—"and we have to run 40 simulations to get each optimization."

Even after all that, the result probably won't be the theoretical optimum. "There are no algorithms that can guarantee you'll find the one global optimum," says Boeing's Dong. "So in industry, optimum just means a much better solution."

In any case, finding the one absolute best solution might not be so great, says Lawrence J. Fogel, president of Natural Selection Inc. in La Jolla, Calif. "It might turn out to have unforeseen side effects that you didn't count on, or be too expensive—and then you'd have to run the whole problem again," he says. "So what you want are the best few."

FAMILY AFFAIR. Fogel is a pioneer of evolutionary computing. He began publishing his ideas in scientific journals in the early 1960s. But his theories went largely ignored until 1992, when they were revived and embellished by his son, David B. Fogel, chief scientist of Natural Selection. That same year, a similar technique, called genetic programming, was unveiled by John R. Koza, a researcher at Stanford University.

Koza insists that evolutionary methods will soon evolve into systems that discover new ideas and inventions. In fact, he has compiled a list of two dozen examples of where genetic programs already have created algorithms and products that match or improve on inventions covered by existing patents. And in two instances, the results of evolutionary computing were actually awarded a patent: an antenna (U.S. Patent 5,719,794) and an unusually shaped airplane wing

AGENTS OF CHANGE ON THE FACTORY FLOOR

In theory, a modern automated factory is a marvel of efficiency. As robots churn out auto parts, for instance, they drill, cut, and weld in an intricate dance. But in the real world, the dance sputters to a halt all too often. A key worker doesn't show up, or a machine breaks down. "All hell breaks loose," says research scientist Katia Sycara at Carnegie Mellon University's Center for Integrated Manufacturing Decision Systems. Suddenly, running the factory "goes from the super-mathematical to the ad hoc."

Soon, however, harried plant managers may get some help from so-called intelligent agents—software emissaries to cyberspace. Equipped with just enough smarts and knowledge to carry out assigned tasks, such virtual aides have already been harnessed for such simple things as enabling Amazon.com Inc. to suggest new books based on a person's purchases.

ZIPPING AROUND. In manufacturing, however, agents offer remarkable benefits. "If you structure them correctly, they can do lots of neat things," says engineer Howell Mitchell of Flavors Technology Inc. in Manchester, N.H. For instance, Mitchell thinks agents could one day spiff up production lines. The basic idea: Equip each factory robot with a software agent. Then, if the robot conks out, the agent zips around the plant's intranet to find another machine that can take over the task. When it does, it triggers a reprogramming of the assembly line—and production hums along.

The agents could also be given bigger tasks. Venturing out into the larger world of cyberspace, they could automatically seek out suppliers, buying parts and raw materials precisely when needed. They would even be made "smart" enough to do such things as pick the supplier with the fastest delivery time in an emergency. Indeed, programmers foresee that there will be whole menageries of agents—production line agents, buyers and sellers, "middle" agents to facilitate transactions, even "reputation" agents to help rank suppliers by quality. "A great deal of business will be mediated automatically by billions of software agents doing the same kinds of transactions humans do now," says Steve White, a senior manager at IBM Research.

With more agile assembly lines, proponents predict improvements in plant efficiency of up to 30%. Parts and materials costs should drop because agents can find suppliers all over the world, not just the handful in the procurement manager's Rolodex. And with agent-assisted factories able to reconfigure production lines on the fly, "we should see drastically reduced cycle times and more mass customization," says Neil Christopher, program manager at the National Institute of Standards & Technology. That's why everyone from Boeing and General Motors to Intel and Deere is exploring the use of agents at various levels of manufacturing.

"UNCHARTED WATERS." Don't expect intelligent agents to revolutionize manufacturing just yet. Flavors' Mitchell learned that agents aren't yet capable of rearranging an assembly line to walk around a broken robot, for instance—the reprogramming is too difficult. Martin Hill, head of e-business development in Britain for Sweden's Intentia International, points out that agents really aren't very adaptive. They may be clever enough to pick a supplier with the best price, but they don't yet have the brains to spot those that offer innovative solutions. "There, the idea breaks down a bit," he says.

What's more, an industry in which decisions are made by millions of pieces of software "is exciting, but it's totally uncharted waters," says Michael Jeng-Ping Shaw, a business professor of the University of Illinois. When White and others at IBM had agents compete to sell goods, they created a never-ending cycle of widely fluctuating prices. "That's not a great solution for consumers," says White. For now, intelligent agents have a lot of potential—but also a lot to prove.

By John Carey in Washington

(D0363696). This facility of genetic design really shouldn't be surprising, Koza says: "Evolution proves how good it is at design all around us."

Maybe. But that doesn't mean people will cotton to the situation. Two years ago, for example, when software giant Computer Associates International Inc. (CA) came up with Neugents, a hybrid neural network and intelligent agent, one of the first applications was to stand guard over CA's worldwide computer network. The Neugents monitor 1,200 data points every five seconds, looking for patterns in the data that coincide with events that led to past computer crashes. "The software can predict when the system is likely to crash within the next 45 minutes," says Gary E. Layton, marketing vice-president for interBiz Solutions, a new division of CA. "But the guys here didn't believe this kind of thing could work, so they ignored the first warning. Sure enough, the system crashed, just like the software said it would."

RAINMAKER. CA has bigger plans for the technology, however—along the lines of Koza's invention machine. With BizWorks, a new software suite marketed by interBiz, "we're trying to apply this predictive capability to business opportunities, not just warnings of failure," says Layton. "We want the software to sift through large volumes of data and find proactive positives—opportunities that we would probably spot later on down the road, but not for a while."

To make tons of money, however, you don't need to probe the actual future, says Steven A. Chien, technical supervisor of the AI group at NASA's Jet Propulsion Laboratory in Pasadena, Calif.: "If you're operating your business on data that's only five days old, but all your competitors are using 30-day-old data, you're effectively predicting the future as far as they are concerned."

Chien's specialty is automated planning and scheduling to maximize return on NASA's investments in space facilities and the logistics maze that surrounds a blast-off.

5

But the principles also apply to manufacturers, especially build-to-order companies such as Dell Computer Corp. "Just bringing together all the different parts and materials you need to fill thousands of orders isn't that hard," says Chien. "What's hard is minimizing your inventory costs."

That's the problem at the root of the explosion in shop-floor scheduling systems and supply-chain management tools. A flock of vendors already offer manufacturing execution systems and enterprise resource planning (ERP) software—Aspen Technology, Camstar, Datasweep, i2 Technologies, Manugistics, Oracle, and Wonderware, to name just a few. This represents just the tip of a brewing supply-chain revolution, says NASA's Chien. Soon, even tiny job shops will be exploiting the new capabilities. "It'll be like computerized payroll systems," he says. "At first, only big companies were able to buy them. Now, they're in every small business."

In addition, as managers get comfortable with evolutionary computation, these programs will gradually become just another everyday technique for analyzing options and improving individual factory operations. At Sandia National Laboratories, researcher Leslie D. Cumiford took two years to develop a software agent for controlling a brazing oven, which is used to solder ceramic parts to metal parts at high temperatures. That's a big-time investment, but Cumiford was breaking new ground. As computers gain more horsepower and the software improves, manufacturers will routinely run genetic programs to help make return-on-investment decisions—not just on major projects such as building a new factory but also on the merits of individual products. Production lines will be continually analyzed to improve flexibility and trim product changeover times.

Not far down the road, manufacturing will become totally digitized and thus more amenable to evolutionary techniques. Israel's Tecnomatix Technologies Ltd., for one, has software that captures a detailed computer model of an entire factory. And supply-chain management and ERP suppliers are starting to revamp their software into smart modules, or so-called object-oriented components, that talk to each other. "At the plant level, a lot of devices now showing up have embedded Web servers," says Kevin E. Prouty, research director of AMR Research. They can relay shop-floor data to any computer with a Net connection. "Now, you have access to information that people once only dreamed of."

Ultimately, predict the seers, every piece of factory equipment will have intelligent agents hovering within. Most office operations will also have associated software agents, from sales and purchasing to customer service and shipping. All of these agents will jabber among themselves to evolve production and delivery schedules. Almost every AI lab and manufacturing research center is working toward this multiagent future. AMR's Prouty probably speaks for many factory engineers when he proclaims: "Nirvana is coming."

One Giant Leap for Machinekind?

■ **Science:** From design to manufacture, nonhuman system creates robotic widgets, and improves itself with every generation.

By USHA LEE McFARLING
TIMES SCIENCE WRITER

A duo of computer scientists has created something science fiction writers have thus far only imagined: self-evolving and self-generating machines. From start to finish, a computer system designs and builds the robot-like creations, described in today's issue of the journal Nature.

"This is a long-awaited and necessary step toward the ultimate dream of self-evolving machines," Rodney Brooks, a leading computer researcher and director of the Artificial Intelligence Lab, wrote in a commentary accompanying the research.

The machines were created by Hod Lipson and Jordan Pollack of Brandeis University in Waltham, Mass.

Made of smooth, white plastic preassembled as a single unit, the robotic creatures are powered by motors and controlled by a neural network on a microchip. Some move by dragging along the ground, or as one visitor described it, "doing the breast stroke on the floor."

Although the devices can't do much more than crawl blindly about the lab, they are considered a huge step for the field of artificial life, which seeks to understand basic biological principles by replicating them synthetically.

The evolution of the machines is surely the stuff of a classic B movie: from the human mind to the computer, which through a self-selection process created the best generations of robot-like machines and ordered another machine to spit them out.

It started with a computer program that contained three building blocks—bars for structure, synthetic muscles and artificial nerve cells— and joined the components in various ways.

A "fitness test" in the computer gauged the creations' movements. Any creatures that moved well in the "virtual tests" were copied multiple times and mutated further by the computer. Those that did not move well were, like virtual Edsels, replaced by more efficient ones. After hundreds of generations, only the best-moving creatures remained.

The designs were then fed to an off-the-shelf 3-D printer, which essentially spits out drops of plastic in layers to create objects depicted on computer screens. These prototyping machines, which cost about $50,000, are used routinely by industrial designers in testing new designs for cell phones, for example.

Most of the creations contained about 20 components and were 8 to 12 inches long. They looked strikingly different from each other—one like an arrow, one like a crab, one like a snake and some like random geometric forms.

"It's interesting to see all the different solutions for a simple task in a simple world," said Lipson, a research scientist at the Volen Center of Complex Systems at Brandeis.

Many of the gadgets ended up, with no guidance from humans, being symmetrical—a useful form for moving in a straight line. "It was surprising to see established engineering ideas in many of our designs," said Pollack, an associate professor who directs the Dynamical and Evolutionary Machine Organization Lab at Brandeis.

The project wasn't completely hands-off. The researchers did have to snap motors on, but nothing more. "That's the only thing we touch," said Pollack. "It's authentic, self-generated, self-organized design."

A major advance in artificial life occurred in 1994 when former Massachusetts Institute of Technology computer scientist Karl Sims created evolving animated creatures that walked and swam through a simulated world where Newtonian rules of physics applied. Though inspiring, they were trapped within the computer that created them.

Other scientists have evolved robot brains, or control systems, within computers and then transferred them to robot bodies. Brooks calls this separation of brain and body a "glaring omission." Pollack agrees, saying, "There is never a body without a brain in nature."

Two years ago, Pollack and graduate student Paolo Funes tried to link the robot brain and body by building cranes and bridges that evolved inside computer programs. But the scientists had to build the structures using Lego blocks; the computer didn't manufacture them.

Now, the lab has taken the next step—one that quite a few labs around the world have been hoping to achieve.

"They've finally bridged that gap between evolution simulation [in computers] and the physical world," said Maja Mataric, who directs USC's Robotics Research Lab. "To evolve the body and brain together in the real world is a first."

Devices Are Not Sophisticated

Mataric said her only caveat is that she would not call the devices robots until they contain sensors for gathering information. But the ability for robots to evolve sensors remains out of reach, at least for now.

Pollack and Lipson are the first to admit—and even to emphasize—the primitive nature of their creations. "These are not Lt. Data. They are not Terminator. They're pretty dumb," said Pollack, who equated their complexity with that of bacteria. Currently, he said, human-created robots are far superior.

A next important step is to develop robots that can design themselves for one task, and with the aid of sensors taking in information, be able to morph into new robots for additional tasks, said Pradeep Khosla, head of the departments of electrical and computer engineering at Carnegie Mellon University in Pittsburgh.

Although he called the new research extremely interesting, he also said any robots deployed in the real world would need to be more robust than those created by a 3-D printer.

Ultimately, the electronic creatures may represent a way to severely cut the high cost of robot production by removing pricier aspects of manufacturing—like human salaries.

"We can be in a situation where there is no cost of development, only the cost of the materials—plastic and motors," said Pollack.

The work also offers the possibility of creating robots exquisitely designed to carry out one task in a specific environment very well—like the ultimate robot vacuum cleaner.

"We'd come to your house with a laser scanner and use it to create a virtual room," mused Pollack. "We'd then use that environment to train the robotic vacuum to avoid your low-slung sofa and the fabric hanging too low because the staples fell out."

The ultimate dream mentioned by Brooks is for machines that can evolve and improve themselves by learning about the world, with no human intervention. Although that is still some way off, such technological visions are inspiring some fear.

"I think it is no exaggeration to say we are on the cusp of the further perfection of extreme evil," Sun Microsystems co-founder Bill Joy wrote in the widely circulating essay "Why the Future Doesn't Need Us," published in Wired magazine in April.

Joy's fears center on the danger of intelligent machines "hugely amplified by the power of self-replication."

Many of these fears are fueled not by science fiction and Terminator movies, but by the forecasts of veteran computer scientist Hans Moravec, who helped found Carnegie Mellon's respected robotics program. In his book "Robot," Moravec suggests that robots will match human intelligence within 50 years. En-

Almost No Assembly Required

A computer designed a series of moving machines by itself, then instructed a prototyping machine to make them. Here are two examples. **For an explanation of how the process works, see graphic, "How It Works."**

What the computer designed:

What the prototyping machine built:

20 inches long

8 inches long

Source: Lipson and Pollack, Brandeis University

Los Angeles Times

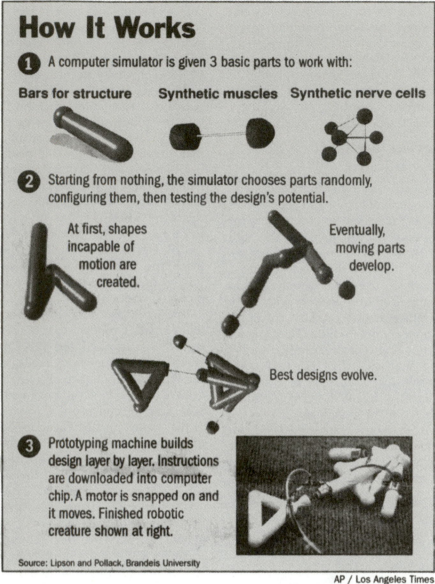

How It Works

1 A computer simulator is given 3 basic parts to work with:

Bars for structure   **Synthetic muscles**   **Synthetic nerve cells**

2 Starting from nothing, the simulator chooses parts randomly, configuring them, then testing the design's potential.

At first, shapes incapable of motion are created.

Eventually, moving parts develop.

Best designs evolve.

3 Prototyping machine builds design layer by layer. Instructions are downloaded into computer chip. A motor is snapped on and it moves. Finished robotic creature shown at right.

Source: Lipson and Pollack, Brandeis University

AP / Los Angeles Times

slavement by robots, some fear, is the next logical step.

Although some roboticists welcome a philosophical debate on such issues, others say such fears are overblown.

"Let's remember, these robots can't even sense the world," said Mataric. Added Khosla: "I'm more concerned about cloning."

Creators Pollack and Lipson wittily acknowledge the debate in the name of their project. It's GOLEM (for Genetically Organized Lifelike Electro Mechanics), named after the Jewish legend of a rabbi who created a being called a Golem out of clay to clean houses and keep order.

As it learned of the world, the Golem grew angry that it couldn't be more like a person, having fun and eating good-tasting things. Finally, in one version, the Golem ran amok. "It's a warning," said Pollack, "about hubris."

Movies of the robots are available at *http://www.demo.cs.brandeis.edu/golem.*

ENVIRONMENTAL MANAGEMENT: NEW CHALLENGES FOR PRODUCTION AND INVENTORY MANAGERS

R. ANTHONY INMAN, CFPIM
College of Administration and Business, Louisiana Tech University

The recent increasing interest in environmental preservation has been remarkable. Many firms have made environmental considerations a fundamental part of their business strategy [1], although others continue to resist changes brought about by government legislation and pressure from the public. Those firms that have made a commitment, however, reluctantly or willingly, are finding that a pro-environment stance can significantly improve cost efficiency, quality, delivery, and flexibility [12].

Changes resulting from environmental considerations are being deeply felt in the area of operations management. For example, product recovery management can have a large impact on the supply chain, specifically affecting production planning, inventory control, and distribution [21]. Key problems resulting from remanufacturing can appear in the areas of inventory availability and management, shop floor scheduling, and capacity planning [11].

Gupta [12] noted that "environmental protection and green consumerism are coming to bear on decision making in operations management as a structured management system." This can have a great impact on the previously mentioned areas of production planning, inventory control, and distribution [2, 21]. We will look at implications and challenges for those three areas and for others resulting from increased environmental interest and change.

PRODUCTION PLANNING AND CONTROL

Production planning under environmental constraints presents a new challenge for industry [3]. The central issue for production planning and control seems to be uncertainty. For environmental issues, great uncertainty is the norm [22], making reliable planning more difficult

[8]. Hence, integration with traditional planning and control models (e.g., MRP) is less obvious because of uncertainty in the time, quality, and quantity of the supply of used products [2, 8].

A number of techniques used to help control environmental damage can complicate the production planning process. We will look at the effects of disassembly, reuse, recycling, repairwork, and remanufacturing.

Repairwork (reuse, recycling, and remanufacturing) implies disassembly [19]. By disassembling the product, securing usable or repairable parts, and reusing as much as possible, the firm protects the environment, regains the value added to products, and avoids future disposal costs [20]. Unfortunately, most MRP logic (and supporting bills of material) fails to provide facilities to plan disassembly [19]. MRP tends to be an assembly-oriented scheduling system that cannot be applied to shop floor operations requiring disassembly [13]. Forms of reuse differ with respect to the production activities to be planned and may involve different levels of coordination [8]. A recovered item can be used in several different ways, thus requiring different disassembly/reassembly bills and routings [19]. The producer typically has little control (i.e., there is a high degree of uncertainty) on the return flow in terms of quantity, quality, and timing [8]. Multiple demand sources create a reverse objective of MRP but one considerably more complicated [13].

Modifications of MRP have recently been proposed for product recovery planning [8]. Most of them use a "reverse" bill of material while documenting every returned product, component content, and reprocessing times [8]. Thierry compares different MRP approaches for remanufacturing with respect to their behavior under uncertainty [8]. Krupp [17] structures bills of material for remanufacturing by utilizing concepts normally used in planning probabilistic demands for end items. Guide [10] proposes the use of drum-buffer-rope to schedule re-manufacturing.

Florida [9] surveyed firms regarding corporate environmental practices (256 responses). Nearly half (48.6%) of the survey respondents say they used closed loop systems (utilized waste from one stage of the process as inputs to other stages of productions). This, of course, means that the recycled goods must be accounted for in the production planning process. According to Jayaraman, et al. [16], "in a closed loop system, new materials are needed to only replace materials which are not received by the system." The problem here is that the number and condition of recovered products are very uncertain. Many recovered parts may be unusable because of paint coating [18], wear, damage, and so on. It may be almost impossible to forecast the degree of work needed to repair recovered products to a "usable" state. To further complicate the situation, recycled material may be used in a totally different process (different from its original use) and used to manufacture a totally different product. Ford Motor Company's program to recycle plastic bumpers into taillight housings provides an example [6]. Even more complex is GE Plastics' experimental recycling of bumpers into internal automotive components, plastic benches, building material, and fuel for incinerators [23].

Even capacity planning is affected. Guide, et al. [11] found that new techniques need to be developed and implemented to replace the standard rough-cut capacity planning techniques if the variability in this environment is to be accounted for.

INVENTORY CONTROL

As in production planning, uncertainty is a problem for inventory control. Difficulty in planning, as a result of uncertainty, may lead to higher safety stock levels [8]. At this time, there is no unifying approach to systematically analyzing the impact of environmental activities on inventory management [8]. Specifically, there are no numerical comparisons of traditional inventory control methods with those adapted to a return flow environment [8].

Disassembly, reuse, recycling, repairwork, and re-manufacturing can create unique problems for those responsible for inventory control. If the firm has a closed loop system, its inventory may include virgin material/purchased parts and material/parts recovered from the system. The parts may serve the same purpose although they come from different sources. Some of the recycled material/parts may require further action, such as disassembly, separation, grading, or sorting, making the inventory control process more complicated [24]. Various classes of repair must be recognized by the sys-

tem, thus causing an expansion of options when inventory is zero [19].

Items that are returned and those that are purchased from outside sources pose an equal challenge. Material/parts may arrive "process-ready" (i.e., sorted, palletized, etc.) or "non process-ready," meaning that they require analyzing (major plastics families contain many different chemical formulas) [18], sorting, grading, or shredding [4]. If disassembly is required, some parts may be found to be of use while others may be worn or damaged beyond repair. Some items, found to be unusable, may be held in inventory until they can be sold as another manufacturer's input or held/sold as refuse-derived fuel (RDF). Again, further complications for inventory control.

DISTRIBUTION AND LOGISTICS

Disassembly, reuse, recycling, repairwork, and re-manufacturing all mean more movement of material. Recyclable material comes from a variety of sources. Some firms may use traditional logistical service providers who have extended their services, while others may use specialized logistical providers [8]. Specific sources include collection banks at retail outlets and supermarkets [5], returns from customers [6], other manufacturers [5], reclamation centers, dismantlers [18], suppliers [9], and internal sources [1]. Each one of these by itself presents a new challenge, but a combination of two or more greatly increases the complexity of logistics. Transportation planning must now take into account both forward and return flows [23]. Warehouses must be designed to deal with two-way movements of products [23]. And distributors should prepare for possible involvement in grading and sorting of used materials [24].

Many firms use reverse logistics, which is based on the idea that manufacturers and distributors should be responsible for cleaning up after themselves [24]. It encompasses the logistics activities from used products no longer required by the user to products again usable in a market [8]. Research is needed on joint routings (i.e., making use of empty rides for collection and return transfer) and on if and how forward and reverse channels should be integrated [8]. Fleischmann, et al. [8] surveyed the field of reverse logistics and found that there was no general framework, comprehensive approaches were rare, and that further research efforts were needed.

OTHER AREAS OF PRODUCTION AND INVENTORY MANAGEMENT

Environmental pressures also affect other areas of production and inventory management but these have not received as much attention in the literature as the areas already discussed. Wallace felt that continuous improvement methods (e.g. kaizen) could create opportunities for

TABLE 1

Environmental Programs	Existing Concepts
keeping pollution under control	SPC
reduction of hazardous inventories	JIT
zero waste	zero defects, TQC
pollution limits	production planning with capacity constraints
cooperating with customers and suppliers to reduce packaging	strategic logistics alliances for time-based competition

pollution prevention and waste as well as emissions reduction [9]. Table 1 shows Corbett and Van Wassenhove's [7, p. 128] comparison of environmental programs to other existing operations management concepts.

Keeping pollution under control is likened to SPC (statistical process control). *Zero waste* is compared to zero defects and TQC (total quality control). Florida [9] found that a number of firms paralleled zero defect approaches with zero emission manufacturing. In this context, it is referred to as total quality environmental management (TQEM). TQEM is based on the premise that pollution prevention is more efficient than pollution cleanup while striving for "zero-discharges" and "zero-risks" to minimize resource wastes [14]. According to Hughes [15], an environmental management system is directly analogous to a total quality culture.

Reduction of hazardous inventories equates with JIT. Hartman and Stafford [14] point out the outbound logistics of Time Inc., which have been greened by employing Just-in-Time (JIT) principles with distributors to reduce the number of unsold magazines. A group of MIT researchers suggest a relationship between lean production and innovative environmental practices [9]. Along those lines, spill and leak prevention can correlate with preventive maintenance [12], an element of a JIT.

Guide, et al. [11] proposed the need for alternative capacity planning techniques. That is reflected in the comparison of *pollution limits* to production planning with capacity constraints. For example, the EPA may allow pollutants to be discharged as long as they do not exceed a maximum allowable amount. This "right to pollute" would need to be "used up" in plant operations but not exceeded [3] to attain the maximum efficient use of capacity.

Finally, *cooperating with customers and suppliers to reduce packaging* corresponds to strategic logistics alliances for time-based competition. General Motors' WECARE (waste elimination and cost awareness reward everyone) program seeks to reduce inbound packaging materials and encourages reusing and recycling them [2].

SUMMARY

It is evident that environmental management trends have a profound impact on production and inventory control. While methods and techniques have been developed to cope with some of these problems [8], for others the solutions have yet to be found.

This article has sought to review the implications presented to production and inventory control practitioners and academicians. "Business as usual" no longer applies for those who care about the world they live in. For managers the challenge is clear.

REFERENCES

1. Arnst, C., S. Reed, G. McWilliams, and D. Weimer. "When Green Begets Green." *Business Week*, November 10, 1997, 98–99, 102, 108.
2. Bloemhof-Ruwaard, J. M., P. van Beek, L. Horkijk, and L. N. Van Wassenhove. "Interactions Between Operational Research and Environmental Management." *European Journal of Operational Research* 85 (1995): 229–243.
3. Bodily, S. E., and H. L. Gabel. "A New Job for Businessmen: Managing the Company's Environmental Resources." *Sloan Management Review* (summer 1982): 3–18.
4. Bowers, W., and R. A. Inman. "Waste Management and Organizational Effectiveness: A Resource-based Conceptualization." Working Paper 1998.
5. Cairncross, F. "How Europe's Companies Reposition to Recycle." *Harvard Business Review* (March–April 1992): 34–45.
6. Cary, J. "A Society That Reuses Almost Everything." *Business Week*, November 10, 1997, 106.
7. Corbett, C. J., and L. N. Van Wassenhove. "The Green Fee: Internalizing and Operationalizing Environmental Issues." *California Management Review* (fall 1993): 116–135.
8. Fleischmann, M., J. M. Bloemhof-Ruwaard, R. Dekker, E. van der Laan, J. A. E. E. Van Nunen, and L. N. Van Wassenhove. "Quantitative Models for Reverse Logistics: A Review." INSEAD Working Paper no97/64/TM.
9. Florida, R. "Lean and Green: The Move To Environmentally Conscious Manufacturing." *California Management Review* 39, no. 1 (1996): 8–105.
10. Guide, V. D. R. "Scheduling Using Drum-Buffer-Rope in a Remanufacturing Environment." *International Journal of Production Research* 34, no. 4 (1996): 1081–1091.
11. Guide, V. D. R., R. Srivastava, and M. S. Spencer. "An Evaluation of Capacity Planning Techniques in a Remanufacturing Environment." *International Journal of Production Research* 35, no. 1 (1997): 67–82.
12. Gupta, M. C. "Environmental Management and Its Impact on the Operations Function." *International Journal of Operations & Production Management* 15, no. 8 (1995): 34–51.

13. Gupta, S. M., and K. N. Taleb. "Scheduling Disassembly." *International Journal of Production Research* 32, no. 8 (1994): 1857–1866.

14. Hartman, C. L, and E. R. Stafford. "Crafting 'Enviropreneurial' Value Chain Strategies Through Green Alliances." *Business Horizons*, March–April 1998, 67–72.

15. Hughes, D. "Environmental Management—An Update." *Quality World*, September 1995, 626–628.

16. Jayaraman, V., D. R. Guide, and R. Srivastava. *Proceedings.* 1997 Decision Sciences Institute Annual Conference, San Diego, 1159–1161.

17. Krupp, J. A. G. "Structuring Bills of Material for Automotive Remanufacturing." *Production and Inventory Management Journal* 34, no. 4 (1993): 46–52.

18. Owen, J. V. "Environmentally Conscious Manufacturing." *Manufacturing Engineering* (October 1993): 44–55.

19. Panisset, B. D. "MRPII for Repair/Refurbish Industries." *Production and Inventory Management Journal* 29, no. 4 (1988): 12–15.

20. Penev, K. D., and A. J. de Ron. "Determination of Disassembly Strategy." *International Journal of Production Research* 34, no. 2 (1996): 495–506.

21. Shrivastava, P. "The Role of Corporations in Achieving Ecological Sustainability." *Academy of Management Review* 20, no. 4 (1995): 936–960.

22. Talcott, F. W. "Environmental Agenda: The Time is Ripe for an Analytical Approach to Policy Problems." *OR/MS Today*, June 1992, 18–24.

23. Thierry, M., M. Salomon, J. Van Nunen, L. and Van Wassenhove. "Strategic Issues In Product Recovery Management." *California Management Review* 37, no. 2 (1995): 114–135.

24. Young, J. "Reverse Logistics: What Goes Around Comes Around." *APICS—The Performance Advantage* (May 1996): 75.

About the Author—

R. ANTHONY INMAN is Ruston Building and Loan Professor of Management at Louisiana Tech University. He has published papers in *Decision Sciences, Interfaces, International Journal of Operations and Production Management, Production and Inventory Management Journal, International Journal of Service Industry Management, Journal of Business and Industrial Marketing,* and *International Journal of Quality and Reliability Management.* He was the recipient of the Shingo Prize for Excellence in Manufacturing: Shingo Prize Research Award for 1993 and was ranked 17th nationally in "POM Research Productivity in U.S. Business Schools" (S. T. Young, B. C. Baird, and M. E. Pullman, *Journal of Operations Management* 14, no. 1, March 1996).

A

acquisitions, in the auto industry, 193–196
activity-based costing (ABC), 130, 132
after-sales service, Saturn and, 172–176, 179
air conditioning manufacturing, JIT and, 146–147
air filter manufacturing, JIT and, 145–146
Airbus Industrie, 141
airlines, customer service by, 18, 19
Alexander Doll Co., 26–27
Allen Bradley Canada, 161, 163
American Dairy Brands, ERP data and, 30
American National Standards Institute, 42
Applied Materials, 160, 161
artificial intelligence, 197–201, 202–204
asset utilization, in manufacturing, 14
Australia, manufacturing managers in, 8–12
auto industry: mergers and acquisitions in, 193–196; multi-tier supply chain and, 15; quality assurance in, 43
automatic insertion process, in printed circuit board assembly, 135–136
Automotive Network Exchange (ANX), 15
autonomous teams, in product development, 92
Avalon Software, 187

B

bankruptcies, of movie theater chains, 122, 123
banks, customer service in, 19
bar codes, 2-D, 49–50
Basic American Foods, ERP planning system and, 29
Bell Canada, 162
best practices, in supply chain management, 168–171
Best Practices LLC, 168–169, 171
BizWorks, 198, 200
Blue Circle Cement, 170–171
BMW, 196; of North America, on the Web, 98–99
Boeing Co.: International Space Station and, 102, 103; 717 jet and, 140–142
bottleneck management, 100, 101, 103
brand loyalty, Saturn and, 172–173
Bridgestone Corp. See Firestone tires
buyer, supply chain management and, 165

C

cable industry, customer service and, 17–18
California, energy crisis in, 124–127
California Independent System Operator (Cal-ISO), 124–127
Canon, 165
carpet manufacturing, JIT and, 148–152
CDS Leopold, 160, 161
celebrations, quality control and, 41
cellular manufacturing, 128–133
Cemex, 181–182
centralized supply chain strategy, 177–178
certification: ISO 9000 and, 44–47; of suppliers, 169–170

change orders, in electronics manufacturing, 186–187
Chrysler Corporation. See DaimlerChrysler Corporation
climate control equipment manufacturing, JIT and, 146–147
Clinton, Bill, 107
closed loop systems, environmental management and, 206
clothes washers, human-factors engineering of, 69–70
collaboration, forecasting and, 112
communication: forecasting and, 112; informal, in teams, 73–74
competency trust, in relationship with suppliers, 162
competitive tension relationships, between suppliers, 159–160, 162–163
computer aided design (CAD): DaimlerChrysler and, 69; in product development, 95
constraints, theory of, 100, 102, 103
cooperative partnerships, with suppliers, 160–162, 163
coordination, forecasting and, 112
cost reduction: ISO 9000 and, 43; JIT and, 152; supply chain management and, 158–159
costs, of ISO 9000 certification, 45–46
crisis management, Ford and, 51–54
Critical Chain (Goldratt), 100, 102, 103–104
critical chain, in project management, 101
critical path, in project management, 100
criticality, of products and services, 177
cross-functional linkages: in forecasting, 112; in manufacturing industry, 8–9
Crown Equipment, 68
CT Express, 67–68
customer demand, sales forecasts of, 111
customer errors: fail-safe procedures and, 36; Firestone tires and, 58–59
customer service, 17–21; ERP data and, 28–31; master production scheduling (MPS) and, 153, 155; poka-yokes and, 34–36; Saturn and, 172–176, 179
customers: of BMW, 98–99; needs of, product development and, 86, 91; quality control and, 39–40; of Saturn, 172, 173, 174; supply chain and, 14
customized products, 180, 181; BMW and, 98–99; carpet manufacturing and, 148–149; furniture manufacturing and, 181
cycle times, for product development, 85–86

D

Daihatsu Motor, 194, 195
DaimlerChrysler Corporation, 193, 194; human-factors engineering and, 69; supply chain and, 15
Davis-Waltermire, Debbie, 167, 168
Deere & Co., 68–69
Dell, 183
demand forecasting, 111, 117–119
of friendly machines, 66–70; tools, in product development process, 93–95
design for manufacturing methods (DFM), 95
disassembly, environmental management and, 205, 206
discontinuous technologies, 103
distributed supply chain strategy, 177–179

distribution network, 177; of Saturn, 173, 175–176
dolls, manufacture of, 26–27
Dunn, Homer, 117, 119

E

Eastman Chemical Co., 167–169
e-business, 180, 189–192; BMW and, 98–99;
electricity, energy crisis in California and, 124–127
Electronic Data Interchange (EDI), 15
electronics manufacturing, JIT and, 145
employee participation programs, legal limitations on, 77–80
employers, legal limits on work teams and, 79–80
enterprise resources planning (ERP): data, customer service and, 28–31; software, 201; systems, master production scheduling (MPS) and, 156
environmental management, of businesses, 205–208
ergonomics. See human-factors engineering
e-supply chain, 189–192
European Community, ISO 9000 and, 44, 47
European Space Agency, 105, 107
evolutionary computation, 197–201, 202–204
expert system, 198
Explorer sport utility vehicles, Firestone tires and, 51–54, 55–59
extranet, e-supply chain and, 190

F

fail-safing, 34–36
Fiat, 195
Firestone tires, Ford and, 51–54, 55–59
First National Maintenance Corp. v. NLRB, 79
flexibility: in product development, 103; in the workplace, stress and, 65
floor-finishing equipment, quality control of, 39–40
flow times, in printed circuit board assembly process, 137–138
Fogel, Lawrence J., 199
food processing, JIT and, 146
Ford Motor Corp., 51–54, 55–59, 193, 194, 199
forecasting, 108–116; of demand, 117–119

G

Gateway, 183
General Electric (GE), 169, 199
General Motors, 194; bar codes and, 49; Saturn and, 172, 173, 175; supply chain management and, 165
genetic algorithms, 198, 199
Goal, The (Goldratt), 100, 102, 128
Goldratt, Eliyahu M., 100–104
goodwill trust, in relationship with suppliers, 162–164
Govindjee, Sanjay, 55, 56, 59
grocery manufacturing, master production scheduling (MPS) and, 155
guarantees, quality control and, 40

H

halogen bulbs, energy efficiency of, 199
Hammer, Michael, 13–16

Herman Miller, customized furniture and, 181
Herzlich, Harold, 55, 57
history: of Boeing's Long Beach Division, 141; of Firestone tire problem, 57
home delivery, of goods, 182
Honda Motor, 194, 195
hospitals, fail-safe procedures in, 34–35
hotels: customer service in, 19; fail-safe procedures in, 35, 36
house of quality. *See* QFD
human-factors engineering, 66–70
humor: quality control and, 40–41; stress and, 65
Hyundai Motor Co., 195

I

IBM: customer service and, 21; supply chain reengineering and, 14
information technology (IT): in electronics manufacturing, 186–188; e-supply chain and, 189–192; supply chain reengineering and, 15
intelligent agents, 198, 200
international cooperation, in space, 105–106
International Organization for Standardization, 42
International Space Station, 105–107
Internet, shopping on, 19, 20, 180; BMW and, 98–99; e-supply chain and, 189–192; for furniture, 181; home delivery and, 182; inventory control and, 117
intranet, e-supply chain and, 190
inventory: control of, 117–119; environmental management and control of, 205, 206; Just-in-Time management of, 144–147; levels, forecasting of, 108; master production scheduling and, 153; performance measurement of, 130; Saturn and, 172–176
islands of analysis, forecasting and, 112–113
ISO 9000, 42–48
ISO 9001, 43
ISO 9002, 43
ISO 9003, 43
ISO 9004, 43
ISO 14000, 43
Israel, Rajasingh S., 199

J

Japan: poka-yokes and, 34; quality in, 37
JAVA, 191, 192
J.C. Penney, selling on the Internet, 19
job content: of production managers, 10; supply chain reengineering and, 16
Juran, Joseph, 37–38
Just-in-Time (JIT), 144–147; performance measurement and, 132

K

Kanban system, 20, 146
Kawai Musical Instrument Manufacturing Co., 62–63
kaizen event, lean manufacturing and, 24
Kia Motors Corp., 195
Kimball Electronics Group, IT system at, 186–188

L

labor organizations, teams as, 78–79
Laval, Bruce, 21
lead times, in carpet manufacturing, 149
lean manufacturing, 85; implementation of, 22–25; of 717 jet, 143
lift trucks, human-factors engineering of, 68
Lilly Software, 30
Lipson, Hod, 202, 203, 204
Longs Drug Stores, inventory control in, 117–119
lot-sizing: in carpet manufactoring, 149, 151; in printed circuit board assembly operations, 134–139

M

machines: evolutionary, 197–201, 202–204; friendly, 66–70; learning, 203
Madame Alexander dolls, 26
magnetic-storage industry, technology and, 159
Malcolm Baldrige Outstanding Quality Award, 148, 168
management: methods, performance measures and, 131–132; of projects, 100–104
managers, performance measurement of, 131
manuals, ISO 9000 and, 44, 45
manufacturing industry, in Australia, 8–12
manufacturing, lean, 22–25
Manugistics, supply chain technology of, 171
MANUPLAN, queueing network software package, 136–139
marketing, of International Space Station, 107
master production scheduling (MPS), in manufacturing companies, 153–156
materials research planning (MRP): in carpet manufacturing, 149, 150, 152; environmental management and, 205; software, in electronics manufacturing, 187–188
Maytag Appliances, 69–70
McCafferty, Terry, 67–68
McDonnell Douglas, 141
media, Ford and, 53, 193
Medtronic Sofamor Danek, ERP system and, 29–30
Mentzer, John T., 108, 114
mergers, in the auto industry, 194
metal machining companies, performance measurement of cellular manufacturing in, 128–133
milestones: in product development, 103; project measurement and, 101
minivans, human-factors engineering of, 69
Mitsubishi Motors Corp., 195
Motorola Inc., 161, 169
movie theaters, 122–123; buying tickets on the Internet for, 20
moving assembly line, for jet production, 140–142
MRP II system, 187–188

N

Nasser, Jacques, 51–54, 193, 194
National Aeronautics and Space Administration (NASA), 106, 107, 200
National Amusements, 123

National Labor Relations Act (NLRA), 77–81
National Labor Relations Board (NLRB), 77–81
natural gas, in California, 125
Natural Selection, 199
net present value techniques, in product development, 89
neural networks, 198, 199, 202
new product development. *See* product development process
Nissan, 195
NLRB v. Cabot Carbon Co., 78–79
Nonstop Solutions, 117–119

O

oil wells, human-factors engineering of, 67–68
operational systems, teams and, 72–73
operations management, 71–75
operations managers, in Australia, 8–12
outsourcing, supply chain management and, 157–166; by Eastman Chemical Co., 167–168

P

parallel development process, 89–90
passport renewal, time-saving and, 20
PDF417, 49–50
performance measurement: of cellular manufacturing, 128–133; of forecasting, 115; by Saturn, 176
pianos, manufacture of, 62–63
plant management, software for, 198
poka-yokes, 34–36
Pollack, Jordan, 202, 203, 204
pollution, environmental management and, 207
power emergency, in California, 124–127
Powerex, energy crisis in California and, 126
printed circuit board assembly operations, 134–139
problem solving, by teams, 73
product development process, management of, 84–97, 103
production managers, in Australia, 8–12
production planning, legal limitations on work teams in, 76–81
production system, 26–27; for carpet manufacturing, 149
productivity, stress and, 64–65
ProfitKey International, ERP system and, 31
profits, quality control and, 39
project management, 100–104
Public Utilities Commission: California, 126; Oregon, 17
pull system, of demand, Saturn and, 175–176

Q

QFD, product development and, 93, 94–95
qualifications, of production managers, 9
quality circles, legal limitations on, 77–81
quality control, 34–36, 37–38, 39–41
quality, in metal machining companies, 129
queueing network models, 134–139
QS-9000, 47

R

recycling, environmental management and, 206

reengineering, of business practices, 13–16
remanufacturing, environmental management and, 205
Renault, 195–196
requests-for-information, to suppliers, 168
research and development (R&D): in product development, 87, 89; in space, 105, 107
resources, in project management, 100–101, 102–103
restaurants: customer service in, 19; fail-safe procedures in, 34, 35, 36
reuse, environmental management and, 205
reverse logistics, environmental management and, 206
Roath, Stephen, 117–119
robots, 202–204
run times, in printed circuit board assembly process, 136–137
Russia, International Space Station and, 105, 106, 107

S

salaries, of production managers, 10
sales force, forecasting and, 110, 111
sales, forecasting of, 108–116
sales plan, sales forecast and, 110
Saturn Corp., supply chain management and, 172–176, 179
Savage Arms, ERP data and, 29
scarce resources, in project management, 100–101
SCE, power emergency in California and, 126–127
schedule performance, measurement of, 131
Schlumberger Ltd., 67–68
Selectica Inc., 98–99
self-certification, quality assurance and, 47
self-directed work teams, legal limitations on, 76–81
sensitive information, supply chain and, 15
setup times: lot sizes and, 134; in metal machining companies, 132
717 jet, production of, 140–142
Shaheen, George, 18–19
Shigeru Kawai grand pianos, 62–63
Shingo, Shigeo, 34
single minute exchange of die method, in metal machining companies, 132
single supplier, supply chain management and, 14–15
six sigma, 169

software: customized furniture design, 181; forecasting, 110, 113–114; inventory control, 117; outsourcing, 167–171; plant management, 198; project management, 101; queueing networks, 135, 136–139; supply chain planning, 187
sole-sourcing, of suppliers, 160
sourcing. See outsourcing
Stage-Gate process, in product development, 93–94
Steinway pianos, 63
strategic alliances, with suppliers, 88–89, 160, 161–162, 163–164; in product development, 88–89
strategic objectives: for product development, 84–97; for supply chain management, 157–159
Streamline.com, 182, 183
stress, productivity and, 64–65
suggestion system, quality control and, 40
Sun Microsystems, 191
suppliers: development of, 160–162; product development process and, 91–92; supply chain management and, 14–15, 158–166, 168–170
supply chain systems: in drug stores, 118; Internet and, 189–192; management of, 157–166; master production scheduling (MPS) and, 153–156; reengineering of 14–16; at Saturn, 172–176; software in electronics manufacturing, 187–188; software tools for, 167–171; strategic opportunities of, 180–183
supply, forecasting and, 111
Supra Products, 160
Symmers, Keith, 169, 170
systems, quality standards for, 42–48

T

Taylor, Frederick Winslow, 17
TBM Consulting, 26–27
teams: cross-functional, in product development process, 90–91; forecasting and, 110; in manufacturing, 71–75; performance measurement of, 132; in product development process, 92–93; self-directed, legal limitations on, 76–77
technology: strategy for, in product development, 86–88; of suppliers, in supply chain management, 159
Tennant Company, 39–40
time buffers, in project management, 101

time-wasting, by companies, of customers' time, 17–21
tire: design, 52–54; manufacturing, JIT and, 146
tools: for outsourcing, 167–171; in product development process, 93–95. See also software
total preventive maintenance (TPM) programs, 130, 132
total quality management (TQM), teams and, 76–77, 79–80
Toyota, 39–40, 193, 194, 195
tracking, of manufacturing performance, 131
tractors, human-factors engineering of, 68–69
training, in forecasting, 110, 113, 114
transportation costs, inventory and, 117
trust, in relationship with suppliers, 162–164
turns, of inventory, 130
2-D bar codes, 49–50

U

United States, economy of, 13
utility companies: poor customer service by, 17; power emergency in California and, 124–127

V

value net, 180–183
vehicle safety, simulations to improve, 199
Volkswagen, 193–194
Volvo, 195

W

Wal-Mart, 158
Walt Disney Co., queueing and, 21
Webango Inc., 167–168
Webvan, 19
work-breakdown structure, in project management, 101
work-in-process (WIP): performance measurement and, 130; reduction of, 134–135
workplace, stress in, 64–65

X

Xerox, quality control and, 38

Z

Zara, clothing retailer, 181
Zemke, Ron, 40
zero gravity research, in space, 105, 107
Zuckerman, A., 44
Zvezda service module, 106, 107

Test Your Knowledge Form

We encourage you to photocopy and use this page as a tool to assess how the articles in **Annual Editions** expand on the information in your textbook. By reflecting on the articles you will gain enhanced text information. You can also access this useful form on a product's book support Web site at **http://www.dushkin.com/ online/.**

NAME: DATE:

_____

TITLE AND NUMBER OF ARTICLE:

_____

BRIEFLY STATE THE MAIN IDEA OF THIS ARTICLE:

_____

LIST THREE IMPORTANT FACTS THAT THE AUTHOR USES TO SUPPORT THE MAIN IDEA:

_____

WHAT INFORMATION OR IDEAS DISCUSSED IN THIS ARTICLE ARE ALSO DISCUSSED IN YOUR TEXTBOOK OR OTHER READINGS THAT YOU HAVE DONE? LIST THE TEXTBOOK CHAPTERS AND PAGE NUMBERS:

_____

LIST ANY EXAMPLES OF BIAS OR FAULTY REASONING THAT YOU FOUND IN THE ARTICLE:

_____

LIST ANY NEW TERMS/CONCEPTS THAT WERE DISCUSSED IN THE ARTICLE, AND WRITE A SHORT DEFINITION:

ANNUAL EDITIONS revisions depend on two major opinion sources: one is our Advisory Board, listed in the front of this volume, which works with us in scanning the thousands of articles published in the public press each year; the other is you—the person actually using the book. Please help us and the users of the next edition by completing the prepaid article rating form on this page and returning it to us. Thank you for your help!

ANNUAL EDITIONS: Production and Operations Management 01/02

ARTICLE RATING FORM

Here is an opportunity for you to have direct input into the next revision of this volume. We would like you to rate each of the 42 articles listed below, using the following scale:

1. Excellent: should definitely be retained
2. Above average: should probably be retained
3. Below average: should probably be deleted
4. Poor: should definitely be deleted

Your ratings will play a vital part in the next revision. So please mail this prepaid form to us just as soon as you complete it. Thanks for your help!

RATING — ARTICLE

1. An Empirical Assessment of the Production/Operations Manager's Job
2. Reengineer or Perish
3. Hurry Up and Wait
4. Do You Have What It Takes to Be Lean?
5. Rally of the Dolls: It Worked for Toyota. Can It Work for Toys?
6. Using ERP Data to Get [Close] to Customers
7. Fool Proof Service: Poka-Yoke
8. A Conversation With Joseph Juran
9. One More Time: Eight Things You Should Remember About Quality
10. ISO 9000 Myth and Reality: A Reasonable Approach to ISO 9000
11. 2-D or Not 2-D?
12. Jac Nasser's Biggest Test
13. Cause of Tire Failures Still a Matter of Dispute
14. How Will Kawai's Hand-Built Grand Play Against Steinway?
15. Less Stress, More Productivity
16. How Great Machines Are Born
17. Characteristics of the Manufacturing Environment That Influence Team Success
18. The Legal Limitations to Self-Directed Work Teams in Production Planning and Control
19. Managing the New Product Development Process: Strategic Imperatives
20. BMW Drives New Web Strategy
21. Bringing Discipline to Project Management
22. New Era About to Dawn for International Space Station
23. Seven Keys to Better Forecasting

RATING — ARTICLE

24. Vitamin Efficiency
25. Not All Projections Bad for Overgrown Theater Chains
26. State Declares First Stage 3 Power Alert
27. Changes in Performance Measures on the Factory Floor
28. Using Queueing Network Models to Set Lot-Sizing Policies for Printed Circuit Board Assembly Operations
29. A New Route for Boeing's Latest Model
30. Introducing JIT Manufacturing: It's Easier Than You Think
31. Tailored Just-In-Time and MRP Systems in Carpet Manufacturing
32. The Critical Importance of Master Production Scheduling
33. The Manager's Guide to Supply Chain Management
34. Squeezing the Most Out of Supply Chains
35. Saturn's Supply-Chain Innovation: High Value in After-Sales Service
36. From Supply Chain to Value Net
37. Electronics Manufacturing: A Well-Integrated IT Approach
38. Are You Ready for the E-Supply Chain?
39. The Global Six
40. Thinking Machines
41. One Giant Leap for Machinekind?
42. Environmental Management: New Challenges for Production and Inventory Managers

(Continued on next page)

BUSINESS REPLY MAIL
FIRST-CLASS MAIL PERMIT NO. 84 GUILFORD CT

POSTAGE WILL BE PAID BY ADDRESSEE

McGraw-Hill/Dushkin
530 Old Whitfield Street
Guilford, CT 06437-9989

ABOUT YOU

Name   Date

Are you a teacher? ☐ A student? ☐

Your school's name

Department

Address   City   State   Zip

School telephone #

YOUR COMMENTS ARE IMPORTANT TO US !

Please fill in the following information:

For which course did you use this book?

Did you use a text with this *ANNUAL EDITION*? ☐ yes ☐ no

What was the title of the text?

What are your general reactions to the *Annual Editions* concept?

Have you read any particular articles recently that you think should be included in the next edition?

Are there any articles you feel should be replaced in the next edition? Why?

Are there any World Wide Web sites you feel should be included in the next edition? Please annotate.

May we contact you for editorial input? ☐ yes ☐ no

May we quote your comments? ☐ yes ☐ no